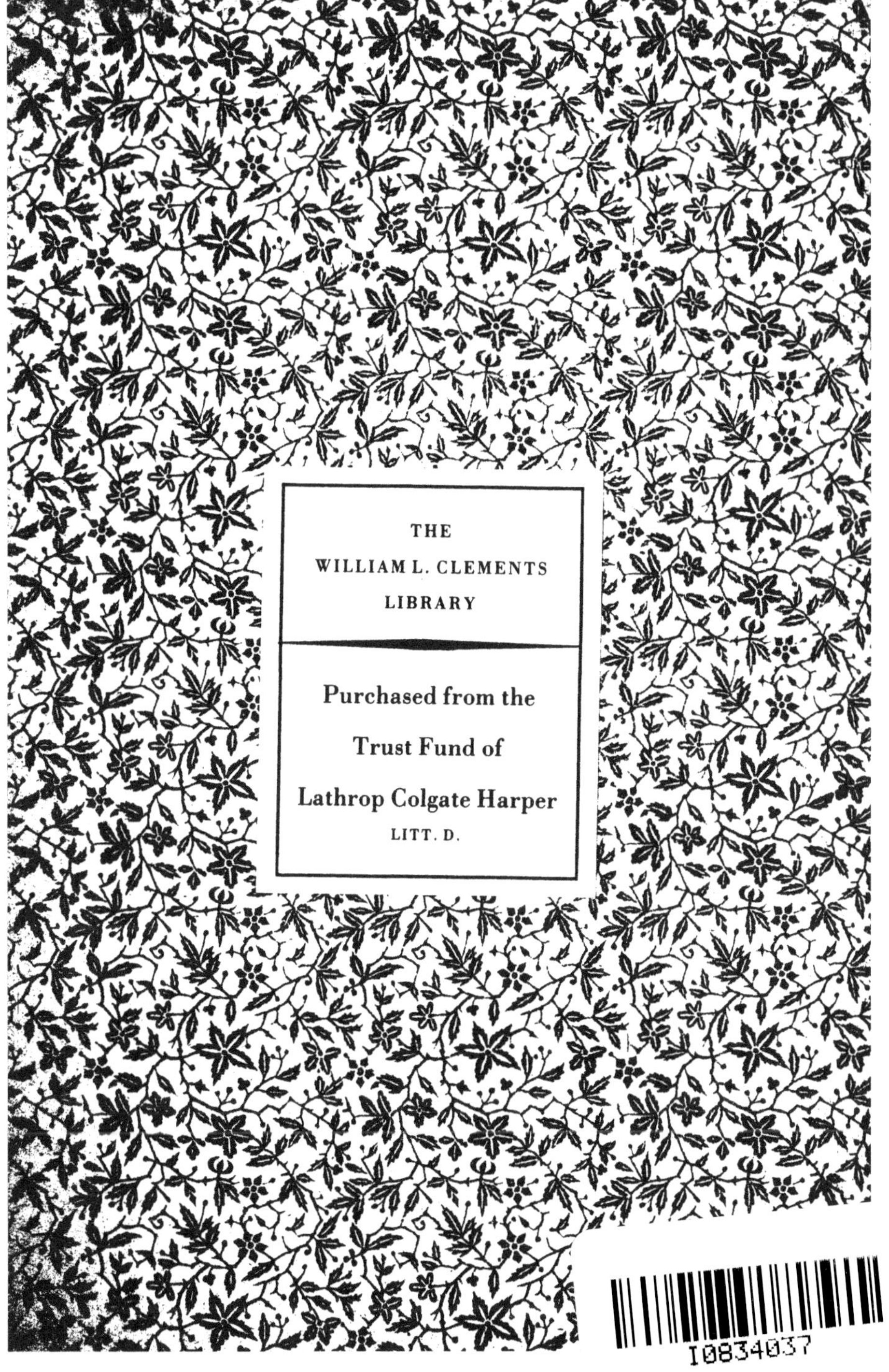

THE OLD MERCHANTS

OF

NEW YORK CITY.

BY

WALTER BARRETT, Clerk.

—The harvest of the river is her revenue, and she is a mart of nations.
—Whose antiquity is of ancient days.
—The Crowning city, whose merchants are princes, whose traffickers are the honorable of the earth.

—*Isaiah xxiii*, 3, 7, 8.

VOL. I.

NEW YORK:
JOHN W. LOVELL COMPANY,
150 Worth Street, corner Mission Place.

To

JOHN CLANCY, Esq.

AS THE PRELIMINARY CHAPTERS

OF

THE OLD MERCHANTS

WERE LAID BEFORE THE PUBLIC THROUGH THE COLUMNS

OF YOUR JOURNAL, IT SEEMS APPROPRIATE THAT

ITS AUTHOR SHOULD DEDICATE THE BOOK

TO YOU, WHICH HE DOES WITH

PLEASURE AND SENTIMENTS

OF REGARD.

PREFACE.

When the writer prepared the first chapters of The Old Merchants for the columns of the *New York Leader*, it was with no intention of subsequently making a book of them; but the unexpected popularity of the papers, and the constantly increasing demand for back numbers, have induced him to revise them carefully and offer them to the reader in their present form.

The author feels justified in saying that he has spared neither time nor expense in rendering the volume valuable as a book of reference; though a work involving so much historical detail, and requiring such laborious research, cannot, necessarily, be entirely free from inaccuracies.

Walter Barrett, Clerk.

INDEX.

B.

C.

D.

E.

F.

G

H

L

M

T

U

V

W

THE

OLD MERCHANTS OF NEW YORK CITY.

CHAPTER I.

The changes in New York life are very wonderful. In no class of society are those changes so extraordinary as among merchants. Commerce has made New York;—kept it up, and will continue to increase it in wealth and population until our city becomes the greatest in the world. Such is her destiny. Thirty years hence we shall be in advance of London! There is no doubt about it. Let us go back thirty years. In 1830 a New Yorker of no very extended acquaintance could tell the names of all the principal merchants, and where they lived. Very few merchants of note lived above Chambers street thirty years ago.

But now it is impossible to tell where they do not live. Thirty years ago there was a court that ran from Wall street to Pine, next to the Bank of New York on Wall, and next to the old Bank Coffee House kept by Billy Niblo on Pine and William street corner. This court was called Wall street court. It was filled with offices, and they were mainly occupied by lawyers. There was a famous pump in the court, that was used by half Wall and all Pine street. In the building fronting Wall street court on Wall street was the New

York Insurance Company, and thirty years ago the venerable Charles McEvers was its President. He was one of the old aristocracy, and his dwelling was in Greenwich street, near the Battery.

The Vice President of this Company was Archibald Gracie, who in his day had been one of the most eminent of New York merchants. He once resided in State street, No. 5, the house with pillars. It was torn down this year. "Valentine's Manual" for 1859 has a picture of it. A few doors below Wall street court entrance in 1830 was a marble building erected by Nathaniel Prime. It had offices in the upper part. The main floor was occupied as the banking rooms of the great banking house of Prime, Ward & King. What a wonderful firm that was thirty years ago! Originally it was "Nathaniel Prime, Stock and Commission Broker, No. 42 Wall street," in 1796. In 1808, he took in Samuel Ward as a partner, and the firm was then Prime & Ward. In 1816 Joseph Sands was made a partner, and the firm was Prime, Ward & Sands, still doing business at the old stand, No. 42 Wall street, until 1825, when the office was temporarily removed, in order that the present building might be erected. That year James G. King was made a partner, and the firm was Prime, Ward, Sands, King & Co. Joseph Sands, of the above firm, was a son of the celebrated Comfort Sands, who died in 1835. In 1826 Joseph left the above firm, and it again became Prime Ward, King & Co. James Gore King, of the above firm, had previously been engaged in business in Liverpool, England, under the firm of King & Gracie. After he returned to this country, he was taken into the great firm for his financial ability, and the firm changed as above stated.

Old Nat Prime was an extraordinary man — stout, thick, short, and heavy in person, yet he was a wonderfully shrewd calculator. It was stated that the original head of this firm was in early life a coachman to the rich William Gray, an eminent merchant in Boston. Mr. Gray loaned him a small sum of money with which to commence the brokerage business in a very small way. The ex-coachman shaved notes, and got bravely ahead He was invited to a dinner party, where there were several gentlemen, and one a planter of wealth from Georgia. The conversation turned upon the best mode of investing money. Mr. Prime took a part in this conversation, and after giving his financial views, added: "If I had $5000, I could invest it to-morrow in a manner that would enable me to double the sum inside of a year."

"What security can you give me, Mr. Prime, if I lend you the sum named?" asked the Georgian planter.

"The word of an honest man," said Mr. Prime.

"You shall have the money on that security alone," said the Georgian. He gave Mr. Prime $5000 the next day. The broker did double the sum, and within a year returned the $5000, with interest, to the generous and confiding lender But there is a sequel to that, not so pleasant to narrate. Some years after the $5000 transaction, the Georgian planter became embarrassed. His plantation and slaves were mortgaged, and he was unable to pay the interest and prevent a foreclosure and sale. He could not raise the money. In this emergency he thought of Mr. Prime, who had meanwhile become the great Wall street banker. He went to him, and recalled himself to the memory of Mr. Prime, and then stated his desperate circumstances. "I need," he added, "about the same amount I once loaned you."

"What security can you give?" asked Prime.

"The word of an honest man," replied the Georgian.

"That will not pass in Wall street," said Prime, and he refused to make the loan, and the planter became a beggar in consequence.

Mr. Prime bought the house on the corner of Broadway and Battery Place, now occupied as the Washington Hotel. He lived there many years, and saw his sons and his daughters intermarrying with the first families in New York. Thirty years ago, Mr. Prime was deemed the *third* richest man in New York, and yet no one set him down as worth over a million! Thirty years ago there was but one man in this town worth over a million; that one was John Jacob Astor. There were four other rich men — Robert Lenox, John G. Coster, Stephen Whitney, and Nat Prime; the latter was regarded as the most wealthy of the last four names.

Country seats were regarded as a necessary appendage to a wealthy man in those days. Mr. Prime bought a house and one hundred and thirty acres of land on the Island near Hurlgate. It has become a valuable property to his heirs.

In 1832, Mr. Prime retired from the great banking firm, and his place was filled by his son, Edward Prime. All seemed fair in the future for old Mr. Prime. Vast wealth, excellent sons, daughters all well married, he had nothing else to do but live and enjoy himself. Did he do so? No. The strange fancy seized upon his mind, that he was becoming poor — that his destiny was to die in the almshouse. Under this singular monomania, and hallucination of mind, he cut his throat with a razor, and died on the instant.

His partner, Samuel Ward, was a splendid specimen

of the old school New Yorker. He stood over six feet, and large in proportion. Fine arts was his *forte.* He lived on the corner of Fourth street and Broadway; the house is still standing; in its rear is a marble building, without windows on Broadway. Thousands in the past thirty years have made enquiry relative to that curious but windowless building. It was the Painting Gallery of Old Sam Ward, of the firm of Prime, Ward & King. Mr. Samuel Ward was supposed to be immensely rich — he died not worth a copper. His son married one of the Astor girls, and has plenty of money, keeps fast horses, is a sort of *diplomat*, and a very good fellow. Old Sam Ward was a brother-in-law of the celebrated Doctor Francis.

James G. King was the business man of Prime, Ward & King. He was a son of Rufus King, once U. S. Senator from New York, Ambassador to England, and a great man in this Union in his day. James G. King had several brothers. One was the late Governor of this state, John A. King. Another brother was Charles King, the President of Columbia College, another was Edward King, an extraordinarily talented person, who went to Ohio, attained great distinction, but died early. Another was Doctor Frederick King, who died in this city. James G. King represented a district in Congress for one term. He was a very useful, but never a brilliant member. For twenty years he was the most intimate friend of Daniel Webster. He left the firm of Prime, Ward & King to found the house of James G. King & Son. Not long after the old firm failed. Mr. King's private residence for a great many years was at Weehawken Heights, New Jersey. He died a few years ago, leaving a large property and a great financial name.

CHAPTER II.

There is an old aristocracy in this city, which is not generally understood. There is no strata of society so difficult to approach or reach. This class makes no noise, no fuss, nor is at all pretentious. If one has qualities and attributes that will place him at the fire-sides of the old set, he will there find all solid and substantial, but no gingerbread or mushroom work. The sideboard is deep shaded, because it is old solid mahogany. On it are real cut glasses, decanters, and solid silver salvers. The wines are old and pure. There are apples, cakes, cider and hickory nuts. The habits of the olden time are kept up. The young man in this set courts the fair girl of the same level, as in the olden time. Origin causes no mark of distinction in this old society. It comprises all countries — old Knickerbocker families or those descended from the original Netherland settlers—from the old English families, who took part in the Revolution as Whigs — those who rose to distinction and political power under the American constitution or during the war, as Generals, or before and during the war as signers of the Declaration of Independence, members of the Continental Congress, or framers of the Constitution.

Among the Dutch names that claim rights among the

old clique I allude to, are found the Van Rensselaers, Le Roys, Schuylers, Stuyvesants, Beeckmans, Bleeckers, Strykers, Anthonys, Van Waggennens, Van Vleicks, Cregiers, Van Horns, Laurenses, Wyckoffs, Van Cliffs Gouverneurs, Stenwycks, Janceys, De Peysters, Nevins, Ruyters, Van Wycks, Hoffinans, Van Cortlandts, Provosts, Kipps, Verplancks, De Kays, Dyckmans, Vermilyeas, Bensons, Van Schaicks, De Forrests, Van Zandts, Brevoorts, Marvins, Vances, Van Horns, &c.

The English descendants and Puritan stock are mixed up with the old Dutch breed in forming the highest class of society, though not the most showy. Originally the set went to New England, and came straggling into New York city in the course of years. They pioneered in the excitement that led to the American Revolution, and took an active part in the seven years war. There were such names as Kent, Jay, Alsop, Lawrence, Laight, Hicks, Phœnix, Post, Perit, Thurston, Jones, Wetmore Hays, Woodward, Bard, Walton, Fleming, Delancy Cruger, Marshall, Gibbs, Deming, Clarkson, Newbold Fuller, Scott, Beach, Aspinwall, Curtiss, Waddington Brooks, Gracie, Savage, Barclay, Goodhue, Grinnell, Ogden, Howland, Davis, Macy, Morton, Ray, Whitlock, Ward, King, Sands, and others. Another class of the old set are descendants of Huguenots who came here prior to the revolution — Lorrillard, Seguine, Masier, Delaplaine, Latourette, Law, De la Montagne, Jumel, Depau, De Rham, Pintard, Delevan, and Purdy.

It was from these names the managers of the "Bachelor Balls," were taken thirty years ago. Then the City Hotel, located on the block in Broadway above Trinity Yard, was the only head-quarters of the pure, genuine aristocracy of which we speak.

Mr. Nathaniel Prime, of the great firm of Prime,

Ward & King, did not legitimately belong to the old set. He claimed a place, however, for his sons and his daughters had intermarried with the Jays, the Rays, the Sands, the Palmers, and the undoubted old families. Aside from this, his partners were of the pure breed.

Prime, Ward & King were the first large genuine private bankers in the city of New York. They allowed interest on all sums deposited with them for either a short or long term. They bought up good bills on Paris or London, and remitted to their bankers, and then every packet day, Prime, Ward & King were large sellers of their own sterling and French bills at *one* per cent. more than they paid for the best private bills. Such was their credit. The firm had no rivals at that time. J. L. & S. Josephs had a banking house on the corner of Wall and Hanover. They were the agents of the Rothschilds, but had no such standing in this town as Prime, Ward & King.

The members of the American banking firm were far-seeing men. The Josephs in this country would have been in their true element, had they done a mercantile instead of a banking business. As bankers, they were in too deep water, and finally made a desperate failure — paying nothing. When the Josephs went to smash, they were succeeded by A. Belmont, who for twenty-two years has managed the banking business of the Rothschilds with great efficiency. Mr. Belmont has not only succeeded in this city as a banker, but as a politician, and but recently we had to admire his patriotic energy, when, as a delegate to the Charleston Convention, he manfully battled for the nomination of Mr. Douglas, in spite of family ties, which might have led him in a contrary direction.

Old Nat Prime was a fearfully long-headed man. He could see through a mill-stone quicker than any other man in Wall street. But he was frequently *sold.* On one occasion a Hartford horse jockey, named Adam Hitchcock, sold him a leopard spotted horse for $ 1500. It was all right until the white and black horse got caught out in a rain, when such a mixing of paints occurred as perfectly astonished him. Mr. Prime left behind him three fine sons — Edward, who succeeded him in the firm in 1831; Rufus, who at one time formed one of the firm of Christmas, Livingston, Prime & Coster. What a firm that was! Charles Christmas (he is now a partner of August Belmont) had been for fifteen years book-keeper, or head clerk, for Prime, Ward & King. He was a long-headed genius. Robert Livingston was a brother of Mortimer Livingston, of the Havre packet line agents, C. Bolton, Fox & Livingston, who married a daughter of Francis Depau, who married Sylvie de Grasse, a daughter of that Count de Grasse who commanded the French fleet on this coast in the Revolutionary war.

Another member of the C. L. P. C. firm was Washington Coster. What a gay boy was Wash. Coster! He married a daughter of old Francis Depau, and there were cart loads of gold on both sides of the house. Wash. was not a son of old John G. Coster — he was a nephew. Poor fellow, he was fond of good eating and good drinking, and he paid the penalty. He died on a sofa at Blançard's Globe Hotel in Broadway near Exchange street, now a dry goods store. Wash. got no sleep for several days, and a celebrated Irish adventurer named John S. Nugent (who was hired by Cozzens as a bar keeper, and wound up his week's work by running away and marrying the sister of Mr. Cozzens,(West

Point Hotel) — gave him a dose of morphine to make him sleep. It was successful, for poor Wash. has not woke up since, unless he made an unknown turn over in the grave.

Mr. Prime had a third son named Frederick. He was a lawyer, and married a grand-daughter of he great John Jay, Chief Justice in Washington's day of the United States.

What funny anecdotes I could tell about some of the members of that firm of C. L. P. & Co. To return to Prime, Ward & King. James G. King was an extraordinary man — a superb financier. He was named after James Gore. Mr. King was a very domestic man — fond of his children, and would make any sacrifice for them. He married a daughter of the celebrated merchant Archibald Gracie, who came to this country in 1765, before the war, and became eminent as one of the first merchants of the day. He had ships trading to the East Indies, to Europe, in fact, everywhere, and continued to do an immense business, until the seizure of several of his ships by France under the Berlin and Milan decrees of Bonaparte forced him to a failure.

What a splendid old merchant was that same grand, god-like white-headed old man, Archibald Gracie. In 1827, 1828 and 1829, until the day he died, day after day, (except Sundays) I used to go to the *Commercial Advertiser*, corner of Pine and William, the *Evening Post*, in William street, where the Bank of America now stands, and to the *New York American*, No. 16 Broad street, and get those evening papers as regularly as clock work. Then when he died in 1829, there was a humble friend but a sincere mourner at his funeral, when they placed his body in the vault, only one foot from the side walk, on the north side of St. Thomas' Church in Broadway.

I have said that James G. King was a great friend of Daniel Webster. So he was of Nicholas Biddle. At one time such was the influence of Mr. King that he held Wall street in his hand, and some profane persons named him "the Almighty of Wall street." He was fond of a little fun occasionally, and liked a good joke or a good story. He held a share in the celebrated "Tontine stock." I have a list of all the original members of the Tontine, and of such as are now living. (I think all the Gracie family and King family had stock in the Tontine.)

Mr. King had a horror of the three and four per cent. a month operations. On one occasion a merchant who was doing a very extensive business, and for whom Mr. King felt a sincere friendship, came to him and said:

"Mr. King, I keep four large bank accounts, and I have offered heavily the best paper for discount. It is flung out as fast as I offer it. I shall have to go on the street, and do as others do — get heavily shaved. Money is worth now three per cent. a month. I have got to pay it. I do not see why I should not pay that to your house as well as on the street. I know you object to such transactions, but I cannot help myself. I will bring down my 'portfolio.' It contains in 'Bills Receivable' for over $200,000 of A No. 1 business paper. You can take your selection. I must have $100,000 in cash before another week."

"No business can stand such a premium for money any length of time. It will use up a million capital very speedily," said Mr. King.

"Oh, not at all. My business will justify my paying any rate of interest, however exorbitant."

"Why discount for a short time? Why not make it for two or three years? I will not discount your good business paper. Pay your debts with it. I will discount your note for $100,000, if you will make it three years."

"Thank you, Mr. King. I will draw it at once. It is very kind in you, but don't you want collateral?"

"No, sir. Mr. Miller (turning to his accountant,) take off the discount at three per cent. a month on $100,000 for three years, and draw a check for the balance for Mr. D. Wait a moment D., or give me your note for $100,000." The conversation became general, both were seated, when Mr. Miller, the accountant, handed the following memorandum to Mr. King:

Note of Mr. D. payable three years after date, for	$100,000
Discount at three per cent. a month is thirty-six per cent. per year, and for three years 108 per cent., or	100,000
Balance due to Prime, Ward & King - - -	$8,000

"D., have you a blank check with you?" pleasantly asked Mr. King.

"A check? What for?"

"Why, Miller has handed me a statement, and I find that if we discount or shave your note for three years for $100,000 at three per cent. a month, you will have to pay us $8,000."

"Why this is absurd. I give you my note for $100,000, and get no cash in return, but have to give you $8,000 cash. Bah!

"Be cool, D., and listen. I have done this purposely to give you a lesson, to show you where your mercantile career will end, if you submit to such extortion. Now if you will pledge me your word of honor that you will curtail your business and never pay more than seven per cent. interest for money to carry on your trade, I will tell you what I will do. You want $100,000. Draw your note for that sum at ninety days, leave with me $100,000 of your best notes receivable, and I will give you the money less the ordinary discount of seven per cent,"

Mr. D. was grateful. He appreciated the lesson taught by Mr. King, and he is at the present moment one of the wealthiest men in the city of New York.

CHAPTER III.

There was a wonderful difference in the manner of advertising by the old merchants thirty years ago and now. Then all the merchants advertised by the year. The regular price was $40 — and that price included the paper, which was left by the carrier. Without the paper it was $30. Strange as it may appear, there was no limit fixed to the amount of advertising in those days. A mercantile firm, like Goodhue & Co., advertised all they desired. No respectable house would overdo the thing. There was a sort of self-respect about the articles advertised. Goodhue & Co. and no other respectable house would have advertised cotton. The reason was that cotton was an article sold altogether through cotton brokers; and to have advertised 1000 bales of cotton by any house, even if they had that quantity for sale, would have appeared like a bom bast or an attempt to show off. A cotton purchaser did not look at the newspapers. He went directly to the offices of the different cotton brokers. The cotton brokers were even then an institution. The principal ones were N. Talcott, G. Merle and D. Crassons.

What aided in making great merchants in this city thirty years ago, was their having foreign or New England connexions. The great shipbuilders and owners were located "down east"—in any state of the five except Vermont. Maine had her Portland and Bangor; Massachusetts had Boston, Salem, New Bedford, Newburyport, and other ports; Rhode Island, her Providence and Newport; Connecticut had New London, Norwich and New Haven. Most all of the shipping was owned in these eastern places, and consequently the merchant in New York who had the most extensive eastern connexions did the largest business. Our readers must understand that to be the New York agents of these eastern shipowners did not confine them to getting freights outward, or the consignment of the ship when she returned from a voyage to the port of New York. That was but a fraction of the business. Many of the large ship owners east were also merchants. They would load their vessels for an outward voyage, and the return cargo would be on "owners' account." If it was an East India cargo, New York was the best port, and the Salem, Boston, or New Bedford owner would order his ship and cargo to New York, consigned to his agent.

The firm of Goodhue & Co., has existed 51 years, having been founded in 1809. The founder of the firm (the Hapsburg of this ancient house) was Jonathan Goodhue. He was a princely merchant: he was a Salem boy, and brought up in the counting room of a Salem merchant and ship owner. When he became of age, his employer sent him to New York to attend to business. Here he established himself as a merchant. Of course, all the Salem business, or a good portion of it, came to one whose integrity, intelligence and business facilities were unquestioned. His first partnership in 1809, was with Mr. Swett, and the firm was Goodhue & Swett. He afterwards formed a partnership with Pelatiah Perit, under the firm of Goodhue & Co., "for the purpose of doing a general commission and commercial business." They located in South street, No. 64. Mr. Perit was a Norwich boy: he, too, had strong connexions; and although the rivals of Goodhue & Co. Gardner G. and Samuel S. Howland, (who formed the firm of G. G. & S. S. Howland) were also from Norwich,) yet Mr. Perit brought to his firm a vast amount of New England connexions and business. Thirty years ago, Goodhue & Co., took in a partner named C. Durand, but he did not remain with them many years. This house has clerks of 45 years standing. There are many who will well remember the old house of Jonathan Goodhue, under the great elm, corner of Whitehall and Pearl street. It was painted yellow and under each window was an iron balcony painted green. It was a great affair in those days, when the aristocracy of New York clustered in State, Pearl, Whitehall, lower Greenwich, Broadway, Beaver and Broad streets.

The growth of the house of Goodhue & Co. was slow but sure. Yankee boys, clerks of the firm, went out to distant parts of the world and formed commercial houses — some in Canton, Calcutta, St. Petersburg, London, &c. Their first strike would be to open a correspondence with the firm of Goodhue & Co. The latter house ran no risk. It did a commission business. It acted as agent for commercial firms in all parts of the world. It has never deviated from its course, never speculated, and consequently stands as firmly as the rock of Gibraltar. It has had correspondents that never changed. Baring Brothers & Co., of London, and Steiglitz of St. Petersburg, hold the same relation to Goodhue & Co., that they did fifty years ago. The elder Goodhue has been long dead, and his sons have succeeded him. The second partner, Perit, is still alive, a very aged but a very good man, and one of the pillars of the Chamber of Commerce. For many years the house of Goodhue & Co., were the agents of the old black ball line of Liverpool packets. A thousand fortunes have been made by that line, and the agency still continues with Goodhue & Co., although managed by one of their old captains, Charles Marshall. I would not swear to the fact, but I think that Goodhue & Co. is the only large commercial house that has not changed the style of the firm in half a century. The old house of G. G. & S. S. Howland changed to the firm of Howland & Aspinwall. Fish, Grinnell & Co., changed to Grinnell, Minturn & Co. In none of these houses remain one of the original partners, except in the great house of Goodhue & Co.

I have previously alluded to the old system of advertising thirty years ago. Those old firms have not changed in their modes of advertising, except when they have had lines of packets or steamships. Thirty years ago, the daily morning journals of New York were, the New York Daily Advertiser, New York Gazette, New York Courier, New York Mercantile Advertiser, New York Journal of Commerce, New York Enquirer. The Evening Papers were the New York American, Evening Post and Commercial Advertiser. The subscription price was ten dollars a-year, and, including advertisements, forty dollars, for all of the above papers.

I doubt whether any of the old houses (those that existed thirty years ago) have become advertisers under the new system. You may look a long time before you will find any of the firms I have named in the Herald, Sun, Tribune or Times. Not a bit of it. None of these old firms will ever go into the new papers. They despise them as advertising mediums of cargoes or parts of cargoes of merchandize.

Goodhue & Co. had many rivals to their line of packets, but none were successful. Robert Kermit once started a line of "Saint" ships. He owned the ship "St. George," and he persuaded Stephen Whitney and old Nat Prime to become owners in a new ship called the "St. Andrew." The line never succeeded, although the latter once made a very short passage in the year 1834, and brought the intelligence of an advance in the price of cotton in Liverpool. She came in late one Christmas Eve. Old Mr. Prime lived at that time at the corner of Broadway and Marketfield street, (now Battery Place). Mr. Whitney lived only a few steps distance on the corner of State street and Bowling Green Row, (where he lived until he died very recently). These *old* heads, and two or three younger ones, had the exclusive news, and they intended to make the most of it. It was certain not to be made public until the day after Christmas. Letters of credit were prepared in the front parlor of No 1. Broadway for one million of dollars. Walter Barrett was selected to leave next morning for New Orleans, by way of Wheeling, hoping that he would outstrip the great Southern mail, leaving two days ahead, carrying these credits in favor of Thomas Barrett and John Hagan, of New Orleans, both eminent merchants in those days. The letters ordered cotton to be bought so long as there was a bale in *first hands* in New Orleans. Mr. Barrett, the bearer of credits and orders, was told to spare no expense in order to beat the mail. It was now eleven o'clock, Christmas Eve. No one had thought about money for the expense of the messenger to New Orleans. Banks were all shut — brokers too. Mr.

Prime seized a blank check, and went up with it to the City Hotel.

"Willard, for what amount can you cash my check to-night?"

"How much do you wish, Mr. Prime?"

"One thousand dollars."

Mr. Willard had the money, and gave it to Mr. Prime. It was in the pocket of Mr. Walter Barrett, the next morning, when he embarked at six o'clock in the boat for Amboy, commanded then by the since famous Capt. Alexander Schultz.

The messenger, by bribing stage drivers, paying Mississippi boat Captains $50 or $75—*not* to stop and receive freight, reached New Orleans in eleven days. It was daylight when he got into the old City Hotel, in New Orleans, kept then by Mr. Bishop. Two hours, after, John Hagan and Thomas Barrett had the letters of credit and orders to purchase cotton. The Southern mail did not arrive for three days. Before night, over 50,000 bales of cotton had been purchased at 11 to 12 cents, or about $60 per bale. That cotton was sold at 17 and 18 cents when cotton went up a few days after. Some was sent to Liverpool. The profit was on some lots over $30 bale, and was divided up among the New Orleans houses of Barrett & Co., and John Hagan Co., and the New York operators. The messenger had the profits of 200 bales awarded him, and his expenses paid. This operation was a lucky one for some of the owners of the St. Andrew, but it did not aid Captain Robert Kermit paticularly, and the "Saint" line went down. Goodhue & Co.'s line of packets met with a more formidable opposition from the celebrated but somewhat unfortunate E. K. Collins. He started a line of packets, nicknamed the "Theatrical line." Few New Yorkers but what will well recollect the "Garrick," the "Siddons," the "Roscius," the "Shakspeare," &c.

This packet line eventually became transient freighting-ships, and Mr. Collins started the famously unfortunate steamship line, consisting of the Atlantic, Pacific, Arctic, Baltic and Adriatic. Two of the ships, the Pacific and Arctic, were steamship coffins for hundreds, and the other ships have been sold and passed into other hands; but the black ball line of Goodhue & Co. still exists, still pays, and exhibits the effect of good management by good merchants, in striking contrast to other lines.

Few persons out of the city and not many in it, have any idea of the immensity of business transacted by such a house as Goodhue & Co. They sell a cargo of teas and China goods (worth perhaps $400,000) at auction or by brokers, with less noise than an eighth avenue dealer in teas and soap displays in an hour. They get their commission of two and a half per cent. and a guarantee commission of two and a half more. In all five per cent, or if the cargo is worth half a million, the commission of Goodhue & Co. would be $25.000. The guarantee commission is against loss to those who send consignments of merchandise to Goodhue & Co. The latter are obliged to sell on time, say four to six months credit to those who buy of them. If they sent the notes so received without endorsing them to the owner of the teas, or endorsing on said notes "*Without recourse*," and if the purchaser failed to pay — then the owner would lose, and naturally be very indignant. So Goodhue & Co. and other commission houses guarantee their notes, and for so doing charge what they call a guarantee commission of about one half per cent. a month. If a note is received by a house like Goodhue & Co. that is worthless they lose it, and not the owner of the teas or other merchandise, for whom Goodhue & Co. have acted and sold goods.

It it said that so many failures occur in New York, that prudent as Goodhue & Co. are, and as well as they know the standing of wholesale merchants and others to whom they sell goods, their guarantee account is a losing one, and that in the last twenty years they have lost largely by it.

At the same time it is safe to say that no foreign merchant would consign goods to Goodhue & Co. or any other commission house, unless they agreed to guarantee and make good the notes taken for merchandize, if not paid at maturity. In giving this brief sketch of Goodhue & Co. I have given a view to the readers of a commercial house of the old school — one known in every part of the world, known to all leading merchants in the great commercial marts of commercial nations, and yet scarcely known to the millions in this city — certainly to but few of them above Wall street or unconnected with its influences.

CHAPTER. IV

It is said, and doubtless truly, that there is not a port in the known world where the American flag has not floated over some American vessel. These vessels and those connected with them are mostly from the New England States. The Eastern built vessels go to every part of the globe. Nearly all of the established American commercial houses in foreign parts, were founded by the supercargoes of American vessels. At first they visited these ports, sold their cargoes, and bought return cargoes. After a while it was found necessary to remain constantly at the foreign ports. For instance, in Canton, China, when it was the only port open to foreign trade, the first supercargoes became in after years the principal merchants. The great Canton house of Russell & Co., was founded by Mr. Russell, originally a supercargo for Mr. Gray of Boston. Goodhue & Co. became the agents of Russell & Co., in New York, except for a period when the brother of Mr. Russell was a partner of George Douglass, who did business thirty years ago at No. 22 Broad street.

Russell was a poor Connecticut boy at the start. He has since erected a palace in his native village, at a cost of a quarter of a million.

The firm of Talbott, Olyphant & Co., in South street,

had a house in Canton — Olyphant & Co. The original supercargo who founded that house in Canton was D. W. C. Olyphant. All connected with this house were pious people. Gutzlaff, who thirty years ago, dressed as a Chinese, and penetrated into the interior of China, always stopped at Olyphant's in the American Hong. Olyphant, the original supercargo, was a Quaker. They had a famed ship named the "Roman."

Another celebrated East India firm was that of Hoyt & Tom. Hoyt died only a few days ago. One of his sons married a daughter of General Scott. Their ship was the famous "Sabina." Goold Hoyt himself was in early years a supercargo for Le Roy, Bayard & Co., the greatest commercial house in the city sixty years ago.

N. L. & G. Griswold was another China house. Their regular ship was the "Panama."

The house that I have alluded to did very little other business except in Canton goods, teas, &c. It was a great business. A house that could raise money enough thirty years ago, to send $260,000 in specie, could soon have an uncommon capital, and this was the working of the old system. The Griswolds owned the ship "Panama." They started her from here in the month of May, with a cargo of perhaps $30,000 worth of ginseng, spelter, lead, iron, &c., and $170,000 in Spanish dollars. The ship goes on the voyage, reaches Whampoa in safety, (a few miles below Canton.) Her supercargo in two months has her loaded with tea, some china ware, a great deal of cassia or false cinnamon, and a few other articles. Suppose the cargo, mainly tea, costing about 37 cents (at that time) per pound on the average.

The duty was enormous in those days. It was twice

the cost of the tea, at least: so that a tea cargo of $200,000, when it had paid duty of 75 cents per lb. (which would be $400,000,) amounted to $600,000. The profit was at least 50 per cent. on the original cost, or $100,000, and would make the cargo worth $700,000.

The cargo of teas would be sold almost on arrival (say eleven or twelve months after the ship left New York in May), to wholesale grocers, for their notes at 4 and 6 months — say for $700,000. In those years there was *credit given by the United States* of 9, 12, and 18 months! So that the East India or Canton merchant, after his ship had made one voyage, had the use of Government capital to the extent of $400,000, on the ordinary cargo of a China ship as stated above.

No sooner had the ship "Panama" arrived, (or any of the regular East Indiamen), than her cargo would be exchanged for grocers' notes for $700,000. These notes could be turned into specie very easily, and the owner had only to pay his bonds for $400,000 duty, at 9, 12 and 18 months, giving him time actually to send two more ships with $200,000 each to Canton, and have them back again in New York before the bonds on the first cargo were due.

John Jacob Astor at one period of his life had several vessels operating in this way. They would go to the Pacific (Oregon) and carry from thence furs to Canton. These would be sold at large profits. Then the cargoes of tea to New York would pay enormous duties, which Astor did not have to pay to the United States for a year and a half. His tea cargoes would be sold for good four and six months paper, or perhaps cash; so that for eighteen or twenty years John Jacob Astor had what was actually a free of interest loan from government of over *five millions* of dollars. Astor was prudent and lucky in his operations, and such an enormous government loan did not ruin him as it did many others. One house was Thomas H. Smith & Sons. This firm also went enormously into the Canton trade, and although possessing originally but a few thousand dollars, Smith imported teas to such an extent that when he failed he owed the United States three millions, and not a cent has ever been paid.

Thomas H. Smith built an enormous tea store in South street, up by Dover. It extended through to Water, and was a hundred feet wide. It was the wonder of the city when it was built. The docks near it were named India wharf. Smith also built famous stores at Perth Amboy, and had his tea ships land tea cargoes there. The travelers to Philadelphia by the old route must often have wondered what those immense brick stores were doing in such an insignificant place as Perth Amboy. Thomas H. Smith, besides being the greatest tea merchant of his day, was also the greatest *Spreeite* of his day. He was the President of a Club called "The Fire Club." It held its meetings in Franklin square on the corner of Dover street. Boys have a mode of amusement called "Follow your leader." This was adopted by the Club of which Smith was President. Many men who are now aged and respected men, or dead, belonged to the "Fire Club." Joseph Foulke, a trader at Curacoa, a Dutch Island in the West Indies, and the Staggs. There was old Peter Stagg, cashier of the City Bank, and John and Benjamin Stagg. There was old Matthias Bruen, and many more whose names were on the Club list. They gave grand suppers, and their entertainments were very expensive. They would invite a guest to these suppers, explain the rules, and if he refused to join, or could not carry out the idea, the fine was one dozen of champagne. These fines were occasioned by a refusal to follow the leader. On one occasion a great cotton merchant from New Orleans was a guest. He agreed to all the conditions. It was late in the evening, in the dead of winter. The ice in the East river was floating up and down with every flood or ebb of the tide. "Follow leader," shouted Smith, and out of the warm, luxurious club-rooms poured the members of the Club. Out of the Square, around the corner into Dover street. "Follow leader," and on rushed Smith, the President of the Club, with thirty men behind him, down Dover, past Water, past Front, into South, and thence on to the pier. One of Smith's own ships lay at the dock. A lighter lay inside of the main wharf. The ice was loose and dashed up around the vessels. "Follow leader," exclaimed Smith, as he plunged from the dock into water. Some drew back, but others followed the leader, who succeeded in getting out of the ice water on to the lighter, and from thence to the dock: and shouting "Follow leader," he led off with frozen clothes, up Dover and into the room of the Club. Plunge, plunge, plunge, one after another, and so on until all had successfully accomplished the terrible and dangerous feat. The Southern cotton merchant was last. Some of the regular club members remained until they saw him reach the dock again safely, and there they left him shivering. He did not remain long. As he walked up from the dock, he noticed a large store open in South street. He entered. It was a wholesale and retail ship stores. "I have met with an accident — give me a glass of cognac, hot, with sugar and water." It was done, and he drank it. "Do you keep gunpowder?" he asked.

Receiving an affirmative reply, he bought and paid for half a keg, and then took his way to the club room. At the door were standing Mr. Lowe and Mr. Town, two members of the Club. The latter exclaimed, "Brave Southern stranger — you have passed the ordeal safely. You are now *leader*, and we are deputed to place the Club under your command, if you choose to exert your sacred privilege."

"Thanks, my friends, I shall do so, but I will not ask you to go out of the room this cold night. Let us drink!" and as he entered the room, he sought a side closet where hung his cloak. There he placed the keg, and then returned and took a seat at the long solid mahogany table. President Smith called the Club to order. The stewards for the night opened a dozen of champagne amid shouts, calls, and songs of the most stirring character. "Order, come to order!" exclaimed President Smith. When order was partially restored, he said; "members of the club, our guest has passed the icy ordeal. He has now the right of becoming leader for the balance of the night, or until a failure in our sacred rites. What says he?"

The cotton merchant took from his bosom a bundle of tow, and laid it on the table. All eyes were fixed upon him. "I accept the command. I will lead now. Wait until I give the word and then do as you see me do." By this time, he had spun the tow into a string, that would reach from the table to the grate. He placed a tumbler on one end of the tow, to hold it on the table, and then passed the other to the pan under the grate, and made that fast with a piece of coal from the coal scuttle. Not a word was spoke. All felt that something unusual was to occur. Cotton merchant now deliberately went to the closet and returning with the keg took his seat. Then he went to work and removed the hoops, until he could take out the head of the little keg. Not a soul moved. Then he took a very little of what appeared to be black sand in his hand, walked to the fire, and flung it in. The considerable explosion that followed started all. "Powder, by Jupiter," exclaimed Smith. Cotton merchant took the end of the tow line from the glass, and pushed it down deep into the powder in the keg, and there reseated himself. "Now, Mr. President and members of the club, I wish you to hear what I have to say."

"You have tried my pluck, I come from a hot climate, and you have made me go through an icy ordeal. It is my time now, but I will not be so cruel. I will give you a *fiery ordeal* to go through. If you stand it, you will never need more wine ; and if you do not, the fines will amount to a small fortune, and you will have wine enough to last your club a year. Look at me. He walked to the fire, kicked off the coal lump, and placed the other end of the tow-line in the red hot coals. Then he walked back, and as he brought his fist down upon the table said in tones of thunder as he sat down, "Keep your seats, and thus follow your leader." The fire curled up in fitful spouts from the burning tar — it burnt over the grate pan, and began to crawl along the carpet. It had eighteen feet to go. Sixty and odd single eyes, watched the burning train. One rose from his seat, then another, finally one exclaimed, "we shall all be blown to old Nick," and made for the door. The panic increased. Down stairs the club members plunged like a flock of sheep. Even old Smith the President, was among the first to bolt from the room. Before the tow-line had burned as far as the table all were gone but the cotton merchant. As soon as he saw that he was alone, he placed his foot upon the burning tow, and extinguished it. Then he opened the window and emptied the keg into the snow, and again resumed his seat. He waited long for the return of the club members: one by one they did come back. There Cotton sat, until Smith took his seat as President. "Now call for the fines," he said, and a severe lecture he gave them for their follies and real cowardice. The club died long ago.

Thomas H. Smith & Son, when they failed owed the Government over three millions. Their book-keeper was old Matthew Bruen. His son, George W. Bruen, married old Thomas Smith's daughter. Matthew Bruen was assignee of old Tom, and must have put away some millions. Thomas Smith left a son — young Tom Smith, as he used to be called — who is now a farmer somewhere on Long Island. Old Smith had another daughter, who married Frank Waddell, recently deceased. Of course, the gift and assignment of property by old Tom Smith to Matt Bruen was absolute and unqualified, or the United States would have seized it. The result was that the only way young Tom and Frank Waddell could make old Matthew Bruen disgorge was by scaring him. This was done so effectually that it is supposed by Doctor John Carnochan, Minthorne Tompkins, John Coster and others, who are posted, that Frank Waddell in twenty-five years made him shell out over four hundred thousand dollars at different periods. Frank ran away with Miss Smith. He was an awfully fast man — not a bad man, but heartless as a shark. He was at one time a great crony of Henry W. Herbert and William McLeod.

CHAPTER V.

In a former chapter, George Douglas was alluded to as having done a very large East India commission business; but the firm of George Douglas & Co., did a heavy business independent of India. This house was one of the very few that, in the contest between General Jackson and the United States Bank, sided with the President against the Bank. Almost all the merchants opposed Jackson. Not so George Douglas, who in 1832 held bank credits to the extent of $300,000. He was advised to sink politics, or not let his political opinions be ventilated until he no longer needed the credits; but Mr. Douglas was not that kind of a man. He avowed his opinions openly and above board. It is needless to add, that the Bank of the United States very speedily closed its accounts with the independent New York Jackson merchant. The stoppage of his credits injured him seriously, but he stood up under it, and although staggered did not fall.

Mr. Douglas was equally independent in other mattars. He was the first merchant who ever refused to receive the consignment of a cargo of brandy or wine, because he was a temperance man and meant to be consistent. But this did Mr. Donglas: — He actually sacrificed $20,000 or $30,000 worth of commission because he would not sell wines or liquors even by the cargo. He never said, "others *will* do it if I refuse, and I may as well earn the commission as any other merchant!"

Mr. D. has always allowed his name to be used, whenever and wherever it could do good to the cause of democracy. In 1844 he was one of the democratic electors at large, and voted for James K. Polk. In 1845, James Hagarty, the United States consul at Liverpool died, and Mr. Douglas became an applicant for his post. John Tyler was at that time rewarding Tyler men as fast as it was possible for him to do. He had only one month more to do it in; and so he rejected Mr. Douglas, appointing a Connecticut Yankee named Joel White. White's claims were irresistible, for he was post master of a small town, and "an original Tyler man." His appointment was upheld by two special post-office agents, and also by Mr. Holbrook, now special agent of New York and New England, but who was then a Tyler editor in the Connecticut village of Norwich.

But to return to the East India merchants. The large capital required in this business kept the mass of merchants from operating in that quarter of the world. A large tea firm, Smith & Nicoll, were very heavy importers until they failed. The sons however carried on the business for some years, as the old concern had the good fortune to owe the United States a few hundred thousand dollars — never since paid. One of these sons, Henry T. Nicoll, represented State street and Bowling Green in Congress for two years.

About twenty-five years ago the China trade underwent a complete change. A new class of men entered into it, and enlarged it very much. Up to 1834, the cargo of an East Indiaman, from China, was principally tea. A small quantity of China ware, ditto preserved ginger in cases of six jars each, costing in Canton $4,25, but sold here to-day for $9; a few hundred boxes of fire crackers, forty packages in each box, costing sixty cents in Canton, and sold here then for $1 to $1,12, but now worth from $2,50 to $3; a few thousand mats of cassia or Chinese cinnamon, weighing a pound or more, and used in stowing cargoes. This trash cinnamon is the only kind used in the United States, the real cinnamon from Ceylon, such as is used in London by the great families, coming too high for American use. It can only be had here of druggists. The nasty stuff from China called cinnamon, impregnated with bilge water, is ground up and sold as cinnamon by all the grocers in the United States. It costs about one cent per pound in Canton. The cargo was commonly completed with silks.

A house called F. & N. G. Carnes, two brothers, had a firm in Paris and one in this city. Frank Carnes resided in Paris, and N. G. in New York. They had made a fortune by importing drugs, fancy goods &c., from Paris. These gentlemen took it into their heads that as the Chinese were a very imitative people, they could send out samples of every fancy article made in Paris, and have it made in China at one-tenth part of the cost. An experienced clerk in their employ was sent out in a ship which they purchased called the "Howard." The speculation succeeded, and such a cargo was never brought to this country before. The profit was immense. Very small quantities of Chinese matting had been brought in any one ship up to that time. But the "Howard" had on board 4-4 6-4 5-4 7-4 of all sizes, patterns and colors — black, white, checker goods, fine, coarse, and so forth. Over 6,000 rolls came in, and the owners doubled their money.

The next trip of the "Howard" was to be a great one. N. G. Carnes had a tongue, great energy, and plans sufficient in his head to load and employ ten Chinese ships; but he lacked the needful money; so he inveigled two other houses, both blessed with plenty of money, into the Chinese trade. One of these firms Gracie, Prime & Co., composed of A. Gracie, Rufus Prime, and John C. Jay; the other firm was Henry & William Delafield, two twin brothers, red-headed and perfect images of each other. The arrangement for a fair share of profits was duly made, and N. G. Carnes was told he might "sail in." He did. The ships "Washington," "Romulus," and "Thomas Dickinson," were respectively chartered, and added to the China fleet, of which the "Howard" was No. 1. B. T. Obear, who commanded the "Howard" was changed to the "Washington," and a Captain Wainwright to the "Howard," a Mr. Butler being sent out as supercargo of the "Romulus." That ship made an awful business of it. She was gone eighteen months. The captain, one Haring, was one of the boys, i. e. mad as a March hare. Once when he thought the ship was sinking, he locked up Supercargo Butler in his cabin while he and the crew fled to the boats. Seeing however that the ship did not sink, they shortly after returned and brought her home. But Butler got the best of the old fellow in a trial which occurred in New York, after the arrival of the ship. He made the old captain pay swinging damages. The "Romulus" however brought home a very valuable cargo, and did well.

The "Thomas Dickinson" carried out a supercargo, younger than the rest; but what he lacked in experience he made up in luck. The ship made the passage out in 97 days, and re urned home in 90. But such cargoes were never heard of before, and in most cases the quantity of articles ordered was so extensive that the market was overstocked, and prices actually soon ranged lower in New York than in Canton! P. L. Mills — who died up in Connecticut last May — was the auctioneer for the concern. Philo Mills had two partners —a brother, who became insane about the Westchester prophet, Mathias, and Thomas M. Hooker, who married a daughter of John H. Howland.

In these cargoes every fan ever made in France was re-copied by the Chinese, and hundreds of cases of feather, palm, silk, ivory, mother-of-pearl and peacock fans included. Palm leaf fans were abundant; and one of these ships brought $20,000 worth of those articles alone. Some of the finer fans cost $5 each. In addition to this every drug known in Europe, Carnes had imitated in China. There is a wood in China, which when cut up into proper sizes resembles the real Turkey rhubarb. It is yellowish and has a taste like our American sumach. Carnes ordered a hundred tin cans (just as the genuine Turkey rhubarb is packed) to be packed with this yellow wood, and sold it for the original article, thus clearing several hundred times its cost. Since then this mock China-wood, called rhubarb, has become a regular article of trade, and has superseded the genuine Turkey rhubarb. The latter has not probably been seen in this country for ten years, unless brought over by some family from London or Paris for domestic use. Of course the yellow dog-wood, or China rhubarb, is harmless, and so is sawdust; but if as large a quantity of sawdust were to be poked down children as there is of this mock rhubarb, deaths would be (as they are) fearfully large from this cause alone.

Carnes also sent out a sample of pure attar of roses,

worth $25 an ounce. The Chinese Samski made a capital imitation, costing about sixpence an ounce, for imitation attar of roses. About 10,000 ounces came out in one ship, and druggists and perfumers bought it up rap idly at from ten to fifteen dollars an ounce. Cassia buds, Chinese cammomile flowers, and in fact every known drug, were imported.

From Paris and London the most famous sauces, condiments, preserves, sweetmeats, syrups, etc., were procured. The Chinese imitated them all, even to the fac similes of the printed London or Paris labels, and $20,000 worth at least of these imitations were imported at prices underselling the London and Paris manufacturers. An immense profit was realized. But the fireworks that Carnes ordered were tremendous. Every pattern, shade and name appeared. Fire-crackers, rockets, revolving wheels, and all the rest. But these did not take so well, and some of these fireworks are still remaining in the market unsold.

The writer, who happened to be mixed up in these events, bought fifty cases of jos sticks and fifty cases of punk, with flint, steel, pouch, and so forth ; and he sold to Madame Newcombe, who kept her tobacco store in Broadway, between Liberty and Cedar streets, a large lot. She probably has some yet.

Every species of lacquer ware, basket, or card case, ever made in London or Paris, was imitated closely by the Chinese ; and New York was flooded. Chessmen, back-gammon boards, fifty in a case ; they came in cargoes almost.

Every article of horn was imitated — one invoice being 100,000 horn scoops, to be used in the drawers of grocers and druggists to ladle out sugar, salt, or any powdered stuff. There is hardly a druggist in this city to-day who does not possess some samples of the Chinese horn scoops.

For the first time, rice paintings were brought out to this country as an article of commerce. Who does not remember old Aaron Levy, who held night auctions on the second floor, between Cedar and Liberty, opposite Mrs. Newcombe's and the City Hotel? Levy was as great a humbug, with his "old master paintings," as Leeds is by some regarded at the present day; but he was a pretty honest old fellow, as auctioneers go. The supercargo of the "Thomas Dickinson" gave Mr. Levy a thousand of them, assorted, large and small sized silk books, each containing twelve plates of Chinese paintings, chiefly of birds, beasts, fish, prisoners, games, whipping-scenes, Chinese punishments, laborers, flowers, fruits, &c. Well, they took amazingly. They cost the supercargo twelve dollars per hundred in China; but old Levy ran off every book at over a dollar each on the average, making a snug profit of about eight hundred lollars nett on this small matter.

There had been, up to 1833, but a few varieties of China silks imported. Carnes sent samples of Italian, English and French silks, and the Chinese imitated them not only to perfection, but actually improved on the patterns sent. But the tendency of these importations from China was to reduce the price of all silks. The shawls imported by the Carnes concern were never equalled, and the South American markets were supplied from New York for ten years after with the most costly crimson, scarlet, white, cream-colored and pink shawls, at prices varying from fifty to two hundred and fifty dollars each. The result of the combination was not such as was expected; the business was overdone. Some few articles paid enormous profits, others did not bring here the first cost in Canton. Duty was high, and of course, the freight on such cases of goods as fans, woodenware, and baskets, was enormous. It was decided by these firms to close up, and to abandon the China trade. Their losses were heavy ; and so the old ship "Howard" was sold, and bought in by Gracie, Prime & Co., to place in the Liverpool line of packets.

It is hardly necessary for me to say that the great Canton merchants looked with scorn on these irregular interlopers — such men as the Griswolds, Olyphants, Russels, Hoyts, &c., these old India traders of New York. In Rhode Island, was the house of Edward Carrington & Co., immensely in the India trade. The Wetmores were connected with this house, and formed a New York concern called Wetmore, Cryder & Co. Cryder was from London. The China trade to America was not confined to New York and Eastern ports. The city of Philadelphia had merchants extensively engaged in the trade. They had great advantages iu capital while the United States Bank was in existence, but labored under a corresponding, disadvantage in regard to market. The China cargoes, although owned in Philadelphia, had to be sold in New York, and a heavy commission paid to New York commission merchants. There were immense operators in Philadelphia twenty-five years ago. Bevan & Humphreys, Samuel Comly, John McCrea, Henry Toland, and such men are the names that occur to me. John McCrea owned nineteen ships at one time, or rather he had them mortgaged at one time. His agents in New York were Rogers & Co., one of the most remarkable houses that ever existed in New York. Lewis Rogers was a Virginian by birth, and he had a house in Havre (France) called Lewis Rogers & Co. In Paris, he was connected with the great bankers Fould & Fould Oppenheim. The Monsieur Fould of that concern is now the great finance minister of the Emperor Napoleon. Through this combination, Lewis Rogers got certain immense contracts to supply the French government with tobacco — what is called "The Regie contract," and the profits were immense. Rogers was a very handsome man, and it is said his influence at the Court of Louis Philippe to get tobacco contracts, was more owing to his good looks than to his mercantile sagacity. In New York, the house of Rogers & Co. was managed by one of the shrewdest merchants that ever lived in New York — Charles Sagory, to wit. This gentleman came from France in the time of the elder Napoleon, to escape the conscription. He became connected with the then greatest firm ever known in New York. I allude to Le Roy, Bayard & Co. In that house Mr. Sagory acquired a vast mercantile experience, and when he became a partner of the branch house of Rogers & Co., he brought to it a capital superior to money.

In Richmond, the firm was Rogers, Harrison & Gray. In New Orleans, James Gray & Co. In London, (England) the connection was Warwick & Claggett. W. S. Warwick was from Richmond also, and the largest tobacco dealer in London.

CHAPTER VI.

The house of Rogers & Co. was conducted by Charles Sagory. While Mr. Rogers held the French contract for tobacco, his agents at Richmond and New Orleans were constantly purchasing tobacco, and drawing upon the New York house for money to pay for their purchases. Consequently, the New York house was a drawer of bills on Paris and on London, to meet the payment of the Southern drafts. Sometimes this business amounted to a million a month, and Chas. Sagory would be the largest drawer of foreign bills in the market. Brokers were employed to sell bills of exchange, but this house had its regular buyers, and principally among French houses.

A great business was this advancing money on consignments of cargoes of foreign produce. A voyage for instance, would be made for the "Liberty," or any of John McCrea's ships. The money would be advanced by Rogers & Co. to pay for the cargo, provided it came freight-free. There was rarely any loss on such advances. It required of course an immense capital to be able to advance $250,000 to purchase a cargo in Canton. Yet it was easily done. Letters of credit were furnished to draw on London, at Canton. Suppose Rogers & Co. applied for these London credits.

They had only to remit to London, when they heard of the drafts being drawn in Canton. These drafts would be at four or six months, so that the ship containing the cargo, which the proceeds of these drafts were used to purchase, would be in New York with the cargo before it was needful to remit to London. Consequently, Rogers & Co. were often in their transactions not out of money for a day. Mr. Sagory had two large houses that were always his friends — gave him the use of their bonds at the Custom House, and endorsement when he needed it. These houses were French. One was A. C. Rossire & Co., deeply engaged for thirty-five years in the St. Domingo trade. The other was Bouchaud & Thebaud, also commission merchants, very old in business, and very rich. When Mr. Thebaud died, Joseph Bouchaud, his partner, carried on business on his own account. He was very rich, and resided for many years, in a house in Duane street, corner of Staples street.

Joseph Bouchaud had two daughters. One married A. Voisin, of the firm of Voisin & Tardy, French importing merchants. They were rich and respected men. Tom Quick, thus alludes to Mr. John A. Tardy, one of the firm : —

" Jim was one of the old pillars of the Carlton House in Leonard street, and was always on hand in the evening to have a ' little draught ' with his old friend Tardy. I asked Barney where old man Tardy held forth now-a-days, but he was unable to answer. I wonder if Bates can tell me, as I would like to see the old gentleman, and pass the rosy just once, for old acquaintance sake."

Those who meet " Old Man Tardy " in these later years of his decadence little dream what a gay, gallant popular man and merchant he was in his palmy days. Oh, how sadly that changeful damsel Miss-Fortune used Tardy! He married a beautiful girl. She was Miss Eustaphieve, the daughter of the Russian consul, and a great belle. She died long ago. The partner of Mr. Tardy was a fine French boy. His mother was a widow, and supported herself and him for many years by working at millinery at the shop of Miss Miller, No. 128 William street, where ex-mayor Tieman's paint store now stands. That same Kate Miller was great in her way. She made men of all her young brothers. One, Andrew Miller, was, and is the largest leather dealer in the Swamp. Her forewoman was a Mrs. Ives. She had one son, who clerked it in old John Greacen's cloth store, until he got ahead and married the daughter of Ralph Olmstead, a rich dry goods merchant. George R. Ives had a friend. He was a little brainless counter-jumper at a small dry goods store, and used to get his six-penny dinners at Seely Brown's eating-house, No. 51 Nassau street (Brown keeps it yet, and has for thirty-one years,) and had a cot bed in a room No. 60 Dey street for $2,00 a week, including breakfast and tea. This friend of George Ives was named Homer Ramsdell. He lacked everything but the impudence of Satan. He was pious in order to prosper; taught in the Sunday school of the Rev. Dr. Potts in order to have a good shye at girls of fortune. This Ramsdell combed his hair beautifully. He dressed to kill, but a man would have been deemed the veriest maniac outside of a lunatic asylum, had he whispered that the nice young man in the dry goods store in Maiden Lane — so harmless, so pleasant and kitten-like in his way of acting — so soft did he speak, and say, "Miss, what shall I show you to-day?" — that that half simpleton would be at the head of a mighty corporation and wield property worth tens of millions! Merchants, listen! Bankers of Wall street, hearken! This poor devil in intellect, in experience — who could just count two and two makes four, could fix a silly girl — he was good looking, he was pious, and he cast his eyes around to make a match for money. He found a partner in Miss Powell of Newburgh, a daughter of that rich Thomas Powell who placed the son-in-law, Homer Ramsdell, ex-dry-goods clerk, as President of the Erie railroad and its vast interests! Great heavens! is it a wonder that under such a trifling chap that superb road should have gone to ruin, and carried with it thousands and tens of thousands of innocent people? No. Now, brokers, why was it done? Because a little chit of a girl fell in love with a brainless counter jumper, and then persuaded her father to impose the son-in-law upon the directors of a mighty corporation. Nobody knew this Homer Ramsdell but a few fellow dry good clerks and members of Potts' church, until Powell made him president of the Erie road; and the silly president set road and stock-brokers on the road to general ruin.

There were about ten of the young counter-jumpers that formed a society to marry rich girls. They swore to protect and aid each other. All succeeded. Ramsdell was one; Ives was another, and the rest I will not now mention. One of the set, named ——, made a dead set at the only daughter of Frank Olmstead, who was rich, (owned then the American Museum buildings, and daughter does now.) It was not to be. Miss Olmstead was destined for a higher class man. She mittened Mr. ——, and married Henry W. Sargent, of the firm of Gracie & Sargent, the agents of Welles & Co., bankers in Paris. The society of young clerks boarded generally at twenty shilling boarding houses, curled each other's hair on Saturday night, went to Sunday school as teachers, and became members of the Presbyterian church that had the richest members and prettiest daugh ters. Their piety game was the card that won in every instance.

I have digressed, but as it is truthful and amusing, I will let it go, and once more return to the Old Merchants.

Rogers & Co., whom I am speaking of, must not be confounded or mixed up with the great sugar house of David Rogers & Co. That firm failed many years ago. The old Rogers was once a sea captain and traded afterwards to Santa Cruz, one of the Danish Islands in the West Indies, where old David resided, was consul, and owned vast sugar plantations. That Rogers did no other business than in sugars. His large stores were over in Greenwich street.

Rogers & Co. had their counting room at 42 Exchange Place, directly opposite the Garden street church of Dr. Mathews, and all were burned out together in the great fire of 1835. At the time that fire occurred, there were few notes to be paid. Money was easy. It was in December. Business had been for years magnificent. Everybody engaged in commerce was making a fortune. Insurance stocks were deemed as good as gold. But that fiery night taught merchants a fearful esson. At least thirty millions of property went off in smoke and ashes in a few hours. It was a bitter cold night. The counting house of Rogers & Co. had not been closed that night, when the alarm was given. The chief clerk was writing in the cash book. When the alarm sounded, he went to the vault and deposited the books. In that vault was what is called a " por' folio." It contained nearly one million of dollars, or what represented that sum. There were bills of exchange, notes or bills receivable of merchants for a vast sum. In another pigeon hole in the vault were policies of insurance for a quarter of a million, for at that time Rogers & Co. had large quantities of foreign merchandise stored in different warehouses.

The clerk smiled, for he thought how little a fire could injure Rogers & Co. in a pecuniary point of view. The bells were ringing, and the clerk stepped out into the keen cold to see where the fire was. It had then reached the west end of Exchange street, a little crooked corner that elbowed around into Pearl street. He watched the fire as it burned fiercer and fiercer. It spread so rapidly, that he began to think the Merchant's Exchange (then deemed fire proof) might catch. Bells ceased to ring, and were rung no more that night. Bell ringers were paralyzed — firemen were aghast — the water froze. About midnight, when the fire was most grand, there was comparative stillness, except its roar. It was an awful silence. The clerk determined to go up town, and find Mr. Sagory. As he passed along the silent streets, he was surprised at the apparent indifference of people up town to the burning city. The fact was, that few people in the upper wards had the least idea that there was a fire down town. The clerk did not find his employer, and hurried back, just in time to enter the store of Ro gers & Co., and secure the portfolio with its valuabl contents. Then came the fiery deluge down Exchange street, sweeping stores, churches and dwellings, like chaff. It was near Broad street. The church of Doctor Mathews, though surrounded by a graveyard, caught in twenty places, and was a mass of ruins inside of thirty minutes. Then more stores, and the sea of fire would move on, all ready to cross Broad street, and then — God have mercy on the devoted city! — the fire would have swept up to Broadway and down to the North River. A building in Exchange street, near Broad, and opposite to the Reformed Church, was blown up, and the fire was stayed. Had it not been stopped, it would have in less then ten minutes more reached the stores of Stebbins, Brouwer & Co., 41 Broad street. In these cellars were nearly 1000 pipes and half pipes of brandy, belonging to Charles Squires. That brandy would have scattered the fire, or sent it across Broad street.

It was a horrid sight next morning to witness the arrival of old merchants down town at about their usual hour. Their faces were pictures of consternation. But little did these merchants, when they witnessed their warehouses a pile of ruins, dream of the extent of the damage. As prudent merchants generally act, so had they. "I am fully insured," were the words of each. Insured! Bah! Every fire insurance company was broken ten times over, and their capitals could not pay ten cents on the dollar. Mr. Sagory came down town among others. He had not heard of the fire until he reached Wall street, and soon after he found himself in front of the ruins where the store of Rogers & Co. had stood, when he had left it the night previous. The books of the house had been saved, and what was of more consequence than all, that "portfolio" with its great value. He, too, relied upon fire insurance policies to make good his losses, and like hundreds of other merchants was doomed to grievous disappointment.

It was some days before merchants realized the extent of the fire calamity in 1835. It was not felt at once, nor for some months, but finally it came, and such a panic as followed — such failures, were never known before nor since. But bravely and manfully that house of Rogers & Co. stood up, engineered as it was by Mr. Sagory. Drafts for tobacco poured in from the South. They were accepted and paid at maturity. By and by the news came that the London tobacco house of Warwick & Claggett had failed, and if so, Rogers & Co. had reason to expect at least half a million of dollars of bills to be returned, and on which they would have to pay 10 per cent. damage. But no. This did not happen. Mr. Rogers himself crossed from France to London and paid the drafts of his New York house as they became due. All this while Rogers & Co. had to sustain not only their own Southern house, but their Philadelphia connections.

John McCrea was a most curious man. I have spoken of him as owning so many ships. He seemed to do all his extensive business himself. He purchased a ship or built her, and would at once come to New York, and with Rogers & Co. make up a voyage for her. The mode of operating was ingenious, and while the United States Bank of Pennsylvania was in existence, could be done to any extent. We will say that McCrea purchased a ship for $30,000, (without a cent in his pocket) cash. He would go to Bevan & Humphreys (old Mat. Bevan was president, "to close up the concern" of the old United States Bank.)

"I want to raise $25,000 on such a ship on the usual terms. I have got her a freight to Liverpool of $9,000, and I want to raise $5,000 on that freight list."

Mr. Bevan would consent to the arrangement, and discount the notes of Mr. McCrea for six months. Mr. McCrea would take the sums and go and pay for the ship and receive a bill of sale for her. He would give another bill of sale to Bevan & Humphreys, and the reg ister would of course be issued to B. & H. as collateral security for McCrea's notes. Bevan & Humphreys charged two per cent. for making these advances. McCrea would plan his voyage well, and when the ship returned she perhaps had half paid for herself, and notes would be renewed until she was clear, when he would make her the basis of a new mercantile operation, and so it went on for years.

Now and then McCrea would make an enormous sum. He really owned nineteen or twenty ships, and yet their registers were all acting as collateral security to some other operation, an iron mine in Juniata county, or a speculation of $250,000 in domestics, in New York, purchased by William Stewart, the dry goods broker. Millions on millions of business was done in this apparent loose way by Mr. McCrea. So long as he had cash for a *margin* he cared not. He kept no books, unless pencil figures on the back of old letters, and little slips of paper in his pockets, could be called books. This extraordinary man had to be kept straight by Rogers & Co., for McCrea was always ready for an operation of $100,000 or $1,000,000, and would carry it through, and that, too, when he had to borrow a five dollar bill to carry him back to Philadelphia. Mr. McCrea had another great financial friend in this city. It was John N. Gossler, the New York agent of the great bankers in London, Thomas Wilson & Co. Mr McCrea named one of his new ships the "John N Gossler." She made several very lucky voyages.

CHAPTER VII.

I have alluded on several occasions when writing about old merchants to the vast number that have come to this city from the six New England States. The immigration has been going on ever since the Revolution. At that time, or about eighty or ninety years ago, Boston, Salem and several other along-shore places did a heavy business in navigation. A great part of the tonnage of the United States was owned East. These ambitious young men could stay at home. Not so in after years, when New York city, like a fast race-horse, took the bit in her mouth, and went ahead with terrific commercial speed. Every city has been distanced in this mercantile race. Philadelphia, Boston, Baltimore, and all other Atlantic ports are nowhere when mentioned in contrast with New York. So soon as this last city fairly started ahead, the talent, enterprise, genius and smartness of the entire Union began to pour into New York, so that now, if a pestilence was to break out in this city to-morrow, there is not a house however lofty, nor a cottage so humble, but would be affected by the sad news. All are represented or connected in some way with the Empire City. This is particularly the case in the New England towns. Almost every family has sent here one or more representatives. All do not succeed, but some do, and this is quite sufficient to keep the ambition to get a clerkship in New York alive.

It is not deemed essential, as a general rule, that anything more is required to enter the mercantile career than a sound district school education. This consists in going to school in winter to a male teacher, and in summer to a female teacher, until the future great merchant is eight years old. After that, if the lad is located in the interior of New England, he goes to school in the winter only, and in the summer works on a farm.

His winter schooling generally ends when the boy is fourteen years old. He can by that time (if he is smart) parse pretty well, and has reached the "double rule of three" in Daboll. He needs no more towards his future success than a trunk, "Sunday-go-to-meeting" clothes, and a Bible. This the family provide, and with a few dollars and a mother's prayer, the young hero goes forth to seek his fortune in the great mart of commerce. He needs but a foothold. He asks no more, and he is as sure to keep it as that light will dispel darkness. He gets a place somewhere in a "store." It is all store to him. He hardly comprehends the difference between the business of the great South street house, that send ships over the world, and the Bowery dry goods shop with three or four spruce clerks. He rather thinks the Bowery or Canal street store the biggest, as they make more show. But wherever this boy strikes, he fastens. He is honest, determined and intelligent. From the word "go" he begins to learn. to compare, and no matter what the commercial business he is engaged in, he will not rest until he knows all about it, its details, — in fact, as much as the principals.

Another characteristic of the future merchant is this – no sooner has he got a foothold, than the New England boy begins to look for standing room for others. Perhaps he is the son of a small farmer who has several other children. The pioneer boy, if true blue, does not rest until one by one he has procured situations for all of his brothers. If he has none, he has friends in the village, and ere a year, Bill, Jo and Jim have been seduced off to New York. Such a boy must have been one of the firm of Fitch & Co., a large house that have a counting room in New street, and at present own nearly an *acre* of buildings, bounded by Broadway, New and Exchange streets.

I believe the father of Mr. Asa Fitch, Jr., the senior of the firm, is still alive ; and if so, must be nearly ninety-five years old. He was born at Bean Hill, near Norwich, Connecticut. It is hardly necessary to go into the details of the career of the former Fitch boy. After a faithful clerkship of some years (as necessary to make a skilful merchant, as an apprenticeship to a trade of any kind is to eventual success) he was sent out by his employer to France. He there founded the house of Fitch, Brothers & Co., having (as soon as he was fairly established, himself) sent for two younger brothers, one named Douglas and the other William Fitch. Thirty years ago Fitch, Brothers & Co. of Marseilles, were established, and doing an immense business. Nearly all the American vessels and American produce sent from ports in the union to Marseilles, were consigned to the great firm. The United States government, also, found it necessary to appoint this house the agents of the Navy ; and it had the supplying of all the provisions, making all the payments, &c., of the American squadron stationed in the Mediterranean. This business gave Fitch, Brothers & Co., a large capital to operate upon, and immense commissions every year. No French house in Marseilles could, or can now, compete with this old American house. It has its agents in New York, Philadelphia, Baltimore, Richmond, Charleston, Savannah, Mobile and New Orleans. Their agents would advance to shippers of cotton, rice, pot and pearl ashes almost the invoice cost in the American markets, to get the consignments of vessels and cargoes to Fitch, Brothers & Co.

This is a very curious sort of business, and can hardly be comprehended by the large mass of American readers.

There are merchants who hardly make any noise in the cities where they dwell, who are constantly shippers They watch foreign markets, and are constant buyers and shippers to ports where they think money can be made Still there is a limit to this shipper's capital. I will call him Kennedy. Mr. K. thinks 300 tierces of rice and 100 bales of upland cotton, would pay him to purchase here and ship it to Marseilles. He has watched prices in both markets — he knows that very little rice and cotton have been shipped, and the chances are that both will command high prices in Marseilles. He goes to Mr. A. the agent of Fitch, Brothers & Co., and tells him what he thinks.

"You will do well to ship," says the agent. "What will you advance me?" asks Kennedy, and adds, "my invoice for rice and cotton will amount to about $16,000. I have bought at a bargain, and freights are very low. I will consign it to Fitch, Brothers & Co. I expect to make at least 20 per cent. on this shipment if prices keep up in Marseilles, but I tell you candidly, unless you advance me pretty near cost, I can't ship." Says the agent, "Well, Kennedy, I'll tell you what I will do. I will advance you seven-eighths of the invoice cost, that will be $14,000, as soon as you hand me invoice and bills of lading.

Mr. Kennedy at once goes to work, buys the rice and cotton. Ships it. Gets bill of lading, goes to the agent, and gets the advance of $14,000. He has bought the rice and cotton for cash. He pays for it with this money and $2,000 of his own. He insures the same for cost and a profit, say $18,000 in all, and transfers the policy of insurance to the agent of Fitch, Brothers & Co. The agent draws for the sum he has advanced after converting the dollars into francs, and sells his bills on the Paris banker of Fitch, Brothers & Co.

A few weeks pass away. The invoice of rice and cotton reaches Marseilles. Fitch, Brothers & Co. sell it at good prices, and make out sales. The profit, say, has been twenty-five per cent. They make out the accounts, deducting the advance of $14,000, and pay over through the New York agent, $4,000 profit, and $2,000, difference between cost and advance. The shrewd shipper pockets $4, 000 clear profit on an actual outlay of only $2,000.

There are many of these quiet shippers in New York. They make no noise—rarely keep an office. Sometimes they have a desk, a tin sign, and a place in some other merchant's office, and yet, with a small capital, they are operating as buyers and shippers of cotton, rice and other prodnce to an extent of three or four million of dollars annually. The foreign houses who make such liberal advances through their agents aim but to get the American interest of seven per cent. for the use of money, and their regular commission.

In this way, by means of active agents in 1830 and up to 1840, Fitch Brothers & Co., cleared annually from $50,000 to 100,000 per annum by their commissions on vessels, cargoes and invoices of American produce consigned to them in Marseilles.

Another branch of business was equally important. It was the reverse of the operations enumerated. Large wine manufacturers and dealers in France would wish to ship to the States. "Consign your cargo to our agent in New York, and we will advance you three fourths of the invoice cost," would say Fitch, Brothers & Co. Every year this business was enormous, and the agent in New York had to divide the commission he charged, and gave one half back to Fitch, Brothers & Co.

A third branch of the business was American orders for drugs, fruits, wines, &c., to be bought in Marseilles. A large drug house, for instance, in New York, could go to the New York agent of Fitch and get him to order out $20,000 worth of madders, brimstone, or any other product of the Mediterranean. Knowing that the house giving such orders was as good as gold, Fitch, Brothers & Co., would execute the order, and ship it, consigned to "Order." The bills of lading, so filled up, accompanied by an invoice, including Fitch, Brothers & Co.'s commission, would be sent to the agent. He at once sent a bill for the amount. It would be paid, or secured, and then the real orderers of the goods would be handed the bill of lading to order, endorsed over by Fitch, Brothers & Co.

So large were the operations of the New York agent, so important were they, that the elder Fitch (Asa Fitch, Jr.,) decided that he would cross the Atlantic and superintend the agency himself.

His next brother, Douglas Fitch, had become *au fait* at the business in Marseilles, and had married a French lady of wealth, showing a disposition to make Marseilles his home for life. Asa Fitch, Jr., had an awful dread of the sea. It was extremely curious that the moment he got out of sight of land, he dropped a helpless man, unable to raise his head until once more on land. It mattered little how long or how short was the passage, or whether rough or mild weather prevailed. In the fall of 1828 he left Havre for New York. He reached here more dead than alive, and was carried to the Atlantic Hotel, No. 5 Broadway. He remained at that hotel for some years, occupying the two front rooms on the second floor. During that period Mr. Fitch was making his arrangements for establishing a new commercial house in New York. He had a brother named William, and three favorite nephews. One of the last was the late somewhat celebrated Colonel William D. Lee, who was so deeply interested in the Tehuantepec route operations with Colonel A. G. Sloo. Robert Lee was killed in Texas. The other nephew, George Washington Lee, is still living and doing good in the world.

Mr. Asa Fitch opened his New York commercial house in Exchange street, under the firm of Fitch & Co. He had become immensely wealthy, and having a larger capital than he could use profitably in his business, he began to invest in real estate. On the South corner of Broadway and Exchange Place was a large double house, extending back to New street. Next to it was a house, and at the back of it a livery stable. Mr. Fitch purchased all that property from the corner of Exchange Place (Garden street formerly) down Broadway at least 150 feet, if not 200. He had put up an immense store on the New street corner, the summer previous to the great fire in December, 1835. When that fire occurred, the merchants hired the building of him for an Exchange. Then he rented the property on Broadway for the Waverly Hotel. At last he built the public stores, covering all that part of the block, and I have no doubt that, in one shape or another, that property has produced in rents from the U. S. Government, $800,000 to $1,000,000. Some say that he received $50,000 a year from these public stores, for twenty years. It may be so.

Asa Fitch was a gay and gallant bachelor, extremely polite to everybody, and especially so to ladies. He was once the most popular man in town. Neither has he in his great prosperity neglected the spot where he was born. One brother remained at home, and in place of the stony farm of 110 acres, worth about $4,000 when Asa left home, it is now the town of Fitchville, and factories loom up in it, worth a million of money. All belong to Asa Fitch.

Asa Fitch, Jr., must now be 75 years old, and when he dies will leave at least six millions of dollars worth of property. What a career! What fun he must have had in his day, and even now he is a jolly joker. What an amusing biography could be written of such a man! What novel could begin to equal it? Talk of the lives of statesmen, politicians, divines and medical men, there is no comparison between any one of them and the career of one of our great merchants.

Truthfully and forcibly written, a life of an eminent merchant would be the book of the day. Particularly of any New York merchant. What a life would be one of P. Perit, written under his own dictation, or of Wm. H. Aspinwall. The life of Asa Fitch, Jr., with all his early struggles before he made a great bank account, would be a model book for unknown millions of young Americans who have to follow in his footsteps and struggle, and — succeed.

CHAPTER VIII.

The old merchants had a different way of doing business thirty years ago than now. They were more careful and more prudent. Perhaps it was owing to the fact that the law abolishing imprisonment for debt had not then been passed; and a large shipping merchant, if he did not pay his debts promptly, could be locked up in the old jail. That building is now nearly forgotten. It stood at the east of the City Hall, on the very ground now occupied by the Hall of Records. It was a square brick building, and had on the top a cupola and a bell. I remember that old jail bell's tones as well as if it were swinging now. Up in the cupola the poor debtors used to sit for hours, and sun themselves. Some of the prisoners were allowed to go on what was called the "jail limits." I have read signs at particular points in the lower parts of the city with "jail limits" painted on the board, and nailed up in a conspicuous spots.

The system of credits places a prudent merchant, if his business is at all extended, at the mercy of other persons. To do business, he gives large credits of from six to eight months. If these time buyers are reckless, or if a panic comes along, and they go by the board, the large merchant is also shaken, and perhaps fails, or is forced to ask an extension from his creditors.

Among other merchants whose names arise in my memory this morning are two, who were very singular men. Their names were James A. Moore, and J. W. Hinton. They did business for many years at 95 Front street, under the firm of Hinton & Moore. Mr Hinton was a large, full-faced Englishman. He was a princely-hearted man in the days of his prosperity. His residence was in Dey street, at that time a street that contained no stores. It was filled with dwelling houses.

Hinton & Moore failed. They had a meeting of creditors, and as it was quite evident that their business would be ruined by an assignment, one creditor proposed that Hinton & Moore should pay a certain amount on each dollar due. The sum so named was forty cents. All the creditors agreed, and in consideration of this forty cents, signed off, and gave the firm clear legally. I suppose Hinton & Moore owed $500,000 : by paying forty cents on the dollar, they got clear of all their liabilities for $200,000. With some difficulty they raised and paid this compromise sum to their creditors, and then continued their business. They were entirely free of all indebtedness ; their creditors had signed off, the debts were cancelled, and that was supposed to be the last of old matters. The creditors never expected to receive another dollar on the old accounts.

Not so however did the honest firm of Hinton & Moore regard their indebtedness. They were honorable men, and high-minded merchants. Eight years passed away from the day of their failure. Good fortune attended all their operations. They made money hand over fist.

To the surprise of many, the old creditors were called together at the counting-house of Hinton & Moore on a certain occasion. Presently, a clerk delivered [illegible] statement of accounts. One firm that had settled a debt due them by Hinton & Moore, eight years previously of $10,000 for $4,000 — found a statement crediting them $6,000, with eight years compound interest, and a check for the amount. It was so in every instance.

The creditors remarked that it was very unexpected. Hinton & Moore replied to all after this fashion. "Gentlemen, we failed eight years ago. That was one of those commercial calamities to which all are liable. We exhibited to you a fair statement of our affairs — our debts and our assets. You advised us to settle at forty cents. We did so, and you all lost sixty cents on the dollar. You appeared satisfied, and considered the transaction at an end. Not so did we regard it. Legally we owed you nothing, — morally we owed you the balance of sixty cents on each dollar, and the forty cents was only an instalment on our debt. We have been prosperous in closing up our old affairs, and thanks to your liberality, we were fortunate in continuing our old business, and carrying it on without interruption. We are now happy to be able to pay you all we owe you."

It is needless to say that such an honorable course placed that firm high up in the list of honest merchants.

Alas! they failed again, and the aged and honest Hinton could not get credit for a hundred dollars. I believe he finally found a shelter as an inspector in the Custom House, and died very poor. It was his own fault. He need not have paid $300,000 with interest to creditors who had legally released him. But for this absurd folly he might have died rich. James A. Moore had a brother.

John A. Moore was one of the most extraordinary men of his age; he was red headed and freckled in the face; he was small in size; his disposition was entirely mercurial; he had a large store on the corner of Water street and Old Slip, where he sold iron of all descriptions, and sheathing copper. He did a large and very profitable business, but he was not content with that. Mr. John A. Moore believed in controling the market — "cornering" on sugar, copper and coffee. He was a great calculator; he would cypher out to his own satisfaction how a rise in coffee could be obtained.

Luckily, perhaps, for himself, he had not the cash or the credit to buy up all the coffee in first hands in New York. But this small fact never discouraged our bold operator, if he had no other needful. So Mr. Moore would go to a large commission house, and propose that they should buy for his account 100,000 bags of coffee — Rio, Java, St. Domingo, Cuba, La Guayra, Porto Rico, or Mocha. Moore was plausible; he would prove conclusively that coffee must go up — must take a rise. It could not go lower. The crops in the great producing countries of Brazil, Cuba, Java, would be short. "I am willing to give you a mortgage on my store and its contents, worth $100,000, to secure you from loss, if you will make the purchase and hold it for my account a few weeks. I will pay you a commission of five per cent. for purchasing and selling. The amount will be over a million, and you will be sure to make $50,000. Mr. Moore would carry his point, and the coffee would be purchased. Of course none but a house of undoubted credit and means could go into such an immense operation. Such a house existed in Broad street, and in 1832 the operation was consummated. In No. 26 Broad street an immense warehouse was loaded down with coffee. The store belonged to old Mr. Nathaniel Prime, of the firm of Prime, Ward & Co.

The garret was an old fashioned affair, that pointed

almost up to the sky, and would contain more merchandize than all the rest of the lofts added together. Coffee-bags were piled almost to the scuttle. One morning Mr. Moore was up in this garret, examining the coffee. He pointed out to his companion, Mr. Rufus Prime, a box twenty feet long.

" What on earth, Prime, have you got in that funny looking box ? "

" Two paintings," was the reply.

" Paintings ? — what the devil are they doing here ? "

" Well, Moore, I'll tell you the whole story. Two young men named Brette have brought out from London a lot of paintings by the Old Masters. We are bondsmen for the importation. The paintings are on exhibition at the Academy in Barclay street, all but these two. The exhibition is losing money," added Mr. Prime.

" Then why do you not exhibit these ? "

" Oh, they are too immoral. It would not do."

" Do let me see them," said Moore.

" With great pleasure," replied Mr. Prime, and he called up the porter. " Take out those paintings, Henry, and spread them up over the coffee sacks."

It was done. That was the first time that the celebrated paintings of " Adam " and " Eve" were exposed to New York eyes.

" Exhibit them, Prime, by all means. They are scriptural pieces, and they will take," said Mr. Moore. His advice was followed. Adam and Eve were sent up to Barclay street, and the exhibition of them commenced. It was followed by a perfect furore. The money poured in by buckets' full. In a week, the brothers Brette were free from debt. In less than a month, they remitted £500 sterling to London. It was a hit. All New York was agog to see Adam and Eve. Inside of two years $200,000 was received from the exhibition. W. C. Preston of South Carolina, (recently deceased) offered $50,000 for them. It was declined.

To return to John A. Moore and his coffee speculation. The purchase was sixteen millions of pounds, or about $1,140,000. It was sold at an advance of over two cents a pound, and Moore cleared net about $280,000; and he lost that and half as much more, inside of a year, in another speculation, whether sugar, coffee or tea, I do not remember.

Still Moore had a most wonderful streak of luck just after that. Many of our citizens will remember the long lottery law suit between John A. Moore and his creditors.

Moore had a brother-in-law named George ——. He was in the lottery business in Greenwich street, No. —. A great lottery was to be drawn in Virginia; the capital prize was $100,000, and the tickets were $20 each. George —— was poor. He had no capital to enable him to speculate in tickets, and on the occasion of every drawing he hurried in his tickets (left over) so as to be in time. On the day of the great drawing he was too late. He found he had a full ticket, No. 9, 32, 63 in his drawer. He could not afford to lose $20; the drawing would be in next day, and he must get rid of that ticket — 9, 32, 63, somehow or other. He went to everybody he knew who possessed capital, and a speculative disposition. All refused the venture.

There was one more hope for George. It was his sister, Mrs. John A. Moore. He went to her, and with tears in his eyes narrated his unfortunate position. "I can't afford to lose $20, and this week especially."

"Very well, George; here is $20 of my money; I will lose it. Don't say anything about my foolishness to Mr. Moore; now give me the ticket."

He did so, adding, "God bless you, my dearest sister, you have saved me from the greatest anxiety," and he left her home perfectly delighted. He never thought how hard a case it would be for his sister to get stuck.

The next day the drawing arrived.

George's eyes went no further than the three first drawn numbers. There they stood — 63, 9, 32.

"By jingo!" he exclaimed, "my sister has come within an ace of drawing a prize, but her ticket was 9, 32, 63." Again he looked. Now he is as pale as a sheet, as he exclaimed, "She *has* drawn the capital prize of $100,000."

So it proved, but she was not allowed to draw it in peace, or the net amount (about $85,000). Moore's creditors were up in arms. They got out an injunction from the old Chancellor's Court, declaring that the prize really belonged to John A. Moore, and that the wife business was a dodge to cheat. At last it became clearly apparent to Chancellor McCoun that the wife had purchased the ticket with her own money, to oblige a favorite brother, and had concealed it from her husband, fearful of his disapprobation, until after the drawing, when she placed the lucky ticket in his hands to collect.

Poor George! Days, weeks, months and years have passed away, but not for an hour, night or day, has he been able to drown the "penny wise, and pound foolish" arrangement, when to save $20, he lost $100,000. He has tried to have dame Fortune come back again. He has wooed her mild and strong. Lotteries have lingered about George, and he has lingered on trying a solitary chance for more than a quarter of a century. The one *miss* has embittered his existence more than 100,000 other misses could possibly have done.

CHAPTER IX.

The house of John F. Delaplaine & Co. was at one time a commercial house of considerable eminence. John resided in Broadway, nearly opposite the old Grace church, corner of Rector street. He had a brother and partner named Isaac. The counting house of the Delaplaines was on the corner of Old Slip and Water street. Of course this house was a rich one, and had a reputation at home and abroad. The firm was largely in the Mediterranean trade, and dealt in drugs specially, as well as in general merchandise. Both of the Delaplaines died rich, and left sons and daughters. One son, Isaac, married a daughter of the celebrated Billy Post, the paint dealer in Water street. He is now a member of Congress from this city. Post kept for many years in an old shanty that was covered with green moss, and refused to burn whenever there was a fire in the vicinity. Its escapes were almost miraculous, nd it was only torn down after the death of its owner. At one time Mr. Post made all his neighbors laugh, by telling them of his intention to put a granite front to the old wooden store. Post was a miser, and died rich.

Another ancient firm was that of Tucker & Lauries, — all English, or rather Bermudians. Richard Tucker lived for many years in Bond street. He was a stately merchant of the old school. He had sons, well known in New York fashionable life, one was Thomas Tucker, or rather Tom Tucker as he was familiarly called by Ogden Hoffinan, Ned Curtiss, Willis Hall, Charley Hoffman, Sargent, Minthorne Tompkins, and the set of Tom's friend who had rooms at 84 Broadway. When old Richard Tucker died, the style of his house changed; it became the firm of Henry & George Laurie, or in short —H. & G. Laurie. They did a safe commission business, and piled up money, although in small piles at a time. Eventually they became very rich, gave up business — both bachelors — and retired to Geneva in Switzerland, where they live on the income of their American property, real estate, bank and other stocks, for which they draw an interest of $50,000 annually. The Lauries were fashionable men in their day, and regularly attended the City Hall balls, in white and spotless kids.

They had their intimate friends, and cliqued together. Rupert J. Cochrane was one. He was said to be the very looking glass of fashion, and the mould of form. He was a splendid, princely fellow, was Cochrane. He was largely in the coal business. In one of these chapters allusion was made to George Douglas, and to the fact that he did a very heavy business in 1832 at No. 22 Broad st. Cochrane occupied a part of the same store, and he too retired rich, and is ruralizing in the West, if alive.

William MacLeod belonged to the same private set as the Lauries and Cochrane. His firm was Gillespie & MacLeod. He prided himself upon his pure Highland descent, his father, Col. MacLeod, having been killed at Waterloo. MacLeod came to this city with two sisters, from Canada. He had held a commission in the British service, but having a considerable capital was induced to go into mercantile business, throw up his commission, and take up his home in New York.

Handsome, elegant in manners, an ex-British officer, son of a Waterloo hero, rich in purse, and with *hielana blud!* Doing a large business, what could not William MacLeod do? He was beloved by women and envied by men. He despised wealth, except as it enabled him to make others happy. He was surrounded by those who flattered and plucked him. He led the fashion in everything, and no affair of honor could be decided without him. He was the second to Barton when he shot Graham, one of the editors of the New York Cou rier, in a duel at Hoboken. Mr. Barton had married Cora Livingston, a daughter of the Hon. Edward Livingston, minister to France in Jackson's days, and to whom Barton was secretary of legation. Cora Livingston was the great belle of her day in this city before she married Mr. Barton.

I do not remember now the precise matter that occasioned the difficulty between Barton and Graham. The latter was a dead shot, but Barton was lucky in having for his second an experienced man like MacLeod, who had fought several duels on his own account. The duel was fought on the old duelling ground at Hoboken, and what is very singular, the identical pistols were used that were held by Burr and Hamilton in an earlier part of the century, when the great statesman was shot.

MacLeod's instructions to Barton were graphic. His opponent was on a footpath, in a dead straight line. Mac told him to place the butt of the pistol to his middle, and when the word was given to elevate the barrel to a level and fire along the line. He did so, and Graham had to turn up his toes in consequence. MacLeod, when in his glory, courted a fair lady, the daughter of one of our richest merchants, said to be the late John G. Coster. Mac was a favored suitor, and the damsel referred him to papa. To properly understand the point of Mr. Coster's reply, it is necessary to say that MacLeod had, like other fashionable men, committed the great folly of keeping a mistress. Mr. Coster, unknown to Mac, was aware of it when MacLeod made his proposition for the hand of the "fair daughter." He stated that he was doing well in business, possessed property, a name unquestioned, old family, and all that sort of thing. Old John G. looked at him quietly and listened calmly to all Mac had to say. When it was finished, the old merchant replied:

"That is doubtless all so. I should be pleased under certain circumstances to have you for a son-in-law, but, as a prudent man, I shall be forced to decline your flattering offer in a most positive manner. I will not give my consent."

Mac was taken all aback. He was perfectly astounded. Mr. Coster was asked for his reasons. He would not give any for a long time. At last he said:

"You may be wealthy. I do not dispute it. I hope so. I am rich, but I will tell you what it is, Mr. MacLeod, neither you, or me, or any other man, is rich enough to support two families.

"Good morning, Mr. Coster," replied Mac.

"I am perfectly satisfied with your reasons. I will never repeat the application, and I am too proud to attempt clandestinely to become your son-in-law against your wishes."

And he never did.

Mr. MacLeod was afterwards unfortunate in his commercial affairs, and failed. He left children when he died, and they are wealthy from their Scotch aunts, who allowed Mr. MacLeod an income while he lived. He died at his old favorite haunt, the City Hotel. The friends of his later years were Henry W. Herbert, Dr. John Carnochan, and Frank Waddell. Very few English, Irish or Scotch officers visited New York that did not find out and make the acquaintance of MacLeod.

Two other intimates of MacLeod and the Lauries, were the brothers Oldfield. Granville Sharp Oldfield, was a grandson of the English Granville Sharp. He came to New York and formed a commercial House, under the firm of Oldfield, Bernard & Co. They had a large old-fashioned store, corner of Broad and Garden streets, (now Exchange Place). The senior Oldfield was a real merchant — devoted to business, and yet could be pleased with a good dinner, and good company. All the English notables stopped with Oldfield. When the Keans (father and son) were in New York, they were daily with Oldfield. He did a very heavy commission business. He was forced to suspend in consequence of acts of his partner. Mr. Bernard had a habit of pinching women in public places. He was a Dutch Jew, and did not believe there was a virtuous Christian woman in the United States. On one occasion, when the Woods were playing at the old Park theatre, in opera, Bernard was present. The opera was La "Somnambula." Mrs. Wood was singing "False one, I love thee still," when a thump was followed by a maddening shriek, to the astonishment of the whole house. The cause was known to but few. Mr. Bernard was seated in the rear of a lady and her husband. He commenced his curious antics. She whispered to her husband. The latter turned around, and discovered the aggressor Bernard, who wore a pair of gold spectacles. The offence was repeated, and the wife again told her lord: he rose, and dashed his fist at the right eye of Monsieur Bernard, smashing the glass and driving the particles into the eye-ball of the maddened Bernard, who screamed with horror.

Mr. Bernard became insane, and was sent to the Bloomingdale or some other mad-house, where I believe he died, after a straight-jacket discipline of two years. The house of Oldfield, Bernard & Co. was dissolved, and the head of it, Mr. Oldfield, removed to Baltimore, where he acquired again a large fortune. His only son, Granville, had his arm shot off and died, and the senior Oldfield, although very wealthy, is to-day an inmate of the Baltimore Lunatic Asylum, and yet signs mad checks for the expense!

The other brother, "Tom," was a great favorite in New York with all who knew him, but Tom detested business. He was a genius, and would have made a fortune on the stage. Every actor in New York loved Tom. So did Rupert I. Cochran and William McLeod. So did Doctor Carnochan, and so did Tom's brother. It was of no use to try to change Tom's habits. W. D. Cuthbertson, an extensive merchant in Water street, (recently Vice President of the St George's Society,) employed Tom Oldfield at a high salary as a book-keeper. Tom would make his appearance at precisely two o'clock in the afternoon.

This went on for a week, when the merchant remarked the lateness of the hour when he arrived, and remonstrated.

"But, my dear sir, I don't get my breakfast until one o'clock; how can I come earlier?"

"Get your breakfast earlier," said the merchant.

"How can I? I don't get up until past twelve."

"Then get up earlier," said the merchant.

"How can I?" pleaded Tom, when I don't go to bed until daylight."

Further argument was useless, and Thomas left the employ of Mr. Cuthbertson. Poor Tom! He caught the small pox, and died at the small pox hospital on Staten Island. Among the set who adored him was the late Lewis C. Levin, who died in a hospital recently. They were nearly all "Washington Hall boys"— MacLeod, Cochran, Oldfield, Herbert, Waddell, the Wolcotts, and many others whose names occur to me, and who are indirectly, if not directly, connected with these old merchants.

CHAPTER X.

Some strange coincidences occur occasionally. This day week, the author took his pen in hand, (Tuesday morning last) to write the ninth chapter of this book. Little did he dream, when he was writing about Granville Sharp Oldfield, formerly of the firm of Oldfield, Bernard & Co., that then, on that very day, within an hour of his writing, he, Mr. Oldfield, was dying in the lunatic asylum at Baltimore. So it was.

Mr. Oldfield, as we mentioned last week, became insane some time ago, and yet he signed checks until within a few days of his death, when he became unconscious of what was passing around him, and last Tuesday, the 3d of July, quietly died. About checks he was eccentric. Whenever he drew one in his prosperous days, it was made payable to "order," and he never failed to accompany the person to whom he gave the check, to the bank, and see it paid.

Now that he is dead, all his faults will be buried with him. He had two children — a son and a daughter. He believed as many fathers in England do, that children should obey parents in all things — even in the matter of marrying. That a father of standing should select a wife for his son, and a husband for a daughter, and that love was absurd nonsense, if the match brought wealth, connection, or mutual advantages.

Mr. Oldfield was a lover of the fine arts ; that is, he spent about $60,000 in purchasing a choice and rare collection of paintings. They were sold about a year ago, and brought fabulous prices. His son, upon whom he had lavished all his affections, was killed. His daughter Isabella married Mr. John Wright, of the great American firm of Maxwell, Wright & Co., of Rio Janeiro. Mr. Oldfield was a regular John Bull. He was for a long time the agent at Baltimore, of " Lloyds, London, " and of Barclay & Livingston, of this city.

The firm of Barclay & Livingston is English and ancient. It was originally " Henry & George Barclay." They were sons of Thomas Barclay, who was British consul in New York in the early years of the Republic, when Washington, Adams and Jefferson were Presidents. Although born in this city, yet the Barclays claim to be and are " British born," for they were born under the flag of the British consulate, their father being consul. Henry Barclay left the house about twenty-eight years ago, and retired up the river to a place called Saugerties. There he became a principal stockholder in a paper manufactory, called the " Saugerties Paper Company. " About this time he picked up a smart foreman named Moses Y. Beach, who has since become famous in connection with the Daily Sun now owned by his son Moses S. Beach. The agent in the city was Robert Gracie, then doing business at No. 20 Broad street, as Gracie & Co. The advances made by Mr. Gracie were enormous. He purchased the rags needed, or imported them in large quantitles from Italian ports. To make a long story short, the paper company got behind-hand with Mr. Gracie about $45,000, when he placed the *papers* in the hands of Robert Sedgwick. An injunction from the Chancellor followed, and was served upon Moses Y. Beach in 1833. Shortly after he came to New York, and the paper used by the *Sun* he would buy in small parcels from the old stock stuck upon Mr. Robert Gracie.

H. & G. Barclay had a smart clerk named Schuyler Livingston. When Henry Barclay retired, this clerk was made a partner, and the firm changed to Barclay & Livingston. Some time after, Colonel Anthony Barclay, another brother, came from Savannah, where he had married a wealthy widow named Glen, and became a partner, and the firm was changed to Barclays & Livingston. Anthony Barclay lived in Dey street, near Greenwich, for a long time. Then he moved up to College Place. When James Buchanan gave up, Anthony Barclay succeeded him as British consul. The widow Glen had one son, named Tom Glen; he died many years ago; but few young men were so well known about town as poor Tom Glen. Barclay's own sons were a splendid set of fine fellows. There was Clarence, Henry, Delancy, and others whose names I forget — where are they all now? Their fine figures are seen no more in the haunts they once frequented. They are all dead save one. One daughter remains, and she I notice was recently presented to the Queen of England.

George Barclay had but one child, and she married Frank Rives, a son of the Hon. William C. Rives of Virginia.

The Barclays prided themselves on being English, and at the head of a commercial house of the first class. They were "Lloyd's Agents" for the City of New York. They never meddled with politics. Mr. Schuyler Livingston, the American partner, was a Democrat.

It is a very common fact, that for thirty-four years (since 1828) very few merchants of the first class have been Democrats. The mass of large and little merchants have like a flock of sheep gathered either in the Federal, Whig, Clay, or Republican folds. The Democratic merchants could have easily been stowed in a large Eighth avenue railroad car. Schuyler Livingston, George Douglas, Moses Taylor, Charles Secor, James Lee, August Belmont, are about all the prominent names that I can remember, or who were found as officers at the great Douglas ratification meeting at old Tammany a few nights ago.

I am by no means certain that Anthony Barclay, when he became British consul, continued a partner in the firm of Barclay & Livingston. I think he gave way in favor of one of his sons.

He was removed as consul at the request of the American government, for trying to enlist men for the Crimea. It was understood very well in England, that while he was publicly reproved by a removal, he was privately rewarded with a retiring pension of £10,000, which he will draw while he lives. In fact he is better off, in a pecuniary point of view, than when rushing about New York as British consul.

There were to be found in this great city, thirty years and odd ago, experienced merchants who have retired from active mercantile business, and engaged in pursuits equally important. I have in my eye now the very form and figure of one of these, William O'Brien, who was engaged in the ship broker business, or rather in adjusting the claims of merchants or other insurers, upon insurance companies. In the days I speak of, Mr. O'Brien was the only person in the city who did that particular but important *specialitie*. He made up "general averages" for ships and cargoes lost, and such was the confidence in his capacity, integrity, and correctness, that his adjustments were never disputed by port wardens, insurers, or insurance companies. He was a true Irish gentleman, and possessed great conversational powers. His office was in Wall street, between (what is now) Hanover and Pearl streets. His residence was in Broome street, around the corner from Broadway toward Crosby. He was very jovial and social, and held his *levees* regularly once or twice a week. His house was always open to his friends. No Irish gentleman of any note ever passed through New York, without making his appearance at the residence of Mr. O'Brien in Broome street. The best wines and liquors in the United States could be found in perfection upon Mr. O'Brien's good old fashioned mahogany side board. No man died more regretted; he left several children. Two of his sons, William and John O'Brien, were for many years engaged in the Mechanics Bank — one as book-keeper and one as first teller. They left the bank to found the house of W. & J. O'Brien, some years ago, and are now doing a very extensive brokerage business in Wall street. In fact, the O'Briens are probably as much respected, and do as large a business as any financial house in Wall street.

Another old and well known name in the haunts of commerce was Peter H. Schenck. His store was in Maiden Lane, just below Pearl street. The sign wa "P. A. Schenck & Co." His partner's name was Samuel G. Wheeler. Mr. W. was the step-father of D. B. Allen, the agent, and son-in-law of the world renowned Commodore Vanderbilt, who in those days had hardly emerged from the shell of an oyster boat captain.

Peter H. Schenck was the first man that ever started

a manufactory for domestic fabrics in this State. Before the war, he and Henry Cowing started a cotton factory at Fishkill Landing, up the North River. It is now called Mattewan. In 1812 these two enterprising men had got the factory fully under weigh when the war broke out. A large British fleet was off the entrance of the port of New York. A strict blockade was carried on by the British, for every other Atlantic port. But these men were not to be subdued. While the war lasted they had all the cotton they required at their factory *wagoned from Charleston, South Carolina, to Fishkill Landing, New York*, a distance of over 900 miles, and when the roads were not what they are now.

There were two of the brothers Cowing — Henry and Ward. They originated in Rhode Island; and Henry went from Providence to Charleston as a sort of tin, clock, or Yankee notion pedlar. He married in Charleston a niece of the celebrated Langdon Cheeves, who was the president of the old United States Bank until Nick Biddle was elected in his place. The other brother, Ward Cowing, used to go out to Mobile and New Orleans every year, to purchase cotton for the celebrated firm of Dudley & Stuyvesant. While P. H. Schenck went on steadily making money, the Cowings, with all their great advantages, partly broke down. Their sister, Jane Cowing, started a large boarding house at Nos. 5, 7 and 9 Murray street. Henry Cowing had two daughters, Anne and Mary. The latter married little William Powell, the artist, who has painted a painting called "De Soto landing at the mouth of the Mississippi," now in the possession of the government at Washington.

What a funny lot of boarders there was at the Cowing fashionable boarding house. Among them was the now famous Dr. Peckham, who lives up at the corner of Fifth avenue and Twenty-third street, in massy, magnificent style. When he lived at Cowing's he paid $3 50 a week, slept in an attic, (two beds in the room) but mealed with the high class $14 boarders. He married by means of his boarding house connection, the widow Stuyvesant, of the Stuyvesant who was of the firm of Dudley & Stuyvesant, and settled with her relations for her dower at the sum (cash down) of $60,000. Her maiden name was Milderberger. With the $60,000 Peckham went to work and purchased a large quantity of land where the Fifth Avenue Hotel now stands. Then he got some money from his wife's father. He has slowly accumulated until he is worth at least $500,000.

Peter H. Schenck was a truly great man. He continued his factory at Mattawan until he died. He also erected a machine factory. He started a cloth (woollen) factory called the "Rocky Glen Cloth Co.," but Clay's compromise tariff knocked spots out of that. He died leaving a large property behind him.

For many years a house heavily in the Mediterranean trade was Davis & Brooks. They occupied the same store in Broad street (north east corner of Garden or Exchange street,) that had been previously occupied by Oldfield, Bernard & Co. Davis & Brooks sold largely every year fruits and wines, principally at auction. Their auctioneer was the celebrated William F. Pell, in Coffee House Slip. This is a favorite way with many large commission houses to get rid of goods easily, and save their commission. If owners of goods abroad knew how faithlessly their consignments were managed here, they would never consign merchandise to what are called the large commission houses, but consign at once to an auctioneer, and save large commissions. These large commission houses, as a general rule, do not pay devoted attention to the sales of merchandise consigned to them. It is left to inexperienced clerks or sent to auction, and the charges made on the account sales are not such as occur, but according to a tariff fixed by the house.

To return to Davis & Brooks. Charles A. Davis made for himself a great but ephemeral literary fame in 1830 to 1836, as the writer of the famous "Major Jack Downing letters." These letters appeared in the New York Daily Advertiser. They were supposed to be written by a Yankee major, who represented himself as sleeping with Gen. Andrew Jackson, the President of the United States.

It was considered so remarkable that a commission merchant should create a sensation with his pen, aside from the legitimate way of signing checks, that Mr. Davis, (though he never wrote a line besides the Downing letters) took rank at once among the literary stars of America, and ranked with Bryant, Irving, Halleck or Bancroft; and no literary society could get over a dinner without author Davis being present.

General Jackson regarded the author of these letters as a silly person; and if he could have caught would have drowned him.

Mr. Brooks, the other member of the firm, never attempted a greater sensation than to be the partner of the literary Davis. In the same firm, Mr. Downing Davis had a nephew named Charles Davis, a glorious fellow years ago. He married a daughter of Mr. Elihu Townsend, of the highly respectable and rich Wall street broker firm, Nevins & Townsend. The lady was rich, and Charles Davis retired a millionaire. Few persons have more sincere and more devoted friends. Young Charles Davis is amiable, accomplished, and had he devoted himself to commerce, would have been one of the most eminent merchants of 1860.

Another partner in the firm of Davis & Brooks, was Theodore Dehon, a son of the late Bishop of South Carolina.

When the firm of Davis & Brooks ceased to exist by the retirement of the two principal partners, Mr. Dehon continued the business and with great success.

Davis, Brooks & Co. became very largely engaged in the iron trade during the last twenty years of their commercial existence.

CHAPTER XI.

The Mediterranean trade is ever a large oı e to this city. Davis & Brooks, years ago, had a large share of it, but not all. The principal part of it was divided between Davis & Brooks, and the house of G. W. & H. Bruen.

I have already mentioned that G. W. Bruen married a daughter of Thomas H. Smith, the great tea merchant in this city. Both G. W. and his brother Herman were sons of old Matthias Bruen, of Perth Amboy; he, who in after years was the famous assignee of old Thomas H. Smith,

The firm of G. W. & H. Bruen commenced business in 1822, the year famous for the yellow fever, and would have done an immense business for years had not the young firm been allied with the old one. The way and method of this entanglement happened after this fashion:

There were three great tea houses in America at the period of which we write — Thompson, of Philadelphia; Perkins, of Boston; and Thomas H. Smith, of New York. In 1826, the market became overstocked, the tea cargoes had come in so fast that the government got scared about the duties. At that time the credit given to tea importers was twelve, eighteen and twenty-four months — one third at each period before they were made to pay the heavy duties. Thomas H. Smith had imported immensely. He owed the United States a large sum, probably two millions, and old Jonathan Thompson,(who was then Collector of the port of New York, under John Quincy Adams' Presidency) refused to take his bonds for a larger amount, even with his bondsmen Matthias Bruen, and his two sons, George and Herman. Collector Thompson regarded the Bruens as mere men of straw.

The Collector of Philadelphia also got frightened in respect to Thompson, and refused to take his bonds any longer. He had overstocked the market. Finally, it was agreed that Thompson should place his tea importation under the Custom House lock, as security, and when he wanted teas he should enter only the quantity needed, pay the duty, and take it out of the government charge. This was all very well so far as it went. But Thompson had a plan to carry out — a game to play, and for a time it succeeded. He would enter and pay duty on (say) one hundred chests, and then forge a *permit* for one thousand chests, or five thousand packages and at once ship them on to his New York agents, Smith & Nicoll. There was no sale in Philadelphia for such a quantity of teas, and there was great danger of Mr. Thompson being detected, if he had sold it in that city.

These teas as fast as they arrived here were offered at auction by John Hone & Sons, the great auctioneers of their day. Thompson sent on seven cargoes.

John Jacob Astor at that time held a large quantity of teas. So did Thomas H. Smith. To keep the market from being entirely broken down by the terrific quantity of tea Philadelphia Thompson was forcing upon it, both

Astor and Smith became buyers, and bought nearly all that was offered, with the intention of re-exporting the tea so purchased to the Mediterranean, thus relieving the New York tea market, and enhancing greatly the value of their own tea cargoes. The teas so sold by Thompson were bought by Astor & Smith, for the duty, without debenture, when it was discovered that Thompson was a defaulter. The duty was more than the cost of the tea in China. When the Government seized in Philadelphia and New York all the teas imported by Thompson, they sold them *entitled to debenture*, and Astor & Smith purchased teas at such a low price that when they were exported, and they received from Government the face of the *dedenture*, the teas had really *cost nothing shipped.*

Strange as it may seem, even under these favorable circumstances, the teas shipped to Europe were a loss, for they did not sell in the Mediterranean ports for a sum sufficient to pay freight, duties and other charges.

The only way the purchasers were benefitted was by the relief of the New York tea market. The tea business now became so stagnant that the Perkins withdrew from it. They could not compete with the Philadelphia and New York houses.

Thompson, of Philadelphia, when his enormous fraud was discovered, was locked up in prison, where he died about the time of the forced sale of his tea in New York by the Government.

The book-keeper of Thomas H. Smith & Son was Charles Henry Hall, for a long period. He had a certain share in the business, and it was his duty to make out the statement at the close of the year. It was said that by valuing the stock of teas very high, Hall made his profits about $150,000 higher than in justice they should have been. At any rate he retired at that time, and has been rich ever since.

Charles Henry Hall was succeeded as book-keeper by William Roberts. After the house of Thomas H. Smith & Son failed, Mr. Roberts kept a wine and liquor cellar on the corner of Wall street and Broadway for many years.

He died not long ago. An adopted daughter of his, married the late Doctor Alexander F. Vaché. I shall have more to say about Mr. Roberts before I finish this volume.

When Jonathan Thompson, the upright Collector of the port of New York, refused to take the bonds of Smith for tea duties, Smith went at once to New Jersey, and was told by the collector of the trifling port of Perth Amboy that he would take Smith's bonds for any amount. Assured of this, Mr. Smith went to work at once and erected those large warehouses alluded to in a former article, and then sent out pilot boats with orders to his captains, when they reached the Narrows, to go to Perth Amboy with his ships and their valuable cargoes. It was as broad as it was long. It mattered very little to Uncle Sam whether he was cheated at Perth Amboy, New Jersey, or at New York city. At last Mr. Smith failed, owing the Government the sum of three millions of dollars. This failure carried down his son-in-law, of the firm of G. W. & H. Bruen, who were bondsmen of his to the United States.

This failure upset the tea business for five years, and ruined nearly every person engaged in it.

It did not affect John Jacob Astor, for his tea business was a sort of secondary affair to his great Northwest fur business. His ships traded on the Pacific coast for furs and skins, and then went to China, were the fur cargoes were exchanged for teas, and these were brought to New York. Astor probably made by the voyages of his ships four times as much as the regular tea merchants even in the most prosperous days of the tea trade.

At that time there were not so many kinds of fancy teas as now. The black tea was called souchong, and the green, hyson skin. Now and then a ship would have a few packages of young hyson, or hyson.

Thomas H. Smith assigned to Matthias Bruen, of Perth Amboy. He at once went to work to compromse with the Government for the three million dollars worth of bonds due by Smith. The world never knew precisely how the matter was settled, but the people of this city were probably well satisfied that the assignee made about two millions of dollars by the compromise. It never did old Thomas Smith any good. He died. The three children he left behind; his son Thomas, and his son-in-law, George W. Bruen, and Frank Waddell, about once in three years, would make a joint, and sometimes an individual descent upon old Matt. Bruen, and scare him into making a forced payment of $100,000 to each. When this was done, a hollow peace would be patched up between the belligerents, until Waddell or his relatives needed more money. Evidently old Mr. Bruen felt that he was in their power, or he would not have disgorged so easily. Smith assigned in 1828, and died not long after.

The business office of John Jacob Astor at that time was in Vesey street, where the Astor House rear is now located. Mr. Astor owned an immense tea warehouse on the east side of Greenwich, between Liberty and Courtlandt. His son owns it still, or rather the ground upon which it was built, and where now stands a new building.

The great grocers and heavy wholesale tea purchasers resided mainly in Front street. Among them all, I do not know of more than three houses, or any members of grocery houses, who are still in business.

The largest grocers thirty years ago, in Front street or in the city, were Reed & Sturgis, and Lee, Dater & Miller. The first firm changed to Reed, Hempstead & Sturgis, and is to-day Sturgis, Bennet & Co.

Luman Reed was a game old grocer; he built a palace (for his day) in Greenwich street, No. 13, close to the Atlantic Garden. The large pavement stones in front of his door, were the wonder of his age. His great house was filled with paintings, and he never dreamed that the lower part of Greenwich street would be desecrated by Dutch emigrant houses and *rum* shops!

Of the great grocers Lee, Dater & Miller, that kept in a (then) mammoth store in Front street, between Maiden Lane and Burling Slip, on the corner of Fletcher street, only one, Philip Dater, is alive or in business. Next door to Lee, Dater & Miller, was the firm of Jackson & McJimsey. They failed. Jackson lived in Liberty street, and had a large family of daughters. One of them married George W. Tyson. Another daughter married Henry H. Leeds, formerly of the house of Amory Leeds & Co., but now Henry H. Leeds & Co., the auctioneers of note on Nassau street.

To return to grocers. Harper & Sons are still left, and doing as large a business now as in 1838.

The three partners are the only ones in business now, that were doing business in Front street thirty years ago, when that street was lined with such firms as Pomeroy & Bull, Wisner & Gale, S. Whitney, Smith, Mills & Co., Isaac Van Cleef, A. V. Winans and others.

CHAPTER. XII.

A glorious occupation on this continent is that of a merchant! He has no superior. There is no class of citizens that excel, or even equal him, except it be editors. Lawyers are respectable, if they conduct their business properly; but in this community they rarely raise their heads, unless so lucky as to become patronized by merchants.

Take Daniel Lord, Jr., the late George Griffin or George Wood, Charles O'Connor, Francis B. Cutting, Francis R. Tilyon, John H. Power, James T. Brady, or Lewis B. Woodruff, or Charles P. Daly. Would these men, however great may be their abilities, ever have risen to the distinction they have reached, unless they had received the patronage and confidence of merchants? No. They are all rich. Would they have become so, but for the business afforded by merchants? No.

Take our lawyers who have turned their attention to politics — a class that the live merchant despises — but still men who have got a right to attach the doubtful meaning word "Honorable" to their names, say, W. B. McClay, John McKeon, Elisha Ward, Horace Clark, Judge James I. Roosevelt and that class. As practising lawyers they are dead. Having been in Congress, the Administration gives an office to some of them, if asked for. I could name five hundred men — political lawyers — if I had a Directory before me, who could not pay the fractional office rents by their regular la business. No. In rank, the lawyer occupies a secondary position, for he lives and thrives off the business created for him by the more planning, combining genius of the great merchant.

So too, it is with the physician. How slow and dreary is the progress of every great medical man for weeks, months and years, until he becomes a favored protege of the merchant princes in our midst?

Is it not so, Doctors Cheeseman, Mott, Hosack, Bush, Buck, Carnochan, and 500 other M. D. gentleman? You now keep carriages and gigs, but until you obtained commerical patronage you could not have kept a good-sized cat in a thriving condition.

No man in the medical ranks has fairly thriven, until he has got a chance to operate upon the pocket books, as well as bodies of our great merchants. Consequently the learned medical faculty do, and ever will, play second fiddle to the great merchants.

The clergymen, in this city, never get on and become very great, very good, or very popular, until they can spot in their congregations and audiences fifty or a hundred extensive merchants. Dr. Tyng says so; and Henry Ward Beecher, with all his comicality, would be a small party in Plymouth Church, but for his wealthy mercantile congregation. So it is with Doctors Potts, Hawks, Cheever, &c., &c.

Save and except the Catholic churches, and rich old Trinity and her four chapels, no congregation in the city would get on, and be self-sustaining, except it numbered in its communion wealthy merchants. It is all very fine to talk of the inspiration of ministers of the

Gospel. Their propelling power in this city, the steam, is in the merchants; and consequently the clergy are a secondary class of the community, no matter how gifted they may be.

There is no nobility in this country. There is a class of princes, and they are the highest in the city. These princes can be seen every day (except Sundays) at a daily Congress in the Merchant's Exchange, between one and two o'clock. There can be seen princes of commerce, and such names as are *good* in Asia, Africa, Europe, or in any part of America. There are the princes Goodhue, Aspinwall, Aymar, Perit, King, Grinnell, Minturn, Howland, Boorman, Griswold, and a pit full of other names of world-wide renown.

What do such men as these care for the ephemeral four year names of Buchanan, Pierce, Polk, Cass, Cobb, Tyler, Fillmore, Everett, Floyd, and some five hundred others equally notorious names that have figured in politics.

No, sir! The merchant princes despise such names. They are not good in Wall street, nor would the bearers be received in the social domestic circles of the self-satisfied merchant unless they could be regularly introduced by an equal or by some regular correspondent of "the firm" in this or other cities.

Few of this generation will remember the name of Hone. Yet there are readers of this book who will recollect a day when that name was as highly honored and as extensively known in this city as it possibly could be.

As far back as I can recollect, there were two brothers in the auction business of the name of Hone. The firm was "Philip & John Hone." Their auction store was up in Fulton street around the corner from

Pearl. John Hone lived in one of the seven houses fronting the Bowling Green. Stephen Whitney lived and died on one end of Bowling Green Row, and John Hone on the other.

Both brothers were magnificent specimens of American men. Philip Hone lived up Broadway, one door this side of the South corner of Park place. The corner at that time was covered by a small wooden tenement, and on the first floor thread and needles were sold.

The Hones were the *creme de la creme* of society in those days. Philip and John Hone had made large fortunes. In 1826 they dissolved, and Philip was elected Mayor of the City of New York.

John Hone for the sake of his sons determined to continue the auction business under the name of "John Hone & Sons." They built a store on the northeast corner of Wall and Pearl, where the Seamen's Savings Bank now stands.

Never had New York merchant so fine a collection of sons. They were noble looking fellows. Henry was the handsomest man, in 1830, in the United States. John Jr., was a noble fellow. He died in Rome, and his widow afterward married lawyer Frederick De-Peyster.

Isaac Hone, another son, was of this firm, and after a variety of mercantile ups and downs, disasters and successes, became a deputy collector under Collector Hugh Maxwell. At one time Isaac was of the firm of Hone & Fleming. His partner, John B. Fleming, drew a prize in the lottery, of thirty thousand dollars. Two other sons were members of the rich firm of John Hone & Sons. Henry was one. He lived up opposite St John's Park in Varick street, a few doors from the church. What dinner parties that man gave. What choice "Chateaux Margeaux," and Lynch's "Sauterne.' Poor Dominick Lynch. Henry was elected a member of the Legislature at one time. He married as his second wife Miss Haywood. Although opposed by her father Henry Haywood of Charleston S. C. (who owned 2,500 negroes and who resided in the old mansion with pillars, seen by the Democratic delegates as they came out of Charleston last April, on the line of the North Eastern Railroad,) and who did not like Hone at all. It was of no use, this opposition. Harry Hone was a dashing fellow and he carried the day. Miss Haywood ran away from her father and married handsome Harry. She was rich, and loved her husband; but he, alas, poor Harry -- down, down, down he went, and finally died in a low rum shop in Chatham street. All gone — used up — his death a mercy, for his wife allowed him so much a year to keep clear of her.

Another of the firm of John Hone & Sons, was the now well-known Myndert Van Schaick; he married a daughter of John Hone. John Anthon, the lawyer, married another daughter. Van Schaick was the indoor man, and used to hand down the pieces of dry goods from the shelves during a sale at auction. Of all that crowd, Van Schaick is the only one left.

Old James Buchanan, the British consul in those years, had several sons. One was a clerk with John Hone & Sons. One night, previous to a large trade sale, the clerks were very busy opening boxes, taking out goods, and putting them on the shelves; the store doors were closed, it was near eleven o'clock at night, and the clerks got to sky-larking among themselves. One young fellow says to young Buchanan, "Give me that chisel, I want to pry open this box." Young Buchanan playfully tossed it at him, never dreaming of harm. It entered the young man's right side, and he fell dead. It was an accident, but it preyed upon young Buchanan's mind so greatly, that his father sent him off traveling.

John Hone died in the cholera year of 1832, and for some time the style of the firm remained unchanged.

About that time, an evil had grown up in this city, or at least, our wise legislature twenty-five years ago so deemed it. Many firms were doing business under old names not in the firm. The legislature passed a law, that no name should appear in a mercantile firm, unless there really was such a person in the firm. This law made a stir. "John Hone & Sons," was a well established firm, but John Hone was dead, and this style came under the new law penalty. The sons got over it by changing the firm to "John Hone's Sons," consisting then of Isaac, Henry and Myndert Van-Schaick.

One of the Hone merchants firm, Mr. Van Schaick, retired rich, or rather the moderate sum with which he left business, has in real estate become vastly valuable. He for a long time lived up in Broadway between Anthony and Leonard streets. On that same side, and row, lived also John Mason, James Heard, John G. Warren, Jacob Le Roy and John H. Howland. Afterwards, on one corner, Ned Windust kept his celebrated Athenæum Hotel, then the resort of everybody who was any body.

One of the most remarkable houses of the present day is Grinnell, Minturn & Co. Originally, it was Fish & Grinnell, fifty years ago. The members of the firm came here from New Bedford to attend to the oil and candle business of New Bedford whale oil merchants The head of the firm was Preserved Fish. He had been, while a babe, found floating by a New Bedford fisherman, who named the interesting modern Moses, Preserved Fish. The original Grinnell was the honorable Moses. The junior partner was the celebrated Saul Alley, who was a famed man in after years as a politician. When Fish, Grinnell & Co. dissolved, the firm was changed to Grinnell, Minturn & Co., and Robert B. Minturn was taken in the concern. R. B. was the son of Edward Minturn, of the firm of Champlin & Minturn, the great house before the war of 1812. In 1815, the firm failed. There were three Minturns in that old firm, Nat, Jonas and Edward.

Jonas also had a son named Richard R. Minturn. His melancholy death from jumping out of a window of a third story, some years ago, will be well remembered. Jonas Minturn went into the auction business under the firm of Franklin & Minturn. Franklin was the father and grandfather of the present firm of Franklin & Sons, in Broad street. Old Franklin was a Quaker, short and thick set. The firm of Franklin & Minturn was succeeded by R. R. Minturn & Co., being the suicide above named and his brother Thomas. The Minturns were and are a good-looking race of men. Six foot men with rosy cheeks and curly black hair.

Robert B., who is the head of Grinnell, Minturn & Co. to-day, used to live in Beach street opposite St. John's Park. He is not only celebrated as a merchant, but has a daughter of sweet seventeen that has just written and published a novel called "Rutledge." A Philadelphia correspondent says:

"THE AUTHOR OF RUTLEDGE.—Not a little curiosity has been expressed to learn who the young lady is who wrote 'Rutledge,' one of the best novels of American society that have been published in a long while. The publishers (Derby & Jackson) have been teased to death by all sorts of people to know who did it. The senior partner answers all askers by saying that the author is a young woman of twenty, (more or less), a church woman educated at Bishop Doane's school.

I will go just a step further, and "guess" it is the production of Miss Minturn, a daughter of one of our merchant princes — Mr. Robert B. Minturn. The Minturns, aside from being one of our historical families, (the firm of Grinnell, Minturn & Co., has stood unchanged for over forty years) have made their mark in literature. Young Minturn, who has just been admitted a partner in the firm, is the author of a clever book of travels — "New York to Delhi."

Unchanged for forty years! That is not so. The firm was changed in 1832, after the new law alluded to in a previous paragraph was passed. Fish not being in the firm: Fish, Grinnell & Co. had to be changed to Grinnell, Minturn & Co. The last has stood unchanged twenty-eight years. The junior partner of this firm was young Delano, a son of the old packet Captain. Frank Delano was a handsome fellow, and captivated a daughter of William B. Astor.

Grinnell, Minturn & Co. do all sorts of commercial business now. All is fish that gets into their nets, although in the early days of Fish, Grinnell & Co. it was not so. They sell oil, and they operate in Canton. They send packet ships to London, and act as agents of "Great Easterns."

Fish, Grinnell & Co., when they first opened shop in this city did nothing but an oil business. They sold two kinds of oil, good and bad. Among the regular customers was a pedlar named Samuel Judd. At first he kept no shop, but peddled his oil, poor and good, which he mixed to suit himself, about town. After a while his peddling perseverance was rewarded, and he was able to take a 6x9 store down near the old Fly Market.

Finally Samuel Judd obtained contracts and became vastly rich. James F. Penniman who sold his large house up by Union Square to Ben Wood, married one of Sam Judd's daughters. Lewis K. Bridge married another, and J. C. Baldwin, of the firm of Baldwin & Forbes, in Coffee House Slip, married another. He is now the President of the Merchant's Exchange Company. They were the most beautiful girls ever grown in New York, were old Sam Judd the oil pedler's daughters. Poor old fellow, he ought to have been spared to see his son-in-law, James F. Penniman, become the leader of society, both in New York and in Paris.

CHAPTER XIII.

About eleven months ago, the author of these chapters received a note and a ticket from Daniel Lynch, James Swords, Daniel F. Sullivan, John White, Daniel Lucy and Peter Brady, inviting him to attend a grand soiree of the Walton club, to take place at the old Walton House, 326 Pearl street, on Thursday evening, March 14, 1861. The writer could not go, and from then until now has heard no more of the matter; but he supposes it is a club got up to do honor to an honored old merchant name, for such were the "Waltons." So believing, he at the time determined to recognise the intended kindness, by giving one chapter at least to those "Waltons." I have frequently said something about them; in this chapter I will say more, and if the club is in existence yet, I hope they will take it as a sort of acknowledgement of past favors, and if I throw any more light upon the Waltons, I shall be glad of it.

There seems to have been a family of William Waltons flourishing in London, as well as New York, for two hundred years back, and mixed up, too, with South American affairs. One wrote a "History of South America" many years ago; and one William Walton, as late as the regency of George IV. of England, wrote an "Appeal" — quite a book, showing how beneficial it would be to Great Britain if she would aid the South American republics in getting rid of the wretched Spanish authority. I dare say, these London Waltons, who must have resided long in South America, to be able to write so learnedly about those matters, were nearly related to our New York family. They were merchants as well as statesmen. So, too, in New York city. Among our great merchants of the olden time we have numbered several Waltons. The first of the name was Robert Walton, a counsellor to the Earl of Belmont. He had his ship yards then and as late as 1728. The "Walton" house, now 328 Pearl (formerly 68 Queen,) had a garden that reached the river. At that time the river came up to where Water street now is, and all along from Peck slip to what is now Roosevelt street, were ship-yards. In 1728, the first ship-yard was Mr. Roosevelt's — the next, Mr. Walton's — the next Van Horn's. Walton's grounds extended up on Peck's hill, which was thirty feet higher than Franklin square now is, where he built in 1764. Benjamin Peck's wharf was on the south side of the slip, and at that time there was but one house (Peck's) on the south side of the slip. In 1800, it was called Walton wharf. There were four houses on Pearl between Peck slip and Beekman, and but one on the block where the Walton house now is. The ship-builder Walton, was the father of William Walton, who built the house in 1757, after the English model, and avoided the Dutch style. In 1762, it was illuminated in celebration of the Stamp Act repeal. It has five windows in front, is constructed of yellow Holland brick, has a double pitched roof covered with tiles, and a double row of balustrades thereon. Its garden extended to the river. William Walton was a merchant descendant from the ship-builder. He was one of the Council, and made his wealth by trading among the Spaniards of South America and Cuba.

Old William Walton was one of the first trustees of the New York Society Library, in 1754, and was associated with John Watts, Hon. Joseph Murray, Peter Van Brugh Livingston and Peter Ketteltas, merchants. He was then one of His Majesty's council. His famous "Walton House" is even yet the pride of old New York. The entrance hall is in the centre of the building, and has large, old fashioned parlors. The portico is supported by two fluted columns, and surmounted with the armorial bearings of the Walton family. It is fifty feet in front, three stories high, the brick relieved by brown stone water tables, lintels and jams. The old man was a bachelor. He left it to his nephew, the late Hon. William Walton, in 1846.

The first William was called "Boss" Walton. The word *Bos* had a meaning in Dutch, in 1754, not since as well understood. It was originally *Baas*, and means master — a name repugnant to democrats, although few object to recognize a *Boss*.

William Walton, the nephew of old Boss William Walton, lived at No. 67 Queen street, in 1792, and his brother Gerard at No. 68 Queen. The elder William, in 1745 resided in Hanover square. He in that locality made a contract with Spaniards in St. Augustine, and made a large fortune. He built his house out of town. The reason of his choice was that he owned the land, it being the ship-yard of the Waltons. The elder Walton was a prince of a merchant. He was very hospitable, and he gave the most splendid entertainments, even for the bountiful age in which he lived.

In 1759 the city had over 10,000 inhabitants. That year the old French war terminated, and Canada was conquered for the British, and the province of New York relieved from all danger of any more French or Indian incursions and massacres. Of course the city of New York was joyful, and celebrated the event. The British army came from Canada to New York, and all were received as heroes. "Boss" Walton opened his house, and gave the most costly entertainments. His table was spread with a feast of decanters filled with the choicest liquors and wines. The sideboard groaned with its weight of brilliant, massive silver.

Afterwards, when the Bank of New York was chartered, and when it began business in June 9, 1784, it opened in one of the parlors of the Walton House. A. McDougal was the President, and William Seton the cashier. William Walton No. 2 was a director.

I believe the name of the ship-yard owner Walton was Robert. He was, as I have stated, a member of the Council when the Earl of Belmont was the Governor, and then attended the Council meetings that were held at Fort William Henry.

It was while the same Robert Walton was mayor, from 1720 to 1724, that the first regular duties on imported European goods were laid. It was but two per cent., but it was the first tariff in this city.

To be sure, his ship-yard in 1796 must have been in striking contrast with one of the present day. Yet, I dare say, he made as much money then as a ship-builder does now. The whole tonnage that came into New York in those years was about one hundred, of which forty were square-rigged, and sixty sloops. Boats were extensively used in those years, and of course were all built here. The square-rigged vessels did not probably average over 110 tons each, and not over one quarter were built or owned in New York. Most of the ships were built at Walton's and other ship-yards. From 1720 to 1724 Robert Walton was mayor of the city of New York. Abraham Walton, who figured in the Revolution, and who was one of the committee of safety for the city and county of New York in 1775, was a brother of William Walton, who was also a member of that committee, and both were nephews of Boss Walton. Abraham was a vestryman of Trinity church from 1782 to 1784. He was also in the first Provincial Congress in 1775, from New York city.

Gerard Walton was a brother of William, also. He was governor of the New York Hospital from 1789 to 1799 — ten years. He was Vice-President and also President of the board of governors. During a portion of that time, Jacob was also a governor until 1777. William was a life member, but now a governor.

All the Waltons were connected with the chamber of commerce. William was treasurer from 1771 to 1772. He was Vice-President from 1772 to 1774, and again from 1783 to 1784. He was President from 1774 to 1785. Gerard was Vice-President from 1783 to 1785. Jacob was Vice-President from 1781 to 1783.

Gerard Walton stood six feet two inches high. He ttended Trinity church, and sat in the family pew.

I am inclined to think that during the Revolution the Waltons — William, Gerard, and Abraham — sided with the English; for, as soon as it was over, they all joined the St. George's Society, in 1786. Jacob had died, or he would have joined it too.

Abraham, after the war, did merchandizing at 137

Water street. His son, Abraham M., was a lawyer, and lived with his father, afterwards, for many years — 1796 to 1801 — at 59 Wall street. He died wealthy. Old Abraham died in 1794, but his widow lived in that house, which would now be 269 Water street, being a part of the old Walton ship-yard property; as it was, of course, a water front, they continued to own as it was filled up.

About the time Abraham died, in 1795, old William Walton, who has figured so extensively, and who was in so many grand institutions, and who was nephew to the "Boss," moved to 220 William street, and resided there for two years.

Gerard Walton, in 1796, was Vice-President of the New York Western and Northern Canal Company.

In 1806, William Walton died, and the old mansion came into the possession of his heir, James De Lancey Walton, who lived in No. 326 until 1835, where, I believe, he died. He was morose, and no one ever was intimate with or knew aught about him.

Admiral Gerard Walton died in 1821. Among many curious things is the receipt book of William Walton.

This William Walton, who died in 1806, was one of the original founders of the Marine Society of New York. He is named as one of the original incorporators by George the Third, in 1770. His funeral was a grand affair. It took place at the old mansion, and from thence where the body had lain in state for several days. All the rooms were flung open in that house, and also in the adjoining house, occupied by the Admiral. Refreshments of cakes and meats were served, and the choicest wines, for the Waltons were celebrated for their old wines. There was no religious service at the house, but the body was conveyed to St. George's Church in Beekman street, where a public funeral service was performed. I think the body was buried there in one of the vaults. William Walton was a vestryman in the church. He was a short, thick-set man. Neighbors used to designate them as the "short" and the "long" Waltons. He was a single man. James De Lancey was a nephew of this William Walton. James, a son of old Isaac Roosevelt, who was President of the Bank of New York, when it was in the Walton mansion, married a Miss Walton. I think she was a niece of this William, and a daughter of the Admiral Gerard.

The Rev. Dr. William Walton, who married the daughter of Dr. Seabury, is a son of this Gerard Walton, who was a half-pay Admiral in the British Navy. His widow still lives with her son at 39 West Twenty-second street.

After the death of William Walton there was a grand sale of choice wines at the old mansion, such as was never before or since.

The Waltons were a singular, proud race. They had their dignified style of amusement, but the mass of the community knew no more about them than if they had lived in London.

The last of the Waltons who used to dwell in the old mansion, used frequently to visit and make purchases at the store of the celebrated Bonafanti, now nearly forgotten. Excellent Bonafanti, favorite child of the Muses! Those chaps, Smith Brothers, who keep a poet, did not originate poetical ideas in partnership with trade. Bonafanti kept everything in the fancy line. His was the original variety store. So remarkable was he is this regard, on one occasion he was made the sub ject of a bet.

"You cannot name an article," said an enthusiastic New Yorker, "that our Joe Bonafanti don't keep."

"I'll bet you ten dollars that I can," said a southerner from Charleston, to whom the boast was made.

"Done!" said the New Yorker. "Now let us go up to Bonafanti's."

Up they went. Mr. Bonafanti was, as usual, all smiles. He handed to each a new poem on a sheet just printed that day.

"Vat kan I do for you, sair?"

"Mr. Bonafanti, I wish to purchase a second-hand pulpit; can you supply me?"

"Segond-hand pulpit. Oh, yees sir. Sammee," (calling out to some one up stairs,) "get out a segond-hand pulpit for de gentleman to see."

"Yes, sir; all ready," replied Sam.

"Here, Bob, take this ten," said South Carolina. "I've lost. Now, Mr. Bonafanti, I will buy some goods of you, but not pulpits."

The joke was told Bonafanti, who was quite delighted. Bonafanti and his splendid stock and harmonious poetry made him a great favorite with the fashionable dames of New York. A fan, or opera gloves, card case, pocket-book, purse, eye-glass must be purchased of Bonafanti. Lucky was this for the young beginner. It brought grist to his mill. That poetry was deemed wonderful, and it would have been had it been written by Bonafanti. But it was not. The mad poet, McDonald Clark, wrote it, or Woodworth, the poet. The author of "The Old Oaken Bucket" was alive and poor at that time, and I think he was one of Bonafanti's poets, for in after years the sons of the poet Woodworth succeeded to the business of Bonafanti. I could write a book about Bonafanti, but it would be a "*sealed* book" to all but old time New Yorkers.

The Waltons, as well as all of the very old merchants in this city, were extremely methodical. It was much more so one hundred years ago than is the case now. I speak of merchants in this city. Every young man or boy in those days, who wished to become a merchant, was obliged to go through a few years of preparatory education as he would have to do if intended for what is called a learned profession. The system of the colleges are not as strict as was the discipline of an old New York merchant. The lad was practiced in writing month after month, until he was capable of writing rapidly and correctly that grand old round commercial handwriting we see among ancient books or documents, such as John Hancock used when he signed the Declaration of Independence, for he was a merchant, and had been regularly brought up to business.

I presume that the habit of thoroughly educating young clerks was copied from the customs in the counting houses of the old merchants, in Amsterdam or London In fact, many of our leading merchants, sixty or eighty years ago had received their education abroad. Compared with those years, there is scarcely any pains taken now to make a merchant of the old school. In former years a clerk took his regular degrees. He was first set to delivering goods from the store—taking ac counts of the marks and the number of the packages. He was also obliged to recevie goods and to keep correct accounts of such as he received in store or delivered to purchasers. In doors he was obliged to copy letters; when the clerk could do that correctly and neatly without making an error or a blot, then he was promoted to making duplicates of letters to go by the packet ships. Then he was promoted to copying accounts. Next, he was trusted with the responsible duty of making these accounts. All was a perfect system. One clerk instructed and one inspected the work of another. It was impossible to make mistakes. The book-keeper too was an institution in the olden time. He was more important than he is now, as the older a commercial firm is even now, the greater is the consideration with which they treat the book-keeper.

In other years the retail business was nothing to what it is now. Those who did that kind of business were not regarded as merchants. They were called shopkeepers, or in some cases "mongers." Of course there were not any such immense retail stores as Stewart's. Our ancestors could hardly have conceived of such an establishment as Stewart & Co.'s, that employs 200 to 300 clerks. I do not suppose that up to 1780, there were three retail stores in New York, that employed over three clerks to wait upon their customers.

Ireland has been the birthplace of many remarkable men, but never has she sent from her shore a more sagacious one than A. T. Stewart. Our land has fostered the Frenchman Girard, of Philadelphia, and the German Astor, and they died worth millions; but they never, even at a great age, reached the wealth of the Merchant Stewart. He is yet in the gristle of his success, and not hardened into the bone of mammoth, overgrown wealth. Stewart is this day worth fourteen to twenty millions of dollars. He owns more real estate than Astor, and if he lives ten years longer, Mr. Stewart will probably be worth from twenty to thirty millions of dollars.

In 1848 he moved to his present marble palace. He

had bought Washington Hall of young John Coster for $60,000, and for a few thousand dollars more two additional buildings and lots on Broadway, corner of Chambers street. Upon this magnificent site he erected the present store. The whole cost of the ground and the palace erected did not reach $300,000. To-day it would sell at auction for from $800,000 to 1,000,000.

He paid patroon Van Rensselaer $530,000 for the Metropolitan Hotel and out-buildings. It is now worth and pays an interest of ten. per cent. on $1,000,000, and would bring at auction $800,000. He owns nearly all of Bleecker street, between Broadway and his present residence, and in fact owns more real estate than any other man in New York, except it may be Mr. Wm. B. Astor.

CHAPTER XIV.

"Do you class Mr. A. T. Stewart among the Old Merchants?" asked a very aged merchant of the author. I replied "if a man who has been engaged in commercial business under his own name steadily for forty years, less one, is not an old merchant, it will be difficult to find one." It is true that a merchant who conducts his business, as does Mr. Stewart, does not run much risk. Mr. Stewart sells for cash. He adds a moderate profit to his cost price, and while he keeps insured is not likely to lose much. The shipping merchant runs far more risk. The fluctuations in foreign markets may ruin him in a brief space. So too with the great commission merchant, who sells large amounts on time. A severe pressure in the money market, may cause an unusual number of failures, and he may lose beyond his ability to pay what he has guarantied. There are risks and there are losses in every kind of business. Some cannot be avoided.

A very remarkable firm once existed in this city under the style of Hicks, Lawrence & Co. They were the great domestic dry goods auctioneers of their day. Their store was in Pearl street, between Fulton and Beekman streets. It was a Quaker firm. The head of the house was Willet Hicks. He was the father of the wife of Dr. Cheeseman. Another of the firm was Cornelius W. Lawrence, who was many years mayor, and also Collector of the Port. In the firm was his brother Joseph Lawrence (now of the firm of Lawrence & Trimble), also Richard Lawrence. Cornelius W. Lawrence retired from this firm with a large fortune. Old Mr. Hicks was very rich and wished to retire. The other members begged him not to do so, or at least to leave his name in the firm. Mr. Hicks complied, unfortunately for himself, and let his name remain, although he did not attend to the business. At that time Joseph retired rich, leaving only Mr. Hicks and Richard Lawrence in the firm.

The panic of 1837 burst upon them, and they broke all to smithereens. Old Mr. Hicks, who had so kindly consented to let his name remain, became a ruined man He was stripped of everything. Luckily he had a daughter, and the last years of his life were spent under the roof of his son-in-law, Dr. Cheeseman, who has achieved as high and well-deserved a reputation as any medical man in this city or in the Union. Another daughter of Mr. Hicks married C. W. Lawrence. She died, and Lawrence then married a Miss Prall. She died, and the ex-mayor then married his cousin, a Miss Lawrence.

The Ex-Collector and ex-mayor, old Cornelius, had the ice cream and strawberries of everything in life — in commerce, in politics, in wives, in finances and in religion. Mr. Lawrence lived for a long time up Broadway, near the old Tabernacle. He had a peculiar way of carrying his spectacles in his hand, behind his back while he looked at all the pretty girls he met.

One of them led him a sad dance. Mr. Lawrence, the most respected man in this city, was led into an ambuscade and made the victim of a plot. It was a sad business, lost the old gentlemen a great amount of money, and caused him any quantity of mental misery.

C.W. Lawrence, who has been so successful in all of his undertakings, is now dead. What a melancholy history is that of Hicks, Lawrence & Co.

Another auction concern was that of Corlies, Hay dock & Co. They sold crockery ware as well as dry goods. They were all Quakers. Their store was at the corner of Pine and Pearl streets. All of the old members of the firm are dead except two. They died rich, if that is any consolation to the families left behind, which it must be undoubtedly. The living are Thomas Pearsall and Joseph Corlies; the latter lives up near Madison park.

While talking of auctioneers, I will mention that there was a large auction house once, composed of Haggerty, Austin & Co. This house separated in 1836. Old John Haggerty formed a firm called John Haggerty & Sons. David Austin formed a firm called Austin, Spicer & Co., and William E. Wilmerding, lately deceased, formed a firm called Wilmerding, Priest & Mount — three auction firms out of what had been one. Mount had been a clerk with Adee, Timpson & Co. Mr. Priest had been a book-keeper to Haggerty, Austin & Co., and W. E. Wilmerding was one of the partners in that firm.

John Haggerty took into partnership his sons John A. Haggerty, J. Ogden Haggerty, and Clement Haggerty.

Afterward the firm was changed to Haggerty, Draper & Jones, the old John not being in it, but his place was supplied by J. Ogden Haggerty. Simeon Draper, a son-in-law of old Mr. Haggerty, was of this firm. The other partner was Arthur T. Jones. Simeon Draper had previously been in business under the firm of S. Crumby & Draper.

I have prepared a lengthy sketch of Mr. John Haggerty, and it will be found before this book is finished. He was a merchant in the city sixty years ago. His family stands among the first. It is ancient and it is aristocratic. His boys were all great dandies thirty years ago; and many a lovely girl has "set her cap," for one of the sons of Mr. John Haggerty. He lived in Broadway, where the Astor House now stands, for many years, until he sold his house and lot to Astor, and then he moved into Chambers street, opposite the Park. He was an intensely smart and energetic man. His children were all counted among the fashionables, and were frequenters of the balls at the old City Hotel in the palmy days of New York, before it got crowded.

Old Mr. Haggerty is still alive, living on a splendid farm near Flushing, Long Island. He is now nearly ninety years old, and as active and industrious as a man of thirty. He is the first man on his place to get up in the morning, and invariably wakes up his hired men.

A great copper merchant in former years was old Harman Hendricks. His store was in Mill street, where the old Jewish synagogue used to be, but is now called South William street. His manufactory was at Belleville, New Jersey. Mr. Hendricks was a born New Yorker, of the Jewish persuasion — honest, upright, prudent, and a very cautious man. He lived in Greenwich, near Morris street, for many years — in fact, until he died. That was twenty years ago. He died immensely rich, leaving over three millions of dollars. His real estate was in the Sixth to Seventh avenues, from Twentieth to Twenty-second streets; also out near where Mayor Wood lives, thirty acres on Broadway. Had he lived until now, as he never sold property, he would have been worth twelve millions. His heirs are worth at least seven millions. His sons continue the same business, in the same store, (except being rebuilt) where they have kept for fifty years. The firm is changed from Hendricks & Son to Hendricks Brothers. He had four sons, Uriah, Washington, (dead,) Henry and Montague. The three living sons comprise that firm now. Uriah is worth three millions. He was the original partner of his father, and is rich in his purse and rich in his family, having eighteen living children, and the finest and handsomest set in the country. They are from five to twenty-six years old. He married a Miss Tobias, and his brother Henry married a sister.

Mr. T. J. Tobias is a very aged man, was once an eminent merchant, and is now engaged in the wine and liquor trade, and has on hand now some of the oldest and choicest wines to be found in the United States. He recently celebrated his golden wedding, having been married fifty years.

Mr. Tobias is English by birth, a nephew of Morris Tobias, the celebrated watch and chronometer maker of London. His store is in New street, near Fitch's great stores. He died since the above was written.

Mr. Hendricks left several daughters. One married Mr. Gomez, (recently dead.) One married Benjamin Nathan, a broker in Wall street. Another, (since deceased,) married Benjamin Hart, a brother of E. B. Hart, Surveyor of the port. One married Mr. Tobias, and one is not married. With all the revulsions in trade, the credit of the house for half a century has never been questioned, either in this country or in Europe, and to-day in Wall street, their obligations would sell quite as readily as government securities bearing the same rates of interest. No man stood higher in this community while he lived, and no man has left a memory more revered than Harman Hendricks. When he died, the synagogue which he attended lost one of its best friends, and the rising generation of that numerous family could not have a better example.

CHAPTER XV.

The writer of these Recollections would be a very arrogant person were he to assume that they were perfect, or in every particular correct, or that they tell everything that could be told about any one merchant or firm. Thirty years ago is a long time to recollect.

I frequently am reminded of errors. A friend points them out. I correct as soon as I have a chance, and it may not be amiss here to state, that any errors that the reader may discover in this book will be cheerfully corrected in future editions. A note addressed to the author, will be attended to.

Among the recent deaths is Benjamin Welles, of Boston, aged eighty years. He was a son of Samuel Welles, and was born in 1780. Benjamin Welles was a companion of and traveled in Europe with Washington Allston in 1804. Mr. Benjamin Welles was a cousin to Hon. John Welles; and in 1816 they became partners in Boston under the firm of John & Benjamin Welles, and acted as active agents in the United States to Welles & Co., the great Paris bankers, until the 31st of August, 1841, when Mr. Samuel Welles died.

There is not an importer in New York, who does not remember that banking house. For twenty-five years at least it was without a rival, and issued credits to an almost unlimited extent. When the panic of 1837 occurred in New York, and almost everybody failed, there was at one time due Welles & Co., beween two and three millions of dollars. Sam Welles came over himself to try and arrange this enormous indebtedness, leaving his Paris business in charge of his wife, Mrs. A. Welles. He often did so. He stopped at the Globe Hotel in Broadway, then kept by Blançard.

He settled promptly with every creditor at his (the creditor's offer), whether it was ten cents or fifty cents on a dollar. When such an offer was made Mr. Welles insisted upon its being paid cash, or to be secured in the most ample manner by real estate. In this way, a large amount of real estate came into his possession. He had much in Brooklyn. The property he unfortuntely sold before it commenced rising. In many cases Mr. Welles had to pay off previous mortgages before getting possession, and thus realized nothing. His loss was $600,000 by New York creditors.

H. Hollis Hunnewell, the former partner of Welles & Co., and who married a daughter of John Welles, is worth several millions of dollars. He has a country seat at Natick, about eighteen miles from Boston. It is unequalled in the United States. Mr. H. is executor of the estate of John Welles.

Ben Welles, one of the firm, who died last month, left a vast property. He entailed it as far as to his his grand children. He left one son, Benjamin Welles, who married a Miss Schermerhorn. He resides at Islip, Long Island. One of the daughters of Ben Welles married John O. Sargent. Another a Perkins, and another Russel Sturgis, Jr.

In New York there was a very capable man named E. Thayer, who aided Mr. Welles to settle up his busi ness in this country. Mr. Thayer had been many years a confidential clerk in the Boston house of J. & B. Welles, but came to New York, and is still extensively engaged in business here.

Madam Welles the wife of Samuel Welles above alluded to was one of four beautiful sisters named Fowle, born in Watertown, Massachusetts, it gave rise to the following popular couplet:

"The Fowles of Watertown
Is the Fair of every town."

One of the Misses Fowle married Captain Charles Smith of Lowell. Their son changed his name to Davenant, and is now one of the most distinguished lawyers in Boston.

One sister married Mr. Britton, and was mother to Lloyd L. Britton, the proprietor of the Everett House. Another sister married Mr. Timothy Wiggin, the great London banker for many years. (Every one will recollect the three great W.'s, or three great American banking houses abroad, viz. — Welles & Co., Paris; Wiggins, and Thomas Wilson & Co., London. American losses brought down flat the two last named. Another sister married Mr. Samuel Welles. He died in 1841, leaving behind only one child, a son named Samuel.

Madame Welles, sometime after the death of her husband, married, and is now the wife of the Marquis Lavalette, the present Ambasssdor of the Emperor Napoleon at Constantinople. She is a very remarkable woman even now, anc it is said that during her first husband's lifetime it was to her he owed the suggestions that enabled him to make some of his most successful financial combinations.

For the last three or four years of his life, Gracie & Sargent were his agents in New York. Mr. H. W. Sargent was his nephew, and when he gave up business he married Miss Olmsted, the only child of Frank Olmsted, who owned, while he lived, the now celebrated building occupied by Barnum for his museum. That property now belongs to Mr. Sargent.

In reference to the property of Frank Olmstead. His first wife was a Miss Wykoff. Old Alderman Wykoff was the grandfather of Mrs. Henry W. Sargent. The first Mrs. Olmstead died in Italy; his second wife was a Widow Douglass, and she gets a portion of the rent of the American Museum. It is $10,000 nett per annum.

Just before Alderman Wykoff died, his son Henry failed, and the old gentleman altered his will, and made Henry W. Sargent trustee for his son Henry's portion, and Mr. Sargent paid off all young Wykoff's debts.

Henry W. Sargent gets a fine income from property left him by his father, who married a sister of John and Sam Welles. Old Sargent was a portrait painter; he died fifteen years ago, very well off, indeed.

Another son of the old painter was John Turner Welles Sargent. He married the only daughter of George Phillips Parker, a great beauty and belle twenty years ago, when she and her parents made their home occasionally at the old Carlton House. Her aunt, Mrs. Boardman, left her $132,000 not long ago. Mr. and Mrs. John T. Sargent are at present in Europe.

The position of a Paris banker in reference to New York importers of French goods is something after this fashion. The New York agent writes that A B C wish a credit opened to a silk house in Lyons, or in Paris, for 100,000 francs. Welles & Co. are satisfied and agree to it. The goods are shipped, and sometimes a bill of lading to "order" is taken to Havre, and the advance of Welles & Co. has to be received before the bill of lading is handed over to the New York house. But this is often done. A house in good standing in New York, order as many goods as they please, and Welles & Co. pay the cost. The New York importers then remit at their convenience. In this way, a very large amount would soon accumulate. The business was a profitable one. By leaving money on this side, a higher rate of interest was obtained, and if the New York house was regarded as A No. 1, all went on smoothly until a panic occurred. So it was in 1837. Thirty millions of property were destroyed in December 1835, by the great fire. It was not felt so greatly at the moment as it was in the two succeeding years. In 1837, all the commercial difficulties culminated, and merchants failed, not singly but in platoons. Among other houses, was the firm of Manice, Gould & Co. They were very heavy importers and occupied a large store in William street, opposite the Merchants Exchange. They failed owing Welles & Co. an immense amount.

When old Sam Welles reached New York, he addressed a note to D. F. Manice, requesting him to call upon him at the Globe Hotel.

Manice complied.

"Well, sir, what are you going to do about the large amount you owe my house?" said Mr, Welles.

"I'll give you thirty cents on the dollar," was the reply of Mr. Manice, very carelessly, as though he didn't care a fiddler's curse whether old Welles accepted it or not.

Mr. Welles looked at his customer for a moment and then replied promptly:

"I accept your offer, sir, and the sooner the matter is settled and off my mind, the better I shall like it."

Manice was not a man or a merchant who cared a straw whether he made money by successful business, or by a successful failure and settlement with creditors He was neither scrupulous nor conscientious. His motto was "get money — honestly if you can, and if not, get money anyhow." He acted up to it.

After all was squared up, and the creditor was about leaving the room at the Globe Hotel occupied by the great banker, Mr. Manice turned to him and said: —

"By the way, Welles, suppose you come up and dine with me at my house on Thursday."

"Damn his impudence," thought Mr. Welles, but he replied: —

"Very well, sir, I will."

He went up and dined with Manice. Welles had seen and been at some superb dinners in Europe, but never had sat down to a more magnificent set-out than was made by his creditor, who diddled him out of tens of thousands of dollars. A servant in white kids stood behind the chair of each guest. The dinner service was of solid silver. Mr. Welles appeared pleased, and so he was, for when he reached his hotel, he met a friend, and told him, "I never made a more fortunate settlement than with that man Manice; if he had not settled with me when he did, I would have settled with him to-day for five cents on the dollar. His 'cheek' is beyond belief. To give a grand dinner with money robbed from me, and then invite me to it!"

Such conduct killed old Welles. He had many other

customers I may give some of their names in future chapters. It broke the banker's heart. He died not long after, and did not know the full extent of the rise of Brooklyn property that he had taken for debts.

The combination agents and business connections of Welles & Co. were very extensive. As they made large advances on goods in France that had to be shipped from Havre, Mr. Welles established a commercial house at Havre, under the firm of Welles & Greene.

The partner was J. B. Greene, of Boston. They received packages from Paris and all parts of France and Germany to be forwarded to New York in the Havre Packet Line. The business of forwarding was immense. The consul's certificate had to be attached to all invoices, and the fees of that consulate were second only to Liverpool.

Welles & Greene also did a very large commission business from the United States, especially in cotton, rice, &c., from the Southern Atlantic cities. They had agents in all parts of the Union.

No American traveler went upon the continent without a letter of credit from Welles & Co. The Boston brothers were members of the great Paris firm. All are dead now.

J. B. Greene, of the firm of Welles & Greene, was from New Hampshire. The successors of Welles & Co. are the following firm:

That Charles G. Greene is no connection of old J. B Greene, except by marriage. He is a son of the famous Charles G. Greene, the Boston *Post* editor, and married the second daughter of J. B. Greene.

Frederick Van Den Broek married Charlotte, the eldest daughter of J. B. Greene. These two daughters held interests in the firm of Greene & Co., bankers, Paris, on account of their father's death. That house suspended in 1857.

Then, John Van Den Broek, the brother of Fred, came from Batavia, Island of Java, and opened the new house, putting in it a cash capital of one million of francs.

The Van Den Broek family in Java have an income from their estates of $300,000 annually. They are immensely rich.

E. Thayer is still their agent in New York, as he formerly was of Welles & Co.

In a former number I have spoken extensively of Fitch & Co., of this city, and of Fitch Brothers & Co., of Marseilles. This house was one of the connections of Welles & Co., and an immense business was done through Fitch Brothers & Co. All drafts for advances made to shippers who consigned goods to the United States, or ordered goods shipped from Marseilles, passed through Welles & Co.

So too all drafts in the United States to make advance to parties shipping to Marseilles, were made upon Welles & Co. The banking commission is small, but when the monstrous sums are considered, this small commission makes an enormous income every year. It is well it is so. Were it not, no European house could stand the awful wipes it gets occasionally by New York failures. It has ever been so, and ever will be so.

The most risky business in the world is that of giving credits in New York, whether it be the banker who gives a line of credit of half a million to a house in the importing trade, or the grog seller who trusts his three-cent customer. It is a losing business, is the New York credit business.

CHAPTER XVI.

In the preceding chapter, I alluded to the celebrated Misses Fowle of Watertown, and stated, that one of them married Mr. Britton of New Hampshire, and that she was mother to Lloyd L. Britton, the present proprietor of the Everett House in this city. Few are aware that young Mr. Britton has had one of the most extraordinary of mercantile careers. His mother's sister, Mrs. Welles of Paris persuaded her to send young Britton abroad. He remained in Europe some time. On his return to New York city he entered the counting house of Fitch & Co., already spoken of. While there in 1838 Mr. Samuel Welles came out from Paris. Wishing to see his nephew John Turner Welles Sargent of Boston, established in business as his other nephew Henry W. Sargent had been, and to see the nephew of his wife established also, he consented to the establishment of the partnership of "Scoville & Britton." One nephew being the general and the other the special partner. The senior partner was Joseph A. Scoville, who had been regularly educated in a counting-house Mr. Welles Sargent remained in Boston, Mr. Scoville in New York, and Mr. Britton went abroad. He visited every port and city of note in Europe, and made business connections for the New York house. Its bankers in London were Prescott, Grote, Ames & Co., and in Paris, Welles & Co. The business that was done by the New York house was immense. William Gracie, who in early years was the " Son " in the great house of " Archibald Gracie & Son " in 1808, was their bondsman at the Custom House. Business poured in from every quarter. They had been conversant with the negotiation made by the Hon. Edmund Roberts, a merchant and a personal friend of General Jackson, who, when he was President of the United States, sent out Mr. Roberts to make treaties for this country with Japan, Muscat and Siam. He succeded in the two latter countries, and shortly after died. His papers were in the possession of his son-in-law, the Hon. Amasa J. Parker of this State. " Scoville & Britton had access to all the knowledge of the Arabian traffic possessed by Mr. Roberts. They opened a trade with Muscat, first building a barque, they named her the " Archibald Gracie," after the old merchant who had educated Mr. Scoville, loaded and sent her out to Zanzibar, and also to Muscat. In the counting house of Scoville & Britton were several persons who afterwards distinguished themselves. John C. Loescher, Henry P. Marshall, Andrew Nottebohm, Richard S. Ely, Edward Stucken, (afterwards of the firm of Meyer & Stucken,) Peter S. Parker, Edgar Botsford and Walter P. Marshall.

Mr. Van Buren, who was President, appointed Mr. Marshall a consul at Muscat, and Mr. P. S. Parker a consul to Bombay. The latter with Mr. Edgar Bottsford, went out in the barque "Archibald Gracie."

Scoville & Britton also owned the ship " William Brown," the ship " Virginia,"and the brig " Wyoming."

Misfortunes never come single. The ship " William Brown," struck an iceberg, on her voyage from Liver pool to New York, and sank in ha.f an hour, with many passengers. Scoville & Britton never received a dollar of insurance. The "Virginia" was lost on the bar at Galveston. In a week more she would have had a freight of $13,000 to Liverpool!

The brig "Wyoming" was captured off the Cape de Verd Islands by the British brig of War "Buzzard" under the frivolous charge that she was suspected of being about to engage in the slave trade. Meanwhile, the barque "Archibald Gracie" was on the other side of the Cape of Good Hope with $250,000 on board, when the adverse circumstances already alluded to, rendered it of importance that she should be here. Her funds were needed. The barque came in at last, and loaded with a valuable cargo — but too late. The house that had not made a bad debt, or a loss except as stated, had been obliged to suspend. Not long after came another ship to their consignment loaded with a valuable cargo. This was the Arab ship sent over by the Sultan of Muscat, and consigned to Scoville & Britton. Of course, this first fruit of their energy and enterprize was reaped by others. The forced sale of the barque "Archibald Gracie," afterwards ended their mercantile career. Not long after Mr. Scoville went to Holland. Mr. J. Turner Welles Sargent was wealthy. Mr. Britton went into business again. He afterwards married Miss Mary A. Ming, a daughter of Alexander Ming of this city, a man of great worth and an old Knickerbocker. Mr. Britton went to Albany, established the Stanwix Hall, and became wealthy. He has for some years owned the "Everett House" in this city. He has two children — a son, Edward Ming Britton, now sixteen, and a daughter Ada L. Britton now about fourteen.

The senior partner, Mr. Scoville, married a Miss Caroline Schaub, of St. Johns Berkley, S. C. He has but one child, a daughter, Mary. He was private secretary to John C. Calhoun until the great statesman died in 1850. He once owned the "Pick," and afterwards the "Daily State Register." He went to South Carolina in 1857, and there was a report that he died there, but I have the very best reasons for believing that it was not true.

It will be impossible for me to please all. Some will find fault with this personal historical book, because it goes too earnestly into details, while others will not be satisfied, unless I tell the whole story — all I know. Others will say, that they know more than I do about a particular merchant. I grant it, and will merely add that I write about thousands, and they think of but one.

There are few persons living in New York who have not heard the name of Gebhard. There is a firm of Schuchard & Gebhard. There is also a Gebhard Insurance Company.

Old Frederick Gebhard came from Amsterdam, in Holland, to New York in 1800. He acted at first as agent for a Dutch house, but after a while commenced business upon his own account. For many years the old man Gebhard lived on the corner of Greenwich and Rector streets. It was an old fashioned house, with a low stoop. Mr. Gebhard had his office on the first floor, and lived up stairs, as was the custom of many of our first families thirty or forty years ago. He kept in Greenwich street until 1832, when he moved to 21 Nassau street. Gebhard was the first importer of the celebrated Swan gin. He formed a connection in Amsterdam with the great gin distillers, Meder & Zoon.

When Mr. Gebhard left the agency business, he formed a partnership with his brother in Amsterdam, where the firm was Gebhard & Co. That house is still in existence. The firm in New York was Frederick Gebhard until 1822, when his nephew Frederick Schuchardt was taken into partnership, and then the firm was altered to F. Gebhard & Co.

In 1835 Mr. Gebhard died. The business was carried on afterward under the firm of Suchard, Favre and Co. Mr. F. had married a daughter of old Mr. Gebhard. The Company was the Amsterdam Gebhard.

When the son of old Mr. Gebhard (Fred. Gebhard) was of age, he became one of the firm, and it was again changed to Schuchard & Gebhard. This was in 1845. At that time, besides the gin trade, S. & G. did a very large silk business. They also did a large fur trade. They imported furs and also bought them and shipped to Europe. In addition, they were large importers of German and other hardware. Their principal business now is banking and operating in railroad stocks. They do the largest Dutch banking business in New York, and their bills on Holland sell higher than those of any other house. They still occupy No. 21 Nassau street. The old building cost Mr. Gebhard $18,000. The present firm put up a double building in connection with Wm. Bloodgood. It covers Nos. 19 and 21, and is worth $200,000.

Mr. Schuchard married Miss Remsen, who had a large property. He is worth $800,000 at least. Young Gebhard is one of the smartest business men in New York. He is highly educated, and a very gentlemanly man. He married a daughter of Thomas E. Davies, who although not a merchant, is one of the cleverest men in New York city. Mr. Davies is an Englishman He married a sister of the very Rev. Doctor Powers, of the Catholic Church, now deceased. She had a brother who came to this country to pick up an heiress. He succeeded, and married Miss Livingston. He went back to Ireland, and his money procured him a seat in the English House of Commons.

When Thomas E. Davies came from England, he settled in New Brunswick, New Jersey. There he was engaged in the distillery business, but did not make out very well. In 1830 he removed to the City of New York. Being a cool, shrewd, far-seeing man, he soon made up his mind that the city was destined in thirty years to reach the brilliant destiny and the high prices of real estate in 1860. He acted upon his opinion, and began to purchase real estate in large quantities. He was a man of more brains than means, but found an equivalent in the latter deficiency by making the acquaintance of the celebrated J. L. & S. Josephs, then the rich bankers and agents of the Rothschilds. Under their auspices, Mr. Davies went to work in the land speculation in St. Mark's Place. He bought and he built up all of that street. He next tried Bleecker street, and built up Carroll Place. His grand *coup* came next in the New Brighton Association, got up under his plans. That company purchased all the land from Quarantine, two miles back, and running up to the Sailor's Snug Harbor two miles. In 1836, the company got a loan from the United States Bank of $479,000. They erected buildings, hotels, &c., &c.

Will it be believed that all this property, now worth five millions, was sold under foreclosure, and bought in by Thomas E. Davies, the late George Griffin, Francis B. Cutting, and George Griswold, who formed a copartnership, and (lucky fellows) bought it all in for $200,000?

As a sample of the energetic character of Mr. Davies, let me say this: In 1837, when the great revulsion came, he found himself carrying an enormous amount of real estate. He promptly sacrificed one and a half million of dollars to get through, and he succeeded.

In 1840, there was a large sale of real estate at auction. The ground to be sold commenced at Twentieth street, and extended up to Murray Hill, on both sides of the Fifth avenue. Davies purchased, in connection with Frank Griffin, (old George's son) over 400 lots at $200 to $400 each. Mr. Davies has since sold some of those lots at $15,000 each.

He built up a whole block in Fifth avenue, between Thirty-first and Thirty-second streets.

He bought Nos. 82 and 84 Nassau street, the old Baptist Church, of Sarsaparilla Townsend, for a trifle, $80,000, and it is now worth nearly half a million.

To-day, as real estate owners, Astor is No. 1, A. T. Stewart is No. 2, and Davies is No. 3.

He is worth a few millions. Mr. Davies lives in Union Square, next to Seventeenth street. He gives good dinners, receives in magnificent style, and his house is visited by all the great foreigners that come to New York City.

But to return to his son-in-law Gebhard. The old Gebhard was a genuine Dutch school merchant. He had regular packets trading between Amsterdam and New York. His "Swan" gin was regarded by the grocers and dealers as the best in the market for many years. In 1836, Gebhard imported 4,000 pipes. No such importation was ever reached by any one gin importer.

Mr. Gebhard's store for many years was the only one upon that side of Nassau street.

CHAPTER XVII.

It does not seem possible to the author of these chapters that nearly three months have passed away since he penned chapter sixteen, the last written. The eminent name of Frederick Gebhard was last upon the list.

For three months the entire city as well as nation has been engaged by politics. That is all over now. Many of the merchants of the city, whose names will unquestionably figure in these columns hereafter, have been actively engaged in the recent political campaign. It was somewhat unusual. Merchants rarely trouble their heads about politics. This year two merchants were up for Congress. One was nominated by Tammany Hall—Udolopho Wolfe; and the other, Augustus F. Dow, by the Republicans. Through the instrumentality of another merchant, Joshua J. Henry, the Beaver street merchant, Mr. Wolfe, was forced to back down to give place to a regular politician, Gen. Ward, who was elected.

A commercial city like New York ought to send merchants as her delegates to Congress at every election They are the proper persons to represent her. By commerce she lives, and moves, and yet she sends all classes to legislate for her except her merchants. This ought not to be. Since the Constitution was adopted, or for more than eighty years, New York city has had but few merchants to represent her in Congress. M. H.

Grinnell was the last of any note. James G. King, the emiment merchant and banker, was in Congress, but he was elected from New Jersey.

Isaac Delaplaine, recently elected from the Eighth District, is the son of an old New York merchant, but instead of following in the footsteps of his excellent ather, he pursues the circuitous track of a lawyer.

Ben Wood, elected in the Third District, may claim to be a merchant, or rather what he sells is "people" not, merchandize.

We have spoken in some of the earlier chapters, of the quantity of merchants sent to this town by Connecticut. In this issue we shall speak of a few more. Probably one of the most extensive grocery establishments in this city at the present moment, is Sherman & Collins, No. 65 Front street. About thirty years ago, George Collins and four other boys, viz: E. D. Morgan, Morris Earle, John J. Phelps and Amos R. Eno, emigrated from Hartford, Connecticut, to New York.

Halleck, in a poem called "Connecticut," writes of her people as a race that

"Love their land, because it is their own,
And scorn to give aught other reason why;
Would shake hands with a King upon his throne,
And think it kindness to his majesty.
A stubborn race fearing and flattering none,
Such are they nurtured — such they live and die.
All but a few apostates, who are meddling
With merchandise, pounds, shillings, pence, and peddling,
Or wandering through the Southern counties teaching
The A B C from Webster's Spelling Book;
Gallant and godly, making love and preaching,
And gaining by what they call "hook and crook,"
And what the moralists call over-reaching,
A decent living. Southerners look
Upon them with as favorable eyes
As Gabriel on the devil in Paradise."

Halleck further says:

"But these are but their outcasts

Certainly among these were not the young men I have named. They were all Connecticut boys, and came here to try their fortunes. But to return to Sherman & Collins. B. B. Sherman was originally from New Jersey. His father was a farmer at Long Branch. Young S. came to New York in 1828, when a boy, and entered as a junior clerk the extensive grocery house of Waddell & McCoon. In 1831 he became a partner under the firm of Waddell, McCoon & Co. Mr. Waddell retired with a fortune in 1833, and then the firm was changed to McCoon & Sherman. It continued so until about 1850, when McCoon retired as an active, and became a special partner. Collins then became a partner, and the firm was changed to Sherman & Collins They have always stood high in the community. Both partners possess great business capacity and integrity of character. Mr. Collins "traveled through the Southern States, not teaching the A. B. C. from Webster's spelling book," but he was "gallant and godly," and was a clerk in a Mobile house with the great cotton merchant, twenty-five years ago, Barrett Ames. The latter was an enormous cotton shipper to all parts of Europe, as also to the North. He retired many years since from his extensive cotton operations in Mobile, came North, and now lives at Craigsville, up back of Newburgh, where he owns a large cotton manufactory. At this moment no grocery house in this city or country stands higher, or enjoys a greater credit than Sherman & Collins. They have lived through all sorts of panics, and never made a stop. They are about the oldest grocery merchants in Front street. Mr. Sherman, like the majority of long shore Jerseymen, is of small stature, stout built, but very quick in his movements. He is regarded as one of the best grocery merchants in the street, Mr.

Collins is slender built, and carries Connecticut in his face.

Two other boys connected with the Connecticut emigration were Amos R. Eno and J. J. Phelps. They came in company, and in 1831 went into partnership in the dry goods business in Exchange Place, in the rear of the old Merchants' Exchange. Their store was about 20x30 feet. They had small means, small credit, but big hopes. The principal purchases they made were at auction, and they bought of all the great auction houses — John Hone & Sons, Hicks, Lawrence & Co., Adee, Timpson & Co., Mills & Minturn, John Haggerty & Sons, Boggs, Thompson & Co., Corlies, Mabbitt & Co. In those days almost every purchaser was required to give an endorsed note for the amount of his purchase. Eno & Phelps could not do it. Nobody would endorse for them. So they purchased for cash (payable in thirty days). In less than one year from their start, by their strict attention to business, their indomitable perseverance, and their economical habits, they gained a high position and became the largest auction purchasers. In fact, when present at a sale, auctioneers became anxious for them to buy, and would call upon them to bid. In the great fire of December, 1835, Eno & Phelps were burnt out. They then removed to Hanover Square, near the store of Arthur Tappan & Co. After accumulating a large property by this business, they entered into real estate speculation. They were the first persons who took hold of property in Dey, Barclay, Warren and Chambers streets, and also in Broadway. When Eno & Phelps withdrew from commercial business in 1850, they were supposed to be worth over a half million of dollars each. Mr. Phelps has again gone into business at No. 340 Broadway, near where the old Taber nacle used to stand. His new firm is Phelps, Bliss & Co., and they do an enormous dry goods business.

Mr. Eno built the Fifth Avenue Hotel. The ground and building cost him over one million of dollars. They were both good merchants, prudent and economical in their habits, and their uprightness was beyond question.

Two more of those five Connecticut boys must be handled by me. E. D. Morgan has reached the position of Governor of this State, and has just been re-elected. He left Hartford with the rest named, in 1830. Morris Earle was along, and from the same place. In 1834 they formed a partnership under the firm of Morgan & Earle, and did a grocery business. There is a romance about the private history of these young men; their first loves, their piety, Sunday school teaching, and success, that would make a novel. But we have only room to deal with the rough outline of all of them.

The means and credit of Morgan & Earle were very limited, and their grocery business was confined principally to the section of Connecticut from whence they came. In 1837 Morgan & Earle dissolved partnership. Morris Earle put up his own single shingle, and E. D. Morgan was left alone. He at once turned his attention to speculation in the great articles of sugar and coffee, rather than try to extend his grocery business. His operations in sugar were principally with the South. He spent nearly all of the winters in the city of New Orleans. He visited every sugar plantation in the vicinity, and purchased the crops in advance of their being sent to the New Orleans market. In these immense operations he coined money. It was at this period of the future Governor's life, that he became sc familiar with the domestic habits of the African negro while in servitude, and no one probably understands the negro character better than our Governor.

It is a very curious fact, that while E. D. Morgan made his wealth out of the Southern planters, he should have turned against them in after years, and became a King Pin in the ranks of the Republicans. Of late years grocer and Governor E. D. Morgan has engaged in various speculations, especially in railroads. He has the credit of being, to a certain extent, intimate with both Democrats and Republicans. He is fifty-five years old, and worth $300,000.

Morris Earle, the old partner of the Governor, died two years ago. He was a hard working, energetic man, but only left $100,000 behind him. He had one very singular rule in his business. He required his clerks to be at the store before seven o'clock summer mornings, and kept them there until nine o'clock at night; in winter, 8 A. M. to 9 P. M. were the regular hours. By such hard work he shortened his own days. He overtaxed his mind, and it weakened until he died.

Passing down Wall street yesterday, I met E. K. Collins, and exchanged salutations with him. He looked rosy, hearty, and not as care-worn as when he had those mighty American steamships resting upon his single shoulders.

"You are not living here now?" I asked.

"No. Only occasionally I come here. I am off again to-morrow."

We parted. He was once an old merchant, and the son of an old merchant, who existed even in my day. He was E. K. Collins, Jr., thirty years ago; then the firm was E. K. Collins & Son. Their counting house was in South street, near Burling Slip. The father was old

Captain Collins, who was for many years in the Vera Cruz trade, and commanded a vessel. Then he stopped going to sea, and in 1820 started as a merchant, and became the part owner and sole agent to a line of packet schooners and hermaphrodite brigs that traded between New York and Vera Cruz. The old house als established a line of packets to New Orleans. Old E K. Collins died about 1830; then the firm still continued E. K. Collins, afterwards E. K. Collins & Co. I believe Count Foster, of New Orleans, was the Company.

Mr. Collins became one of the most successful packet agents in the Liverpool line. He was agent of the theatrical line, as it was called, viz. the "Roscius," the "Sheridan," the "Siddons," and others whose names I forget. His success in this line led to the establishment of the line of steamers, the "Pacific," the "Arctic," the "Atlantic," the "Baltic," and the "Adriatic." Millions of dollars were sunk in that line; it ruined Mr. Collins.

At one time he had a house in New Orleans and another in St. Louis. Mr. Woodruff, who was killed a few years ago, was his partner in the provision trade. The firm of Woodruff is still in existence in Broad street. For nearly fifty years the sign-board of E. K. Collins (father and son) was elevated in New York, and they did an immense business.

Another old concern, more fortunate than the Collins' (for it is still in existence) is the tobacco establishment of A. H. Mickle & Son. Mr. Mickle was born in the Sixth Ward, in Cross street, between Duane and Pearl. The house, a two story modern shanty, was standing until within a few years ago, and we have watched for hours the admirable discipline of about twenty lusty porkers, who used to inhabit it, and went out regularly for grub in the morning, returned about sundown, and then marched up stairs to their place in the attic.

Mr. Mickle has had a great success in life. When a boy, he was a clerk in a counting house up at the opposite corner to where the Custom House now stands. On the opposite side, lived a concern in which Schuyler Livingston, of the firm of Barclay & Livingston, was a clerk. In those days the boys in a store or office, used to clean the desks, inkstands, sweep out the office, &c. Also there was a City Ordinance that required all dirt to be swept to the very middle of the street. An artist, in those days, could have sketched the future Mayor Mickle, and the renowned merchant and agent of Lloyds, London, Mr. S. Livingston, each armed with a broom, and threatening vengeance upon the other for encroaching his dirt too far beyond the middle of the street, and trespassing upon the private sweeping dominion of one or the other. Such is life, or *telle est la vie*, as the Frenchman translated it.

Mr. Mickle when nearly grown, became a clerk with Mr. Miller, the great tobacconist in Water street, near Wall. He was very attentive to business — was a good salesman, and soon gained the entire confidence of the old man, and became his head-clerk. After Mr. Miller died, Mrs. Miller carried on the business, and made snuff, cigar and chewing tobacco under her own name, "Mrs G. B. Miller." Mr. Mickle married a daughter, and was made a partner in the heavy concern. After her death he changed the firm to A. H. Mickle & Son, and has a store or manufactory running from Broadway to New street.

A Mr. Lawrence married his daughter, and for his second wife, Mr. Mickle married a sister of Mr. Lawrence. Mr. Cornelius W. Lawrence married another sister.

When Edward Prime sold his father's old house, corner of Broadway and Battery Place, Mr. Mickle bought it and resided there while mayor of the city. When he reached that elevation Mr. M. saw the elephant, and has since retired altogether from the political field. Mr. Mickle has a high position among the merchants and financial men of the city. His word is as good as his bond. He has acquired a fortune of over a million of dollars, and that he may long enjoy it, is the wish of every person who has ever been brought into pleasant contact with him.

CHAPTER XVIII.

Teh history of the names of some of the old mercnants is very curious. The large grocery houses of Bininger is an example of our statement.

The eldest, or founder of the name that came to this country, was a native of Zurich, Switzerland. The father, Christian, his wife and son Abraham, came in a brig from a port in Europe to Savannah, Georgia. On board the vessel came the celebrated John Wesley.

The vessel was within two days' sail of her port when Mr. C. Bininger and his wife died, and their bodies were committed to the great deep. Abraham Bininger, then a lad, was educated in the great Methodist Whitfield Orphan School in Savannah. A large crowd of Moravians had settled in this Southern city. They afterwards emigrated north to Philadelphia, and carried young Bininger with them. The Rev. Mr. Whitfield came North also. He had bought a large tract of land (about five thousand acres) at Nazareth, near Bethlehem, Pennsylvania. This land he sold to the Moravians, and they, after a short stay in Philadelphia, removed to it. The young Abraham Bininger was educated in the Moravian tenets, and with the intention of becoming a preacher in that faith.

When of age, he settled at Christian Spring, a mile from

Nazareth, and there began his preaching. He married at the same time, and became the father of four sons. One named Abraham, (who was destined to found the great grocery house in New York city in after years,) and of Isaac, Christian and Joseph. The old father went out as a Moravian missionary to St. Thomas, in the West Indies. While there, he was told that "none but slaves were allowed to preach to slaves." He forthwith sent a letter to the Governor of St. Thomas, offering to become a slave, in order to save the souls of the black race. His letter was transmitted to the King of Denmark, who, as a mark of his appreciation of such devotion, gave permission for the Moravian parson to preach to any class in St. Thomas.

On his return from the West Indies, the old pastor started off with Mr. Whitfield as a missionary among the Indians. His success was very great. He returned to New York. That year Mr. Embury, the first Methodist, came to this city. He got up a society, and they erected a church in John street. In this labor the Rev. Abraham Bininger was very active, and his name appears upon the early records of John street church.

From New York city Mr. Bininger went to Camden Valley, (now Salem, in Washington County in New York.) Mr. Embury moved up with him. They took up a large quantity of land there, and then was erected the old family mansion, that is still in existence, and still in the possession of A. M. Bininger, of this city, who is the grandson of the old Moravian minister. The furniture in that house in 1862 is the same as it was in 1760 — 102 years ago. That year Abraham, the eldest son, was dispatched to New York to begin an apprenticeship at the tanner and leather dresser trade, in the Swamp. He served there seven years, but did not like the business, and declared he would never engage in it for a living. He was at that time 21 years old, having been born in 1740.

After his apprenticeship was finished, he commenced getting a living by working at day's work as a common laborer. He hired out wherever he could get a job. He had at this time a friend named Peter Embury, who was a nephew of the Methodist minister, the founder of John street Church. Peter (afterwards celebrated as a great grocer and wine merchant) was then learning the chair making trade. Peter had a sister, and she married Abraham Bininger about the time he left the tanning business. Peter Embury went early into the grocery line, and was located at the corner of Beekman and Nassau streets, opposite the old Brick Church, now the *Times* Buildings. This Mr. Peter Embury lived in Greenwich street, not far from Duane, and died only four years ago, a very aged man.

Miss Kate Embury was a beautiful, buxom girl, and as smart as a steel trap. She soon discovered (after she became Mrs. Bininger) that it was up hill work for a white man to support a family with the earnings of a day laborer, and she proposed to assist him by taking in washing and ironing. This was agreed to, and their stock increased. The ambitious lady then proposed that he should purchase a table to stand outside of the door, and she would while washing keep her eyes looking out of the window at this table and its contents of merchandise.

Their place, a little shanty, was in old Agustus street, now City Hall Place. At first the buxom young wife only sold a few cakes, cookies and sugar plums. From that it changed to cabbages, potatoes, fruits — tobacco, snuff, and finally a few groceries. Here was the foundation of the great Bininger grocery house.

In after years, when Abraham Bininger was enjoying the fruit of his early planting, he took quite a delight in narrating all the incidents of his early days, especially to such men as De Witt Clinton and the other political great men of the day.

Abraham, after his little store was started, found that day labor was precarious. He plodded along contentedly for some time, and then he bought a buck and saw, and took up the business of sawing wood, then a very money making employment.

When Mr. Embury, his brother-in-law, built the store in Beekman street, Abraham carried a hod ; and afterwards pointing to the house, boasted that the greater portion of the bricks were carried on his shoulders. In those days, hod-carrying was not at all disreputable. Even masons carried it ; it had not been monopolized by the Irish laborer, as now. After a while he became so "forehanded," that he was able to buy a horse and cart. This he drove for some years. Meanwhile, his grocery department prospered under the careful management of his "Katy." The sales increased, and he frequently was called upon to purchase seven pounds of sugar a day, and carry it home, to be retailed out by the pennyworth. Up to this time all his stock of groceries has been carried on his own back, but an important change was soon to occur. The old pastor was settled at Camden Valley, as has been narrated: it had become quite a place. Isaac Bininger, the brother of Abraham, after the war, lived with his father at Camden Valley. He had been finely educated — Abraham had not received an education. Isaac opened a store at Camden Valley. It was the most extensive store between Albany and

Montreal, and was the wonder of the primitive inhabitants.

We have heard the aged and venerable Doctor Matthews, of this city, (he who preached so long and so faithfully to the members of the Garden Street Church — Exchange street — burnt in 1835), state that the great event of his boy life was, when once dressed up in clouded stockings, he was permitted to ride five miles from home on a load of wheat to visit the great store of Bininger.

So successful was Isaac, that he sent down to New York city for his brother Abe to come up and share in the mercantile prosperity of the old Bininger stock. Abraham departed from New York, leaving Katy Bininger in charge of the shop in Augustus street, and joined his brother at Camden Valley. He was taken into partnership. After a short time the brothers decided that Abraham should come back to New York and sell or barter away the produce, pot ashes, &c., received at the country store, and buy the return goods. At that period it took two weeks to do a journey now made in a few hours. Abraham, in accordance with the agreement, returned to New York, never to leave it more; and here may fairly be said to be the start of the great grocer house, for up to this period the merchandize had not gone greatly beyond the sale of a few penny's worth of snuff, sugar, tobacco, candies and vegetables — a mere huckster business. After acting with his brother Isaac for some time, and being the sole agent, they concluded to dissolve, and Abraham received his share of the profits.

He then opened on his own hook a small grocery store in Maiden Lane, opposite the old Oswego market, that then came nearly up to Broadway where the Howard

Hotel now stands. It was a great stand in those days. The centre of produce, fruits and groceries. Prosperity flowed in upon the prudent grocer. He bought two lots opposite the market, Nos. 10 and 12 Maiden Lane (now.) They were 25 x 80 feet deep each. He paid 250 pounds for each, equal to $750 now.

Splendid marble stores now stand upon them, and they are still owned by the descendants of the early grocer who bought them.

Back of these stores at that time, fronting on Liberty street, or rather in the very middle of the block, stood the old Quaker church. Many of our readers will remember a later period, say thirty years ago, when it was occupied by the pleasant little Grant Thorburn as a flower garden and seed store. That Grant Thorburn is still alive—probably a hundred years old, if not more. His descendant still carries on the business in John street, near Broadway.

But the store and the Quaker church thirty and thirty-five years ago! Such a wonder. The building was about forty feet back of Liberty street. But in front of it were long beds of beautiful flowers, the admiration of all our city. Then, old Grant kept every kind of plants and flowers known. He had cages of Canary birds and lots of gold fishes, then a wonderfully rare affair.

How many times the writer has been run out of that place by "little Scotchy," as the Liberty street boys used to call him.

But to return to Abraham Bininger. While in business in Maiden Lane—in fact until he died, he lived in a most moderate two story brick house at No. 164 William street, between Beekman and Ann streets. He was a wonderfully sprightly old gentleman, and only died in 1836, a very aged man.

After being in Maiden Lane for years, he bought the property on the west side of Broadway, 25 x 100, on the lot next from the corner of Liberty street. He paid for it $11,000. No building upon it. Everybody said he was crazy to pay such a price. That no man could stand it. It is still owned by the family.

Abraham had a son named Jacob Bininger. His health was wretched. He traveled in Europe many years, and died in Charleston in 1840, leaving one son named Abraham, after his grandfather, the shrewd grocer, and his great-grandfather, the determined minister of the gospel.

Twenty years ago no house in the United States had such a stock of choice wines, liquors and cigars, &c., as this famed house. Out of the old stock has arisen two distinct houses, both dating far back into the past, but continuing the same kind of business.

A. M. Bininger — the grand-son of the old man who settled the town of Salem, and who was the son of Isaac, who started the mercantile business in that town in 1774, and established an agency in New York city in 1776, to which the old country store was finally removed about 1778, and is still carried on by Abraham at No. 19 Broad street, under the firm of A. M. Bininger & Co.— claims to be the most ancient — in fact, th original Hapsburg Bininger, as he no doubt is, for he is the hereditary owner of Bininger Castle, its portraits, old furniture, and rare old wills and title deeds, at Salem, New York, and possesses the original letter of the King of Denmark, replying to the offer of the Moravian missionary, at St. Thomas, to wear chains, and go into slavery in order to preach Christ crucified to the slaves of that Island.

The Broad street A. M. Bininger claims precedence as son and grandson of the oldest Abraham and his son Isaac, who started the store in 1774.

The A. Bininger, of Thames street and Liberty, claims only from his father Jacob, who evidently was not the "Original Jacobs" of the old grocery house of Bininger.

The house of A. M. Bininger & Co., No. 19 Broad street, the ancients, have adopted the great modern invention of advertising, and use this fearful lever to make sales, doing a monster business in thousands of papers.

The house of A. Bininger, in Liberty street, have never done anything in the way of advertising beyond the old style of $40 per annum for an advertisement in the *Courier and Enquirer*, and the antediluvian sheets for which the subscription of $10 for the daily paper is thrown in.

My task is not to judge. I have given a faithful record of a grocery house as "Old as the Hills." We have gone back in this instance 160 years to 1700, when the little boy Bininger, after his father and mother had been tossed into the deep blue sea, landed in Savannah, and became the founder of that name on this continent.

CHAPTER XIX.

There are few merchants in this city who retain the same firm or style of doing business for half or even quarter of a century.

About one of the oldest, wealthiest and most extensive commercial houses, is that of Boorman, Johnston & Co. When that house commenced is beyond my personal knowledge, but I believe it to have been before the war of 1812. Originally the firm was Boorman & Johnston. Both of the partners were Scotchmen, and must have come over to this country when they had just reached manhood, as agents for some old established Scotch house. This was the case with many other Scotch youths who made a successful start in the great city, and we presume it was the case with James Boorman and John Johnston.

Their business at first was selling Scotch goods, bagging from Dundee &c. The firm did a very large business with Virginia, and at one time sold nearly all the tobacco that came to this market from Richmond.

They also did a large iron business, and received cargoes from England and Sweden. They always had Swedish vessels coming in loaded with cargoes of iron to their consignment.

The store of Boorman & Johnston was in South street

a long time. They then removed about thirty years ago to Greenwich street directly opposite Albany street. It was an immense store, with a very large yard. Here were erected sheds and iron bins.

In 1835 Boorman, Johnston & Co. received a consignment of immense iron pillars. I believe they came from Stockholm. They did their best to sell what nobody wanted. Finally, they set a mason to work, took out the under front wall of their great store in Greenwich street and placed the pillars underneath. There they remain to this day to be seen by any curious person, and I fancy those were the first iron pillars ever made use of in this city.

In 1828 Adam Norrie came out from Scotland, and was taken in as a partner of B. & J., and the firm had Company attached to it.

Adam Norrie, when he arrived, was not remarkable for his beauty, and has not grown more handsome since ; but New York has never seen a more energetic and intelligent merchant. Scotch to the back bone — that is, filled with ideas of stern honesty, sagacity, prudence and rapid determination, Mr. Norrie has never been beat. He probably was remarked for these great mercantile qualities before he left Scotland, for with them he also brought to the firm he joined in this city a most splendid connection and correspondence in the old country, and greatly added to the business of Boorman, Johnston & Co.

The business of this mammoth concern became so large about twenty-five years ago, that they had to give up portions of it. They were the largest Madeira merchants, and received immense quantities of that wine every year. From Italian ports they received large consignments.

Mr. John Johnston had a brother who was doing a large dry goods business in Richmond, Va., under the firm of Triplett & Johnston. Mr. Johnston retired from that firm, came on to New York, and formed with Silas Wood and Francis Burritt the firm of Wood, Johnston & Burritt. The new house took all the dry goods business formerly done by Boorman, Johnston & Co. for some years, and did the largest business in the city.

That house was dissolved long ago. Silas Wood and Mr. Johnston, of that firm, both died. Mr. Burritt is still living, and the business is carried on at No. 69 Broad street, by Francis Burritt & Co.

Probably there are more merchants in this city, who were once clerks with Boorman, Johnston & Co., than with any other house. It would be a curious matter to see the list. Among others were two young men, one of whom was named William Wilson, and the other Francis Brown.

Wilson was the son of a Scotch friend of James Boorman, but had been unfortunate, failed and died. He left his children to the guardianship of James Boorman. The latter never had any children of his own, but he adopted a daughter of his friend Wilson. The son he took in his counting room, and in 1838 started him in business with another clerk of his, Mr. Brown, under the firm of Wilson & Brown. To the new house he gave up all the wine and Italian business of Boorman Johnston & Co.

Mr. Wilson married Susan Ripley, a daughter of Frederick A. Tracy, a very extensive broker in Wall street, forty-five years ago. Mr. Brown married Eliza, another daughter. Mr. Tracy left several sons and daughters when he died. A son of Mr. Tracy, Frederick Jr., married Miss Wilson, the adopted daughter of

Mr. Boorman. He is now, although a young man, the head of the immense dry goods house of Tracy, Irwin, & Co. in Broadway. Young Tracy was for many years a clerk in the great silk house of Nelson, Carleton & Co. Their store was in Pearl street, about three doors from Wall, and where Beaver now enters Pearl. It was among the first stores burned on the night of the great fire in December, 1835.

John G. Nelson was one of the best silk merchants of this city. He was superior to Stewart in his knowledge of silk. He had married Miss Eunice Ripley, a sister of Mrs. Frederick A. Tracy, and was so far connected with the younger Tracy.

In those days most of our merchants and prominent business men were men of piety, and were religiously useful. They were attached to some church — were usually engaged in the process of Sunday school teaching. Business and money-making were not the only objects of life. Not a person have we named in this article as yet, who was not devotedly pious. Old Frederick A. Tracy, though a Wall street broker, was a pure, devoted, sincere Christian, if ever there lived such a man. He was a member of Dr. Milnor's church — St. George's, in Beekman street (now Dr. Tyng's, up town). Great credit is paid to Dr. Tyng for his knowledge of Sunday schools. Dr. Milnor forgot more in five minutes about Sunday schools than Docter Tyng ever knew, or ever will know, if he lives to be as old in years as the antique Methusaleh.

Frederick S. Winston, once a merchant, now I believe president of an insurance company, was superintendent of the main Sunday school at St. George's in Beekman street. He was able, energetic and devotedly pious. Dr. Milnor had a sort of branch Sunday school up in Duane street, between Church and West Broad way — about 133 and 135 — where the public school recently stood, but where new stores are just now finished.

There were two schools in that building. One was a negro Sunday school below, and a white school above. It was a hard old neighborhood, and ranked in sin next to the Five Points. West Broadway was then called Chapel street.

Jeremiah H. Taylor, an energetic Christian, though a hardware merchant near Pearl street, was the superintendent of the colored part, and Mr. Tracy of the white school. Nearly all the teachers belonged to Dr. Milnor's church, and after the Sunday school hour was over, adjourned to Beekman street.

Dr. Potts at that time preached in Duane street, and I believe John G. Nelson and old James Boorman both belonged to that church.

Dr. Milnor was an extraordinary man, as well as clergyman. He truly was "as wise as a serpent, and as harmless as a dove." He had once been in Congress — a member of the House of Representatives from Philadelphia, in the same Congress with Clay, Calhoun and Randolph. He evidently made a great impression upon Randolph, for in one of his letters, published in his life, he makes the following allusion to him:

JOHN RANDOLPH TO DR. JOHN BROCKENBROUGH.

"*Roanoke, Va., June 2d*, 1813.

"What you tell me of Milnor is quite unexpected. He was one of the last men I should have expected to take orders; not so much on account of his quitting a lucrative profession, as from his fondness for a gay life.

I am not sure but that it is the safest path. The responsibility is awful — it is tremendous."

The attachment to him formed by those who came in contact with Dr. Milnor, was very remarkable. He was a true shepherd to his flock. Among his congregation he numbered some of the most wealthy merchants of the city. There was Hubert Van Waggenen, Wm. S. Johnson, Wm. Whitlock, R. B. Minturn, and others.

James Boorman has a history worth reading, if it is ever written. A more remarkable man never lived. By commerce he became rich, and has never abandoned the pursuit by which he thrived, and probably never will.

The firm is still Boorman, Johnston & Co., and is composed of James Boorman, a son of Mr. Johnston, (for the old John Johnston died in 1849), and Mr. Adam Norrie. They occupy a counting room over the Bank of the Republic.

Probably no merchant now alive has been more active in schemes of benevolence than Mr. Boorman. He has been honored with being made chief of every corporation with which he would connect himself, and at this moment is the principal man, as he was the originator, of the Hudson River Railroad.

Adam Norrie, one of the great firm above, lived for a long time in Chambers street, opposite the Park, and only a few doors from where Stewart's great store stands. At that time it was regarded as one of the most desirable streets for private residences. John Haggerty lived on that range, and few thought commerce would ever trouble Chambers street.

Mr. John G. Nelson is now one of the largest wire manufacturers in the United States; under the firm of

Nelson & Richmond. Their wire mill is in Twenty-fifth street, and their warehouse at 81 John street.

The firm of Tracy, Irwin & Co., has been very nearly a quarter of a century in existence and without a change until quite recently. It is said that matrimony is a lottery, or if it was, a man's chance of securing a partner would be better than by actual acquaintance. So it would seem in mercantile partnership, for it has been said that when young Tracy wished to go into business on his account after leaving the house of Nelson, Carleton & Co., he drew up an advertisement and inserted in the daily newspapers. It was replied to by Mr. Irwin, neither of them had ever been previously acquainted with the other. It led to a partnership, and the new dry goods firm commenced business in Hanover Square.

Booraem another name, has been frequently mixed up with Boorman. It was another house altogether. Henry Booraem was the head of a great silk house many years ago. He was a very elegant man in his manners, and died rich. The store of H. Booraem & Co., was in Pearl street near Wall. His partner was Jacob Rathbun, at one time considered the handsomest man in New York, save one. That one was handsome Harry Hone. When Henry Booraem died, his wife put in the concern $60,000, and the business was carried on for some time. Mr. Booraem left sons and daughters. One of the sons married a daughter of old parson Lyle, who preached for so many years in Christ Church, Anthony street, opposite the hospital grounds. A sister married Mr. Leni, and one of the sons is with the latter person.

CHAPTER XX.

There is an old dwelling-house down Broadway, No. 55, that is very remarkable. It has its history, and a curious one it will be found if it is ever published, and I intend it shall be.

It was inhabited for many years — in fact was built by a Mr. Douglas. His widow resided there, and several of her daughters were old maids. One married a Mr. Cruger, and a Miss Cruger married James Monroe, who was once a member of Congress from this city, and is a nephew of the James Monroe who was once President of the United States.

Mr. Cruger refused to sell No. 55 Broadway, and there it stands on the lower side of the alley, surrounded by high stores, and looks wonderfully out of place. Mrs. C. refused to desecrate the house where she was born by allowing it to be used for the purposes of trade.

The Douglas maids were extremely civil. In those days, when a person called to collect a bill, they used to give the young clerk-collecter a piece of cake and a glass of wine, from out and off one of those solid mahogany side-boards. All was real in those days. The wine was old and good. The cake, lemonade, and the glasses, real *cut*, and the furniture solid. There was no jim-crackery then.

There is another monument left of the olden time,

It is located at No. 7 Broadway, and was long the residence of old Herman Le Roy, who built it. He was the founder of Le Roy, Bayard & Co. He had a large family of sons and daughters. One daughter, Caroline, married the Hon. Daniel Webster in that same house. Another married Mr. Newbold, of Philadelphia. He died in 1818, and after her father's death Mrs. Newbold lived with her children at No. 7 Broadway. Another daughter married William Edgar, a son of a former distinguished merchant in this city. He was a lawyer. Another daughter, Mary, died very young, and unmarried. There were several sons of old Herman Le Roy.

His mercantile firm was Le Roy, Bayard & Co. The store was in Washington street, two doors from Rector street.

He had a brother, Jacob, who was also in business under the firm of Jacob Le Roy & Son. Their store was on the corner of Rector and Washington streets. Roswell L. Colt was a partner in the last house.

Almost in the rear of No. 7 Broadway is a duplicate marble building at No. 7 Greenwich street. Old Herman Le Roy built that for his daughter, Mrs William Edgar. I passed it yesterday. Shorn of its glory, it is now rented out to poor families, and yet often in the early years of this century, it has had inside its walls nearly all the fashion, the beauty, the wealth and the talent of the city. It is melancholy to look at it. Not much better off is the once famed and beautiful residence of Mrs. Newbold. It is occupied mainly with offices. Sleepy-looking clerks seated on high cane stools before a great desk, occupy the room where the great Webster upon a gorgeously canopied bedstead passed his bridal night.

My readers can go next Sunday and look upon both these once merchant palaces now in their decay. There are no houses in the lower part of the city that can compare with them.

William Edgar was a great merchant n his day. Gardner G. Howland married a daughter for his first wife, and his eldest son is named William Edgar Howland.

At No. 9 Broadway lived John Watts, a rich man in those days — worth perhaps $300,000 — who had a good income.

Old William Edgar lived in Greenwich street, near the Battery, on the west side. His store was on Washington street, in the rear of his house. At that time Washington street overlooked the river. Many merchants of great renown occupied similar stores and dwellings. It was the case with G. G. & S. Howland, Le Roy, Bayard & Co., as well as old Mr. Edgar. This was where the Howlands started business, and before they removed to South street, where they are at present located.

G. G. Howland, Willian Edgar, A. M. Bininger and William B. Astor all belonged to the same military company, commanded by Captain Titus. The company belonged to the second regiment of N. Y. State artillery, Colonel Robert G. Manly, a gay, dashing officer in his day. It is an old Fifth Ward family, and Manly Frisbee was a nephew of Colonel Manly.

The Edgars, Le Roys, Newbolds, McEvers, Bayards, Howlands, were all intermarried, and were the *creme de la creme* of those days. Old Jacob Le Roy lived in Broadway near the Tabernacle. There was the Bayard farm where Mr. William Bayard lived, and where Alex ander Hamilton was taken after being mortally wounded by Burr. It was near Fort Gansevoort.

The old firm of Le Roy, Bayard & Co. was one of the most remarkable commercial houses in this or any other American city. The firm existed before the commencement of this century. They traded to all parts of the world. Robert Bayard, one of the firm, married a Miss McEvers, a daughter of Mr. McEvers.

The Mr. Newbold who married Miss Le Roy, was son of the very rich Calcutta merchant in Philadelphia, and the head of the Newbold family in this country.

Young Jacob Le Roy was nicknamed "Black Jake." The old house made immense fortunes. In the war of 1812 they owned and sent out fast sailing vessels to Europe and to the East Indies. If they escaped capture and got safely to New York, of course the profits were immense.

The house failed in 1827, but they had no Le Roy in it at the time; although the firm was kept up as Le Roy, Bayard & Co. That house built the frigates for the Greek Government in connection with G. G. & S. S. Howland. I will give a full account of the transaction in a future chapter.

There are anecdotes connected with this house of a very amusing character. In their palmy days, there was in New York a famous man named Salles. He was always spoken of as old Salles. He was a glove-maker by profession. He had in that business a partner named Tonnelly. It is after him is called the Tonnelly estate, up near the Sixth avenue. They made the old fashioned deer-skin suspender, and after Salles dissolved partnership, Tonnelly carried on business in the old slow but sure way.

Old Salles was a plain man; in fact, those who can

now recall him to memory must say he was very sloven ly in his appearance. He appeared to be a poor man. On one occasion, about the time of the war, Le Roy, Bayard & Co. had one of their fast clippers arrive. She had escaped capture, and brought in a large quantity of silks. The value was immense. At that time the counting room of Le Roy, Bayard & Co. was in Washington street. William Bayard knew old Salles by sight, but to the clerks he was not known. At that time old Mr. Salles was a great shaver of notes, but it is certain he never would shave higher than seven per cent. per annum, the legal interest of the State.

When this clipper arrived, old Mr. Salles went down to the office of Le Roy & Co. He was a capital judge of silks. There was no better in this city. He asked the young salesman to show him the samples. He did so. Old Salles selected lot after lot, amounting to thousands of dollars. The clerks thought him crazy. Finally he stopped, and the bill was made out. "Send the goods to mine shtore, and I vil pay de bill," said old Salles. The clerks laughed, and old Mr. Salles left, and went to get his dinner. He boarded in Pearl street, and took his meals under the old Tontine Coffee House. He was a terrible eater, and dreaded by all private boarding house or hotel keepers. He ate three plates of turkey, and other things in proportion, at a meal. He stood six feet three inches high, and wore a white hat, *a la* Greeley. When it was three o'clock, the time for the goods he had bought of Le Roy, Bayard & Co., to be at his store, old Salles went there. No silks had come. Down he went to the office of Le Roy, Bayard & Co.

"Did I not buy goods here?" he asked.

"Yes, but we want pay!" said the clerk. But at

this moment Mr. Wm. Bayard came in, and Mr. Salles narrated what occurred.

"You shall have the goods immediately, Mr. Salles." The clerk started, but the silks were sent round to Salles's store, and he gave a check for them.

The next time that a vessel of Le Roy, Bayard & Co. came in, Salles was sent for, and again he purchased the entire cargo. He made a monstrous amount of money in such purchases. Old Salles would re-sell to King & Mead, (the A. T. Stewart of 1812,) the largest dry goods jobbers in America, and other retail dealers.

There are some curious anecdotes about the awful eating habits of old Salles. At one time he went to a boarding-house in Pearl street, kept by Mr. and Mrs. Conrad. He had been turned out of various places, where his voracity became too great for any profit. At the new place he was unknown, and terms were agreed upon for one month. When it expired, the bill was handed to him, with a request to leave. The proprietor informed Mr. Salles that he could not afford to keep him at *that* price.

"Is dat de matter? Den chargee more," said Salles. The previous price was $4 a week; $2 were added, making it $6 per week, and another month was commenced. At its expiration, a bill was presented to Mr. Salles, and he was again told he must leave. The bill was paid. Another month was entered upon at $8 a week. Another month, and it was raised to $10 per week. When that expired, the unhappy landlord received the sum due, and again asked Mr. Salles to leave. Salles says: "D — it, chargee more. Chargee all you want."

With tears in his eyes, the man replied:

"It is no use, Mr. Salles. I will not have you any

longer, any how. The more I charge, the more you eat."

In the account of the Bininger family, their early start, and detailed history, that I wrote about in a former chapter, I omitted matter that I had forgotten.

I said that the old grocer, Abraham Bininger, when working at days work, lived in Augustus street, now City Hall Place. That his wife Aunt Katy, kept a little shop, sold candy, sugar, snuff, tobacco, pipes, cookies and other cakes from a little table in front of the shop. I omitted to mention, that the cookies, cakes, and tea rusk, were daily supplied from a basket carried by a young man, who peddled tea rusks, &c. The name of the boy peddler was John Jacob Astor, who was then eighteen or twenty years of age, and had not been long arrived in this country, and before he had fairly started in that wonderful rise in the world, that Astor afterwards made.

John Jacob Astor had a sister, who came out from Germany with him previous to the Revolution. Her name at that early period was not Mrs. Miller, but Mrs. Ehninger, she having married a person of that name previous to her departure from Europe.

Old Mr. Ehninger was a cordial distiller, and he died from the effects of an accident caused by burning spirits. His descendants still reside in the city. After his death, the widow married Michael Miller, and having taught him the secrets of the business, she, in company with him continued to carry it on. She had several children by her first husband, Mr. Ehninger.

Old Mr. Miller had a nephew George, who was from Pennsylvania, and when the distiller died, carried on the business until he (the younger) died in 1846.

In after years, John Jacob rather turned up his nose

at a distiller. Mrs. Miller resented it, and upon one occasion observed: "Yacob vas noting put a paker poy, und solt preat und kak." She spoke mongrel Dutch until the day of her death.

Of course, when Mr. Astor peddled cakes was long before he went into the baking business upon his own account, and longer still before he became a fur peddler, and eventually the founder of the North-West fur company, or American fur company, located in Vesey street, on the block where the Astor House now stands.

A very old wholesale grocery house in this city is that of Philip Dater & Co. For years it was Lee, Dater & Miller, and at one time they occupied a large store in Front street, corner of Fletcher.

Philip Dater was the son of a farmer in moderate circumstances in Rensselaer county, in this State. He did chores, and was occupied about his father's farm until he was thirteen years old, when he up stick and came to New York somewhere about 1815. He is now a man sixty-four years old. He got employment as a clerk in a small store, and after a few years of experience, he started business on his own account near Coenties Slip. Then he engaged in business with Mr. Miller, under the firm of Dater & Miller. Finding that more capital could be usefully employed, they entered into copartnership with a capitalist named Lee, and the firm was changed to Lee, Dater & Miller. Mr. Lee lived in College Place, where he had built a handsome house.

All the daughters of Mr. Lee, who once kept a retail grocery in Coenties Slip, have married noblemen or sons of noblemen. One of them married a grandson of the haughty Duke of Athol, the proprietor of Glen Tilf, and distinguished himself in the Crimean war; another married a French nobleman of lofty lineage.

After years of great success, Mr. Lee died, Mr. Miller went out of the firm, and it then became what it now is — Philip Dater & Co.

Mr. Dater has had a large family of children. Several sons are in business with him. One is at Chicago, doing a large grocery business. For many years Mr. Dater lived in Cliff street, between John and Fulton. Then he bought a large farm at Morrisania, about two miles from Harlem. He bought that property very low. It is worth now ten times what he gave for it. Upon it Mr. Dater has erected a superb house, and has lived in it since he left Cliff street until now.

He is perfectly devoted to his business. He fairly loves it. He gets his breakfast long before daylight goes to the depot, and reaches his store by seven o'clock; and this he does all the year round, beating his clerks. He is like most of our old school merchants — pious. He is a prominent member of the Episcopal church. Take Philip Dater all in all, he is a noble specimen of a man. He has a heart like an ox. He is good to the poor. He is a warm friend, and carries out his christian professions. His wife is like him, and they are well matched. Philip Dater and old Abe Bininger were quite intimate when the old man lived in William street.

The latter had adopted a niece named Catharine Bininger. The couple were very old and very infirm. She was young and gay. They liked old society. She liked new, and was about to leave them, when Mr. Bininger arrested her going, by saying, "Kate, if you stop with me until I die, you shall inherit the same as one of my own children." This was agreed to, and Kate spent some of the best years of her life waiting upon the old folks. Philip Dater knew all about this transaction.

Well, Abraham Bininger died. George W. Miller and Philip Dater were pall bearers at the old man's funeral. He died of apoplexy, and had not thought to add a codicil to his will, providing as he had agreed to do for his niece.

Jacob Bininger and his wife, who had not troubled the infirm old man, refused to allow the devoted niece a cent, although they knew the circumstances. Then it was that Mr. and Mrs. Dater showed their friendship. They advised the niece to sue for wages, and during the trial, day after day, they sat by her side in Court, encouraging and sustaining her by their presence.

Jacob Bininger, the son of old Abraham, had married a Miss Harriet Burger. She lived sometime in the family of David Rogers, the great Santa Cruz sugar merchant. She was daughter of old Mr. Burger, of Staten Island, one of the most extensive clam dealers in his day. She was the mother of the present Abraham Bininger, of Liberty street. She was very vindictive, and decidedly opposed to Miss Kate Bininger coming in for any share, even servant's wages, of the old grocer's tin. She looked so savage that James R. Whiting, in summing up, remarked of her, "That woman, if it was in her power, would annihilate my client with a look, if it could have been done." Miss Bininger recovered "servant's wages" from the estate of her uncle, but nothing more. That was all she could sue for.

CHAPTER XXI.

Few persons are aware how intimately and how extensively are interwoven the fortunes, the business, the social life and destiny of our leading merchants with those of Europe, Asia, and even Africa. Our great merchants do not make any noise. Many of them are less known here than in the great cities of London, Liverpool, Paris, Amsterdam and St. Petersburg.

One of the most extraordinary men of his day was Dominick Lynch. He was a merchant of wines — an extensive importer and a connoisseur in all nice things. He was a perfect gentleman, and thirty-two years ago, was the envy of all the ambitious youths of New York. Whatever Dominick Lynch said was "good," must have been. He was the most fashionable man in New York. His taste of wines was exquisite, and he made mere common clay pay for his own unequaled wisdom and judgment.

Dominick had a brother named James. The latter was a lawyer, and had his office at No. 5 Wall street Court. Not many citizens will remember that court, and yet what a wonderful place it was. It had a pump in it, and the finest water in the city. It ran through the buildings of the old New York Insurance company, (next to the present Bank of New York) from Wall to Pine street, and on the latter street came out next to the old Bank Coffee House, on the corner of Pine and William streets, then kept by William Niblo.

James Lynch resided in the Court, and lived in the Sixth Ward. He afterwards became a Judge. One of his daughters married the Count Tasistro, and the latter was exposed by Dominick Lynch, who was a perfect living dictionary of the European as well as American peerage. Another brother was Henry Lynch, a famous man in Wall street, who had an affair of honor with Colonel Webb, and who was challenged by Mr. Tasistro and posted by that gentleman for refusing to fight.

Dominick Lynch kept a very large wine store in William street, three doors from Wall, and opposite the Merchants' Exchange. In 1829 he was burned out, and a splendid stock of wines was consumed. I was at that fire, and never did the firemen of New York suck such delicious wines as then.

The fire did not burn up Dominick Lynch. He was more energetic after than before the fire. He commenced in 1830 his importations of the great Lynch's "Chateau Margeaux." A man was nobody in those days if he had not subscribed for a box of that almost inaccessible wine to any body but Lynch. The subscription lists for three hundred cases contained all the principal people of New York. The cases were about three feet long and four feet round, and contained four dozen quart bottles. A smaller size contained four dozen pints. The price, I believe, was about $75 per case.

Then Lynch's "Sauterne" was another great wine, delivered upon subscription lists. He had great success also with Lynch's "Lucca Oil." It commanded an unheard of price. Mr. Lynch had it manufactured in some part of Italy after his own idea; it was put up in "bettys," and was really an oil that our first families used as if it had been strained honey. Dominick Lynch coined money; he spent it, with the freedom of a prince. He was a high liver, gave royal dinners, and went into the best society. He was an extraordinary judge of wines.

He had a lovely family of daughters, and bought a place on Staten Island, next door to the Pavilion Hotel at New Brighton, where he lived until he died in 1844. He never saved anything, and consequently died poor. Of his daughters, two married naval commanders, one the celebrated Commodore Wilkes; another married William Watson, a lawyer, who died last winter. One married Julius Pringle of South Carolina. One married a Mr. Luqueer of Brooklyn. One son was a distinguished naval officer. Another who was once our Deputy Surveyor is now a distinguished lawyer at Rome, N. Y. Another of the daughters married Stewart Maitland, of the firm of Maitland, Phelps & Co. — once Maitland & Co., Maitland & Kennedy, Maitland, Kennedy & Maitland, and lastly Maitland, Phelps & Co. Another memorable circumstance in the history of Dominick Lynch, is the fact that Mr. Lynch brought to this country the first Italian opera troupe, of which Garcia, the greatest tenor then living, Angrisani, the greatest basso, and Malibran, the greatest prime donne, were members. Malibran was then only Signorina Garcia, but she married Malibran soon after her arrival here. Still another interesting fact about Dominick Lynch is, he was a very strong Roman Catholic, his father, also a Roman Catholic, having been the original settler of the town of Rome in this State, but all of his children have become Protestants.

The house of Maitland & Co. was founded before the American Revolution by Scotch supercargoes, and has existed under the above firms nearly one hundred years. At present there is no partner of the name of Maitland in that house, the late partner, James William Maitland, having died recently.

The Dumfries (Scotland) *Courier* of Oct. 30th, thus notices him:

BEQUEST TO THE POOR. The late William Maitland, Esq., New York, has bequeathed the sum of $250 to the poor of each of the parishes in which the estates of his father, the late Lord Dundrennan, were situated, viz: Berrick, Tonglan and Twyaholm, in the Stewartry of Kirkendbright, and West Calder in Mid Lothian. The legacies are directed to be paid "to the minister of the established Church of Scotland in each parish, to be distributed according to his discretion among the poor of all religious sects and denominations within the bounds of his parish."

Stewart Maitland who married Miss Lynch is a brother of the above named James, and a son of the late Lord Dundrennan. Stewart retired from the house of Maitland, Phelps & Co., upon the death of his father, the late Lord Dundrennan, and he now resides in Scotland with his lady, formerly Miss Lynch.

Lord Dundrennan was but a Scotch law bred lord, whose title was only a courtesy one, like that of Lord Jeffreys, and was not transmissible; consequently at his death it became extinct. Mr. Maitland, who was of the firm of Maitland, Kennedy & Co., removed from New York to Edinburgh about ten years since. The summer before he left an affair of his caused some talk in New York, and among gambling and mercantile people generally. In playing cards with a gentlemanly Philadelphia black sporting adventurer, named Meredith, he lost one evening in Saratoga something over one hundred thousand dollars. Mr. Meredith was a brother of the Secretary of the Treasury, and held the appointment of measurer in our Custom House. Mr. Maitland, being a man of scrupulous ideas of honor, would have paid every dollar he lost, but his friends would not permit him to do it, and compromised the matter for a very small sum with Meredith.

Old David Maitland was of the house of Maitland, Kennedy & Maitland when it was in Front street. He was an old bachelor, but the father of the present house, and uncle to Stewart and James Maitland. Old David retired some years ago to his estates in Scotland, where he now resides. He was succeeded by Stewart (now in Scotland), who formed a copartnership with the now somewhat celebrated Royal Phelps, a very wealthy gentleman, who but then recently returned from South America. A Mr. Cumrie was also one of that firm.

He was succeeded by his brother James, as I have already stated. He was very much beloved and respected for his many amiable qualities. He married the daughter of James A. O'Reilly, Esq. During the early part of last summer he was seized with rheumatic fever, of which he died in the thirtieth year of his age.

His entire fortune, with the exception of about $20,000 in small legacies (as stated by the Scotch paper above), he bequeathed to his wife as residuary legatee.

On the retirement of Mr. Cumrie from the firm of Maitland, Phelps & Co., Mr. Robert Gordon, a former clerk in the establishment, was taken into the partnership, purely owing to his mercantile merit and good conduct.

When James William Maitland died, Benjamin F. Butler, the cashier of the house, became a partner.

Royal Phelps married a South American lady, by whom he had one child, a daughter. The latter married, a few years ago, a Mr. Carroll, of Baltimore. Mr. Phelps himself was a clerk on the Pacific coast for many years.

Jacob and Herman Le Roy, who are mentioned in our last chapter, were sons of Daniel Le Roy, an old New York merchant, who died in September, 1791.

I am aiding all those who do not wish prominent merchants to be buried in oblivion forever. I am rescuing men and things from such a fate, and I have a right occasionally to ask assistance in my efforts.

Is there any one alive who can explain to me a matter of deep interest?

In 1791 the Tammany Society, or Columbian Order, established an American Museum. The object was to collect and preserve everything relating to the history of America, — likewise, every American production of nature or art; for which purpose part of the funds of the Tammany Society were appropriated.

The Corporation of the city so far favored the enterprise as to grant a room in the City Hall (the City Hall was in the rear of the present one), on a range with the library. The Museum was opened every Tuesday and Friday afternoon.

Articles could be sent there on those days, or to Mr. John Pintard, No. 57 King street (not the present King street), but Pine street that was called King street from 1728 to 1797, and previous to 1728 was Queen street.

The trustees of the Museum were William Pitt Smith, chairman; James Tyler, John R. B. Rodgers, Jacob Morton, Effingham Embree, William W. Gilbert, treasurer; John Pintard, secretary; Gardner Baker, keeper.

At that time the Tammany Society had their great wigwam in Broad street.

Now, what has become of that Museum? We have in our possession the

"LAWS AND REGULATIONS OF THE AMERICAN MUSEUM BELONGING TO THE TAMMANY SOCIETY, OR COLUMBIAN ORDER."

Number one to eight. — We have also a bit of several articles contributed to that Museum. What became of it?

We remember going to the old City Hall building, (back of the present City Hall), to Scudder's Museum.

Was that the original American Museum established under the auspices of Tammany Society?

Is not that the same Museum bought by Phineas T. Barnum of Doctor Scudder, and by him called the American Museum?

What right had any body to sell the Museum of old Tammany Society, made up as it was, by presents?

Have not the heirs of old Samuel L. Mitchell, or any other person who presented the American Museum in 1791 with a specified article, a right to walk into Barnum's Museum, and seize that article if it is to be found there?

Are none of the trustees alive now? Are none of the Smiths, Tylers, Rogers, Mortons, Embrees, Gilberts, Pintards, or Bakers' descendants capable of giving us some information?

We have no doubt but that Barnum, by some hocus pocus arrangement, is the present possessor of the chosen jewels of old Tammany. What is his right to them?

The following is a copy of the laws alluded to:

1. *Of the Election of Officers.* — The trustees of the American Museum, as by law elected, shall, on the first stated meeting after their election, choose from out their number a chairman, treasurer and a secretary.

2. *Of the Chairman.* — The chairman is to preside at all meetings, to preserve order, to regulate the debates, and to state and put questions agreeably to the sense and intentions of the trustees. In the absence of the chairman, his place shall be supplied by one of the trustees, chosen *pro hac vice.*

3. *Of the Treasurer.* — The treasurer shall receive all moneys that may become due to the Museum, and shall pay the same, by an order from the chairman, which shall be his voucher. The treasurer shall keep a regular account of all moneys received and paid by him, as aforesaid. And once every year, or oftener if required by the trustees, he shall render an account to them of the stock in his hands, and the disbursements made by their order, and shall deliver up to his successor the books and all papers belonging to them, together with the balance of cash in his hands.

4. *Of the Secretary.* — The secretary shall take the minutes, and read all letters and papers that may be communicated to the trustees. He shall enter into a book, to be provided for the purpose, an account of all donations made to the Museum, together with the names of the donors. He shall take charge of and preserve all books, pamphlets and works presented to the Museum, or purchased by it; all curiosities, whether of nature or art, presented or purchased, and shall class and arrange them in their proper order.

5. *Of the Meetings of the Trustees.* — The ordinary meetings of the trustees shall be on the second and fourth Fridays of every month, from October tc

May, both inclusive, at six o'clock in the evening; on the fourth Friday of each of the other four months, at seven o'clock. No meeting shall be continued after ten o'clock. Five trustees shall constitute a quorum.

6. *Of the Distribution of Money and making New Laws.* — No part of the funds shall be disposed of but by regular motion, seconded and agreed to by a majority of the trustees present. And all orders for payment shall be signed by the chairman. No new law shall be made until the same shall have been proposed at one meeting, and agreed to by a majority of trustees (giving a quorum) present at a subsequent meeting.

7. *Of a Keeper.* — The trustees shall elect a keeper of the Museum, whose duty shall be to summon all meetings called by the chairman, to attend the same, and perform such necessary offices as may be required. He shall receive all presents made to the Society, and deposit them in the Museum, giving an account thereof to the secretary. He shall admit all members into the Museum, at such times as shall be apportioned for that purpose, and shall take care that no visitor shall remove or injure any of the articles belonging to the Museum. For all which services he shall be entitled to such compensation as the trustees shall see fit to grant.

8. *Of access to, and use of the Museum.* — The intention of the Tammany Society or Columbian Order in establishing an American Museum, being for the sole purpose of collecting and preserving whatever may relate to the history of our country, and serve to perpetuate the same, as also all American curiosities of nature or of art. In order to answer this end, it is evident that every article presented to or purchased by the Society, ought to be carefully deposited in the Museum, and never be allowed to be taken out of the same, lest

it should be mislaid, and perhaps irretrievably lost. Nevertheless, in order to render the Museum serviceable to the great interests of the society, every member of the Tammany Society shall have free access thereto, through means of the keeper, and shall be permitted to examine all the natural or artificial curiosities and read all books, pamphlets and papers, and take extracts therefrom, as far as may suit his purposes, but shall not be allowed to take away anything whatever, out of the Museum, on any pretext whatever.

The Museum shall also be accessible to any other person not a member of the society, but who shall be introduced by a member, who shall be alike indulged and alike subject to the same regulations as the members of the Tammany society.

Although sixty-nine years have elapsed since that American Museum was started, I have no doubt but that I shall be able to pick up a good many of the books, documents, and curiosities alluded to above. They must be found somewhere. I mean to find out whether there was any legality exercised in their sale or disposal.

Every particle of interest that I can obtain from those of my readers who are posted in these matters, and who are descended from the old Tammany founders and members, I shall be thankful for.

CHAPTER XXII.

When I forget any thing about an old merchant, I insert it as it comes to my mind. All that the reader of this work has to do is to refer to the *Index*, at the end of this volume. I have already written something about the Biningers. Here is more. A son of Jacob Bininger certainly did marry the daughter of a high ex-official at Paris. Abraham B. married Miss Draper, a daughter of Lorenzo Draper, by his first wife. He was formerly dry goods importer, and appointed consul at Paris by John Tyler, when President. Lorenzo is brother to William and Simeon Draper. Both of the latter brothers married daughters of John Haggerty.

Mr. Abraham Bininger had a brother William, whose history, unfortunate and romantic, would form the ground work of a tale to rend the hearts and bring tears to the eyes of the most hardened and unsympathising of merchants.

William Bininger was a noble fellow. He was educated at Nazareth, Penn., and was intended to be a Moravian minister. He was a glorious soul. His prospects were bright, when in a sad hour he fell in love with a charming, beautiful girl, who lived in Liberty street, just around the corner from the Bininger store in

Broadway. She had but one fault — she was poor. The mother of the youth, who was Mrs. Harriet Burger Bininger, herself the daughter of the aristocratic clam-digger Burger of Staten Island, did not consider the match a suitable one, and she deliberately went to work to break it up. She swore it should never be, and she kept her oath. William Bininger was as noble a fellow as God ever allowed to breathe. But he wished to be an obedient son — to mind his parents. Disgusted with maternal interference, he bade farewell to his lady-love and embarked for Europe. Dispirited and disheartened, he died of a broken heart in a port of France. His body was placed in a pipe of old Cognac brandy, the cask was marked A. B. & Co., New York, and shipped by a vessel bound to this port.

The vessel in which the melancholy package was shipped was wrecked off Barnegat, but the pipe and its contents were picked up on the Barnegat beach, and eventually reached Bininger & Co.

Before he died, William made his will, and gave every dollar that he was or would be worth (for it was before his father Jacob died) to the beautiful but poor girl to whom he was attached. His fortune, so willed away, was then worth about $100,000; it would now be worth $400,000. So soon as the mother received the news of his death, and of the will, she was fearfully angry. Previously, she never would acknowledge acquaintance with the poor girl her son loved; but as soon as she became the heiress of her son, she sought her out, invited her to their magnificent residence in Chambers street, where Jacob Bininger lived in splendid style, and coaxed and wheedled the young lady to take $20,000 and relinquish all claims upon the Bininger property.

The first Miss Bininger, Agnes, married Richard Clark, who was once a dry goods merchant, and latterly a Third Ward constable, in which high official capacity, he died. He was the father of Abraham Clark, one of the present firm.

Martha, another sister of Jacob Bininger, married a Frenchman, Andrew Gautier. He was a well known broker down town. When he died, his widow married Isaiah Mankin, a merchant in Baltimore. He was concerned with W. W. Todd of this city, the great salt merchant, in a line of coasters between the two cities. Old Abe Bininger bought for him a house in Baltimore, and the widow Mankin still owns it.

Rebecca married Nathan Sands of Orange county, and was mother to the sarsaparilla Sands, A. B. & D. Sands in Fulton street, druggists. Old Nathan Sands was a Quaker preacher.

Jacob Bininger left three daughters. Harriet married Doctor Smith, a son of Professor Smith of the Medical College. Charlotte married David Wagstaff, a grocer in Courtlandt street near West street.

Mary Catherine (since dead), married John B. Dash, now of the firm of Wolfe, Dash & Spencer, a great hardware house, No. 38 Warren street.

A very old concern is that of John B. Dash. Long before the year 1801, old J. B. D. kept a large hard ware store on the south-west corner of Liberty street and Broadway, and next door to where old Abe Bininger bought a store for $11,000. Old Mr. Dash lived above his store for many years. It was John B. Dash & Son up to 1824, when the old gentleman died. He was a Moravian, and belonged to the Moravian church in Fulton street. It stood one door east of Dutch street. A marble store now stands upon the old site.

In the rear, Mr. Dash was buried. His family was buried there also. When the Moravian church was moved up to Houston street, the bones of the older Dash were put in a box, carried up to Houston street, and placed under the steps of the new edifice. The bones of the young Dash were also removed thither Mrs. Dash, although a strict Moravian, refused ever after to go to the Houston street church, as she said she would not walk over her husband's bones.

J. B. Dash, Jr., kept up the old firm in the old store, corner of Liberty street and Broadway, as late as 1830.

The whole family became wealthy by the rise of real estate, originally belonging to the elder Mr. Dash.

The third J. B. Dash became a clerk with Wolfe, Spies & Clark.

The origin of the house was before the War of 1812, when J. D. & Cristopher Wolfe went into the hardware business in Maiden Lane, opposite to Clark & Brown's old coffee house. C. & J. D. Wolfe were on the corner of Gold street. J. D. Wolfe married a Miss Lorillard, and he now lives in Madison avenue, and is supposed to be worth four or five million dollars.

Christopher lived in Broadway, opposite the New York Hotel, for many years. When the house dissolved, it formed two new concerns. One was J. Wolfe, Bishop & Co., and the other Wolfe, Spies & Clark. The firm remained in the old stand, and the latter removed to Pearl street, near Maiden Lane. Mr. Bishop also married a Miss Lorillard, and is extremely rich. Wolfe, Spies & Clark, changed to Wolfe, Dash &.Co., and is now Wolfe, Dash & Spies, No. 38 Warren street. The other firm is still Wolfe, Bishop & Co., in Maiden Lane.

Old Hoffman, who owned the "Swallow," and was connected in the Hudson Steamboat Company, with

Daniel Drew and Isaac Newton, married a Miss Dash, a daughter of old John B. Dash. He has been dead many years. So has Mr. Newton. Daniel Drew yet lives. He will never die until he has obtained sole control and possession of the Erie railroad. He is a great schemer, and has had a wonderful success. Originally a barefooted cattle drover, he has kept traveling until he has acquired immense wealth. He made a great deal of money while he kept the "Bull's Head" house. His assistant was Robinson, who married his daughter. Mr. Drew, when he left hotel keeping, started Robinson in the same business. They are now Drew & Robinson, wealthy brokers in Wall street.

Bradish Johnson was formerly one of the firm of William M. Johnson & Son. He was born on a sugar plantation just below New Orleans. It was bought by his father in 1810, and was called the Bradish plantation. It is now owned by Bradish Johnson. Old Johnson had four sons and one daughter. He was captain of a ship that traded to New Orleans for many years. He always went by the name of Captain Johnson, even when a planter, and also when a merchant. The old captain was a glorious, whole-souled man. He had not one mean idea in his composition.

In 1822 or 1823 Captain Johnson removed to New York city, and here established the distillery business. It is still continued by his son Bradish. The latter was educated for the law. In 1831 he graduated from Columbia College, and commenced studying law. He was admitted to the bar; but his father, the captain, had become old and feeble, and Bradish not having any great fondness for the legal profession, abandoned it, in order to enter into business with his father. They were then doing a moderate business, and their distillery was in Seventeenth street, between the Ninth and Tenth avenues. The old captain was a far-seeing person. When he came to New York he perceived that the city was increasing in the most astonishing manner, and that in a very few years it must equal, if not surpass London. He acted upon this idea, and whenever and wherever he could buy real estate he did it to the utmost limit of his means, especially in the section where the distillery was located, and also in the Sixth avenue. Old Captain Johnson started two of his sons in the rectifying business, in connection with the distillery. In the latter he took in Mr. Lazurus as a partner. When the old gentleman died he left two sons, who were rather gay as well as fast. They never missed a race on Long Island, and owned the finest yacht and fastest horses that money could buy. They retired from the business. Bradish Johnson continued on, under the firm of Johnson & Lazarus. They have the largest whiskey distillery in the United States. The concern sold "swill" to feed a thousand cows, and rented the stalls. It was this house that Frank Leslie pitched into so unmercifully, with pen and pencil, not many years ago.

The distillery and grounds of Johnson & Lazarus occupy two blocks. Michael Tuomey was brought up by Johnson & Sons.

Bradish Johnson married a Miss Lawrence. She was a sister of the wife of the late Wm. E. Wilmerding, of the firm of Haggerty, Austin & Co. once, and who lived many years in Dey street, on the lower side, about eight doors from Broadway.

Johnson & Lazarus have recently established a sugar refinery. It is equal to Stuart's, and in a few years will be the heaviest in the United States.

Bradish Johnson had a brother named Henry. He was located on the sugar plantation near New Orleans, and died two years ago, leaving in his will the plantation to Bradish, and the two hundred and fifty negroes to themselves; that is, at the expiration of three years these negroes were to be called together, and the wil was to be read to them.

They were all to be emancipated and sent to Liberia free of expense to themselves, and each negro was to be furnished with sufficient provisions to last him one year after he arrived in Africa.

When Bradish heard the contents of the will he proceeded at once to New Orleans and to his plantation. He called the negroes together, told them they need not wait for the three years to expire, that its condition could be complied with at once, and that those who wished to go to Africa could do so then.

There were further conditions in the will. Those who did not go to Africa could remain on the plantation, and were never allowed to be sold or removed.

The question was put and a vote was taken whether to go or stay. Not one negro voted to go to Africa. They all begged to remain on the place where nearly all were born and had been brought up. Mr. Bradish Johnson consented. He allowed them Saturday to do their own work, in addition to Sunday. He allowed each one so much ground to cultivate. So matters have worked. Most of the negroes have profited so well by this privilege that the greater part of those slaves could now purchase their own freedom were they so minded.

CHAPTER XXIII.

Among the oldest commercial firms of this city, that of Brown Brothers & Co., looms up proudly and grandly, and has done so for more than a third of a century.

It is a branch of an English house. In Liverpool the firm is William and James Brown & Co. There is also a branch at New Orleans, and another at Mobile.

James and Stewart Brown are the two principal brothers, and members of the firm of Brown Brothers and Co. in this city.

James Brown built for his dwelling-place a magnificent palace in Leonard street. It was a large double house, with a court, and an entrance for horses and carriage from the street. It was located at No. 80 Leonard street, half the block from Broadway towards Church street. Thirty years ago, that part of the city was the residence of the best people in town. A few doors below the residence of James Brown, was the old mansion of Governor Morgan Lewis. Mr. Lewis was a great man in this State. He beat Aaron Burr in the canvass for Governor by 8,000 majority.

In the old place James Brown lived until it was no longer fashionable ground, and then he moved up town with the rest of the world.

Stewart Brown lives in Waverly Place. He married

in Baltimore. James married twice, and his late wife was a Troy lady. The store of Brown Brothers & Co. was formerly in Pine street. They were then largely in the dry goods business.

Samuel Nicholson was for many years a clerk with the firm. About 1833 they retired from the immense dry goods business in favor of Amory, Leeds & Co The latter concern paid a bonus of $100,000 for the good will. It turned out a very "bad will," and Amory, Leeds & Co. soon failed under such peculiar circumstances that their affairs were overhauled by the Law Courts. The manager of the house of A. L. & Co. was Henry H. Leeds, who is now in the auction business.

After getting clear of the dry goods trade, Brown, Brothers & Co. turned their attention and capital to banking and the exchange business. A large and profitable department of it was to make advances to importers of dry goods. The latter hypothecated their business paper to B. B. & Co. for letters of credit in England. The manufacturers drew at six months, the parties here obligating themselves to pay in time to reimburse them on the other side. At that time there were no steamers running. The trade depended upon the packet ships, and calculated on a thirty days passage over.

Brown Brothers & Co. charged to their customers two and a half per cent. for advancing, and two and a half per cent. for accepting those bills on the other side, making the snug commission of five per cent. It is needless to add that they did an enormous business.

In 1842 they established a house in New Orleans, under the name of Samuel Nicholson, (heretofore spoken of,) who had been many years their clerk. Mr. Nicholson had just established himself when a great derangement of the currency occurred — more especially throughout the West and Southwest. During the whole of the winter of 1843 exchanges on New York averaged not less than four to five per cent. Drafts were purchased at those rates in St. Louis, Cincinnati and other places, by the banks, and sent down to New Orleans, and Mr. Nicholson would buy all he could lay his hands upon at four per cent. discount. These drafts he sent to New York. The firm cleared that winter not less than $400,000.

Mr. Garr, a son of old A. S. Garr, of Jersey city was taken into the New Orleans house. He had married a daughter of Mr. Joseph Kernochan. Mr. Nicholson married a sister of William Russel's wife (Charles H. Russell's brother.) Mr. N. retired from business about eight years ago. He built a superb house in the Fifth avenue, near Twenty-first street, the lot running through to Broadway. It is now occupied by Bradish Johnson, to whom we alluded in a late chapter. On the lot facing Broadway, Mr. Johnson erected the store occupied by Park & Tilford.

When Mr. Samuel Nicholson died, he left one million of dollars and no children.

He was a fine looking man in his young days. His hair was as black as jet. He was a gay youth. He clubbed with Alexander Charton, who was in the lace business, and Godfrey Patterson, and they kept open house. They entertained in a most liberal manner, and invited every foreigner of any note who touched the shore.

Mr. Charton went on a farm. Godfrey Patterson went back to Scotland to his father. Sam Nicholson, as he was familiarly called, was one of the old school beaux. He was at every City Hotel ball, and a leader of fashion. He was buried at Greenwood, in a vault, in a large plot of ground, handsomely railed around. His wife lies by his side. Nothing marks the spot, where grass is allowed to grow without stint, except the slab on the entrance of the vault:

"THE VAULT
OF
SAM NICHOLSON."

There is nobody left of his kith or kin to shed a tear over the spot.

Mr. Nicholson conscientiously believed that there never had existed so great and so glorious a commercial house as that of Brown Brothers & Co. He was right.

In 1837, the house was deemed of great importance, and during that disastrous year it was sustained and kept up by the Bank of England. This great financial institution came forward and guaranteed the paper of William and James Brown & Co. to the extent of three millions, and enabled them to go through the crisis untainted. To have allowed that great American house to go by the board would have been a national calamity.

William, of Liverpool, is worth a million of pounds sterling. James, of New York, not less than two millions of dollars. He is a very charitable man, and is a member of the Episcopal church, corner of Eighteenth street and Fifth avenue.

This immense concern does the largest banking business in the United States. They carry on their mammoth operations quietly. They are rarely heard of. They never dabble in stocks except for investment. The main partners, James and Stewart, are the most modest and unassuming of our citizens. There is no show or parade with them. James never rides except in a one-horse coupe. Stewart never rides except in an omnibus. He walks quick — one hand behind the small of his back, and carries a little cane.

James Brown lives at the corner of University Place and Ninth street. His house is a large double one. He has a very large family. At present he is travelling in Europe, with his son Clarence, who, from appearance, gives indication of becoming a very fast young man. Last summer he could have been seen any fine day, either on the road or in the Central Park, with fashionable young ladies, driving *tandem*.

Brown Brothers & Co. must have been in existence over fifty years. They had for twenty-seven years a celebrated mulatto man named Jacob Schermerhorn, a porter, who died about fifteen years ago.

One of the oldest mercantile firms in this city is Peter J. Nevius & Son.

The old man is descended from Johannus Nevius, who was a *schepen* or alderman of this city in 1655.

Our man, Peter Nevius, held the same office, and was alderman of the First Ward, in this city, in 1829, when Walter Bowne was mayor. Mr. Nevius was never a politician. He had no ambition to be other than a merchant. In 1800, he commenced business on his own account at No. 11 South street. On the same spot he does business now, after a period of sixty years has gone by. He was twenty-one years old when he started. He is eighty-one now, and yet is never absent from his counting room, and stands writing at his desk during business hours. Thirty years ago he took his eldest son into the concern, and made it Peter J. Nevius & Son. Different sons have been in the firm at different times. Their business is now and ever has been in produce. They sell flour, produce, etc. on commission. His father was a farmer at White House, New Jersey. The son still owns that farm. General Washington dates many of his dispatches from White House, New Jersey, during the war of the Revolution, and while he was trying to drive out the British.

Mr. Nevius has long been called the *honest merchant.* He is certainly the oldest merchant who continues in active business in this city. He has had a large family of children. Seven are still living. He lives in a house in Waverly Place. He built it himself in 1838. He married Miss Lent, a daughter of James W. Lent, former Recorder of the city and county of New York. She died last spring.

Some of the partners of a very old grocery house in Front street have recently become prominent in connection with an ex-merchant and present mayor.

The firm of Smith & Mills was formed about thirty-two years ago. They did a very heavy trade in Front street, second door from Fletcher street, on the east side. This firm afterwards changed to Smith, Mills & Co. Their purchases of wines, sugars, etc. were very heavy — in fact, they tried to rival their next door neighbors, Lee, Dater & Miller.

S., M. & Co. dealt largely in rice. A brother of Mills being in Charleston, constantly shipped them large quantities for many years.

Ruel Smith is a short, thick-set, active man, and at present traveling about Europe. He is a widower, owns a farm at Skeneatelas in this State, and when in this country, can always be found at the St. Nicholas, where he is called "Little Smith."

The name of the junior partner was Atwater. He

now continues the old business under the firm of Atwater, Munford & Co., at No. 35 Broad street.

Drake Mills was one of the firm, and it laid the foundation of his present fortune of $300,000. He has been twice married. He had several children by his first wife, but one of the offspring of the second marriage has recently risen to greatness, and ranks as the wife of one of the chief magistrates of the empire city. Eugenie of Spain rose to be the wife of Napoleon and empress of France, and Miss Mills, the daughter of one of the old house of Smith, Mills & Co., has become Mrs. Wood and the wife of Fernando, mayor of New York.

In marrying the daughter of an old merchant, Fernando has strengthened his position among our merchants — a class he loves, for he was once one, when he kept the grocery on the north corner of Rector and Washington streets.

Drake Mills has given his daughter an education to fit her to be a President's wife, the position he expects her to occupy before her new mate ends his political career. That bold Fernando deserves a "big honor" none will deny; but it rests an open question among those who know him, and those who do not, whether it will be the "White House" at Washington.

Mills is a brother of the Mills who gives name to the celebrated Mills House in Charleston, South Carolina. It was that southern Mills who shipped such immense quantities of rice to Smith, Mills & Co. when that old grocery house was in their highest glory.

Mrs. Wood, nee Mills, speaks, reads and writes five different languages, viz: French, Spanish, German, Italian and English. She spent twelve years of her young life at the best schools in Europe, where she was accompanied by her excellent mother.

Mr. Drake Mills is an excellent business man, and a prudent one. Although out of regular business at present, yet he recently gave evidence he had not forgotten his old prudent methods, for he made Fernando Wood carefully place $100,000 in good Croton Water stock, where the income, $5,500, can go for pin money for his daughter; and in case of her death, the principal reverts to the parents of the aforesaid lady.

Mrs. Mayoress Wood will eventually be the richest lady in New York. Wood is immensely rich — some say three millions. She is sixteen; he was fifty-six years old last 24th November. Wood will wear out. He will never rust out, and will live ten years more certainly, and then the daughter of our old mercantile friend, Drake Mills, may find herself a one-thirder in vast wealth, and a charming widow of twenty-six.

Mr. Drake Mills is one of the directors of the Phœnix Bank, and I presume would have been nominated as City Chamberlain in place of Mr. Devlin, the clothing merchant, had not Mr. Alderman Peck, the acting mayor, assumed doubtful powers.

CHAPTER XXIV

Our largest merchants, or those doing the most extensive commercial business at the present day, did not all commence with large capitals and credits or extensive connections. On the contrary very many of the heaviest capitalists commenced their course in the most humble and limited manner. The old John Jacob Astor commenced with peddling cookies and cakes. In those days, it was not so humble to do that as now. Then the largest bakers sent their apprentices out to peddle the luxuries from the oven, and it was probably in this capacity that Astor peddled cakes.

Many of our afterward large merchants commenced life as porters in the large mercantile establishments. Such was the case with Barney Graham, who became a partner in the heavy foreign house of Peter Harmony & Co. Mr. Graham was an excessively hard-featured man, at the same time he was a capital business man, and Mr. Harmony was obliged to take him into the firm or lose his services altogether. He made himself useful. He never put on airs. It is a singular fact, that a foreign-born boy, or one from the New England States, will succeed in this city, and become a partner in our largest firms, much oftener than a born New York boy. The great secret of this success is the perfect willingness to be useful and do what they are required to do, and cheerfully.

Take for instance such a firm as Grinnell, Minturn & Co. In their counting-room, they have New York boys, and New England boys. Moses H. Grinnell comes down in the morning and says to John, a New York boy, — "Charley, take my overcoat up to my house in Fifth Avenue." Mr. Charley takes the coat, mutters something about "I'm not an errand boy. I came here to learn business," and moves reluctantly. Mr. Grinnell sees it, and at the same time, one of his New England clerks says, "I'll take it up." "That is right. Do so," says Mr. G., and to himself he says, "that boy is smart, will work," and he gives him plenty to do. He gets promoted — gets the confidence of chief clerk and employers, and eventually gets into the firm as a partner. It's so all over the city. It is so in nearly every store, counting-room or office. Outside boys get on faster than New York boys, owing to two reasons. One is, they are not afraid to work, or to run of errands, or do cheerfully what they are told to do. A second reason, they do their work quickly. A New York boy has many acquaintances — New England boy has none, and is not called upon to stop and talk, when sent out by the merchant.

The histories of many of the merchants in this city are quite romantic.

How many of the thousands who pass up and down the Sixth Avenue, and at No. 200, between Thirteenth and Fourteenth streets, notice the sign of Joseph Batten, over a moderate hosiery store, would ever dream that volumes could be written about the man who started that store?

I remember the aged John Batten as well as if he had

called upon me yesterday. What a spry old gentleman he was! He used to be one of the "Old Battery walkers," or "Peep o' day boys," that up to 1837 used to go down to the lonely Battery by day-light, and walk about there until breakfast, and then the same class would go to their stores.

I remember these old gentlemen well. There were many of them, such as John J. Labagh, Peter Harmony, John Laing, Wm. R. Morrill, John Batten, and many more whose names do not occur to me.

Peter Bayard could furnish a list of the old school Battery walkers, for *Peter Bayard's* place on State street next to the old Morton House, was one of the institutions of New York before the Battery, once lively and respectable, became the resort of all that is vile and murderous. The decline of Bayard's House and the Battery began at the same moment, and when both culminated, Peter took it very quietly, and one of our most esteemed New Yorkers, a perfect philosopher in his way, can be seen near the neighborhood of old St. Paul's, noting the cars of the useful Eighth Avenue, as though he had entirely forgotten what a King Pin he ever was, when New York was a moderate city of a quarter of a million of good people, and before the populations of Germany and Ireland had precipitated themselves upon us, and made a monster city of a million who don't know anything about each other, or who is who!

But to return to the hosiery merchant, old John Batten. The last time I saw him he was 101 years old, and came into the store No. 68 Washington street, as spry as a cricket, and addressing the aged Francis Secor, (who was then 75 and is now 96), said "Boy, how are you this morning?"

John Batten was a soldier; he belonged to the body

guard of George the Third, and came out in the early part of the Revolutionary War. He used to say in a pleasant, joking way — "I fought hard for this country," and then after enjoying the patriotic admiration of some of the youngsters, would cock his eye at some old person present who knew his history, and add, "But I didn't get it."

Many a time, days and hours, has the now aged man (who was better educated than the rest of his majesty's soldiers) taught school in the old Dutch Reformed Church, where the post office now is, when it was in the possession of the British troops, and his mates. When the city was evacuated by the British, Mr. Batten slid off to Long Island, a few days previous to the embarkation, and his absence was only discovered when it was too late to arrest and punish him. He at once started on his own account and opened a tavern in Slote lane, — it was afterwards called Exchange street — a little narrow street that commenced at William, where Beaver now is, and crooked around into Pearl street, not very far from where Beaver intersects Pearl street to-day. He kept the Fulton House from 1782, for some time. He afterwards opened a large tavern in Nassau street, No. 37 — on the west side, in the large building afterward occupied by Mrs. Mix and Mrs. Trippe, as a large boarding house. Mr. Batten kept it as a crack tavern many years. He afterwards opened a store in Broadway, on the west side, between Dey and Cortlandt streets. He was there in 1817. From there he removed his store to Greenwich on the west side, and two doors below Warren street. He died in this house. His son Joseph carried on the business, and continues it now in the Sixth avenue. Peter Embury lived near Mr. Batten in Greenwich street; and both were very old men. They were always together — eternally cracking jokes — and those 90 years old boys were daily playing some pranks with each other or the public.

On one occasion, Mr. Batten was repairing the basement, and a plank extended from the walk to the first floor. Mr. Batten had passed across it into the house. Old Mr. Embury came by and removed the plank, and then hid himself behind a box. Mr. Batten wanted to come down the plank, when he missed it, and then discovered Mr. Embury: "Ah, you scamp, let me catch you, and I will give you this cane over your shoulders," said he, shaking his cane at Mr. Embury. Both laughing heartily, they started off for a walk to the Battery. Old Mr. Batten was a noble old fellow. His son resembles him in all his good qualities.

One one occasion a grand dinner was given on the 4th of July, and Mr. Batten was present. Of course he was a revolutionary soldier. Some of the guests got very much excited about the aged man, and drank his health in patriotic toasts. At last the old veteran was called upon to reply. He did so. He spoke of the events of the war very touchingly — some of the female portion of the party cried. All were affected. The old minister got excited. "Yes, I did fight all through the old Revolution. I fought as bravely as the rest. I liked this country — I decided to remain in it, and the day when our commander evacuated this city to the American troops, I was hid on Long Island, and there I remained until my regiment had sailed for old England."

The looks of the astonished company, who by this time had become fully aware of the meaning of the words, and that they had been cheering a fierce old tory and British soldier, reminded old Batten that it was high time for him to hold up.

It may seem strange to many of our readers, that our ancestors would have permitted men besmeared with the blood of Americans, to settle down in our city immediately after the war, and go into business unmolested. It was so, however. It was done in many instances, and it is a convincing proof that all parties must have been tired of the war, and anxious to fraternize, when they could forgive the worst of their oppressors.

Not a child in town even now that has not heard of the horrors of the Jersey Prison ship. Yet one of our most successful and wealthiest merchants made an immense sum as keeper of that ship, and by starving our unfortunate countrymen who fell into his hands. He resided down in Broadway, a few doors from the old Grace Church, south corner of Rector street. There he lived in famous style. He built and owned vessels, and did a large commercial business after the revolution. It was a very frequent occurrence in after years, to meet some of his old prisoners, and to be cursed by them, as the most cruel and inhuman British bloodhound that ever escaped unhung for his toryism.

Mr. Batten escaped reproach. He did his duty bravely, but after the war was over, he was let alone. By-gones became by-gones, and no man was more respected than the ancient British warrior.

A neighbor of Mr. Batten, was Israel Cook. He bought the house next to old Peter Embury's (No. 331), and built and owned by a son of Mr. Embury, who died. Mr. Cook came to this city from Washington county, in this State. He remained here some time, and when quite young commenced business. His first occupation was selling a little butter in the Washington market. Then he married and went to house and "store" keeping on his own hook, directly opposite the market. His rent was $40 — rents were cheap in those days. His store was in the hall bed-room, on the second floor Here they lived, ate, slept, and sold butter. He would go in the market, buy a firkin, take it up-stairs, retail it out, and then go and buy another. This was probably about 1815, just after the war. From that time he kept extending his business, slowly but surely, for many years. He believed that all the property around Washington Market would in a short space of time become very valuable. Acting upon this idea, he bought up all the leases he could find. In this way he buttered his daily bread for himself and family, and in addition accumulated a great deal of money. He has an office now in Chambers street. He lives in style up town, and keeps his carriage.

When old Mr. Cook gave up the butter business, his sons took it up, and went into business, occupying one of their father's stores near the market. After a while, the fancy to get rich suddenly seized upon them, as it does upon many others of the human race. They had money, large credit, and a rich father. With these aids the young Cooks determined to buy up all the sugar in the market, control it, by having a monopoly, and make fabulous sums. They succeeded in buying immense quantities, but not enough to prevent a decline in the price of sugar. They failed, and as old Mr. Cook was heavily upon their paper, his loss was very heavy.

"Never should I have been so disgraced," said the old man, in the bitterness of his heart, "if them boys had been poor, and had to work their way up as I did."

One son of Mr. Cook married a daughter of Charles

Dennison. He started business also in Fulton street, opposite Washington Market, and for a long time kept a retail liquor store and sold liquor in small quantities He followed the business for many years. He was burned out in the old store. He afterwards opened a wholesale grocery under the firm of C. & L. Dennison, and also with a company attached. They did the largest grocery business on the north side of the town for many years. The business is still carried on by the sons. The elder Charles Dennison is President of the Grocers' Bank. They are all rich, and live in splendid mansions up town. Yet, as an evidence of how things once were, there still stands in Franklin street, north side, between Hudson and Greenwich streets, two elegant brick houses, that were ahead of any thing in the house line not many years ago. Those two houses, the father, Charles Dennison, built for his children, and young Charley occupied one, and Mr. White, a son-in-law, the other. In a few years more, they will be pulled down and stores erected upon their sites.

Charles Dennison, Jr. is a thorough-bred merchant. A quarter of a century ago, he used to take an active part in the good and useful Mercantile Library Association, and when it was removed from Cliff street to Clinton Hall, still kept with it, and with Fletcher Westray, and a host of other young clerks we could name, now eminent merchants, struggled successfully to get the institution into the hands of a liberal management.

Another brother of Mr. Charles Dennison, Sen., was Mr. Asher Dennison. I believe he was of the firm of Dennison & Belden. They did an immense grocery trade for many years on the corner of Murray street. That house failed, and settled with their creditors. By the unexpected rise of land in Chicago and other places, he became very rich many years afterwards.

The old house of C. & L. Dennison was kept in Dey street, forming the letter L on West street.

Dominic Hardenbrook, who used to preach in the little Dutch Reformed church in Franklin street near Chapel (in West Broadway) a few doors below the French church — where Appleton's great printing establishment now stands — was very intimate with Asher Dennison, and he became a leading man in that church.

CHAPTER XXV.

In the preceding chapter I alluded to the aged Peter Embury as one of the "Battery walkers." He continued to be so, in the warm season, until he removed up town. The family of Emburys are an old stock. Peter married a sister of old Aymar. The oldest Embury was a Methodist preacher in John street, long before the Revolution. He went up and settled in Camden, Washington county, in this State. During the war of 1776, as the congregation of Mr. Embury were not fighting men, they had to quit the pleasant spot where they had settled, and emigrate to Canada. The pastor himself did not go. One of the number, who came back from Canada, after the war, is now living at Camden, aged 106 years. His name is John Swertzer.

Young Peter Embury was a poor boy in the city. He was early apprenticed to the chair-making trade. He followed chair-making for years. In a former chapter I have mentioned that he opened a grocery store in Beckman street, corner of Nassau. It was on the northeast corner, where the Park Hotel now stands. At that time the ground in front was a common. It was before Dr. Spring's church was erected. Mr. Embury for many years kept the choicest family grocery in this city. He had wines, "rich and rare," not to be found elsewhere. The store was on the first floor, and his family lived in the upper part. It was a good old custom, and if it were followed now by business men they would not be any the worse for it. It was a good old Dutch custom, and to this day, in the great cities of Amsterdam and Rotterdam, the most extensive merchants have their counting rooms in the same building in which their families reside. Why not? Had the custom been continued in New York for the past forty years, what a difference would have been presented in our city. Our shipping merchants would have lived in West, South and the river streets. The upper part of the houses would have made a great display, and probably trees would have lined the river streets. Not only that — canals would have been introduced into such streets as Greenwich, Front, Water and Washington streets, and ships would have been hauled in to unload before the doors of the owner or consignees. But it may be that it is as well as it is, if not decidedly better. The present plan of separating the dwelling house from the stores of our great merchants, gives New York a chance to spread herself. Mr. Embury, after he retired from business, built a splendid house at No. 331 Greenwich street. It was deemed at that time a model house. It is still standing. He never dreamed that it would be in an unfashionable neighborhood. He moved from that house up to Thirty-seventh street. He said he would not live a year after moving from his old home and usual haunts, and he did not. He lived until 1857.

When Prince William, Duke of Clarence — afterwards King William of England — was over here in his boy days, he skated on the "Collect," (below Canal, in the surrounding region of the Tombs at present.) The Prince had an attendant with him, but the latter knew nothing about skates, or skating, and Mr. Embury assisted the Prince to fix on his skates. At that time the "Collect" was an extensive sheet of water, and very deep. People were drowned in it very frequently.

Mr. Embury had a son named Philip. He was a tinsmith in Broad street, and will be remembered by many who read this chapter. He still lives in Thirty-seventh street, with his sister, in the same house occupied while living by his father. Another son of Mr. Embury was in the distillery business in Brooklyn. Another son is an Episcopalian clergyman. The next elder to Philip was Daniel. He is now cashier of a bank in Brooklyn. Another brother of Daniel was named Peter, who is now dead. Both Peter and Daniel were clerks with a large broker, Jacob Barker, for some years.

Old Peter Embury and the late Philip Hone were very intimate friends to the close of the life of the latter in 1851, although they belonged to different stratas of society. Mr. Hone and his family were among the pure aristocratic sets of the day. He had been rich once — had been mayor in 1825 — had traveled largely in Europe, and gave the largest dinners known at the time. Mr. Hone lived on Broadway, one door below Park Place. A wooden house graced the corner; reaching far up above it was Mr. Hone's large house, its northern side boarded and painted red. Over his door could be seen a bust of some remarkable man; it could be seen from the street. Here resided Mr. Hone in his prosperous days, and no one of any note in the city but had been entertained by him at his dinners or evening parties. He was one of the *elite* of our city, but became poor in the after years of his life. Under

General Taylor he received an office in the Custom House. Mr. Embury outlived Mr. Hone six years.

It would be useless to write the lives of men, or to revive recollections of them, unless good can be derived from so doing. I will take the lives of these two men, and their mode of managing. Mr. Hone used to advise with his venerable friend Embury in relation to every matter of great importance. Both had large families of boys. Mr. Embury's sons worked; the sons of Mr. Hone, although amiable, yet relied upon the wealth of the father, and were not remarkable for their activity. One son was a clerk for some time with Brown, Brothers & Co. The fathers used to talk over these matters. One day Mr. Hone asked his friend, "What is the reason that your boys are all smart and hard-working, while mine are good for nothing else except to spend money? How have you brought up your sons, that there should be such a difference?"

"Well," replied old Uncle Peter, somewhat affected, "you are a fashionable man, and you have a fashionable family, and you have brought up your children in the fashionable school. I have brought up mine to work — to take care of themselves. They are all employed, but all board at home. I make them pay me board just as regularly as if they were entire strangers. If they want money, I lend it to them, and take their notes for the amounts, with an understanding that they pay those notes to me when due, the same as if they had been placed in the bank for collection. They pay those notes. I make them know that they must take care of themselves as I did of myself, when I was a boy, and when young.

"As I said, my boys board with me. I live plain. I feed them on good food — lamb, for which I pay one shilling and sixpence per quarter, (price in old times.) I never have any wines or liquors on the table — never, — thus my boys never get a taste of it — never hanker after it. I am not fashionable. I live plain and eat honest food, and by example in eating and drinking I inculcate honest but healthy precepts into the minds of my boys. Now I have given you my method of bringing up a lot of boys. Let me tell you what you have done. You are fashionable — you move in fashionable society. You hold a high position in the community, and you deserve to do so; but my friend Hone, you have done as hundreds of other rich and prosperous men have done. You have brought your sons up under greatly mistaken ideas, if you wished to make men of them. They lived with you; you had upon your table every day the choicest wines that money could procure. They joined in drinking healths day after day, and remained at the table for hours, when they should have been attending to business. You taught them this. Is it strange that by such examples they should have been taught how to spend money, or that they should be anything else than what they are? Stern industry, friend Hone, is all that can rectify in your children the faults and follies of the home education you have given them."

"You are right, old friend, but your advice is too late for me to profit by it. Everybody should hear your experience. There is where I have failed in my family," replied Mr. Hone.

All of Mr. Hone's children are respectable, high-minded men, but I believe none are rich. They lived out their fortunes before they were of age.

I mentioned in another place that Mr. Embury had two sons, who had been for some time doing business in the office of that remarkable man of other days — Jacob Barker. He is still alive and a very aged man. In the days of his prosperity, he must have been a wonderful man, this same Jacob Barker. There is no man of whom so many wonderful things are related as of Jacob Barker. The celebrated Jacob Little was once a clerk with the banker, and if young Jacob should ever get poor, he can rise again by publishing a book to be called "Recollections of the Napoleon of Wall street."

Two sons of old Peter Embury, Daniel and Peter J., were clerks with the famed Jacob Barker. There were seventeen more clerks in the office. Jacob Barker had no equal, on the contrary he was superior to any money broker or banker that ever lived before, in, or since his time. He went ahead — stopped for nothing — not even to go home to dinner. His wife sent his dinner down to his office. His clerks perfectly detested old Jacob Barker. He was a tyrant. When his dinner arrived, it would be on a tin warmer, and wrapped up in a towel. This would be placed on his desk, and then Jacob would sit and eat it, the clerks laughing and making faces at each other in a quiet, subdued way. Sometimes old Jacob would not be in when the dinner arrived. In such a case one of the clerks — who was a great wag — would take Jacob's place, and while he took off the broker in first rate style, amidst screams of laughter from the admiring clerks, would also positively eat up the dinner — put the dishes aside, and Jacob would suppose the dinner had not come. But on one occasion, when this dinner scene was being enacted, old Jacob popped in, and witnessed almost the entire performance before his presence was discovered by the principal perfomer. "Oh, don't let me interrupt you — eat on," said Jacob. The clerk slid. He was not discharged, but remained with Jacob until he went into business on his own account.

Peter Embury kept his great grocery in Beekman street, his family living above it, until he moved to Brooklyn. It was a two-story house, with dormer attic windows, and only three feet of yard. He kept store until 1830, or thereabout.

Then he retired to private life, and to that superb model house he had built at No. 331 Greenwich street. He had built in the yard a little shop where he could make chairs as he had done in his early days. It was a source of real pride to the aged man to speak of his chair-making days. He boasted of them, and showed to his admiring visitors, in his parlor, a set of rush-bottom chairs he had made three-quarters of a century previously, when he was an apprentice boy!

There are chairs now in a residence in this city made by him. I observed a set in a friend's house last New Year's day. His darling house, in Greenwich street, was one of the grandest in its day.

About the year 1826 young Peter carried on business in Fulton street, opposite old Washington Market, under the firm of Vreeland & Embury, grocers. They retired rich. Mr. Vreeland lives at Bergen. Young Peter died at the old house in Greenwich street. He was a bachelor. He built the house next door to his father, and it was sold afterwards to Israel Cook, the butter merchant mentioned in a former chapter.

In connection with merchants and commerce for over two hundred years, stands the name of De Peyster. Old Johannes De Peyster was a merchant before 1650. In 1655 he was schepen. He was Alderman from 1666 to '69, burgomaster in 1673, and mayor in 1677. From that day until now the descendants have been prominent men in the city and connected with the city affairs They have been Mayors (Abraham was Mayor from 1691 to 1694; Johannes, Jr. was mayor in 1698), and there have been aldermen, Johns, Cornelius, Isaacs, Abrahams, Pierres, Williams and Gerards, from 1696 to 1799, and to 1821 in this century.

The De Peysters have been a fine old continuous race, even down to one we shall now name in a more especial manner. Augustus De Peyster (or as he is familiarly known, Captain De Peyster), is probably the oldest Captain that has commanded ships out of New York now alive. A more modest, unassuming man does not breathe, and the young of the present generation who meet him in the street, or on the ferry-boats, never dream of the remarkable scenes that this gentle, but apparently not very aged man, has seen.

Fancy a man who was a boy on one of John Jacob Astor's ships sixty-five or seventy years ago, who has been sailor, mate, and finally captain in the same employ; who has fought French privateers; who has commanded ships for both Astor and Francis Depau, and had his owners on board as passengers to Europe; who commanded the brig "Seneca," belonging to Mr. Astor, that carried the Proclamation of Peace in 1815, in fifty-five days, to the Cape of Good Hope, and then to Java and China, and yet, the man who has been through all these scenes and events is still quite a young man, and sprightly as a cricket — an active man, and bids fair to live forty if not fifty years more. If I could tell all he can, would I not do it?

Augustus De Peyster was born in 1784 or 1786, and took to the sea a few years afterward as naturally as a young duck. He sailed several voyages with Captain Whetten, one of John Jacob Astor's old captains. Mr,

Astor had married a sister of Captain Whetten. The latter died in 1845. Young De Peyster also sailed with Captain Cowman. Mr. Aster called C. his "king of captains." He was a very severe, stern man, but a complete navigator and a good sailor. Captain De Peyster continued in the China trade until about 1828. He after that went into the employ of the celebrated Francis Depau, the merchant who first organized a line of packets from this city to a port in France.

Mr. Depau had married a daughter of the Compte de Grasse, so celebrated in our Revolutionary history. He named one of his Havre packets after her some years later, viz: "The Sylvie de Grasse."

Old Francis Depau must have been in business as an importing and commission merchant long before 1806. When he started the line is not exactly known by me. He ran a regular packet to Havre in 1822. He was a prompt, exact merchant, and very much respected. Two of his clerks, Fox and Livingston, married daughters of Depau. They continued the business long after the death of Mr. Depau. When they failed, they did a good thing — secured all their captains from loss, gave them security on the ships, &c. That is the way Captain Lines came to own such a heavy amount of stock in the Havre line.

Captain De Peyster went into the employ of Francis Depau about the year 1829. He then superintended the building of the ship "De Rham" at old Berg's yard. The ship was named after one of the finest men in the city and county of New York, Henry C. De Rham. The latter was born in Switzerland, but for years he had one of the largest importing houses, and principally in French goods. Forty years ago the firm was De Rham & Iselin; twenty five years ago it was

De Rham, Iselin & Moore, Mr. Moore being of a New York family. The ships of the Havre line in those days averaged 350 tons. The "De Rham" was launched in 1830, and Captain De Peyster commanded her. His name will now become more familiar to the present generation when I say that the commander of the "De Rham" was a long time in her, and was also in the "Sheridan;" and after Captain Whetten's death, in 1845, became governor of the Sailors' Snug Harbor at Staten Island, and has continued so up to the present day, and I hope will continue there for many years longer.

What a wonderful institution is that sailor's arrangement! Nothing like it ever occurred. It seems to be romance.

On the 1st day of June, 1801, an old sea captain, named Robert Richard Randall, made a will. He had as witnesses his friends, Harry Brevoort, Isaac Humbert and Uriah Bridge.

Captain Randall was a bachelor. In his will, he left to his brother Paul's children about five thousand dollars each. The rest of his property he left to trustees to build a "Sailor's Snug Harbor."

The property so left was a farm upon which he lived, (now Fifteenth Ward,) of twenty-one acres.

It was worth at that time about . .	$5,000,00
He also left what he deemed really valuable,	
viz: 50 shares Manhattan stock .	$5,000,00
our lots in First Ward	$5,000,00
In 3 per cent, stocks	
6 do. do.	$6,430,00
	$22,153,00

He expected the Hospital, or Snug Harbor, to be

built upon the twenty-one acres, and that the other property would be used to support the decrepit and worn-out sailors. It was to be so applied as soon as it would support fifty infirm sailors.

Luckily for the fund, the heirs of his brother Paul contested the will. It lasted twenty-nine years. During that time great difficulty existed in effecting leases, and consequently the property became immensely valuable. It is leased to good advantage, and brings in $60,000 a-year. The idea of the donor was not carried out exactly in the way intended, but far better, by purchasing 130 acres of land on Staten Island, and then erecting the present buildings. They were commenced in 1831 and finished in 1834. Some of the most prominent men have been trustees, including De Witt Clinton, Marinus Willett, C. D. Colden, Pierre C. Van Wyck, Peter A. Jay, Cornelius Ray, Wm. Bayard, James De Peyster Ogden, James G. King, Captain John Whetten, Bishops Moore, Hobert & Berrian.

The subject of this sketch, Captain De Peyster, is the Governor, and resides on the Island.

CHAPTER XXVI.

Mrs. Embury the authoress is the wife of Daniel Embury, the President of a Brooklyn Financial Institution. He is the son of Peter Embury.

Jacob Barker used to be an eminent merchant. We remember Mr. Barker very well. He resided in a three-story house in Beekman street, between Gold and Cliff streets. The steps were sideways to the door. On it was a brass plate with his name. That was probably twenty-five years ago. After Mr. Barker removed to New Orleans, the house was occupied by his mother-in-law, and the door-plate had upon it the name of "Mrs. Hazard." At that period the daughters of Mr. Barker were deemed among the most beautiful in the city. They were all married many years ago. Sarah married a Mr. Harrison of Baltimore. I believe an elder sister had previously married a citizen of the State of Maryland. Another daughter, a magnificent girl, married Mr Brower, a very wealthy and extensive merchant in New Orleans. He died. She afterwards married a Mr. Van Zandt of this city. A son of Mr. Barker married into the James family at Albany.

Mr. Barker was a remarkably driving man. If he had an appointment with a man, he waited just five minutes, and not a second longer; then, if the man with whom he had an appointment did not come, Mr. B. left, and never after would he make an appointment with the same man.

Even to this day, every story-teller, who wishes to be smart, tells the story of Jacob Barker and the President of the Insurance Company. It's very stale, and I will not present it to the readers of this volume.

If I had time, I would go back to the panic times of 1826, when Jacob Barker was in his glory. Then the Franklin Bank, Marble Manufacturing Company, Hudson Bank of Jersey City, Jefferson Insurance Company, and other institutions, went to the Old Nick. Jacob was mixed up with them all. So was Henry Eckford, Malipar, George L. Pride and many others.

Henry Eckford and Jacob Barker were both indicted for conspiracy. Hugh Maxwell was the District Attorney in those gay days. Barker plead his own case. He was so successful that it gave him the first idea he ever entertained that he was capable of becoming a clever lawyer. In after years he went to New Orleans, studied law regularly, and made it his profession.

Malipar was President of the Marble Manufacturing Company. He was merely a tool of sharp men behind the curtain. His occupation previous to 1825 was keeping a bar and refreshment saloon at Castle Garden, a favorite resort for our citizens in the summer season.

George L. Pride was the cashier of the Marble Bank arrangement. He flourishes yet, and is the youngest very old man in the city. He is now a Custom House broker in Broad street, near Wall. For many years Mr. Pride held an appointment in the Custom House. No old New Yorker but what is familiar with George L. Pride. He was a gay boy fifty years ago, and danced at old Richard Varick's parties in 1810, being then about thirty years old. Captain Edward Vincent, James B. Glentworth, and Mr. Pride used to drive out to Cato's in the early summer mornings, and drink mint-juleps together previous to the late war with England in 1812.

Never were men kept in such a state of preservation even until now. The only instance is Wagner, the Wehr-Wolf, who was rejuvenated at ninety, and kept young and fresh-looking many years.

The old adage of "Pride must have a fall," is false in the case of George L. He is as young to-day as he was fifty years ago. He has few wrinkles, and crow's feet are unknown in his face. He has led a life of unmitigated enjoyment. Mr. Pride never has known the want of money. He has driven the best horses — had the finest eating — the choicest wines — the oldest brandy — and admired the handsomest women the city ever produced, from the grandmother in 1810, to the great-grand-daughter in 1862. His gratifications have been unlimited. There is not a man in the city of New York who can say aught against this veteran man of the world, and yet a man of business withal. He married a Miss Garr of an old family. Mr. Pride is a pleasant companion, social, and kind. While he enjoys himself without stint, he is always willing to offer enjoyment to others.

Many people mix up the name of Malipar with Mali bran who married the senorita Garcia. It is entirely a different concern. Mr. Malibran was an Italian merchant, at one time possessing great wealth. He figured in this city in 1820 to 1827. In 1826 the Garcia family resided here. Miss Garcia gave singing lessons — taught music, etc. to young ladies of the upper crust. There are many matrons now alive who were taught musical lessons by the Garcias. They went off on a tour to Mexico; when they returned, she sang here in public. The last time Miss Garcia sang in New York was in the opera of "Tancredi," at the Bowery Theatre, in 1828. Hilfert was the manager then. She was soon after married to Mr. Malibran, who settled a large sum of money upon her, and it was agreed to by her that she would not go upon the stage again. Her future history is well known to New York people. Mr. Malibran was separated from her. He died in this city in 1834, very poor.

In former chapters we have alluded to the firm of John & Philip Hone, auctioneers, afterwards John Hone & Sons. One of the concern was George A. Ward. He came here from Salem, Mass., the same town that gave birth to the illustrious Jonathan Goodhue, the founder of the great house of Goodhue & Co. in this city. Mr. Goodhue was sent to New York by William Gray, the eminent Boston merchant. He had been out as supercargo for old Billy Gray to the East Indies. Mr. George A. Ward must now be at least three score and ten years old. He came to this city and began his commercial life as a clerk in 1816, or earlier, perhaps. He prides himself much upon being a descendant from good old stock. He is a believer in thoroughbred "humans" as well as horses. He married a Miss Cushing, and her mother is still alive, al though ninety-two years old. She is one of the finest and most amiable of old ladies. She resides with her son-in-law at Staten Island; the aged dame reads with out the use of spectacles, her hearing is perfect, and she walks about and skips around the house as agile as a young miss of sixteen. Originally well educated, and having been a close reader for seventy years, she is charming; she takes a deep interest also in the politics of the nations; she is older than the Constitution of the United States, and prays God that she may not outlive it; she is a Unitarian and a federalist. So is her son-in-law, Mr. Ward. He prides himself on being called the latter. By the way, as this is a federal government, I think it would be better for the world if we were all federalists.

For a long time Mr. Ward was clerk in the great auctioneer house of J. & P. Hone. When John Hone & Son was firmed, he became a partner in it. After John Hone's death Mr. Ward left the concern. Soon after that, hoping to get a good share of the business of the old house, he started a new auctioneer concern, under the name of Woolsey, Ward & Beach. They kept on the corner of Pine and Pearl streets. On another corner was Shotwell, Fox & Co. On another Adee, Timpson & Co. On the fourth corner was David Adee, & Co. All auctioneer stores. Woolsey, Ward & Beach did a very heavy business for a few years, and in 1830 they dissolved.

After that disconnection Mr. Ward went to Europe to solicit consignments of dry goods to the house of Gracie, Prime & Co. That house, backed up by the celebrated banker, Nathaniel Prime, was doing an extensive business at No. 26 Broad street, a new store recently erected. They determined to go into the dry goods business, and in order to do so, they had made an arrangement with Mr. William Macfarlane, who had been the dry goods manager for G. G. & S. Howland many years. Mr. M. was an excellent judge of goods, and a capital salesman. He is still in New York in business. Mr. Ward went abroad, visited Manchester and different parts of England and Scotland, and was very successful. He moved in the highest of mercantile circles. Mr. Ward always entertained a good opinion of himself and his position. As a sample of his harmless egotism, when he reached England on his mission of dry goods, the cholera on its mission of death had reached Russia. It was expected that it would come to England. Mr. Ward wrote home to his New York correspondents that such was his opinion, but added, "I understand the cholera does not touch the higher classes, and consequently I have no dread of its approach."

True enough, the cholera did not molest Mr. Ward, and after visiting various parts of Europe, and extending his knowledge vastly, he returned to America.

After his return to New York he became a partner in the house of Low, Harriman & Co., and they did a large and successful business. They dissolved in 1837, and Mr. Ward retired with a clear $100,000.

He was and is a fine looking man, and has had many friends. He is quite a literary man, too, and about twenty years ago published a large octavo book, entitled the "Loyalists of America." Price $2. It sold very extensively among his personal friends. Among the things to be desired is a copy of that book, and Mr. Ward cannot perform a greater service than to send a copy to the author of this volume.

After Mr. Ward retired from the house of Low, Harriman & Co., he was induced to go into the Staten Island speculation with J. L. & S. Joseph, Thos. E. Davies, George Griffin, and George Griswold. It was called the New Brighton Association. Ward put in $80,000. They issued superb bonds of $1,000. Such beautiful engravings! Never was anything more magnificent before or since. We will give a dollar for one to frame, as a worthless curiosity. Lots on Rich mond Terrace were sold. Elegant maps were got up of this property. The streets were all laid out in a style far surpassing New York. It was nearer the sea; why should not New Brighton surpass and go ahead of New York? All kinds of fancy names were given to the streets. Then there was a gas company started. Water was to be brought from a long "lake" called Fresh Pond, lying two miles back of New Brighton, up in the highest hills of Staten Island. The pond was two miles long, and filled with fresh water, of course.

This was to supply the "Fountain." Models of all the fountains in Versailles, Berlin, Constantinople, and Vienna, had been secured by Mr. Ward when abroad. The New Brighton fountains were to be copies or superior to old Europe in that regard.

The principal "Village of Fountains" was to be located where Mr. Goodhue now has a place, about half a mile back from Richmond Terrace. These fountains were to play eternally, summer and winter.

All the rich people were to live in "castles." Mr. Ward built the first one. It is sixty feet square, and modelled after one in Switzerland. It still stands as a land mark of old times — still called "Ward's Castle," and he still resides in it.

Those were white days, and Mr. Ward was a king-pin at New Brighton. I recollect on one occasion a grand fancy ball came off. Mr. Ward appeared as General Washington. He was dressed precisely as the old hero, even to the dress when he took the oath as President at the corner of Nassau and Wall street. Anybody who was not posted would have supposed that Mr. Ward was the real General Washington.

Mr. Ward has had the gout for several years; it has kept him closely confined to his house. He is decidedly a literary man of correct taste. He is writing constantly, and has prepared a large mass of valuable manuscripts, that will be published for the benefit of his family after his death, and will be a legacy far more valuable to them than money. Mr. Ward has always been a leading man among the brilliant class with which he associated. He surrounds himself with eminent and learned men.

That venerable lady, Mrs. Alexander Hamilton, the wife of the man killed by Aaron Burr in a duel, up to the time of her death, and for many years previous, was a constant visitor at the residence of Mr. Ward. He must have received a vast mass of historical information from her lips. In fact, she was a literary lady herself. Mr. Ward is notoriously British or toryish in his notions, and has not a particle of confidence in an unfortunate country that has no hereditary aristocracy. At any rate, Mr. Ward's papers, when published, will be found full of interest and of value.

He is the greatest beau in the village of New Brighton at this moment, and will continue to be so while he lives.

Lots at one time sold in that place as high as $1000 for 25 x 100. The United States Bank foreclosed a mortgage for $470,000, and it sold for a song. The purchasers made vast fortunes, but Mr. Ward lost every lollar of his $80,000. He was choused out of every 'ent he had in the world. Did it daunt him? No.

When the gold fever broke out in California, the United States chartered the packet ships Rhone and Sylvia de Grasse to carry our troops to the Pacific. Mr. Ward went to work, and by means of his friends collected merchandise of various kinds, and took it with him in one of the above named vessels, going around

Cape Horn. This was in 1849. He was five months making the voyage. When he reached San Francisco, he found every article he had on board in great demand. He took out $40,000 worth. On that sum he realized $80,000 clear profit. He was content, and returned home to Staten Island, where he has remained quiet ever since, and as his money is judiciously invested, he is contented and happy. He has always resided in his "Castle."

He entertains well, and every body of any note that visits New Brighton when the Pavilion Hotel is opened, is invited to Ward Castle. He holds a levee once a week — winter and summer, and to them come all his neighbors and friends

CHAPTER XXVII.

In the last chapter, when speaking of Mr. George A. Ward, I alluded to his having been a partner in the house of Low, Harriman & Co., and that when that house dissolved in 1836, Mr. Ward retired with the large sum of $100,000. The book-keeper of Low, Harriman & Co. was the celebrated Chevalier George C. de la Figaniere, then merely the Portuguese consul, but now the full Minister of Portugal. The store of Low, Harriman & Co. was in William street, opposite the Exchange. They had a counting-room, and a private office attached. When any one called on business connected with the Portuguese consulate, (captains of vessels, or merchants with papers to be certified,) Mr. Figaniere would retire into the private office, where he kept his uniform, sword and cocked hat, and array himself in the paraphernalia of Portugal — then come out with all the dignity of a King's representative, sign th paper, administer the oath, attach the seal of Portugal and take his fees. He would then undress and resume his old office coat, and return to private life as book-keeper.

Yet who is there in our midst that does not rejoice that we have such a man as this De la Figaniere among us? He is an honor to the merchant class.

When De la Figaniere was elevated from consul to Minister Extraordinary, his successor as consul was first his son Henry, who had been vice consul; then the latter was succeeded by Mr. Phillip N. Searle; and still later by a Mr. Santos. As the latter gentleman resides in Portugal he has a vice consul at No. 92 Pearl street, L. E. Amsinck. The latter is one of the most remarkable men, as well as merchants, in town. Probably he is not yet thirty-five years of age. He represents a class of our great merchants who handle almost fabulous amounts, do an enormous mercantile business, have combinations extending throughout the commercial world, and connections going far back into the past, from one hundred and fifty to two hundred years. Of course, such a mercantile house must have its head in one of the old commercial cities of Europe. There are many such houses here, or rather branches, and yet doing an independent business. Oelrichs & Co., down at 68 Broad street, hardly known above Wall, are agents of the house of Widow John Lang, Son & Co of Bremen. John Lang founded the house in 1642, about the time New York was settled, over two hundred years ago. When he died, at a good old age, his widow took it up, and the firm was Widow John Lang. Then the son came in, and the firm was changed to Widow John Lang & Son. Then some other name came in and a Company was added, and so it has gone on for more than a century, without one of the name or even blood of Lang being in the concern. They have two persons in the firm now named Oelrichs, and another named Lurman. They also have a branch in Baltimore called E. G. Oelrichs & Lurman, and the other Oelrichs & Co., down in Broad street.

Who can forget the first Oelrichs who came to New

York from Bremen to establish the agency, and the house of Oelrichs & Co.? He was the pet of the ladies, and was nicknamed "Fat Oelrichs." He was an open-souled fellow and a smart business man.

Mr. Oelrichs was a gay man. He came to this city bout twenty-five years ago. He married a granddaughter of Harrison Gray Otis of Boston; a niece of James Otis, once of the firm of Otis, Stone & Mason, the great dry goods house. That Otis is now President of the North American Insurace Company.

Mr. Oelrichs, after residing here some time, returned to Europe, where he died.

We will now return to the main subject. L. E. Amsinck, of the firm of L. E. Amsinck & Co. We shall speak of him as a fair representation of this class of merchants, who represent or are connected with the oldest European houses. To those here, who are not familiar with this class of merchants or great financiers, their career and apparent rise seems singular and sudden. It is not so. These young men drop in upon us without notice, but soon they appear to do a large foreign trade. It is because they represent commercial firms who go far back into the past, and are in commerce as ancient as those German Princes of Reuss, who are styled "Henry the 95th" or "97th."

The old house of Nottebohn Brothers, of Rotterdam and Antwerp, a quarter of a century ago (but now widow Nottebohn), sent out one of the family, whose christian name was Andrew. He has done an immense business in those years, but without any fuss or noise. But on "change" it is known who he is, and what great interests he represents.

So, too, with L. E. Amsinck. He came over as recent as 1848, and, as usual, went with a house to clerk it, but really to learn the mode of doing business in New York, in order to do business for his own account. He selected the house of Ebech & Kunhardt as his employers. After an apprenticeship of three years he returned to Hamburg to make arrangements for a final trip here to establish a commercial house This he accomplished in 1851.

The elder Amsinck was the principal partner in the very ancient Hamburg house of John Schuback & Sons, one of the oldest in that free city. Originally from Holland, one or two hundred years ago, this Schuback established himself in Hamburg. All of the original name are dead long ago. The father and brother of L. E., or the American Amsinck, are the principal managers of John Schuback & Sons now.

Of course the connection of a house so long established, and with vast resources and business connections all over the world, could at once throw an immense business into the hands of their new established house in New York, and they did so. The business between Hamburg and Portugal had been large. The Portuguese connection was extended to New York, and Amsinck & Co. became the sole agents of the principal wine trade between Portugal, Spain, and New York. They became the agents of the Royal Oporto Wine Company of Oporto, in Portugal, and of the celebrated brandy and sherry wines of the Widow De X Harmony & Co. of Cadiz.

The name of Harmony, in connection with choice sherry wines, is famed all over the earth.

Many persons suppose it has something to do with the firm of Peter Harmony & Nephews, in this city. It is not so. Old Peter Harmony in his life was once agent of the old house of widow Harmony: but it divided up in Cadiz, and the Harmony house in New York became the agents for Peter Harmony's Nephews in Cadiz The Cadiz house failed last year. Mr. Amsinck was appointed agent of the widow of X. Harmony, one of those antediluvian wine manufacturers in Spain as old as the hills.

By the way, old Peter Harmony was a great merchant in his day. He built a magnificent house on Broadway, just below the corner of Rector street, next but one to the old Grace Church. His lot extendea through to Trinity Place, and his store was back of the dwelling. His counting house was in the rear. Peter was a merchant many years. It was Peter Harmony at one time, and then, "company" was added. It is now Peter Harmony's Nephews.

In connection with Amsinck & Co., and the wine trade, we must mention a very curious fact in reference to Hungarian wines.

A few years ago, none could be sold. In fact no prominent wine dealer would look at the article. It was not deemed worthy of notice. John G. & E. Boker could not sell it to any extent. That firm sent samples to all the dealers, and offered the Hungarian wines for a song. It was useless.

That house of Boker was an old established wine house. The brother John G. came here poor, sent out as an agent of an old wine house. He became wealthy, and notorious in connection with Mr. John Dean who married his daughter. Boker must have done business in this city thirty-eight years ago. He first introduced into this market "the Sparkling Hock." He also undertook to introduce the wines of Hungary into this market as before stated. There is an immense variety. The "Tokay" has been famous in Europe for two hundred years. The best sells for five dollars a bottle in Vienna. The Tokay vineyard belongs to the Emperor of Austria. The old poets allude to it in all their songs.

> "—— Muses young and laughing,
> Dw ll in vineyards of Tokay."

The demand for this wine in America has now become enormous. France only produces at the outside 800 millions of gallons of wine. Hungary produces 500 millions of gallons. The trade to America commenced as recently as 1855, by consignments to J. G. & E. Boker. The originator is an aged Hungarian patriot, by the name of Alois Schwartzer. He is over eighty years of age, and has been over to this country several times. He has a suit with his old agents, the Bokers, involving an immense amount. Mr Schwartzer is the great Hungarian proprietor of vineyards. He has patriotically sunk one million of dollars in five years, in order to introduce the splendid Hungarian wines into this country. He does this for national pride. When he transferred his agency to L. E. Amsinck & Co., they advanced him $100,000 on the stock transferred. The imports increase every year. It has become a permanent institution, and will entirely, or to a great extent, eventually supersede the wines of France. The price varies from sixty cents to six dollars per gallon, by the cask. The sweet wine is very choice, and very high. The Hungarian wines are the finest in the world. Their wines are both white and red. They are sent from the interior of Hungary to Vienna, then to Hamburg, and then to New York city.

CHAPTER XXVIII.

The firm of Arthur Tappan & Co., a large dry goods concern, held a high position in this city thirty-five years ago. We bel.eve that Arthur was in business in this city previous to 1820, and failed. If so, he recovered himself again. But in 1820 he was living in poor circumstances, and bought his family provisions in very small quantities, as many of us have to do in 1862, viz.: half a pound of butter, a pound of sugar, another of coffee, at a time, and pay for it in cash.

In 1826, the house of Arthur Tappan & Co., was in full blast, doing the largest silk business in the city. Their store was at 122 Pearl street, in Hanover square. It was a better class store than any of its neighbors, being built of granite.

Lewis Tappan, a brother of Arthur, was a partner, and so was Alfred Edwards, a nephew of the Tappans.

Alfred Edwards continued business after it was relinquished by the Tappans, who both are living — aged men.

Few are aware that these two men did more to originate and push ahead the abolition movement than any two hundred other men did, or could have done. In connection with David Hale, Gerard Hallock and other original abolitionists, the Tappans started the *Journal of Commerce.* That paper noiselessly instilled abolition ideas among the merchants for many years.

Arthur Tappan was a frank, above board man. He did nothing underhand or secretly. He made proselytes in his store, in his house, in public meetings, and among his neighbors.

He had a large number of pe sons in his employ. Many of his clerks were young men of uncommon ability. Mr. Tappan was the first merchant employer who set the example of attending to the morals and sentiments of his clerks. He wrote rules for their observance, and he made his clerks act up to and comply with those rules, or leave his service. Here are some of them, that I recollect:

1. Every young man was to be a strict temperance man, drink no ardent spirits, or wine of any kind.

2. A clerk was not permitted to visit houses of ill-repute, indulge in fast habits, or stay out late. A moment's thought will inform any one that this rule was an excellent one, and saved Mr. Tappan thousands of dollars of goods every year. Girls are fond of silks, and Tappan kept a silk store. Probably A. T. Stewart & Co. would be worth half a million more had they made all their clerks sign and keep edict No. 2 of Arthur Tappan & Co.

3. No clerk was permitted to visit any theatre, and no forgiveness was accorded if he added to the crime by becoming acquainted with members of the theatrical profession.

4. Each clerk was obliged to attend Divine servic twice on the Sabbath day.

5. Every Monday morning to report to the proper authorities what church they had attended, the name of the clergyman, and the texts.

6. To attend prayer meetings twice a week.

7. Never to be out of the boarding-house or residence of any clerk after 10 o'clock, P. M.

8. Must belong to the Abolition Society, and make as many converts as possible.

Arthur Tappan & Co. went on swimmingly until the negro riots broke out in this city. Mr. Tappan was mixed up with Dr. Cox, who preached at the corner of Varick and Laight streets. The church is still standing. At that time, too, the great wigwam of the Abolitionists and new lights, was what was called the "Chatham Street Chapel." It was the old Chatham Street Theatre, altered into a place for the new Gospelers. It stood on the west side of Chatham, between Pearl and Duane streets. It stood back from the street, upon which was an iron gate. You went back in a passage about twenty-five feet wide and one hundred feet deep. Then you ascended steps to the door of the theatre. When once inside you were startled by its immense size, it having four galleries. Phinney preached there, so did Burchard — both famous sensation Abolition preachers in their day. It is needless to add that Lewis Tappan and Arthur used to be chiefs in the chapel. After the service, the clergyman would ask if any brother or sister would come up to the anxious seats (first row of seats before the pulpit platform) and be prayed for; or "will any parent or pious person name any child or impenitent person to be prayed for?" Of course some persons (females, generally) would go up and take the anxious seats. Then the Tappans would be aroused, take seats with them and talk religion to the weeping women, while the prayers from the preacher went up strong and earnest.

Lewis Tappan lived in the neighborhood in Rose street. His was a nice two story brick house next door (South) to the Quaker Church yard.

The night his house was sacked the mob went first to

the Chatham Street Chapel. After raising Ned there they rushed out, many getting nearly killed (somebody had closed the iron gates) by being crushed in the passage way, and went around to the house of Lewis Tappan. He knew beforehand that such a visit would be made, and his family had removed. The mob entered his house, flung the furniture out of the windows, and the greater proportion was burned in the street.

The police made frequent attempts to stop it, but it was of no use. The cavalry made a charge, passed the sugar house, and drove the mob down Rose to Pearl street.

The Varick street church was mobbed and many windows demolished. So was a church in Spring street, south side, between Hudson and Varick.

The Seventh Regiment, National Guard, Col. Stevens, was called out, and kept moving for two days. That was in 1834.

The house in Rose street occupied by Lewis Tappan became famous. It was afterwards occupied by James Harper, ex-mayor, as late as 1846 or 1848. His wife died in that house.

After the Chatham Street Chapel was given up, a new place for Abolition meetings was built on Broadway on the same principle, viz: the building erected back of the dwelling house, with entrance under one of the houses on Broadway. This was called the "Tabernacle." How it was built I know not. But not long after David Hale, of the *Journal of Commerce*, and the Tappan association, got hold of it and made money by the operation.

Previous to that David Hale was very poor. *The Journal of Commerce* did not pay, and David, to help along, kept a pious boarding-house in Broadway, west side, two doors beyond Morris street, where the Stevens House now stands. We were one of his pious boarders for some time. David was the personification of a Yankee — if there is such a race — long legs, hatchet face, skin and bones, slight, pokey, and keen as a briar He was one of the few men who acted with the Tappans, and sowed the abolition seed that has produced the overshadowing oaks of 1862 — secession, dissolution, anarchy, bloodshed.

That Tabernacle was started as an abolition temple, and it fulfilled its mission. It made money, too, for all hands. Fernando Wood in 1839, when he lived at No. 37 White street with his first wife, was a leader at the Tabernacle, and a deacon there. He has become rich, and married a third wife, who is vastly wealthy. Fernando wanted to get *The Journal of Commerce* support to go to Congress. His dodge succeeded, and next year he got the nomination; and in spite of the robbery of the Greenwich street bank, was elected.

Israel Minor, now a millionaire of this city, was one of that Tabernacle crowd. The history of Minor is a most remarkable one. He was born in the village of Woodbury, Connecticut, and his father, who was a very small farmer, apprenticed him to one Bradley, a tanner.

Young Israel did not like the tanning business, ran away, and walked ninety-eight miles to New York, where he did not know a soul; but the God who looks out for sparrows kept his eye on young Israel. He got a place in a drug store in Maiden Lane, and learned Latin and the drug trade in a few years. He saved up ninety-seven dollars, and with that sum bought a little 0x9 retail drug store in Fulton street, north side, two doors from Greenwich. Then he got married, took a dwelling-house, kept a few boarders, attended prayer meetings, and, next year, took a large drug store on the other side of Fulton street, No. 214. There he commenced raising up for thirty years or more, and he made his ninety-seven dollar store worth $20,000. It is now carried on by his successors.

Mr. Minor bought the Tabernacle a few years ago, and sold it out for mercantile purposes, clearing $80,000. A most worthy man is Israel Minor. He has not forgotten the place of his birth, but has erected there a magnificent country house. It is needless to add that he was one of the Arthur Tappan crowd.

Early in 1830, the southern people made a movement in reference to the Tappans. The pledge was quite natural that no person should, directly or indirectly, have any dealings with the firm of Arthur Tappan &. Co.; that was before the riots broke out. It was the beginning of the end of the great success of the concern.

After the riots the Tappans broke up house-keeping. Lewis went to Mr. Woods, No. 21 Broadway, to board. Edwards, then a bachelor, was already boarding there.

Arthur Tappan & Co. had very stringent rules in reference to time. Every clerk had to be on hand before half-past seven o'clock in summer and eight in winter; and during the business season all the clerks remained until the store closed at night. The goods were packed at night.

There was a book kept of the names of all the clerks and each clerk reported the time of arrival in the morning.

Before commencing the duties of the day, all the bosses and clerks assembled in a large room up stairs, where prayers were offered up. The benediction was,

"Emancipation of the slaves." All joined in. If old Arthur was up to New Haven or absent elsewhere, then Lewis led off in prayer. If he was absent, Mr. Edwards did morning prayer.

Before 1834 Arthur Tappan & Co., were worth not less than $400,000. Then they fell off and broke ir 1837.

Arthur used to give away money for every species of charity; $5, $10, $15, $20 and even $50,000 for educational institutions. To every Abolition society he gave money liberally and constantly. Whether Arthur Tappan abolitionist, would never have made any headway North, President Lincoln ought not to forget the primary cause of his success. Had Arthur Tappan never lived, Abraham Lincoln would never have been President of the United States. The President has appointed the son-in-law of Arthur Tappan, Mr. Hiram Barney, collector of the port.

When Arthur Tappan was in the dry goods business, everybody who called, had to be introduced to him. He would inquire all about such individuals. Finally, if he was satisfied, he would ask him if he would not buy a bill of goods, and on long credit. No detail would be forgotten by the inquisitive merchant. This information Arthur would store away in a very retentive memory. In this way, Mr. Tappan became possessed of a very large information in regard to the means of outside buyers in various parts of the Union.

Even he, when getting this knowledge, had no idea that it would ever lead to anything further than information to be used in his own extensive sales. He was disappointed. When he failed in 1837, Mr. Tappan did not despair, but at once turned his attention to furnishing information to other merchants in relation to the standing of buyers in every part of the Union He relinquished mercantile business for a sterling mercantile agency. He was the founder of a new department in commerce and trade, but probably more useful in saving from loss than any other. He associated with him his brother Lewis Tappan, and afterwards Benjamin Douglas, a son of George Douglas, an ex-merchant of this city. Benjamin was as smart as a steel trap. He was for a long time quite an extensive merchant in Charleston, S. C. but the climate was too enervating, and he returned to New York, which, after all, is the only city fit to dwell in on this side of the Atlantic Ocean.

In the mercantile agency concern the Tappans were first, then B. Douglas & Co., and now it is Dun, Boyd & Co., who were former clerks in what is really a mammoth business.

This mercantile agency is a curiosity. It is a business my readers have but little conception of. It publishes a book of reference. This contains the names of all the principal persons in trade in all the cities of the United States and Canadas.

The charge for these books is $100, $150, or $200 per annum.

Each subscriber pays from one to five hundred dollars every year for information. Some dry goods houses pay as high as $1000 per annum. For this sum, the subscribers are kept posted in reference to almost every trade in the Union. A loss — a death — a change of partnership — failure — or any change, is communicated to the subscribers. Millions are saved to New York merchants every year by this agency.

Before Arthur and Lewis Tappan retired from business, it was openly charged upon them that they hated the South so cordially, that it led to injustice in their reports of the standing of Southern men.

One large dealer South, who deemed himself injured by their report of his standing and resources, sued in a New York Court, and recovered $10,000 damages.

The Tappans, Arthur and Lewis retired from that business, both aged and rich.

Their successors in the business (Dun, Boyd & Co.,) employ about two hundred and fifty clerks. Their reports embrace the Canadas as well as the cities and towns of the United States.

They give the character and standing of the commercial firms of great houses that do a fifty million business in cotton and banking, or of Smith, the pea-nut dealer, on the street corner, whose sales of roasted do not exceed $1 62 per day.

A merchant, named Jones, from Scatwood, Minnesota, calls on Wheeler & Wilson to buy five sewing machines on credit,

"Call back in half an hour," says Wheeler, who at once goes to Dun, Boyd & Co. There he ascertains that Jones is or is not married — that Jones is courting a girl, who will have $10,000 when her father dies — that Jones does or does not drink — that he spends one night at bucking the "Tiger" — that the night previous, Jones did not sleep at the Astor, where he pretends to stop, but at a particular friend's house up town, where he ought not to stop, finally, that Jones is thirty-two years, seven months and three days old — that he voted for Lincoln's election — that he belongs to the local church, and has attended it thirty-three times out of fifty-two Sundays during the year 1861. Of course Wheeler & Co. don't sell to this genius Jones, and consequently, do not lose the cost of five sewing machines

To procure such varied information, and from all sections, Dun, Boyd & Co. employ 10,000 agents. The letters to them daily amount to over 2000.

They do not pay high salaries. Their clerks get $250 to $300. Their business is mostly copying names — changes of firms — suits commenced — mortgages of property — deaths of children — marriage of men on their books — every change, in fact, is noted and recorded in Dun, Boyd & Co.'s books.

An agent of the old concern once called on a merchant in Broad street, and asked him to become a subscriber. He explained its advantages. The merchant hesitated — at last he says, "Tell me all about 'James Samson' and I will subscribe." "The name is not on the agency books, but give me two days and I will find out all about him." The merchant agreed. The clerk got the name correctly and said, "I'll find out all about him if he is in the United States." A week elapsed. The clerk of agency called, and reported as follows: "James Samson is a peddler, aged 30; he comes to Albany to buy his goods, and then peddles them out along the canal from Albany to Buffalo. He is worth $2,000; owns a wooden house at Lockport in his own name; his family reside in it; has a wife and three children, two boys and one girl; boys named Henry and Charles, aged four and six years; girl named Margaret, two years old; no judgment out or mortgage on property; drinks two glasses cider brandy, plain, morning and evening — never more; drinks water after each; chews fine cut; never smokes; good teeth generally; has lost a large double tooth on lower jaw, back, second from throat on left side; has a scar an inch long on his left leg knee-pan; cause, cut himself with a hatchet when only three years old; can be found when in Albany at Pete Mason's, 82 State street; purchases principally jewelry and fancy articles; belongs to the Shoe."

This is evidence of how systematically the business is carried on. The report was conclusive. It satisfied the Broad street merchant. The event was fifteen years ago. The merchant subscribed $150, and has paid it yearly ever since.

Of course other and similar concerns have sprung up in this city, but none so large, so extensive and so valuable, as the great agency of Dun, Boyd & Co., started by Arthur & Lewis Tappan.

The Tappan Brothers have been fearfully abused, North as well as South.

It was but a few days ago that Lewis was again before the public with reference to a little negro boy, under charge of Marshal Rynders, and was subject to the amiability of the famed captain. But he survived it, and yesterday we met Lewis, whose hair is white with the frost of seventy winters, passing smilingly down Broadway towards the South Ferry.

CHAPTER XXIX

There are many points that I could make in these articles were I to go around and make enquiries of this or that one. While the author would be very thankful for any information that will lighten his labors, he is not yet ready to make a personal application for it.

In a former chapter I said Mrs. Hazard's door plate was upon the door of Barker's residence in Beekman street. I did not mean that. The name on the door plate was Thomas Hazard. He was formerly from Nantucket. He made a fortune there in the whaling business, and then came to New York. I never heard that he was in business in this city. He was the father of three children. One was a son. He died early. One daughter married John H. Howland, an extensive merchant in Front street for many years. The other married Jacob Barker, as I have previously stated. The Hazards were all quakers. When in the city, the old man always lived in Beekman street. Old Mr. Hazard deemed Jacob Barker a wonderful person. So he was. He was a great merchant, a great ship owner, the first private banker, the truest patriot, and the best abused man among her old citizens.

Jacob Barker was also a good pilot, and he frequently

piloted his own ships out to sea. He did this for two reasons: the first was, that he saved the pilotage; and the second, he believed that he could do it better and with more safety to his ships than any professed pilot could do.

Fitz Green Halleck, the celebrated poet, was the cashier of Jacob Barker for many years, and he ought to write the history of the old private banker. Halleck was also Secretary of the Duchess County Fire Insurance Company.

I have previously alluded to the four corners of Pearl street and Pine, as being occupied by four great auctioneer houses. I gave the history of Woolsey, Ward and Beach. One of the corners was occupied by Shotwell, Fox & Co.; they had succeeded Leggett, Pearsall & Co., an auction and commission house in 1825.

That house consisted of Samuel Leggett, Thomas W. Pearsall, Joseph S. Shotwell, and George S. Fox. A Mr. Stanton was afterwards taken in.

Of Samuel Leggett I shall have more to say as I get along. He walked through this world treading as softly as any Quaker merchant, yet in his earlier years he trod heavily in the commercial and financial walks. He was President for many years of the famed Franklin Bank, that he got an injunction upon, and stopped it at twenty minutes past ten o'clock on the morning of the 29th May, 1828, thirty-five years ago.

That Franklin Bank was started in 1818. It had good old names among its directors — Henry Astor, Gabriel Furman, James A. Burtis, Israel Corse, James Palmer, Dennis H. Doyle, William Seaman, Thomas Freeborne, Samuel James, Robert Bogardus — most all dead now.

The Leggett family is very old. Samuel was the son of the late Thomas Leggett of West Farms, Westchester county, who among our most ancient merchants left an honored name.

During the Revolution, or about 1780, Thomas Leggett commenced business in a dry grocery, (he did not sell rum) at the corner of Peck Slip and Pearl street. There he was successful in a small way. At that time there was a market in Peck Slip. The Bank of New York was six doors above Thomas Leggett's store on the same side. That was the old location (the Bank was afterwards built on the corner of William and Wall.) It has been since re-built. The builder, George Ireland, is yet alive in the Fifth Ward, ninety and odd years old. He was present when the first corner stone was laid, and was also present many years after when it was taken up, in order to lay the corner stone of the present building. May the old worthy live a century longer.

Walter Franklin lived in the house at the junction of Pearl and Cherry streets, afterwards the residence of General Washington.

Franklin Square is named after Walter, and not after old Benjamin, as is generally supposed. After General Washington left the above house, it was occupied by Samuel Osgood, who married the widow of Walter Franklin, whose daughters married De Witt Clinton, citizens Genet, and John L. Norton.

I mention these facts to show that at that time the Franklin Square and Pearl street neighborhood was the Fifth avenue part of New York. It was the most aristocratic quarter of the town.

As an evidenee of the simplicity of living at that period, as exhibited in the value of rents, Mr. Thomas

Leggett, in anticipation of changing his business, bought in 1781 the house now known as 307 Pearl (then Queen street,) but did not move into it that year. He rented it out to Comfort Sands (then a young gentleman of great pretensions,) for his own occupation with his family, at the rent of $32,50 per annum. This fact will afford us a better idea of the style and cost of living at that time than anything else could do.

A daughter of Comfort Sands married Nathaniel Prime, the founder of the house of Prime & Co., now, and which has been in former time, Prime, Ward & Sands, Prime, Ward, Sands & King, Prime, Ward & King, and Prime, Ward & Co.

Mrs. Philip Hone, formerly Miss Dunscombe, was born and married in the next house to No. 307 Pearl (Queen.) Mr. Leggett moved into his house, No. 307 in 1782, where he conducted a successful dry goods business, and lived until he retired. The firm was at first Thomas Leggett. Then he took into the firm in 1793 his brother Joseph, who left in 1803. Then, in 1803, Joseph retired. He took in his son Samuel, and the firm was Thomas Leggett & Son. He had several sons, -- Samuel, William H., Joseph, and Thomas, Jr. In 1807, the elder Leggett retired from business, and the firm was changed to Leggett, Fox & Co., consisting of Samuel, a brother, and his own brother William. In 1832 or 1833 the concern gave up business and closed up, although doing a large and prosperous business, continued for over forty years. The partners retired well off.

In 1798 New York was afflicted with burglars. One night Mr. Thomas Leggett heard an outcry, in his im mediate neighborhood. "Murder!" "thieves!" was called, and "help" invoked. He rushed out of his own house, and ran across the way, where he saw a light in the store through the chinks of the door, which latter he promptly stove in. He saw three burglars. Two were upon the owner of the store, who was down on the floor. A third was coming towards the door. Mr. Leggett seized him, wheeled about, and jammed him against the wall with his back, and thus held him. Another burglar rushed at Mr. Leggett, but he seized him with his hands, and held him fast. The rear burglar drew a penknife, and commenced stabbing; but he made a mistake, and stabbed his confederate No. 2, that Mr. Leggett was holding on to, while keeping the other fast against the wall. He was relieved from his disagreeable situation by his neighbor, Alderman Theophilus Beekman, who came to his assistance, and the fellows were secured (save burglar No. 3, who escaped,) and afterwards taken to prison, tried, convicted and executed.

Mr. Leggett, in common with all the followers of George Fox and William Penn, was opposed to capital punishment. He was often heard to say that he was glad that he had not been obliged to appear as a witness against the two burglars whom he was mainly instrumental in capturing. (He was absent from the city at the time of their trial, thinking there was sufficient evidence of their guilt for their conviction without his testimony — particularly as one of them was a young offender whom he believed had been seduced to the committal of the deed by his more hardened companion.)

In 1809, as I have before stated, the old gentleman retired from business, and removed to the old homestead, where he died in 1843, aged about eighty-eight years. He was born in 1755. The Leggetts came from an old stock, and we must say something of that old homestead in West Farms, where he died. His ancestors came into West Farms with John Richardson in the year 1661 — two hundred years ago.

In 1664 Mr. Richardson bought from the Indian proprietors the equal half of the township of West Farms, comprising about three thousand acres, bounded by the Sound or East river on the south, Bronx river on the east, Fordham on the north, and what is now known as Morrisania on the west.

The English title came from John Nicolls, the governor of the province in 1666. This was seven years before Morrisania was taken up by Lewis Morris and his brother.

Gabriel Leggett, the grandfather of Thomas, married the daughter of Mr. Richardson, and inherited the lands now occupied (1861) by Joseph Walker, Paul Spofford, Edward Faile, W. W. Fox and George S. Fox.

The two latter married two of the daughters of Thomas Leggett, who lived from 1809 and died in the house now occupied by his daughter, Mrs. George S. Fox, and was the home of his ancestor Gabriel in 1670.

These Foxes were descended from the old Quaker George, who, on the 13th of August, 1658, met Oliver Cromwell, in Hampton Court, at the head of his guards. "I saw and felt," writes honest George, "a waft of leath go forth against him, and when I came to him he ooked like a dead man."

Quaker Fox saw but too truly; the conqueror of all England had bowed, in his turn, to a mightier power. A hand heavier than his own was on him. On September 3d, Oliver Cromwell died.

In the year 1774 Gabriel Leggett, grandfather of Thomas, was driven out of West Farms township by

Colonel Delancy and his partizans, who were arrant tories. The Leggett family then went up on their new lands in Saratoga; from whence they were taken by Burgoyne's Indians. The male part of the family were conveyed to Burgoyne's camp, where they all remained prisoners except Thomas Leggett, who made his escape, swam over the North River in October, and came back to the old homestead in West Farms.

The farm on which the Leggetts lived at Saratoga was a part of the battle-ground afterwards. The wheat fields were manured by many dead bodies; the wheat showed where they lay the following year, when it was harvested! General Frazier was also mortally wounded in a ravine near Mr. Leggett's house.

But to return to Thomas Leggett. After he made his escape and safely reached the homestead, he found it vacated and dismantled, even to the weather boarding, which had been stripped off for kindling wood. The entire neighborhood was a scene of desolation. The negroes belonging to the property had been kept in the house for tory use, and were found entirely destitute. Luckily for all parties, fishing was good. The nets had been left untouched — the fishing season was just approaching. The other proprietors came in about the same time, and they fished as a joint-stock concern. They cleared that season $3,000; one third fell to the share of Thomas Leggett, who, finding it impossible to live in that disturbed region, removed to New York, and went into the grocery business, as already stated, in Peck Slip, corner of Pearl street, in 1780.

When in 1809 Mr. Thomas Leggett left business, he was succeeded by his sons Samuel and W. H. Leggett, and his son-in-law W. W. Fox, under the name of Leggett, Fox & Co., as before stated.

Samuel was the first person in this city who attempted to furnish the city with water from the neighboring river. He proposed the Bronx. From some cause unknown to me, the plan failed. The money subscribed for this object was returned to the subscribers. The idea thus suggested was not lost, however. It culminated in other hands, and the croton was substituted for the Bronx.

Samuel Leggett was a man of enlarged ideas. He possessed great energy and determination, but combined with the most mild and amiable disposition, which sometimes led him into difficulty, as in the case of the unfortunate Franklin Bank. To save the reputation of others, with whose evil doings circumstances had made him acquainted, he permitted scandal to go unrebuked, thinking that time and the full acquittance from every charge of wrong by Chancellor Kent (who gave the entire matter an official examination) would be a sufficient vindication.

In 1831, the Chancellor wrote the following letter:

New York, *March* 4, 1831.

Dear Sir: — I thank you for your pamphlet in vindication of your character and conduct as late President of the Franklin Bank. I was acquainted with the principal facts from the perusal of your journal in the summer of 1828, and your efforts to redeem its credit and promote its stability in a strong and interest ing point of view.

I was never able to discover from my investigation, any ground for the suspicion and calumny against you, in your conduct as President or Director of the institution; and I rejoice that you have been able so completely to vindicate your character, and soothe the lacerated feelings of your family and friends. With my best wishes for your happiness and prosperity, I am, your friend and obedient servant,

JAMES KENT,
Receiver for Franklin Bank.

That same Samuel Leggett was the first originator of a gas company in this city in 1822. He was the first President of the New York Gas Light Company. His brother-in-law, W. W. Fox, succeeded him, and has continued President to this day. He is a man over 70 years of age. This company went into operation on the 26th of March, 1823. Its charter is unlimited. The original capital was $1,000,000.

Samuel Leggett was one of the best men of his time. Like other benevolent men of every age he was persecuted for not exposing the defects of the false and pretentious with whom he had become acquainted. Mr. Leggett had two sons; one of them is Secretary of the Brooklyn Insurance Company. A daughter married Barney Corse.

There are other descendants of the old Gabriel Leggett, the grandfather of Thomas.

William Leggett, at one time connected with the *Post*—editor of the *Plaindealer*—a famous political meteor in the day of General Jackson, and a great friend of Edwin Forrest, was a lineal descendant of old Gabriel. William's great-grandfather was mayor of Westchester many years ago.

As a race, the Leggetts are famed for their agility, strength, indomitable courage and perseverance. Old Thomas Leggett never experienced such a sensation as fear. William, of the *Post*, was also remarkable for his personal disregard of danger.

Thomas Leggett always refused while in business to give an endorser for his auction purchases, in accordance with the customs of auctioneers, which was a source of trouble between him, John Hone, Robert Hunter and David Dunham. He also resisted the tyranny of the banks, at that time, 1800, a great power in the city and for many years afterwards. Even now banks are not quite powerless. He was one of the greatest of the old school merchants who left an unstained name, a comfortable estate, and a large family to enjoy his fortune and give vigor to the State in which they were born.

There were other Leggetts, cousins of this Thomas Leggett's descendants, and at one time numbered among the old merchants. Many of our readers will well recollect Thomas H. Leggett, who lived on the south side of Beekman street, a few doors from Nassau street. It was No. 21. Next door was a lawyer's court filled with offices, and a garden in front between that and Mr. Leggett's house. It belonged to Mr. Leggett. Back of this property, but facing on Ann street, stood the old Catholic Church. The splendid house that our citizens will well remember (it was the handsomest down town) Mr. Leggett quitted in 1836, and rented it as a boarding house to the Misses Wetmore. He retired from business, but afterwards got nearly ruined. He had endorsed for his son and nephew who succeeded him in business. They put him in for $60,000. He did not assign his property, but paid as he could. He owned two houses in Beekman street. One he exchanged with Stephen Allen for a piece of land in Flushing, where he now lives. He has been in the habit of spending his winters South.

Thomas H. Leggett was brother to the famous Aaron Leggett (Mexican Leggett, as he has been nicknamed.)

Never lived such a joker as Aaron Leggett. He was once in business in Pearl street in dry goods. The firm was Leggett & Hance. Mr. Hance was the Revo. C. — afterwards Revo. C. Hance & Co.

Not a week ago I went up to the Croton Water Office to pay my water dues, where I was very much amazed to see Revo. C. Hance, and get his signature for my small amount of money. He has died since.

If I was to pen all I know about Aaron Leggett, it would take a year. To cut it as short as possible, he went out to Mexico. I believe he started a steamboat. At any rate, he was as intimate as a pickpocket, with old Santa Anna. Leggett got upset, and then commenced his celebrated claims. He may have lost $10,000. He claimed a million, and certainly got considerable. The way Aaron made out his bills, was as follows : —

Value of steamboat.	$5,000
What she would have made in one year had not the Mexicans seized her. . . .	500,000
Interest for three years at 33⅓ per annum.	510,000
Total.	$1,015 000

While floating about Washington City, Aaron Leggett fixed his eyes upon about two thousand acres of the Mount Vernon estate belonging to George Washington. He bought it for about $5 an acre, and when he died held it at $50.

When he died he left his brother Thomas H. about $60,000 ; in other words, quite comfortable.

CHAPTER XXX.

Poor Charles Leupp, who died suddenly, not long ago, belonged to the hide and leather merchants, whose sphere of action is called "The Swamp." Alluding upon one occasion to the great men from that locality — such as Jacob Lorillard, Abraham Bloodgood, Israel Corse, David Bryson, Gideon Lee, Peter McCartee, William Kumbel, Abraham Polhemus, Richard Cunningham, Hugh McCormick, Shepherd Knapp, Thomas Everett, Jonathan Thorne, the Brookses, James George and Thomas, Peter Bonnett, Henry Orttery, Daniel Tooker, and other lights, the lamented Charles — (who was also a great leather merchant, and had been at one time a partner and son-in-law, of Gideon Lee and Shepherd Knapp) said:

"The Roman mother Cornelia, when asked to display her jewels, pointed to her sons. So can we, to these (leather and hide) fathers and claim them as ours. Let us cherish their example, and emulate their noble qualities, so that hereafter our successors may, in like manner, be not ashamed of any of us, but exclaim:

"He, too, was a Swamper!"

That Swamp is a wonderful place. I can remember it well, when it was all a lot of tan vats. I have seen some of those great names above alluded to. They were great in their day and generation. But long before their time tanneries existed in the "Swamp."

A couple of hundred years ago, when people talked Dutch in the small town, they called that part of the town, "*Greppel Bosch*," which means in English a "swamp or marsh covered with wood." The trees were cut down long ago, but the name "Swamp" is retained to this day.

The land adjoining the Swamp, extending to Pearl and Rose, including what is now called Vandewater street, belonged in 1683 to Balthazar Bayard. A part of it afterwards in 1783 — a hundred years later — was sold to the widow of Hendrick Vandewater, after whom that street was named.

I cannot tell how early the tan-yards were commenced there, but in 1744, Van Hook, Anthony & Stevens, and Becine & Rips, all had tan-yards in the "Swamp."

Jacob street and Skinner street existed at the time, and the other boundaries of the "Swamp" were Gold, Frankfort, Ferry, and Queen (Pearl). Frankfort only came to Skinner street (one part changed to Cliff and the other part to Hague street). Flack street ran from Skinner to Queen (now Pearl). Flack is now changed to Frankfort street.

Jacob street was named after Gov. Jacob Leisler, whose farm or estate adjoined the "Swamp," and extended as far as Chatham street, half way from Frankfort to Pearl, on that line. It was confiscated in 1691, upon conviction of his attainder, and afterwards restored to him by the act of parliament, reversing his attainder. Poor Jacob was hung and buried in his own garden. The grave was about fifty feet from Chatham, near the spot where French's Hotel now stands. No houses stood nearer than Beekman street to the spot as late as 1732. About that time his body was dug up and removed to the Dutch Reformed church burying ground in Garden (Exchange street,) where Dr. Mathews, who still lives, preached so many years.

These streets were all in the "Montgomerie Ward" in 1744.

Within the recollection of many of our readers, the space bounded by Jacob, Gold, Ferry and Frankfort streets, was nothing but tan yards or vats. There were no houses. The houses on the opposite sides to the vat square were small buildings. There was not a three story house in that vicinity. How changed now!

Among the tanners or leather dealers that I recollect, was Israel Corse. He was Quaker, and born in Chestertown, Maryland, in 1769. He lost his father when an infant. His mother married again; and when young Israel arrived at the age of seventeen years, not liking the new male parent, he ran away from home, and apprenticed himself to a tannery in Camden, Delaware. There he served out his time, and when he had finished he was worth seventy-five cents. Nothing daunted, he commenced business upon that small capital. Not long after, he married Lydia Troth, a farmer's daughter, residing at Dover Bridge, near Easton, in Maryland. She brought him some $4,000 or $5,000, besides being a most amiable, prudent, and industrious wife. Mr. Corse remained in Camden until he accumulated by his own honest exertion the sum of $10,000. He lost several children by death; only one, Barney, survived, and came to New York when his father Israel removed thither in 1803. In New York

Israel Corse went into business in the Swamp with George Ferguson, under the firm of Ferguson & Corse, at No. 14 Jacob street. His residence was at No. 6 Vandewater street, then a very respectable part of the town. The house is still standing. Some years after he bought No. 7, (opposite,) where he lived many years, until he removed to a house he bought in East Broadway, near Rutgers, where he died in 1842. The house was afterwards sold to, and is now occupied by Dr. Leveredge.

Mr. Corse soon found that Ferguson was sadly embarrassed with old affairs, so he dissolved the concern after a partnership of five years, and in 1808 continued the business under his own name. Mr. Ferguson never got into business again, and died a few years ago at the advanced age of 84 years.

Israel Corse had a son (Barney) and a daughter (Lydia) by his first wife. He married a second wife after he reached New York. By her he had two more children, Israel and Mary, who survive.

Barney Corse married a daughter of the late Samuel Leggett. Lydia Corse married Jonathan Thorne.

Israel married a daughter of Morris Ketchum ; Mary married W. H. Polk, the pet brother of President James K. Polk. She died in 1849, leaving one son, Jas. K. Polk, Jr. Wm. H. Polk is known in this community as the wildest sort of a fast man. So he was at one time in his career. But now, all that is changed ; he neither drinks, swears, or gambles. He is a teetotaller, and a member of the church.

John Tyler appointed him minister to Naples (Charge d'Affaires.) He raised Ned out there, and at last resigned and came home. His brother willingly gave him a commission in the army, when war raged with Mex ico, (the only favor he willingly granted, as he hoped his brother would die a glorious death, instead of an ignominious one.) He did not, however; and has, since the war, been elected to Congress from Tennessee. When James K. Polk found that he was going to die in the summer of 1849, he called his wife into the room, where he had a lawyer, and requested her to dictate a will. She refused. He said, "I shall leave all to you." She begged him not to do so, and suggested that his brother William was the true heir. "He will go to the devil fast enough without any property to squander," said the dying chief, and added, "if he ever reforms you can use your own judgment in letting him have money." Finally Mrs. Polk consented (they had no children of their own) and the property of the President went to his wife. William H. Polk is now an honor to the President. He annoyed the latter awfully in his life time.

To return to the firm of old Israel Corse. He kept on business at 14 Jacob street for many years in his own name. In 1821 he took into the concern his son Barney, and the firm was Israel Corse & Son, until 1830, when the old gentleman retired, and B. Corse invited his brother-in-law, Jonathan Thorne, to come into the concern, and the firm was continued for two years, when Barney retired. Then Jonathan continued the business alone for a few years, when he took in his brother-in-law Israel, and Anson Lapham, who married his sister, and the firm was Jonathan Thorne & Co. They did business at 14 Jacob street. In 1840 the firm removed from 14 Jacob street to a new store at 18 Ferry street, that cost $27,000, where the business is still continued by Jonathan Thorne and partner, who is very rich. Jonathan was from Dutchess county, and he was in the dry goods business some years.

In 1840 Thorne & Corse took in a Mr. Watson, who had purchased the interest of Lapham, and the firm was changed to Corse, Thorne & Co.

Some time after Israel retired, and Mr. Thorne took into partnership his eldest son Edwin and his book-keeper Mr. Ely, who had bought Israel Corse's share, now Watson, Thorne & Co.

The Thorne name has been made famous by this family, not only for the connection with the selling of cattle, skins, hides, etc., but with the raising of cattle. The elder Thorne always had a remarkable attachment to splendid cattle. He has a place called Thornedale.

One son devoted himself to this sole business. He imports the best breeds of cattle, such as Durham, etc., to be found in Europe, and pays prices almost fabulous.

He recently married Miss Van Cowenhoven, a step-daughter of Joel Wolfe in the Fifth avenue. Among the presents old Jonathan Thorne and others gave to the bride were massive sets of silver, ornamented with "bull's heads." The plate presented by the father of the groom amounted to $20,000. Mr. Thorne the elder is a most excellent man. He is an honor to the city and the "Swamp." Old Israel Corse thought the world of him. He is shrewd. So are all Quakers, for that matter. A soft Quaker would be as great a curiosity as a dissipated Hebrew.

When Israel Corse was an apprentice to the tan yard business, a thief stole a mare in the village. She had a colt and it was following her. "Stop thief," cried the neighbors. "Catch the colt," cried Israel. The colt was caught, and the quick wit of the young Quaker was apparent. The thief was caught, for the mare would not move a step after she missed her colt.

For forty and odd years Israel Corse was a most inveterate tobacco chewer. He chewed at all times, except when asleep, and before breakfast in the morning. He made up his mind that it injured him and left it off, and improved his good health, and lived to a good old age. Few tobacco chewers are aware how much they shorten their lives by the awful and fearful practice.

Israel Corse was one of that devoted band that rid New York of the curse of lotteries, and made the selling of lottery tickets a crime. One celebrated man named Aaron Clark was made mayor. He was a great lottery seller, and made a fortune by it. So did Gregory of Jersey City — so did many others. Ever since, it has become a crime to deal in lotteries. People in this city have coined money in it. Witness the celebrated brothers, Ben and Fernando Wood, — one a member of Congress and the other mayor! Ben, it is said, has often spouted a pair of boots to obtain fifty cents with which to operate in policies, and finally, when he became a policy dealer himself and the backer, made a sum sufficient to buy a few illegal lottery privileges down South, and out of it clears annually a few hundred thousand dollars, ruining thousands of virtuous but poor families. What a pity that no Israel Corse is alive now, to follow up such men with the law, and prosecute them for their criminality.

The Swamp was once the scene of a great deal of fun, in consequence of the discovery of a well in Jacob street, that contained "mineral water." I think it was in 1826 or thereabouts. The citizens all ran wild. Saratoga was forgotten. A mineral spring was found in Jacob street! "Sixpence" a drink, was charged.

Old Jacob Hays, high constable of the city, was a great believer in that new found mineral water. He drank it himself, and he carried it to his home in bottles, and believed that he derived great benefits from its use. At last it was blown; the excitement was subdued by the fact that the well was supplied from the old tan vats that had been covered over.

Among other great men of the Swamp, was Jacob Lorillard, tanner, currier and hide dealer. He died about twenty-two years ago, a man about sixty-eight or seventy years old. He had brothers who were in the tobacco business in Chatham street, and their sons are still so. I believe there were three brothers in the tobacco business — George, Peter, and another whose name I forget. I have a faint recollection that Peter was wounded in Chatham street, near the Hall of Records. The old debtor's jail stood there, and one night the prisoners tried to make their escape. Peter Lorillard came over from the tobacco store to assist in securing them, and was shot.

I may be wrong. It is among my earliest recollections.

Doctor Francis could tell all about it, but poor old gentleman, he stepped out at three in the morning of the dreadful hurricane performance of the 7th and 8th inst. The doctor was as jovial a good old soul as ever breathed. He could tell amusing stories. He will be a pleasant fellow for a chat in the other world, if talking is allowed there and will have the pleasure of renewing his acquaintance with Abernethy, Cuvier, Gall, Brewester and Walter Scott, men of note, that the doctor could tell famous anecdotes about, for he had known them personally. To return to Jacob Lorillard, of the Swamp. In his day he had a large tannery on the corner of Pearl and Ferry streets and his currying shop was in Jacob street. He had a clerk — Ogden E. Edwards — who succeeded him in business.

Ogden Edwards, a son, I believe, of William Edwards, a tanner in Elizabethtown, N. J. The latter in 1784, was apprenticed to his uncle, Colonel Matthias Ogden, who was also a tanner and currier.

Colonel Edwards was a very smart man. When twenty years old he went from Elizabethtown, in 1790, to Northampton, Mass., and there commenced a tannery, erected a bank, mill, etc. In 1794 he sent the first leather ever sent from old Hampshire to Boston. He invented the copper heater so long used by the trade. When dry hides began to appear, he commenced his hide mill and perfected his rolling machine. The appearance of the new leather in this city startled the Swamp, and induced Jacob Lorillard to make a long journey to the works to see how the thing was done. It was probably on this visit that Jacob became acquainted with the young Ogden Edwards, who was to succeed him in his business.

Colonel Edwards induced a young shoemaker, who bought leather of him in Northampton in 1836, to come to New York. He offered him a salary of a thousand dollars a year. It was accepted. That young shoemaker was Gideon Lee. A year after he reached here he commenced business in the Swamp as a currier, tanner and leather dealer, in a Ferry street wooden shanty.

Gideon Lee had in after years a clerk and afterwards partner, named Shepherd Knapp. The latter reached the city about 1815. For a long time (to 1839) he did business under the firm of Gideon Lee & Co. Mr.

Knapp is one of the most useful of our citizens. He is President of the Mechanics' Bank.

Old Gideon Lee was a stern man. For many years he lived in Bond street, in a marble front house, nearly opposite where Burdell was killed. That street in 1830 was the fashionable part of the town. At No. 1 lived Dr. Francis before alluded to, and his brother-in-law Samuel Ward, of the firm of Prime, Ward & King. Eli Hart, the great flour merchant, lived next door to Mr. Lee. James G. King also lived in Bond street.

Most of the people who live in that street now are surgeon dentists. It is proposed that it shall be called Dentist street.

Mr. Lee was alderman of the twelfth ward (then — 1828 — comprising Bond street as well as up to Harlem river). He was once a member of the State legislature in 1822. In 1833 he was our mayor.

When Mr. Lee was run for alderman, Peter Cooper was elected assistant alderman.

Mr. Lee was the last mayor elected by the common council. That year (1833) the system of election of mayor was amended, and in 1834, for the first time, was submitted to the people. The contest was between G. C. Verplanck and Cornelius W. Lawrence. The latter was elected, receiving 17,575 votes; the other received 17,372.

In 1836 Mr. Lee was elected to Congress. In 1838 he left New York and went to reside at Geneva, where he had purchased a splendid property. He died in that village in August 1841, aged sixty-four. He left sons and daughters and a large fortune.

Peter McCartee was a famed Swamp man in his day. He died about twenty-five years ago. He was a currier and resided at No. 12 Jacob street, on the east side.

He was at least seventy-eight years old when he died, in 1835.

Richard Cunningham was a tanner and currier, and also "morocco manufacturer." He had his tannery and manufactory near the old powder house and sun fish pond, at the foot of Murray Hill. He died as late as 1840, aged seventy-five years.

He had two partners. One was named Hugh McCormick, and the other was John Murray. They did business under the firm of Cunningham & McCormick, at the place above named. Mr. McCormick died in 1827, aged about fifty-two years.

Thomas Everett was a tanner, having his tannery at Brooklyn and his hide store in the Swamp. He died about twenty years ago, aged seventy. His son, Valentine Everett, succeeded him in the same business.

Thomas Brooks was a general dealer, and did business in Partition street. He retired about twenty years ago, and died in 1855, aged sixty-eight years.

William Kumbell is probably the oldest merchant in the Swamp. He is a tanner and currier and patent band manufacturer, and has done business in Ferry street since 1812 — forty-eight years ago — and continues to do business there yet.

James and George Brooks, tanners and leather dealers, did business in Greenwich street for a long time, and afterwards removed to the Swamp. They commenced about 1820, and James continues business yet in Spruce street, under the firm of James Brooks & Co.

Some of the more ancient dwellers in the Swamp, whose names belong to the history of the city, were:

First, Abraham Polhemus. He was a famed tanner and currier. His tannery was in Ferry street, and extended to Jacob street. He and two others named below — Tooker and Ortley — occupied with their tanneries nearly the whole block bounded by Ferry, Jacob, Frankfort, and Gold streets. Mr. Polhemus died in 1815, aged eighty years.

Henry Ortley, before mentioned, was a tanner and had his tannery in Frankfort street, extending from the corner of Jacob to the corner of Gold street, on which last corner he had his dwelling-house. He died in 1812, in his sixty-fifth year.

Daniel Tooker died in 1805 (two years after Israel Corse started business), aged eighty-three years. His immense tannery was in Jacob street, and extended through to Gold.

Peter Bonnett had a large tannery on the corner of Skinner street (now Cliff), extending to the present blacksmith shop. This he occupied until 1810. He died in 1854, aged eighty-five years.

"All these men were Swampers."

CHAPTER XXXI.

After I had written somewhat of Jacob Lorillard of "the Swamp," who was many years tanner and currier and hide dealer in that region, and prided himself, when alive, that he was so employed for a long time — a friend called upon me with a book containing "the Life of Jacob Lorillard, by Rev. Mr. Berrian, D. D."

I do not pretend to give the full life of any one merchant, because I have not the materials. The Rev. Mr. Berrian does, for there is evidence that he had access to papers that could only have been afforded to him by the Lorillard family. Without any egotism, or without caring two straws, I will say that there is more of the real, every-day life of Jacob Lorillard in our unpretending chapters than in all the clergyman has written.

No wonder that merchants' biographies are stupid affairs. They are given with their "Sunday-go-to-meetin clothes" on. With rich and rare materials out of which to make a capital life of Jacob Lorillard, and a most readable book, Mr. Berrian has made a "funeral sermon" instead of a life. Will it be believed of the merchant, Jacob Lorillard, whom we wrote about recently, that his biographer, Dr. Berrian, does not even allude to his having been in the leather business?

I gather a few items of wheat from the chaff, and

add it to my own "old merchants;" "Jacob's father was of French and his mother of German descent. He was born in the city of New York in 1774," says Mr. Berrian. I had it that he died in 1839, aged 68 years. Mr. Berrian don't say when he died.

Mr. Berrian states that while Jacob was an apprentice to the tobacco business "the business in which the greater part of his life was spent, he passed his evenings in the patient study of the elements of knowledge which are usually learned in childhood." He adds; "He mastered in the same way the French language and afterwards the German." This could not have been a very hard task if his father was French and his mother German."

Mr. Berrian says; "he entered upon business with a capital of a thousand dollars, increased by a loan from his brothers of double that amount."

Three thousand dollars in cash in 1795 was a pretty good capital for any kind of business.

Mr. Berrian mentions that Mr. Jacob Lorillard was:

"A member of the New York Lyceum and Horticultural society."

"A trustee of the General Theological Seminary."

"A warden of St. Andrews church, Harlem."

"A vestryman of Trinity church."

"President of the German society."

"President of the Mechanics' society."

"President of the Mechanics' Bank."

He forgets that had he never been a swamp tanner and currier, he would have never been in all the subsequent positions.

Can it be possible that Mr. Berrian omitted the great occupation of Jacob Lorillard's early life, because he regarded it as a disagreeable one? So did not Mr.

Lorillard regard it, and so did not the author of this book.

Jacob Lorillard was one of the best judges of leather in the Swamp, and he must have been regularly brought up to the tanning and currying trade, consequently he could not have been an apprentice to the tobacco business. In fact, I know that he was not. In my last chapter I stated that his tannery was on the corner of Pearl and Ferry or Frankfort street. That was an error of the pen. I meant on the corner of Pearl and Cross street (now Park street, and near Centre.)

In that tannery he served his apprenticeship. He afterwards bought and conducted it many years. He frequently boasted that this was the first property in real estate that he ever owned in New York. It is now owned by Dr. Ward of University Place. The doctor married his daughter.

Late in life, Jacob Lorillard kept his store at 16 and 18 Ferry street, and his residence was at No. 14 Ferry street. Fifteen years later, he removed to 48 Hudson street.

Jacob was a most energetic man. It is well known that for a great many years he was President of the "Mechanics' Bank." He took hold of it when its affairs were at a very low ebb — in fact, in a sinking condition. He brought its credit up, and made its stock the best bank stock in the city.

It is some years since he died, but long previous to that event — say twenty-five years ago — he divided up among his children an enormous amount, and yet retained an immense estate for himself. He gave as his reason for so large a distribution in advance of his death, that he wished his children to learn to take care of property, and to share its responsibility with himself.

Jacob was brother to Peter and George Lorillard of 30 Chatham street (old numbering, forty-five years ago, and afterwards 42 Chatham, the same building, but new number.) Old Peter himself lived at 30. Afterwards he removed his residence to 39 Chambers street.

Peter and George — P. & G. Lorillard, fifty years ago, 1810, were so rich, that even then they would never give a note. When they made purchases "on time," they expected to cash them at a good discount, and used every excuse to pay cash, and squirmed out of any note giving. If a concern refused to allow any discount, they would pay cash before giving a "promise to pay."

George died long before either of his brothers. He was a bachelor.

He left one of those queer wills, entailing his property sixty years. He violated a State law passed in 1828, forbidding property to be entailed. There was a step-brother named Hulse mixed up in the case. The will was contested, and finally broken. The result was, the vast estate of George came into good hands again, viz: his two brothers Jacob and Peter. It was over two millions of dollars in value when George died.

Jacob himself, when he divided up, shared twelve hundred houses among his children.

I have already mentioned that there was a brother accidentally wounded. It was Peter.

The deeds and documents held by Peter and George long before they died, can be fancied by a little anecdote.

Jacob went into the store of a neighbor in the Swamp and asked him to dress twelve sheep skins in a particular manner, that Mr. Lorillard described in detail.

Perceiving the astonishment of Col. K---- at so unusual an order, he observed, "The fact is, these skins are for my brothers, Peter and George. They want them to make bags in which to keep the deeds and titles of their real estate."

I am cheered occasionally by an approving letter from some of the old and honored human landmarks in the present century.

The aged Grant Thorburn writes me a letter in his own handwriting. A postscript is written at the foot in the handwriting of a young lady. She says: "Grant does not know any one named Walter Barrett." That is so, nor would Grant know the author, unless the latter could get back the pleasant boy's face he wore a part of a century ago, when in skylarking he used to break the glass panes that covered the flower beds in the open space before Grant's old church flower and seed storehouse in Liberty street.

I give a copy of the letter. The original, in the aged Grant's handwriting, I shall keep as long as I live. About Jacob Barker I shall have a good deal to say in a future chapter.

"I knew every individual mentioned in your list of Old Yorkers.

"It's sixty-six years and seven months since I first saw New York. At that time the city contained only 40,000 inhabitants. Broadway commenced at the Battery and terminated at the head of Warren street. There was only one church in the city, above the Park. Hence, either at church or market, we saw each other often at that period. New York was in fact the city of brotherly love.

"Among our prominent, bustling merchants, was Jacob Barker. He kept a bank of his own in Wall street for some years. It was called the New York Exchange Bank. His notes were as current as any in Wall street. Finally, he stopped payment. A poor widow in my neighborhood came in my store weeping having a ten dollar bill on Jacob's bank in her hand. I told her to be of good cheer. I took the note to the bank—stated the case to Jacob—he cashed the bill at once, like an honest man.

"Jacob Barker and Matthew L. Davis were the last friends that Aaron Burr possessed on earth. When Burr returned from Europe, whither he had fled after his duel with Hamilton, he kept his office on the west corner of Pine and Nassau streets. Having no clients, he was pleased when I stepped in to chat an hour. One day he remarked, 'when stopping in London I was apprehended as a spy under the alien law. I claimed my right as a British subject, having been born before the Revolution, and was discharged.'

GRANT THORBURN.

"Aged 87 years and 11 months."

NEW HAVEN, CONN., JAN. 21, 1862.

That story about Jacob Barker and the $10 bank bill, puts me in mind of another. A young clerk then was made by his employer to go regularly every day, and get the specie for any bills of Jacob's Bank (it was called the New York Exchange Bank) in the possession of the store where he was employed. On one occasion he took down $63 of the Bank. He was late from some cause, and when he entered the building, it was five minutes past bank hours. He saw Jacob Barker.

"Who do you come from?" he asked.

The clerk replied:

"From A. G."

"Give him another bank bill in exchange, said Jacob. It was done. Jacob's bank never opened again after that day.

I recollect Grant Thorburn when he kept around the corner from his old Quaker church store. His garden seed store was then in Nassau, where *The Evening Post* office is now located, and under which John McAuliffe sells his celebrated Irish whisky.

In writing about the Swamp merchants, I should regret not to mention several more than I have yet done.

Within my recollection, James Roosevelt kept at No. 8 Jacob street. It was before Cliff street was opened through. It was in previous years the alley way to the old Roosevelt sugar house.

That property ran back from Jacob street to Franklin square, and was thirty or forty feet wide. In the middle was a large sugar house, which stood where Cliff street now runs. The old sugar house was removed about 1826 or 1827, when Cliff street was cut through from Ferry to Frankfort streets.

Immediately where the street (Cliff) was opened, the Harper Brothers (then J. & J. Harper) occupied a double building at No. 82 Cliff, and also 327 Pearl. Hundreds of young clerks in those days, if they belonged to the "Mercantile Library Association," will recollect the spot, for the Library was for some years kept in the store of J. & J. Harper in Cliff street; and up to the time it was removed to the Clinton Hall, corner of Nassau and Beekman streets.

The locality between Pearl and Jacob was where that old sugar house stood. Many of our readers have frolicked about the old stone pile.

It was famed for a well of the purest spring water,

The alley-way that led up from Jacob street was very wide, and generally contained two or three hundred empty sugar hogsheads.

That old sugar-house was the first erected before the Revolution, and worked during the war and for forty years afterward.

The proprietor who built it, and who manufactured sugar in it, was a great man in his day and generation.

His name was Isaac Roosevelt. His house faced on Queen street, now Pearl, in Franklin square. Harper & Brothers now own that property, and it is No. 333 Pearl street. On the rear of his house and in the centre of the block was the sugar-house. A large alley-way ran up to it from what is now No. 8 Jacob street. The Isaac Roosevelt mansion was originally 159 Queen street. To understand the matter, Queen street in those days of 1786, when the sugar house and the old mansion were in their glory, commenced at Wall street and extended to Chatham, ending there, within a few rods of the great fresh water pond. From Wall street to Smith street, (William,) was Hanover square, from the last to Broad, it was called Dock street. From Broad to the Battery was called Pearl street. Now it is called Pearl from the Battery to Chatham, and even on to Broadway. That part was formerly Magazine street. Almost opposite to Isaac Roosevelt's residence (No. 159 Queen street, now 333 Pearl and part of 331) stood an old building, and it yet stands as 324 and 326 Pearl, and is called now, and has been for sixty years part of the Walton House. In 1786 it was occupied by the Bank of New York, of which Isaac Roosevelt was President.

There were two brothers Walton. One lived at 328,

next door to the double house occupied by the Bank of New York.

After the bank was removed down town, a Walton occupied the double house. Whether he owned and built it, I am unable to say. At any rate, it was occupied by the Bank of New York before the Walton occupied it.

The house next door — No. 328 — was the residence of a Mr. Walton in 1786. It is still standing. Thirty years and more ago, it was kept as a hotel by a Mr. Backus and a worthy man he was, for he was a host to this author about the cholera time of 1832. Abraham Bloodgood bought the old double yellow building or Walton House, occupied by the Bank of New York in 1786. Isaac Roosevelt was President of that bank then the only one in New York. The active old gentleman would get an early breakfast, run into his sugar-house in the rear and direct his son, who was his partner, under the firm of Isaac Roosevelt & Son, and then run across the street to his bank, and there remain and do business from the time it opened at 10 A. M. until it closed at 1 P. M., so that he and his clerk could go home to dinner at 3 P. M., it was opened again for business and was open until 5 P. M. But that was not all old and active Isaac had to do. George Clinton was Governor of the State, and Isaac was one of the seventeen senators of the State of New York. He had legislation to do occasionally. Only a few doors from his house at No. 5 Cherry street, lived John Hancock, for Congress met here in those years and up to 1786. If you wished to find out any Congressman then, you had to apply to "the Congress office, No. 81 Broadway, (old numbering,) corner of King street,

(Pine,) where members are to be heard of." John Anderson & Co. keep a tobacco store there now.

What a lot of great directors president Isaac was surrounded with in his bank! There was Samuel Franklin who lived up at 183 Queen, (corner Pearl and Cherry.) He was son of Walter Franklin, who died in 1780. De Witt Clinton married his daughter. The great merchant, who owned acres thereabout, and who gave his name to the Square.

Another director was Nicholas Low, who did business at 216 Water street. Water street in those days commenced at Burling Slip. Below that point, it was Front street. Mr. Low was father to the Nick Low who died recently, leaving his sister, Mrs. Charles King, wife of the president of Columbia College, $1,000,000.

Another director and vice president too, was William Maxwell. He kept a snuff and tobacco store at No. 4 Wall street. He was the progenitor of the Maxwell family — Hugh and William of our times, but very old they are now.

Another was the great Alexander Hamilton, who lived at No. 57 Wall street, where he practiced law, and even then rivalled Aaron Burr, who also had a law shingle up at No. 10, Little Queen street, (Cedar street,) which many years later Grant Thorburn says, he occupied.

Joshua Waddington was another director. He did business with his brother under the firm of H. & J. Waddington, at No. 30, corner of King and Queen streets, (Pine and Pearl.)

James Buchanan, of the firm of Buchanan & Thompson, 243 Queen street, (Pearl) was a director. He was a great man in our city in his day. The same name is not so popular just now in the new world.

Thomas Randall, who lived at 28 White Hall, was a director. He was of the firm of Randall, Son & Stewarts, merchants at No. 10 Hanover Square.

Comfort Sands, of whom we have spoken in a previous chapter, (Nat Prime married his daughter,) was a director. He was a brother of Joshua Sands, who kept at No. 73 Queen (Pearl) street. He had a rope-walk in Brooklyn also. William Seton was the cashier and lived over the bank. His race and descendants in this city are well known.

The teller in the bank was an humble unassuming young Englishman, who boarded with Mr. Seton, named Charles Wilkes. He arose to be the cashier, and then president of the bank of New York. He was the Hapsburg of the Wilkes family of the town, and uncle of the navy captain who gave a name to "Wilkes Voyages."

This is a bird's eye view upon the past, and now I will go back to the old sugar-house and its owners, Isaac Roosevelt & Son. Their house (now Harper Brothers,) was occupied afterwards by DeWitt Clinton, and many gay scenes were enacted there when he was mayor and recorder. When old Isaac died, I do not know. It was before 1797. The son afterwards kept a sugar refinery at No. 10 Thames street, and resided at No. 18 South street, then containing many dwellings.

The Thames street sugar-house was afterwards occupied by Clark & Co., the Mineral Saratoga Spring water men, who ran opposition to the Jacob street mineral water, and put it down.

Then the old sugar-house was sold, and great buildings were put up there, and called Trinity buildings, by Clafflin, Mellen & Co., who have now removed to their new mammoth store in West Broadway, formerly Chapel street.

That Isaac Roosevelt breed was a proud old stock in New York annals long before the sugar house man. In his day he and his two sons were men of note in the city. He had a son named Oliver, who died young.

James, who lived at 8 Jacob street, another son, was alderman of the Fourth Ward, (present Fourth Ward) in 1809. James Roosevelt lived for some thirty years in Bleecker street, and died at the age of eighty-four, having been married three times. Firstly, to Miss Walton; secondly, to Miss Barclay; and lastly, to a Miss Howland, sister of the late Gardiner G. and Samuel Howland. Although he had numerous children, but two survived him; a son, Isaac Roosevelt, now residing at Hyde Park, and a daughter. Cornelius and James J. Roosevelt are of another branch of the Roosevelt family, not being descended from Isaac Roosevelt.

Isaac left three daughters, the eldest of whom married Richard Varick, once mayor of this city.

A daughter of James Roosevelt, married a Mr. Bailey. A son of the marriage is James Roosevelt Bailey, the honored Catholic bishop of New Jersey. The grandson of James Roosevelt, (the son of Isaac,) inherited nothing from his grandfather, the portion which would otherwise have been his having been willed to a Protestant theological seminary, on account of his having embraced the Catholic religion. Mr. Roosevelt, on hearing his grandson had become a Catholic, put a codicil to his will annulling his former large bequest to him, and cutting him off without a penny. Many of the Bishop's relatives and friends urged him to contest the will, but his indifference to all worldly goods, as well as his amiable, gentle disposition, would not allow it.

Roosevelt Bailey, Bishop of Newark, in a pecuniary point of view, is poor, which would have been otherwise had his grandparent not altered his will. If I mistake not, his reasons for so doing are mentioned in the codicil.

I did not enumerate one quarter of the high offices held by Isaac Roosevelt, the sugar house owner, who was President of the Bank of New York, when the New York Hospital had a charter granted by the State, 13th June, 1771.

In 1792, old Isaac Roosevelt was President of the Board of Governors; and John Murray, mentioned in a former chapter, was treasurer. Their neighbor, Gerard Walton, was also a Governor. These three men all lived in Queen street, and in that part now called Franklin Square. Aaron Burr was also a Governor of the Hospital.

Jacob Roosevelt, bought in 1728 ten lots, each being 25 x 120 feet, "in the Swamp, near the Cripple Bush," for ten pounds each, through which a few years later Roosevelt street was opened. The same Jacob afterwards bought the whole of Beekman Swamp for one hundred pounds, through which his son afterwards opened Ferry street. Isaac, who opened the Sugar House on a part of this property, was a grandson of old Jacob.

Old President, Isaac's father, was named Nicholas. He was an alderman in 1748 to 1767.

Another brother of the last was alderman of a ward from 1659 to 1765. His name was Cornelius. A still elder ancestor was an alderman in 1700.

There is one of the same name since become famed in commerce. James J. started in business in Maiden Lane at 102, (old number) now 94, as early as 1797. He was in the hardware business. He continued business as late as 1824, under the firm of James Roosevelt & Son. He lived at 99 Maiden Lane, and afterwards at 45 Broadway.

He is the father of James J. J., who is now U. S. District Attorney, and has been alderman, member of Congress, judge, &c. He married the daughter of one of the best men I ever knew, and that was good old Governor Van Ness of Vermont.

Judge James J. J. Roosevelt I once met in Holland, and trotted him all about Rotterdam, during a great *Kermis* (Fair) to ascertain whether the New York Dutch, (which he spoke) was the same as spoken in Holland. As the Holland Dutchmen and women could not understand Mr. Roosevelt, I concluded that their dialect had deteriorated from that spoken by the Dutch 200 years previous, when the "original Jacobus" Roosevelt left Holland for New Amsterdam.

There was a widow Margaret Roosevelt lived at 15 (afterwards 19) John street, a great many years. I could never make out whose widow she was.

Another James Roosevelt started in business in old neighborhood, 333 Pearl street near Peck Slip, before 1800. Forty years later the firm of E. J. & H. Roosevelt was doing business at 309 — same place probably, and son of the old James.

A son of James J., of Maiden Lane, is one of the finest men in New York, worth two millions, and a director in the Chemical Bank. His name is C. V. S.

CHAPTER XXXII.

Thomas Musgrove used to live in the Swamp, in Jacob, corner of Frankfort street, where he had a morocco factory.

Henry A. Burr, the great hat man, bought that property of the heirs, and also some lots adjoining, on Cliff street, and has built there an immense building, reaching almost up to the clouds, and as large as the Astor House. In the centre are ponderous wheels moving, and terrible steam engines in operation. Part of the building is used by John A. Gray, a printer of the city in 1862. The other part is used by the owner, Henry A. Burr & Co., in their hat body business. Mr. Burr has a patent for making particular hat bodies, and all the hatters in the United States pay tribute to him. Hence he does an immense business. The great engines do the work for both Burr and Gray.

The old owner of the larger portion of this property was the above named Thomas Musgrove. He was an Englishman, and started in the Swamp very poor. He determined to re-visit England at some future day, but said he would wait "until he could go in his own ship." He realized his determination, for he made a large sum of money. He went to England, and although he came back to his adopted land, he died where he was born. His heirs sold out to Mr. Burr. Mr. Musgrove left no sons. He had three daughters. One married Daniel Braine, who had been a clerk to Mr. Musgrove, and succeeded him in business, on the same spot, but afterwards failed. Her maiden name was Ann Musgrove. The second daughter, Betsey, married a brother of Daniel, named James H. Braine, of the firm of Roland & Braine. They were in the flour business and shipping trade to Nova Scotia. He went to England with his father-in-law, Musgrove. He died well off. He was one of the excutors of Musgrove. The third daughter married a Mr. Griffiths, a leather dealer. His wife died sometime ago. They had no children. Whether he is living or not I do not know. Daniel Braine left several children. His widow is still alive.

James H. Braine left several children.

Another old Swamp resident was Joseph Thompson. He was not a leather dealer, but kept a grocery at 58 Frankfort street, head of Jacob street, as late as 1832. He had a store also at 393 Pearl street. Thompson was originally a shoemaker, before he sold rum. He was the father of the celebrated "One-Eyed Thompson," whose real name was William. Old Joseph had several children. He sold rum in his grocery, and his wife was one of his first victims. He was a great fisherman, and was away on fishing excursions half his time. William, or "One-Eye," was the oldest. When quite a boy he lost the use of his eye by a pin dart sent into it by one of his playmates. A remarkably clever youth, was Thompson, but was mixed up in city criminal matters to an alarming extent. His suicide and remarkable letter to his wife will be remembered by many of our readers. He had an idea that if he were dead, the world would use his wife and family better than if he were alive. I believe he was mistaken. His death was a nine days' wonder, and was then forgotten. His father, old Joseph Thompson, failed in the Swamp, and then retired to East New York (Long Island,) resumed shoemaking, and there died. Old Joe was well off at one time, but never rich.

Another old Swamper was George Gilpin, who kept a leather store at 56 Frankfort street, and resided at No. 31. He also kept at No. 15 Jacob street. Mr. Gilpin was a Quaker from Delaware, and in the Revolutionary War had been a drummer. He used to smile and be very much pleased when he encountered our citizen soldiers with fife and drum. He had married two or three times. His widow lived in Vandewater street, No. 22. She died very recently. One of Mr. Gilpin's daughters is still living. She married Rowland Robinson, an old Quaker. He is dead. Her name was Rachel.

Michael Lowber was a tanner in Philadelphia, and had several brothers in the business. He failed, and came to New York during the last war, and started boot crimping in Higgins' blacksmith shop, in Frankfort street, near Cliff. He afterwards lived at No. 64, and carried on the currier business at No. 66 Frankfort street. He died, leaving several sons. His widow, fifteen years afterwards, kept a boarding house at No. 255 Pearl.

William C. Lowber, one of his sons, kept an ink factory at No. 37 Ferry street, corner of Cliff.

Another son was ship news reporter to the *Courier and Enquirer* for many years. One of his sons is the famed Lowber who dealt in real estate, sold some to the Corporation, sued the city, got judgment, and sold the

City Hall and contents at auction, when A. C. Flagg was comptroller. Old Michael lived in New York. It was proposed to him at one time that he should go to Philadelphia. "No," said he, "I had rather die in New York than live in any other place." His widow died some time ago. A very lovely daughter married Charles Dall, a carpenter, at 39 Chapel street. Another son of old Michael, if I am not mistaken, was commander of the steamer "Ericsson."

Abraham Bloodgood was a remarkable man. He was an old currier and leather merchant in the Swamp, and did a very large business for many years; retired from business in the Swamp about 1815, and resided at No. 52 Frankfort street. His son John M. carried on business at No. 62, afterwards.

Old Abraham died in 1807, aged seventy-five. Up to that time he was President of the Contribution Fire Insurance Company, holding that office at the time of his death.

He had several children; three sons, and, I think, one daughter. John M. was one. Young Abraham was a midshipman, and commanded a gun boat during the last war. He was engaged in the attack made on a British frigate off New Rochelle. He was a great, puffy person. A third son, and the youngest, never did any business, but lived upon his money. I think he is yet living. John M. and Abraham, Jr. are both dead; a daughter was married.

Old Abraham was a stern character, and in his day a great Tammany Hall man, and a leading politician. He commenced as early as the start of the Republican party under Jefferson in 1801. He was eleeted assistant alderman of the Fourth Ward by that party in 1804 and again in 1807.

Previous to that time he had shown his earnestness by deeding away his store to make Republican voters in the Fourth Ward for the election of 1801.

It is very curious that in those days the Federalists nicknamed the Republicans by calling them Democrats, in scorn for their supposed sympathy with the French Jacobins and bloody Democrats of the French Revolution. Nor was the title adopted by the Republican party until the election of Jackson in 1828, when men of that party called themselves Democrats. To carry the election in 1801, the Republicans, and foremost among them Abraham Bloodgood, commenced to make votes. None were voters except freemen and freeholders, and it was necessary that a man should have a freehold estate in landed property to entitle him to the elective franchise for charter officers. The law shut out many worthy citizens. In the Fifth Ward property was purchased by many persons. Mr. Bloodgood in the Fourth deeded his store to thirty citizens. The ward was carried by twenty-five majority for his party.

Among his political friends were David Bryson, John Targee and James Hopson.

Mr. Bryson was a tanner and currier at 48 Frankfort street, and had a house at 46. It was a two story wooden house. His tan yard is now owned by Colonel Kumble.

Targee was a gold and silversmith at 192 Water street, between Burling Slip and Fulton street. His house was in the Fourth Ward, at 27 Frankfort street. They were called the "Swamp clique," and for years ruled the democratic party. Old Mr. Bloodgood's store in Frankfort street was the rendezvous. It was called "Swamp Place." All the leaders of the party could be found at that spot occasionally. Grand schemes were concocted there.

Mr. Bloodgood was a great talker. He always enjoyed the best of credit, and was rich. His ideas in politics were confined. He believed in nobody who did not side with him in his political views. He was devoted body and soul to Jackson.

The David Bryson before alluded to was a great man in his latitude. I believe he was an Irishman, and that he came to this country at the time of the Irish rebellion in 1798, when Dr. McNevin, Emmett, and other Irish patriots came here. He commenced business in the Swamp as a tanner and currier, and made himself well off by 1814. When prosperity dawned upon him in his new home, he displayed the true Irish feeling by sending out funds to Ireland to bring out the rest of his family who were not so well off as himself. His parents came over. David Bryson was a most worthy man, and those who knew him best loved him most.

He had a son Peter M. Bryson, who is cashier of the Phenix Bank. The elder Bryson had much to do with that bank in getting it incorporated. He owned largely of its stock. He was for a long time one of its directors. He died in that capacity. Out of respect to his memory, and regard for his son, who had long been a clerk in the bank, they made him cashier. David Bryson left a large estate. His house, a two story frame building, in Frankfort street, standing back, opposite Gold street, still stands. The son asks for it $30,000. He has the true Knickerbocker feeling about selling. He asks a certain price in advance of the times, when parties get up to it, he adds on another $5,000, and so it has been going on for some time

They never reach his price. This is the way all the old hold-on Knickerbockers become so very wealthy.

Abraham Bloodgood's son John M. was a character in his day. He went by several nicknames: Jack, Justice, and Commissioner. He was a street commissioner in 1830, and resided at 604 Broadway. He married a daughter of a painter, — Cornelius Hoffman, who lived in the Swamp at No. 2 Jacob street. She had some property. J. M. Bloodgood's life would be equal to any romance.

John M. kept in Frankfort street, opposite Jacob. He rebuilt the store on his father's old place, and then carried on boot crimping. He failed in it before 1828, and afterwards took office and left the Swamp. He was a Police Justice a long time. He made a funny magistrate. He was merciful always to good looking girls, that came before him for justice. He rarely committed any female if she was very pretty, but would tell her to fix herself up and be a better girl in future.

He was eccentric. On one, if not more occasions, he started on New Year's day with a large basket, and went around to rich people and collected cakes, pies, meat and any other kind of eatables. When his basket was full, he went with it among the poor and needy, and distributed the contents. Again he would replenish from the able and again dispense food to the needy, and so he kept on doing until after sun down, relieving distress.

What a noble example to follow! How much better than getting silly drunk, and making ninnies of themselves, as thousands of our youths did last New Year's day.

Jack Bloodgood could drink more than a fish; yet he never was seen by any man or woman so drunk as to stagger. He was an immense favorite in this town —

particularly among old New Yorkers, and even now tears will start in some men's eyes when you talk of old Jack. In his way, old Jack was as great a Sport as ever lived in New York city. He was a good-hearted man though rough.

Jack was succeeded in the boot crimping business by Ely J. Lundy, who kept a wooden shanty in Frankfort, opposite Jacob street. He had invented a machine for forcing leather into a kind of shape. Both Lundy and John M. Bloodgood were firemen, and belonged to No. 7.

Justice James Hopkins was also a member of the same company. He was a Swamper and lived in Vandewater street, No. 24. He lived there before the war, and as late as 1844. He died in that house, I believe.

Another fireman belonging to No. 7, was a German named Dieterich, who lived on the corner of Frankfort and Pearl, No. 351. The old German kept a bakery before 1795, under the firm of George Dieterich. His son was taken in forty-five years ago. One son kept at 42 Sixth street. Another son, named Daniel, was a crimper at 64 Frankfort, and lived at 102 Cliff. Old George, (the son in 1815) is still living. Henry was the fireman, and belonged to No. 7 engine, kept in Rose street, just out of Frankfort street.

This Dieterich and James Hopson, (before the latter was a chief magistrate,) were with their engine at a fire in Vesey street, on the north side and below Church James Hopson was the foreman of the company. Dieterich was a dashing, daring fellow, and held the pipe. A chimney fell and buried both Hopson and Dieterich. A fireman got hold of the pipe, and tried to play water upon the burning bricks, when Jack Bloodgood, who belonged to the company, and who was a mighty power ful man, came to the rescue. He scattered the bricks, got hold of the two men, and dragged them out. They were both badly burned and bruised, but luckily no bones were broken, which was very remarkable. Neither Hopson nor Dieterich left their homes for weeks and months.

Daniel Dieterich succeeded Jack Bloodgood in the crimping business, and was in it himself many years after Bloodgood failed and retired.

John Jacob Astor was once in the employ of old George Dieterich and peddled cakes for him.

In Chapter 20, I stated that John Jacob Astor peddled cakes, cookies, and tea rusks, and daily supplied the little shop kept by old Abraham Bininger's wife, aunt Katy, in 20 and 22 Augusta street, now City Hall Place, and that he was then a boy of eighteen or twenty years of age, but recently arrived in this country.

I stated also in another chapter that in the early years of our city, the largest bakeries sent out their apprentices to peddle and cry the luxuries of the oven, and that it was in this capacity that Astor peddled cakes.

I also stated that on one occasion, Mrs. Ehninger (who was John Jacob's sister, and had married a George Ehninger, a distiller of cordials,) got vexed that her brother sneered at her husband's occupation. She replied: " Yakob was noting put a paker poy und sold pread und kak."

Astor was born in 1763, and arrived in New York in the summer of 1784. The first night he ever slept in New York was in the house of old George Dieterich, in Queen street. It is now 351 Pearl street, and stands on the corner of Frankfort. At that time no street had been cut through from Pearl to where Frankfort ended, a few feet past Vandewater street.

Old George Dieterich was a German, and had known Mr. Astor on the other side of the water. For some days he made his home with Mr. Dieterich, in that fashionable neighborhood; found his brother Harry, who was a butcher boy, and hired to a man who sold meat in the Oswego market, then standing on the north-east corner of Broadway and Maiden Lane, where the Howard House now stands.

Old George finding young Jacob anxious to be employed, hired him to peddle cakes, cookies, doughnuts, &c. For a long time young Astor continued with Mr. Dieterich, but seeing an opening for an active young man, he hired a store in Queen street, a little further up, on the opposite side. It was a wooden shanty, and the first building rented by the since great Astor. It was at 362 Pearl street. Here Mr. Astor commenced selling toys and German nicknacks.

Watson, in his "Annals of New York," confirms my statement. He says, in 1841 — "John Jacob Astor, so very rich, is a German who began among us with a store of German toys; can now build a hotel worth half a million, and give it to his son. The brother of John John Jacob Astor was a butcher and was very rich also."

In contrast to these facts, what a lie the "Life of Astor" is. One written by D. R. Jacques, says: "Astor brought over with him a few hundred dollars worth of musical instruments to Baltimore. Among the passengers on the ship was a furrier, very clever in the business, very shrewd, and willing to communicate. Astor made his acquaintance. His attention had been previously directed to the fur trade, and he accordingly addressed numerous inquiries to his new friend in relation to the various kinds and qualities of fur, and the mode of transacting business. The furrier advised him to go to New York, and ultimately accompanied him thither. The proceeds of the musical instruments were, by his advice, invested in furs. With them he hastened back to London, where they were disposed of to great advantage. He at once prepared to cross the Atlantic, and devote himself systematically to the fur trade, as the business of his life. To do this, it was neccessary to study the markets of Leipsic and London, and the other fur markets of Europe."

Peanuts! How ridiculous to write such highfalutin stuff of such a man as Astor. There are hundreds in our midst even now who know better—know that it is not true—know that Mr. Astor's first years in this city, were years of humble struggling—they know that he peddled cakes—know that he dwelt with old German George Dieterich, at 351 Pearl street—know that he started a toy shop afterwards, and when John Jacob got into the fur business, it was not in at the "cabin windows." For a long time he peddled skins, and bought them where he could; and bartered cheap jewelry, birds, &c., from the pack he carried on his back.

A historian says: "When Utica first began its career, John Jacob Astor and Peter Smith traveled the ground from Schenectady to Utica, purchasing furs at the Indian settlements on the route. The Indians aided them in carrying them back to Schenectady. They opened a store in New York city for their sale; and when their stock was exhausted, they again penetrated the lonely forests of the frontiers, and replenished their store. Astor continued this business many years, but Smith purchased land, and died at Schenectady very rich.

Gerritt Smith is the son of this Peter Smith.

What a romance is in Astor's real life, but not in such stuff as cooked up by Jacques.

To return to the residence of old George Dieterich, the baker, where Astor lived. The old gentleman would be a hundred years old, if he were alive now. He was in business as late as 1815, with his son George. That son is now a man, aged over eighty years; very rich, but a bachelor.

The old mansion, 351 Pearl street, stands yet. The upper part is the same, as in the days of the Revolution. Many a party has Washington attended in that old house. It is rich even now in quaint wood carving. The present store underneath is what was once the cellar of the house, that part of Pearl street having been lowered within a few years ten feet. G. Prince & Co., extensive druggists and apothecaries, keep the store 351, which was established in 1825. The upper part is the same as it was seventy years ago. It is occupied as a boarding house.

CHAPTER XXXIII.

Among the most eminent of the commercial names that this city can boast of, stands that of Murray. Prior to the Revolution, Robert Murray in 1769 owned more tons of shipping than any other man in America.

Previous to the advent of Robert, there had lived in this city Joseph Murray, who was a lawyer of note, and after whom Murray street was named. That street was regulated in 1773. This Joseph, from 1720 to 1726, was a vestryman of Trinity Church, and from 1726 to 1758 a warden — 37 years. The street ran through the "King's Farm" owned by Trinity Church, and she had the naming of the street. Mr. Joseph Murray was one of the first trustees of King's (Church) College.

Old Robert, the merchant, is celebrated not only for owning more ships than anybody else, but also for being one of the five persons rich enough to keep a coach. The Governor had a coach — Gerard Walton had another. Colden, the Lieut. Governor kept a coach, which was burnt before his window by a mob. Mrs. Alexander had a coach, and Robert Murray had one. He was a Quaker, or "Friend." He called his carriage "my leather conveniency," in order to avoid the scandal of pride and vain glory.

This Robert was not born in New York. He was from Swetara, near Lancaster, Pennsylvania, where he had a flour mill in 1732 to 1745. He was an enterprising, go-ahead person, and made several voyages to the West Indies in the way of trade. Slowly and by degrees he amassed a large property, and eventually became the greatest of New York merchants. He had extensive concerns in ships, and was engaged in every sort of mercantile business. About 1750, Mr. Murray went to North Carolina to reside, but left that State in 1753, to settle in New York city.

Old Robert Murray had a farm out on the East River, in the neigborhood of old Doctor Gerardus Beekman's place, at the head of Kings Road. There Mrs. Murray entertained General Howe and his staff with refreshments, after their landing at Kipp's Bay, on purpose to afford time to General Putnam to lead off his troops in retreat from the city, which he effected. She was mother to the celebrated Lindley Murray, as well as John, Jr.

Lindley Murray, the grammarian, used often to leap across Burling Slip, twenty-one feet, with a pair of fowls in his hand, as he came from market. His lameness was afterwards imputed to this cause.

I presume Robert Murray resided at one time in Franklin Square, or in that vicinity. His son, John Jr resided at 155 Queen street (now 335) for many years. He occupied that house as early as 1786, and he died there in 1819, leaving two sons and a widowed daughter.

The numbering of streets in those early years must have been curious, and somewhat after the Spanish fashion in Cuba. The houses in Queen street were numbered continuously on each side, and in the order and date of building. For instance, the two Waltons,

William and Gerard, resided next to each other; these houses numbered 67 and 68, now comprise 326 and 328. On the opposite side John Jr. lived at 155, near Isaac Roosevelt, at 159 Queen street, now 333 Pearl street, (Harper's Building) and George Dieterich at 150 Queen now 351 Pearl street. The latter house more up town than the lower numbers, 155 and 159.

Murray & Sansom lived at 188 Queen street. John Murray was also of that firm, and lived in that house. He was a brother of old Robert Murray, and a very eminent merchant. He was uncle to John, Jr.

The bold and daring shipowner, old Robert, died the 22d of July, 1786. He had suffered thirty years. All his living children, except Lindley Murray, who was at York, England, were about the dying bed of old Commerce.

The Murrays were Quakers. I think old Robert died at 188 Queen street, where his brother John, firm of Murray & Sansom, lived in 1792. I presume that 188 Queen was near where the second Quaker church was erected in this city in 1775. It was on Pearl street, between Franklin Square and Oak street. It was torn down in 1824, and stores and dwellings erected in its place.

Another of the name and house of Murray existed in 1786, and founded the concern of Murray, Mumford & Bowen. They did business at Crane Wharf, now Beekman street, from Pearl to the water. Fifteen years later Bowen went out of the concern, and its style was Murray & Mumford, and they kept their counting house at No. 73 Stone street. I have no doubt but that this family descended from the old lawyer, Joseph, who named Murray street.

Murray & Mumford did not dissolve until after 1805,

but in what precise year I do not remember. From that house sprung in after years J. B. Murray & Son, 73 Stone. J. B. lived at 129 Chambers street. Robert Murray was a son. They afterwards did business at 66 South street. Hamilton Murray was in that concern. That J. B. Murray was the only one of the name in this city that dabbled in politics. He was once assistant alderman of the Ninth Ward, and in after years (1831) alderman of the Fifteenth Ward.

From that branch came also the great house Murray & Gallagher, No. 72 South street. That large concern was in existence from 1820 to 1837. It was second to but two or three houses in the city. They did an immense business. In 1834, or thereabouts, old Mr. Gallagher died, and the old Murray went out. Then Hamilton Murray came in with John Gallagher, the brother of the first named Gallagher. The house got embarrassed in 1837. Hamilton Murray had a beautiful sister, who married Judge John G. Mason. She was a most lovely specimen of the American woman.

The old Gallagher was from beautiful Geneva, in this State. His widow went back there and lived in a Paradise with beautiful daughters. Moses Gallagher married Miss Murray. George Gallagher, a son of the old gentleman, was for a long time in the employ of Howland & Aspinwall. In an evil hour he was tempted to go into the political instead of commercial world, and he bough *The True Sun.* He owned it in the disastrous cam paign of 1848, and after George had sunk several thousands, *The True Sun* sunk never to rise more. Poor George, who kept up under all difficulties, was finally reduced to the position of holding a weighmaster's office in the Custom House.

"Ham" Murray, as he was called in his halcyon

days, when he was a leader of fashion, retired from New York to become the president of the leading bank in Oswego. He is the financier of that region, owns a beautiful place, wife and so forth.

I return to Quaker John Murray, Jr. He was connected with a brewery that stood at 13 Oliver and 50 Catherine street. The firm was Murray & Cunningham. He was a great philanthropist, and engaged in every good work. As early as the Revolutionary war there was a society called "the Society for Promoting the Manumission of Slaves, and protecting such of them as have been or may be liberated." — "Meets at the Coffee House." John Jay was president, and John Murray, Jr., was treasurer. Quakers composed the standing committee. Such names as Samuel Franklin, John Keese, Willet and Jacob Seaman, William Shotwell and others. This was the parent of all the Abolition Societies, and flourished seventy-five years ago.

These two John Murrays were both celebrated in that day. John junior resided at No. 155 Queen, (now 335 Pearl street,) and John Murray at 188 Queen, firm of Murray and Sansom.

Both were public men, but I cannot now always distinguish them in their acts for the public good. John, the nephew, was called Junior, to distinguish him from the John who lived at 188, his father's brother.

They flourished in the same years and in the same part of the town. The nephew was the brewer. While John junior flourished in every good work John senior, the uncle, was also prominent in benevolent and other enterprises.

He was a director of the United States Bank in 1804. He was also treasurer to the Governors of the New York

Hospital in 1792. In 1804, John junior held the same office.

Old John Murray was a very large importing merchant. In 1800 he kept at 27 Beekman street, under the firm of John Murray & Son. In 1804 they kept at 209 Pearl street; and yet later in 1815 at foot of Liberty street. John Murray died worth half a millon. He had several clerks who afterwards became leading merchants. Samuel D. Reed, G. W. Somarindyck, and Merrit Pickering were among the number.

In those days to be a bank director made any man a most important citizen and influential person; and when John Murray was made a director of the old United States Branch Bank in this city, he was a made man. He often said that at one period of his life he was on the verge of bankrupcy. He had met with immense losses, and it seemed impossible that he could sustain himself.

Some time previous to his embarrassments he had purchased a ticket in the English lottery. At that time lotteries were permitted in England, and tickets were sent out and sold in the Colonies. There was an agency in Little Queen street, (Cedar.) They were undoubtedly conducted honestly, and in a very different manner from the Ben Wood, Brother & Co's., notorious schemes of the present day, that beggar thousands, engender murder and suicide, to fill the purses and add to the wealth of the parties who own them.

The day previous to the one fixed upon by merchant John Murray to stop payment, a vessel arrived from London, and brought the news of the drawing. Mr. Murray found that he was the holder of the number that had drawn the highest prize. He then lived in a large double house in Pearl street, above Fulton street, then called Beekman Slip, (269 Pearl.) His son lived near St. John's Church. He built up a row on Laight street. I think his son was John R.. The old merchant died in that house in Pearl street. As I said before, he was in 1792 of the firm of Murray & Sansom, and lived and did business at No. 188 Queen street, (Pearl.) He had a country house out by the old Powder House, and Sun-fish pond, (near Twentieth street,) was part of the property. He owned all Murray Hill, named after him. In 1792 he was a director of the Bank of New York. He was also a director of the Mutual Assurance Company. He was in 1792 Vice-President of the Chamber of Commerce, and in 1804, was President of that body. It then met in the Tontine Coffee House. Same year he was director of the United States Bank. He was a director of the Humane Society established for the relief of distressed prisoners.

We, at this period of time (when happily for some of us, there is no imprisonment for debt), can hardly comprehend the value of this Society, of which John Murray was a director. New York was comparatively a small place to what it now is, and yet 131 prisoners would be frequently locked up in the old jail in the Park for debt. The Society furnished these unfortunate individuals with soup and fuel. Fifteen thousand and odd quarts of soup in a few months! Then there were the families of the poor prisoners to look after, and give soup, fuel and rent, too, for when a man is locked up in jail for debt, he cannot provide for the wife and the little folks. "Families of prisoners confined for debt, may be supplied with tickets for soup by applying to the Secretary, Mr. John Nitchie, Jr., at No. 38 Broad street, where contributions will also be thankfully received and faithfully applied by the subscribers."

John Murray, Jacob Morton, James Bleecker, Leonard Bleecker, John Rodgers, William Linn, Thomas Storms, John M. Mason, Divie Bethune, Nathaniel Pendleton, Mathew Clarkson, David Hosack. Good old friends of the debtors, who ought to be remembered.

John Murray's nephew, John Jr., was a Trustee of the City Dispensary, that held its office on the corner of Beekman and Nassau streets.

The John Murray, jr., was an honor to the city. He lived and died at 335 Pearl, where he must have lived thirty or forty years. He had two sons named Robert John and Lindley. The first was named after his father, the great merchant Robert, who owned so many ships in 1769, and the other after his uncle, Lindley Murray, author of "English Grammar," "English Reader," "English Spelling Book," and other books. The history of Lindley Murray is a singular one. Nine persons out of ten suppose the great grammarian who has "English" attached to all of his most remarkable productions, was an Englishman. No such thing. He was a son of old Robert the merchant, and born at Sweetash, Penn. in 1745. He lived to be eighty-one years old, and died February 16, 1826, at York, England. He was buried in the Quaker burying ground in that ancient city, on Washington's birthday, February 22. Not a relation was present. He had no children, and his aged widow was too ill to leave her room. Lindley was older than John. There were twelve children, but only four lived to 1806 — John and Lindley and two sisters, one of whom was named "Beuhlah."

The youngest sister married Gilbert Colden Willett She died in New York in 1808.

Old merchant Robert tried to make a merchant of the future grammarian by placing him in his own count ing room. He did not succeed, and Lindley ran away from New York, and went to Philadelphia. He was coaxed back home, and then a private tutor was hired. Finally, law was decided upon, and young Murray was placed in the law office of Benjamin Kissam. He had a chum named John Jay, afterwards a man of some note in the great world; and the two met in London, when John Jay was ambassador from the new Republic. Lindley studied law four years, got a license to practice "in all the courts of the province," was twenty years old, and commenced courting a lovely girl, with good sense, good disposition, and good family. He married, and fifty years of experience justified his first impression.

In 1767, old Robert the merchant went to England for health and commercial purposes. Lindley followed him. The whole family, save the two Johns, followed, but with no intent of a long stay. 1771, Lindley and wife returned to New York. Old Robert remained in London until 1775, managing his extended trade.

When war broke out Lindley's law business was used up. So he retired forty miles from New York to Islip, Long Island, to a snug cottage, and determined to stay there until the war storm had passed away. He kept a pleasure boat, kept quiet four years, and then went to New York to try commerce instead of law. His father gave him a large credit to import goods from London in 1779. The goods arrived. He sold them at great profits, and kept on doing so until the war closed. Every year added largely to his capital, and when Independence was established he was well off and able to retire from business. He did so, and purchased a country seat three miles from New York, at Bellevue. Alas! after a few months his health failed in this Para dise, and he removed to Bethlehem, Pennsylvania. Finding his health feeble, he consulted one of the first physicians of New York. He advised a permanent change of climate, where the summers were more temperate and less relaxing, and where he would not lose in warm weather the bracing effects produced by th regions of winter. Yorkshire, in England, was thought a proper place. The advice was accepted. The voyage was made in 1784. He selected and bought a place at Holdgate, near York, and that became his habitation for many years of his life. There he wrote the books that have immortalized his name. There he died. His affairs in America were managed by his father, until he died, in 1786; then his brother John managed them until Lindley died, in 1826.

In 1810 our glorious Historical Society elected him an honorary member.

John Murray, Jr., the brewer, was very much like his brother Lindley. In the prime of life he had amassed a fortune. From that time he devoted himself to the service of religion and humanity. He not only tried to abolish slavery, but he tried to ameliorate the condition of the Indian. As I have shown, he tried to establish and support various institutions in New York for the relief of poverty and the improvement of public morals.

A short time before his death in 1819, he was up a Albany, pushing some of his plans; the streets were covered with ice, and he had a fall, from the effects of which he never recovered. He died while making a prayer. He left two sons and a widowed daughter. The names of the sons were Robert and Lindley. They are both dead now. For many years they were in the drug business, in partnership under the firm of Robert and L. Murray, 313 Pearl street, forty-five years ago, and Lindley lived at No. 337, next door to his father, No. 335 Pearl street — Robert's house was at No. 292. Afterwards the drug store of Lindley was kept at No. 72 Vesey, and he lived in Mott street. Both Robert and Lindley lived at the old mansion as late as twenty years ago. Robert died in 1859. The father Quaker, John, Jr., although a liberal man, yet he practiced strict economy. There was no public charity to which he did not belong, and towards any and everything that promised to do good or benefit the human family, he was always a ready and a cheerful giver.

On one occasion some ladies were deputed to call upon him for aid to a deserving object. They were shown up to the second floor of the old 335 Pearl Street House, and into his parlor. He was busily engaged in writing at a table, upon which was placed two lighted candles. When they entered he arose, begged them to be seated, and blew out one of the candles. One lady laughed and whispered to her neighbor, "We shan't get much here." She thought his conduct indicated meanness. He listened patiently to their statement, and then generously handed them $100. The lady who had spoken sneeringly when one of the candles was extinguished, turned towards him, and with a noble frankness said, "Mr. Murray, I am very much disappointed. I did not expect to receive a cent from you. I calculated on getting nothing." Surprised, the old Quaker asked the eason why,

She then narrated the story, and referred to the act of blowing out one of the candle lights.

"That, ladies, is the reason I am able to let you have the $100. It is by practicing economy that I save up money with which to do charitable actions," and the old man went on and gave the lady visitors a most excellent discourse upon charity and economy.

The Old Brewery, started before the Revolutionary war by John Murray, Jr., still stands. At the commencement of the century the proprietors were Murray & Cunningham. It ran from 13 Oliver street back to the centre of the block. In 1803 it was extended through to Catherine street.

It stands back from Madison street about twenty-five feet, and the passer-by can see this relict of a past age looming up above the small tenements, and the sign "C. & S. Milbank."

It is somewhat diminished in its proportions. On the corner of Madison and Catherine streets stands a Mariners' Church; half of the rear of that Church and Nos. 50, 50½, and 52 buildings stand on the site of the old Brewery House of 1792.

It opens now at 70 Madison street, and is carried on by the descendants of one of the original proprietors. Murray & Milbank succeeded to Murray & Cunningham. Mr. Samuel Milbank was a Philadelphian, a brewer, and came to New York long before the last war. When John Murray, Jr., left the concern, Samuel carried it on as Milbank & Co. Now it is Samuel Milbank & Son, the "son" of to-day being the grandson of old John Murray's partner.

I love these old solid monuments of the past; they are rapidly passing away from us. Many a Sunday I have walked five miles to take a good outside look of that same old Brewery, which has often furnished gallons of good old ale to General Washington when he resided in New York. Old John Hancock, when he lived at 5 Cherry street, drank ale, made in the same Brewery that we can see to-day.

The ale from that time-stained old brewery, is ale. One pewter mug full of that, is more precious than a big Missouri river full of lager. I am bursting with patriotism as I close this chapter, and am determined never to touch or taste a glass of porter or ale, unless the patriotic vender of it can exhibit a certificate that it comes from John Murray's old brewery up at 70 Madison, or 48 Oliver street.

I cannot recollect where old John Murray, jr., was buried. He died seven years before his sickly brother Lindley Murray, who outlived him and their three sisters. Lindley earned an immense sum by his various works, but the profit he invariably devoted to benevolent purposes. When he died he left by will several bequests to charities in England. After his wife deceased, the residue of his property was to be transferred to New York city, and vested in trustees, so as to form a permanent fund, the yearly income or produce of which was to be appropriated in the following manner: "In liberating black people who may be held in slavery, assisting them when freed, and giving their descendants or the descendants of other black persons, suitable education." What became of the money to do this, is a question of mere curiosity that arises to one's mind, when he reads this.

CHAPTER XXXIV.

I have alluded several times to the great House of G. & S. S. Howland, now Howland & Aspinwall. The two Howlands that come to this city were Gardner Greene and Samuel Shaw Howland. They founded the great commercial house of G. G. & S. S. Howland, now Howland & Aspinwall. They were sons of Joseph Howland, of New London, Connecticut. He was in the whaling business.

Both sons came to New York while boys to learn business, Gardner G. became a clerk with the house of Leroy, Bayard & McEvers. I have alluded to this house in another chapter under the firm of Leroy & Bayard. The house started in 1790 under that style. Herman Leroy was of the firm then. They did business at No. 3 Hanover Square. Herman lived over the store, as was then the custom. William Bayard lived at No. 43 Wall street. They took in Charles McEvers, who had previously done business upon his own account at 194 Water street, and lived at 34 Wall street. This last residence was famed for many years as the McEvers mansion. Through it led Wall street Court to

Pine street. The mansion was next door to the Bank of New York.

The old man Charles McEvers was of the house of Le Roy, Bayard & McEvers from before 1804 to long after 1815. Their counting house for many years was at 66 Broadway, where old Herman Le Roy lived, and afterwards the office and store was at 66 Washington street.

It was with this great house Gardner G. Howland clerked it for many years, rose to be head clerk, and when he left them was a thorough business man. G. G. at first went alone, and after the war he became prominent as a merchant. Then he did business at 77 Washington street, and his residence was in the rear at No. 64 Greenwich street. The firm was G. G. Howland. Samuel had been a clerk in the auction business. When he commenced business on his own account it was as a coffee broker.

While a clerk with Le Roy, Bayard & McEvers, Gardner G. Howland was sent out to Matanzas as supercargo of a little brig. He then probably formed many connections that in after years added to his commercial grandeur. While in Cuba he visited St. Jago de Cuba, and there formed the business acquaintance of the great house of Wright, Shelton & Co. Few can have an idea what a business that house of Wright, Shelton & Co. did for many years, forty or fifty years ago. Wright was an Englishman, a monstrous large man. The Sheltons were from about Derby, Connecticut. Stephen was the senior brother. He died in a boarding house in State street. Henry Shelton was a large man. He came to New York finally and married a daughter of Elisha W. King of Westchester County. Mr. King was a renowned lawyer in this city in the early part of this century.

Henry Shelton's beautiful widow afterwards married Doctor Watson. Philo S. Shelton married and settled in Boston, where he is or was one of the "solid men," owns a few Guano Islands, and has recently recovered from Venezuela a few hundred thousands of dollars, thanks to Senator Westcott of Florida, "who worked up the case," and has received the trifling check of $50,000 for his trouble.

One of the Shelton brothers kept a tin shop down by the bridge in New Haven in the olden time. Many of the graduates of Old Yale have visited old Shelton's tin shop, and will recollect it.

A Miss Shelton married Nehemiah Sanford, who kept a tin shop at Woodbury, Connecticut. He made all sorts of tin ware, and employed several tin peddlers to dispose of his wares in other States. But old Nehemiah is more remarkable for being the father of Henry Shelton Sanford, his only son, recently appointed Minister to Belgium by our new President, Abraham Lincoln. H. S. Sanford was named after his uncle, Henry Shelton, of the great house at St. Jago de Cuba, who made immense sums by importing cargoes of unchristianized Africans to that island.

To go back to G. G. Howland. He spent several days at the Gran Sofia the largest coffee plantation in Cuba, and owned by old Wright. It is located about thirty miles from the city of St. Jago.

When Gardner returned to New York, he made arrangements to commence on his own account. He did business for three years before Samuel joined him. Meanwhile he had married a daughter of the rich William Edgar, a wealthy old merchant, who commenced business at 7 Wall street in 1786, and continued there for some years after. For twenty years and more, commencing at 1800, he lived at 39 Broadway; and in that house the friends assembled at Gardner G. Howland's wedding. From Miss Edgar he received capital and credit sufficient to establish the firm of G. G. & S. S. Howland.

The first vessel the firm owned was a schooner, and she was named the "Edgar." She lasted many years, and they kept her running in the Matanzas trade.

This schooner was built and named the same year that William Edgar Howland (the eldest son of G. G. Howland) was born.

G. G. & S. S. Howland worked along by degrees, until they got into a very heavy Mexican and West India business, Vera Cruz, Campeachy, &c., &c.

The house suffered heavily by placing too great confidence in a person (I suppress his name) it sent out as agent. It nearly broke them. The firm suffered terribly, and came very near failing. Nothing saved them but the indomitable courage of G. G. Howland. He mastered all the difficulties. He frequently said, that on but two occasions was his house in danger. One by the rascality of their agent in Mexico, and again in the "Greek business."

The concern stretched out and made new commercial connections in all directions. The house opened a trade with the Mediterranean, and also became largely connected with England.

From the time of the shock owing to the Swartwouting of their agent; to the Greek business, the second crisis in their affairs, the Howlands went on swimmingly.

The Greek business nearly broke them. The firm contracted to build two men-of-war for the unfortunate Greeks. Le Roy Bayard & Co. shared in this contract. I shall allude to it in detail in another chapter. They employed Commodore Chancy, under whose inspectioı ths Greek frigates were built. But one was sent out to Greece. The other was bought by our Government, and eventually rotted in the house at the Brooklyn navy yard.

The Howlands went through the cotton panic in 1826, when hundreds of houses failed. After this difficulty, Gardner G. Howland went to England. He afterwards traveled all over Europe. His pleasing address, and encouraging mode of talking, made him very popular, and he procured an enormous business both from England and from the continental cities That business has never decreased.

William H. Aspinwall was a nephew. He was brought up in the house as a clerk. About 1832, he was taken into the house of G. G. & S. S. Howland as a partner. They gave Mr. A. one quarter of the profits of the commission business (which that year was $60,000.) The same offer was made at the same time to Moses Taylor, who was also a clerk with G. G. & S. S. Howland.

Moses declined the offer, and started next door to G. G. & S. S. H., who kept then at Nos. 49 and 50 South street, where the office is still kept.

G. G. Howland lived for many years at No. 18 Greenwich street. Afterwards Sam lived in the same house, and Gardner moved to the splendid house with pillars at No. 7 State street. It is still standing.

The firm of G. G. & S. S. Howland was changed in 1836 or 1837, to Howland & Aspinwall. The two old Howlands retired as active partners, each one putting in a cash capital of $100,000. The general partners were William Edgar Howland, the eldest son of Gardner G., by his first wife, and William H. Aspinwall.

CHAPTER XXXV.

G. G. & S. S. Howland did an immense business in all those ye rs alluded to, and after the firm was changed to Howland & Aspinwall their extensive operations did not decrease.

In the Pacific trade these merchants had no equals. From 1831 to 1840, they did the largest general business of any firm in the city of New York.

They did a heavy business from both the East and West Indies; also from the Mediterranean and England. They owned several Liverpool packets, among them the "John Jay," "William Brown," and "Crawford." They owned at least seventeen or eighteen ships.

I have read in the papers of to-day that old General Paez has just safely reached La Guayra, on his return from the United States, where he has long been an exile.

Twenty-eight years ago, old Paez was in his glory and President of Venezuela. At that time the Howland concern did the largest business with that country. They had a resident agent, John M. Foster, at Carraccas, and traded regularly at Puerto Cavello and La

Guayra. Old Doctor Litchfield was their agent at the former port, and J. S. McKaighen at the latter. Both were United States consuls.

Packets owned by the Howlands sailed between these two ports and New York regularly. One was the brig "Elizabeth," another the "Flight," another the brig "Stag."

Captain Anderson, as nice a little fellow as ever trod a deck, commanded the "Stag" for a long time. Howland & Aspinwall, when the civil war broke out, sold her to the government of Venezuela for $14,000. She was made a man-of-war in that service. Captain Anderson fell over her taffrail at sea and was drowned.

John S. Manson was also agent of this great house at La Guayra.

Mr. Briggs, of the large grocery house of J. & N. Briggs, in South street, was one of their captains (brig "Elizabeth.") So was Captain Munday, who is still in New York, and one of our oldest and most respected sea captains.

The brig "Elizabeth" was sold to the house of March & Schermerhorn, who had been clerks in other years to the Howlands. Schermerhorn is dead, and March is buried somewhere West in a lead mine.

The Pacific business of the Howlands was an immense concern. They sent out cargoes valued as high as $250,000 each. The voyage was made up to Valparaiso, Lima, and up to Mazatlan. These ships took cargoes composed of everything, from a cambric needle to a hoop pole. Iron ware, bars, steel, provisions, salt, brandies — in small barrels to go on mules' backs — wines, bales of domestics, fireworks, Chinese crackers, gunpowder, muskets, lead, spelter, costly flaming crimson and scarlet crape shawls, crockery ware, and in fact a country store on a mammoth scale.

There is only one place in this wide world where such a cargo can be made up, and that place is the city of New York.

The Howlands sent out supercargoes with these ships. They were in most cases clerks in the employ of the house, and who had lived with them some time. In this way Samuel M. Comstock (once of the firm,) became connected with the house. He was sent out supercargo to the Pacific.

At Mazatlan, Barr & Kennedy did business for Howland & Aspinwall. Mr. Barr is now in New York, and Mr. Kennedy, of whom we have written very liberally in a previous chapter, is in Scotland.

Samuel Shaw Howland married a daughter of John Hone. One of his sons, Meredith, is in the present concern. William Edgar, the general partner with W. H. Aspinwall, is now in Paris. He married a Miss Parsons, for his first wife. His second was a Parisian lady.

One daughter of Mr. Howland, Anabella, married Rufus Leavitt. The Leavitts, David, Rufus and John, were originally from Bethlehem, Conn., and came to New York poor boys. John and Rufus Leavitt, were for many years the greatest dry goods concern in the city.

Abbey Howland, another daughter, married a Wolcott. He was a son of Judge Frederick Wolcott, of Litchfield, Conn., who was a brother of Oliver Wolcott, one of General Washington's Secretaries of the Treasury, and son of the first Governor of Connecticut. His brother Oliver was also Governor of Connecticut. Oliver's descendants are all dead.

Another Miss Howland, Louisa, married James Brown, of the firm of Brown, Brothers & Co. Young

Brown was accidentally shot on the fourth of July on the piazza of his father-in-law's house at Flushing. He was slinging a grass hammock, when one of his little brothers-in-law accidentally fired off a pistol loaded with a marble. It killed him dead.

Gardner G. Howland for his first wife married Miss Edgar. His second wife was the beautiful Louisa Meredith, a daughter of William Meredith, one of the most eminent men in Baltimore. She was a great belle in the city of belles. She is now a widow, and resides in Washington Square, next to Fifth avenue, and is mother of two children. The son is named G. G., after his father, and is a member of the present firm of Howland & Aspinwall. The other child is a little girl.

When Gardner G. Howland retired from the great house as an active partner, he went to work to get up the Hudson River Railroad. He was a director in 1840. He was a great deal of his time at his country seat at Flushing, and in fact, he never interfered with the affairs of the old house. He died one Sunday morning. He was taken ill in church seven or eight years ago, and died half an hour after he reached home. Samuel died two years later in Rome. His body was brought home.

When G. G. lived at 8 State street, on one occasion old Joseph, his father, and his mother were there on a visit. One evening a quadrille was got up, and in it danced the grand-parents, the parents, and the grand-children.

A brother of G. G. and S. S. Howland was named Joseph. He died on a coffee estate, owned by G. G. and S. S., near Matanzas. He was never married. He had been a clerk with his father at New London, but never with his brothers in New York. A sister of the Howlands married James Roosevelt, (his third wife.)

Wm. H. Aspinwall had a brother, G. Woolsey Aspinwall, who was a long time clerk in the South street house. He joined a Mr. Pope in Philadelphia, and established a house there, under the firm of Pope & Aspinwall. Mr. Pope had been some years the agent of G. G. & S. S. Howland, at Tobasco, where he had made $20,000. Woolsey Aspinwall married Miss Hare, a great Philadelphia beauty. Never was a commercial house started under more favorable auspices, but alas! it did not last. The new house in Philadelphia was anxious to outdo Howland & Aspinwall, the old house in New York. But the place was not equal, and they had neither the means nor the talent. So Pope & Aspinwall suspended, after a short but exciting mercantile career in the Quaker City. Mr. A. died, and Mr. Pope went to New Orleans.

W. H. Aspinwall left the active management of the affairs of Howland & Aspinwall in 1850 and '51 to go into the Pacific Railroad and Panama Steamship Company. He founded the city of Aspinwall and gave his own name to it.

In connection with his new enterprise, there was one time when his vast fortune was in jeopardy. It was saved by sheer luck. The California operations made an immense fortune for himself as well as many others.

All the members of the firm, since its foundation fifty years ago by G. G., have been relatives, brothers, cousins and nephews, except Mr. Comstock, who is now interested with Mr. Aspinwall.

At one time they had Mr. Samuel Byerly in the concern, but it was only for a short time, and then he went West. He had been very much overrated. He led the firm into a speculation in furs, by which they lost $200,000. His partners at once were satisfied he should leave.

W. H. Aspinwall is a good man, and he is a great merchant. Good fortune sits gracefully upon his shoulders. He is a generous-hearted man. He is remarkable for his generosity, and his lenience to the debtors to his house. The amounts due such a concern every year by important parties who have failed, are enormous. Holding a high idea of man's honesty, Mr. Aspinwall has a general rule permitting all such debtors to settle up in their own way, and pay ten cents or one hundred on the dollar, as they see fit, and promptly signs their release.

Mr. W. H. A. is a great patron of the fine arts, and owns a gallery of paintings. He is vastly rich. He has had the benefit of much foreign travel, and commenced his career with a good solid education. He is very courteous. Once a week his gallery is open to those who have more taste than money.

Of course there is no commercial honor that the various Howlands and Aspinwalls have not received during the past half century.

By this I mean they have been honored by being directors in every bank, insurance company, railroad or other monopoly, when they could be induced to accept office; but in their cases it was generally to get their powerful names and active enterprise.

They have flourished too, in the annals of the Chamber of Commerce.

I have never known any of the members of the great firm to be politicians. The founder Gardner G., was a "King on Change." Nobody outranked him there, and that was his highest ambition. He had an utter contempt for any person who became a merchant without having served a regular apprenticeship as clerk.

On one occasion, when a person bearing the aristocratic name of Jay had been transferred from a doctor's office to a partnership in a large mercantile house, owing to the influence of a rich father-in-law, Mr. Howland entered their counting-room one day, and taking up a sample of cotton said:

"Look here, John. Do you know what this is?"

"Cotton," replied the amazed junior partner.

"Bless your heart, I did not think you knew so much," was the sarcastic reply of the thoroughbred Howland.

The business done now by Howland & Aspinwall is entirely different from what it was years ago. They are more bankers than merchants, and are immensely rich and responsible.

There are two Howlands in the concern. One is G. G., a son of the founder, Meredith, a son of Sam, and J. Lloyd Aspinwall is a son of W. H.

The graduates from the great house are not to be counted. I refer particularly to young men who have clerked it with the Howlands for some time, until they had acquired a thorough knowledge of business, and then gone into it on their own account. Many of them I remember, but not all.

There was a Mr. Carrington. He was of the firm of John Hone & Co. afterwards.

There was a W. A. Lawrence, of the firm of W. A. Lawrence & Munsell, in Pine street. They dealt heavily in silks. Mr. Lawrence finally went out to Canton. He was drowned off the poop of the ship "Rainbow," and was smoking a cigar when he fell overboard. He struck his head, was killed, and his body was shipped for New York. The ship was lost, but the body was recovered and brought home by another vessel, and buried in Greenwood.

Schermerhorn and March were both clerks. Samuel Comstock, partner now with W. H. Aspinwall. Pope & Aspinwall, alluded to before.

George Hart of the firm of Pinkerton & Hart, in the Mediterranean trade.

Jonathan Thompson, son of the old Collector of the Port of same name. He is of the firm of Thompson & Adams.

William Macfarlane, a broker in Wall street. Geogre Gallagher, a son of one of the firm of Murray & Gallagher, alluded to before.

Wm. Newton Adams, descendant of an old family of Fairfax County, Virginia; was afterwards United States and Venezuelan Consul at Santiago de Cuba, and a partner in the well-known house of Messrs. Brooks & Co. of that place. His uprightness and great business talents gained for him universal respect and esteem, being invariably appointed arbitrator in disputes among his fellow-merchants. He is now a member of the firm of Messrs. Moses Taylor & Co. of this city.

Murdock Mathewson, a nephew of Charles Edmonston & Co., of Charleston, South Carolina, where M. is now in business.

Moses Taylor, a son of the rent collector of John Jacob Astor, was also a clerk with G. G. & S. S. Howland. I alluded to him in the last chapter. His father died in the employ of Mr. Astor. Moses went with G G. & S. S. H. when very young, and served his time out, and then left for causes already explained. He at first started a little Matanzas business, and imported sugars from other ports of Cuba.

Old Mr. Astor also always backed up Moses when he needed aid. Moses worked hard for many years. He became rich, and in 1837, when others failed, Moses was reaping a harvest of gold. He was a speculator in notes at two or three per cent. a month — a most excellent and easy way of making money. Finally he became a millionaire and President of the City Bank.

His partner was named Pyne, a son of Thomas Pyne, the old seal skin broker in Wall street.

Peter V. King was a clerk with Moses. He was a brother of Mrs. Henry Shelton, alluded to in a former chapter.

CHAPTER XXXVI.

Who would not do honor to the merchants of New York? What a glorious class of our citizens in peace or war, and especially in war! What have not our hero merchants done within a few weeks? Their names should be immortal. We note passing events with a recording pen. Our old merchants are a credit to the city — the nation — the age. How they have disappointed those who barely showed their patriotism a few weeks ago, by stating that love of gold and traffic would absorb their love of country.

At the meeting of merchants a few days ago, one old merchant, P. Perit, of the firm of Goodhue & Co., called the attention of his hearers to the fact, that he and another one (then present) had attended a meeting of merchants for the same purpose, in the War of 1812 — 49 years ago.

Among other eminent merchants, there was one here once, named Samson V. S. Wilder. He at one time lived in Chambers street, No. 151 — and afterward, when wealth moved up town, Mr. Wilder moved too, and located in Washington Place. His counting-room was for many years at 42 Wall street. He was the agent of the great French banking-house of Henry Hottinguer & Co., of Paris and Havre. In his office Mr. Wilder had a portrait of old Baron Hottinguer, and he certainly much resembled him. Mr. Hottinguer has been long dead, but the widow married the cashier, and continues the firm to this day.

Mr. Wilder not only represented this great house, and advanced millions of money on consignments to their address from New York, and every other port of importance, but he was also the agent in this city of the Bank of the United States. Of course he controlled millions. To day he has not a penny to bless himself with, and resides near Boston. He has a large family—many daughters. On one occasion when one of them was married, the wedding created as much of a stir as if she had been a Princess of England. In the days of Mr. Wilder's glory, had any one hinted to him that *he* could fail, the idea would have been scouted. Yet he once said to a friend: "Griswold, how many merchants have succeeded among all those you have known for fifty years?"

Old Nat Griswold replied: "The average who have succeeded have been about seven in the hundred. All the rest, ninety-three in the hundred of untold thousands, have been bankrupts."

Mr. Wilder was brought up by Hottinguer and Co., and sent out to this country. He failed twenty years ago, and then lost his agency. He was regarded as a very shrewd man. So in fact are most men while their commercial prosperity lasts, but let that leave them, and they are called fools, or at best are "imprudent" men. As a general rule, success is the only true test of commercial merit.

Mr. Wilder made advances to an immense extent,

In the terrible times of 1837 he over-advanced on cotton, and the losses of his house were fearful. The worst claim in the world is for *reclamation.* Some of our readers may not understand the meaning of this commercial term. Suppose I had shipped 1,000 bales of cotton, costing me $100,000, to Hottinguer & Co. The agent, Mr. Wilder, advances me $90,000. The cotton sells in Havre for only $80,000. I not only lose the difference between cost and the advance, but Mr. Wilder makes a reclamation upon me for $10,000 more, and charges, interest, etc.

There have been sometimes claims made by European houses, when not a dollar had been advanced by the shipper of the goods. Such cases are not frequent, and arise from holding goods a long time, and then selling them at a price that don't pay charges.

Of that class of merchants who come under the head of agents special of great European houses was Mr. Wilder. While such men make liberal advances, in order to get consignments to their friends on the other side of the Atlantic, there are always a large number of *strictly* shipping merchants (not merchants who own ships) ready to ship cotton, tobacco, or any other species of merchandize that the advices afforded a fair margin for profit. Many of these houses do an immense business on a very small personal capital. They are enabled to do so owing to the liberal facilities afforded by the New York agents of the wealthy foreign houses.

I have, in one of these chapters, merely alluded to Dudley & Stuyvesant. That house was a large shipping concern. Mr. Dudley was a business man, and married Miss Stuyvesant, sister of his partner, Nicholas W. Stuyvesant, Jr., who resided up Broadway, near St. Thomas' Church. Their counting-room was at

90 South street. They were for many years heavy cotton shippers.

Their book keeper was named George G. Root. After the death of Dudley, Mr. Root became a partner with Mr. Stuyvesant, and their history for a few years is wonderful.

They held in 1837, at one time, 35,000 bales of cotton, worth over $3,000,000. There was every prospect of its going to 20 cents a pound. Wilder was making unheard of liberal advances for the United States Bank. Stuyvesant & Root had shipped to William & James Brown, of Liverpool, an immense amount of cotton; and the concern of Brown, Brothers & Co., had advanced largely on these cotton shipments. How largely can be estimated, when I say that after these cotton shipments were closed up, Stuyvesant & Root owed Brown, Brothers & Co., £70,000, or about $350,000. Yet, in order to show the uncertainty of cotton shipments, Root & Stuyvesant at one time were offered $250,000 for their chances of profit on the 35,000 bales. They refused it. Even Brown, Brothers & Co., at a later period, offered to take this cotton on their own account, and release R. & S. from any loss. But no. Cotton went down by the run. Mr. Wilder had pledged to many that the United States Bank would go into the market here and in Liverpool, and buy up 200,000 bales of cotton, so as to stiffen up prices, instead of doing which they put in the Liverpool market unexpectedly 250,000 bales, and sold for any price. Cotton fell 6 to 8 cents a pound, and all engaged in it were ruined beyond redemption. Root & Stuyvesant lost $1,000,000.

Mr. Root caved as a merchant. He for many years lived at the celebrated boarding house of Miss Jane Cowing, 5, 7 and 9 Murray street. People now-a-days can have no idea of the extent of that boarding house. It was the resort of the very *elite* of the United States Whenever John Forsyth, or any of the great guns of the South, came North, they went with their families to the Cowings. There was to be had the finest wines. At the sale of the choice wines of the old City Hotel, Mr. Root bought $4,000 worth of the best for Miss Cowing.

Mr. Root was beloved and respected by every one who knew him. He was one of the fashionable young men of the town. He married a lovely girl, but I believe she died before misfortune laid her heavy hand upon him. He who has negotiated his thousands now has hard work to negotiate weekly $1 50 to pay for humble lodgings, somewhere in the Bowery. He passes along the streets scarcely known to the present race of wealthy citizens, and forgotten by most of those who were his admirers and friends when fortune smiled upon him.

Woe to the great merchant who comes down! He has hardly a resource left, if poor and unprovided for: those who knew him when well off, will see him starve before they would give him a five dollar a-week clerkship. It is hard, very hard, and very cruel in a community so wealthy as New York.

There should be a home founded for the broken-down merchants in New York. Frequently the most deserving, the most energetic and the most honest, are the most unfortunate. Refuges are provided for all classes. The old captains have a Sailor's Snug Harbor to go to. The merchant who has failed has no place to go except the poor house. This is not right. It ought to be remedied. No merchant is beyond the reach of poverty. It has long arms. Many a proud and prosperous young merchant could spare $5,000 for an institution such as we allude to, who will, in all human probability, yet be glad to get inside of the hospitable portals before he reaches old age.

To be an Odd Fellow or Mason is an advantage when poverty comes, but how rarely does the merchant, who signs his check for $5,000 or a million, ever dream that $5 will be a perfect God-send to him! Yet so it is. I hope yet to see towering aloft the tower of "A Home for the Unfortunate Merchant." Commercial New York owes her glory to commercial individuals. When they become hopeless and helpless there should be a better refuge for them in their old age than the mammoth poor house,

It is impossible to be perfect in these chapters. If I were to attempt to record all the important events in the life of those merchants whose names figure in these chapters it would fill a library. With what I recollect, I add that which I pick up, and find correct. The best lives of merchants will be found in my collection.

The following is an addition to what I said in a late chapter about Howland & Aspinwall. Their friends in Mazatlan were Messrs. Barre & Kennedy. One of that firm, Mr. James Lennox Kennedy, is now residing in Jalapa, Mexico, where he has been since 1835, when that firm dissolved. Mr. Lewis P. Barre is in this city. Neither of the parties have been engaged in business since that year. Mr. Kennedy is a Scotchman, and Mr. Barre a Frenchman. He was born in Cahors, France. Both were sent out by the Howlands as supercargoes to the Pacific coast, and being honest, upright, and hard-working men, soon made themselves indispensable to their employers, who conceived the idea to have them start on their own hook. Accordingly, they were dispatched

14*

with a valuable shipment, and after trading along the coast, found their way up to Mazatlan. By their strict industry and business habits, they built up a large Mexican trade with the States, and were the heaviest traders on the Western coast.

Immense cargoes were sent to them by the Howlands, and in return all kinds of Mexican produce found its way to this market, upon which fabulous amounts were realized. B. & K., after a brilliant career of about 15 years, retired from business, well satisfied with their gains.

They were succeeded by Mott, Talbot & Co., who also coined money, but owing to extravagances, wound up with the "shorts." Mott was a sea captain. I saw him in San Francisco a few years since, a cripple by gout, and greatly reduced in funds. Poor fellow! he had a good run of luck, but did not know how to profit by it.

The names of Barre & Kennedy are still spoken of in Mexico in the highest terms, and especially among the poorer class, whom they were ever ready to assist. In 1848, while at Mazatlan, I happened to stumble over an old native woman, surnamed "Maria la Infortunada," who related to me the many charities received at their hands.

CHAPTER XXXVII.

So many importers of brandy, wines, and other choice fluids, are now in existence, that it is hardly possible to realize so far back as when the business was confined to a very few persons.

Mr. Kennedy, of the firm of Barre & Kennedy, was a nephew of Robert Lenox, and was named James Lenox Kennedy. As before stated, he resided at Jalapa, Mexico. An anecdote is told of him in connection with the American army during the war with Mexico. When it was approaching Jalapa, under General Scott, with the evident design of capturing that ill-fated city, a deputation of the citizens was sent to Scott to beg off. At the head of the delegation was J. L. Kennedy. Scott had known him from the time of boyhood. They asked the great American commander to make a detour, and pass Jalapa harmlessly. The General, probably out of good feeling to an old New Yorker, as much as from any other cause, granted their request.

When this determination became known in Jalapa, the inhabitants loaded every animal they could find with the most luscious fruits, and everything eatable or drinkable, and dispatched the caravan to the troops.

Two of the principal importers, in the early part of this century, were two Frenchmen. One was named

Stephen Jumel. He came out from France in 1798, and for many years kept a store at 39 Stone street, where he did a heavy business. He kept the same 15 years. He was afterward, for a long time, at No. 69 Liberty street near Broadway; and, still later, in Pearl street, corner of Whitehall. He coined money. He was twice married. For his second wife he married his housekeeper, and when he died — as he had no children by either wife — he left the last all his money and real estate.

His country mansion is still standing out of town, near the High Bridge. Madam Jumel sold three acres of it for bridge purposes at a high figure.

Madam Jumel, since her first husband's death, has been twice married. Once to the celebrated Aaron Burr. The latter kept his law office at the time, and up to 1836, at 23 Nassau street, where he practiced law.

Dr. J. Xavier Chabert, the Fire King, once so celebrated, and who was a benefactor to the city in the sad times of 1832, also married a wealthy lady. Dr. Cha bert was a very remarkable man. His profession was botanic physician. I do not know when the Doctor came here. I think he was a brother or son of Etienne Chabert, a tailor who kept at 103 Chambers street, about forty-six years ago. The Doctor exhibited himself up to the year 1831. After the cholera he opened a regular shop at 322 Broadway, next to corner of Pearl, and where Bowen, McNamee & Co. have their marble palace dry goods store. After Dr. Chabert's death, his wife remained a widow.

Stephen Jumel was a fine, noble-hearted old Frenchman as ever lived. As I have said before, his great rival in the brandy and wine trade was another Frenchman named John Juhel. He was almost the same name as Jumel — an *h* instead of an *m* made the only difference. Mr. Juhel came over before 1800, and kept his store at 160 Greenwich, next to Courtlandt street. He afterward moved up to 42 Warren street, in the war time, and there kept until he died. He left no children.

For the information of my readers, I here insert a catalogue of the articles sold in the war time (1813) in the liquor line:

Wines: — Maderia, Sherry, Tenneriffe, Lisbon, Mal aga, Fayal, Port, Claret. No Champagne was ever advertised.

Brandy: — Cogniac, Spanish, Cette, Peach, Country.

Cordials: — York Rum, All Fours, Stoughton Bitters, Metheglin, Cherry Bounce, Cherry Brandy, Raspberry, Liquor d'Or, Creme de Caffe, Anizette, Pennyroyal, Baum, Wintergreen, Mint, Aqua Mirables, Noyeau, Rosa Solis, Mount Pelieur, Rattifia, Citron, Cinnamon, Ladies Comfort, Usquebaugh, Orange, Life of Man, double distilled, Life of Man, single distilled, Peppermint, double and single distilled.

Spirits: — Jamaica, Antigua, St. Croix, W. I. Island, N. England.

Gin: — Holland, York Anchor, Country, Old Irish Whisky, Old Shrub, Cider Spirits, Alcohol, Highwines, Spirits of Wine.

And iron liquor for leather dressers' use.

Most of these articles were imported, although cordial making had been carried on some time by Michael Miller, who married the sister of John Jacob Astor, and who came out with the latter. Miller went first into the tailor business, in Elizabeth street, Bowery in 1792. Afterward, about twelve years, he went into the business of distilling cordials at 11 Barley street. It ran from Broadway to Church street (now Duane.) Some years later he removed to 80 Duane street, where he kept within the recollection of many of my readers, and lived next door. After his death, his son carried on the cordial distillery until he died, in 1846. Michael Miller left tailoring to get into the distillery business in a singular manner. J. J. Astor's sister married in Germany, before she came out here, a Mr. George Ehninger, who was a cordial distiller. He was about the first to commence that kind of business in the United States, and was extremely clever. He died from the effects of an accident caused while burning spirits. After his death, his widow married Michael Miller, taught him the secrets of the business, and carried it on with him for years. I have said part of this before.

Still, the real French cordials were so far superior to those manufactured here, that the sale of the latter was very limited. I presume both Jumel and Juhel kept them.

One cold winter afternoon, a cart was passing the store of old Mr. Jumel, when he kept corner of Pearl and Whitehall. It was very slippery. The horse slipped, fell, and broke his leg. The cart contained a pipe of brandy, belonging to Mr. Juhel. The pipe rolled off, and was smashed. This was worth a great deal of money in those days. Juhel's cartman was hurt himself, and had lost a horse worth $150. Old Jumel came out of his store and joined the crowd, who were expressing their sympathy and regrets. "Poor fellow!" said one. "What a pity!" exclaimed another. Old Jumel pulled off his hat, and exclaimed, "Aha! You all pitty, eh! — how much you pitty? — I pitty ten dollar!" and he put that amount in the hat. Then he passed it around among the crowd. His generous sympathy was extensively imitated, and he collected in his hat over $150

He gave it to the worthy cartman of his rival, Mr. Juhel

I am not aware that either of these French worthies and merchants of the olden time have left any descendants. I think not.

As we are on the eve of a war that will try the resources of the kings of commerce before it is through with, it is curious to look back and remember the names of the great commercial firms who survived the war of 1812. That war tried the merchants of this city. Many survived it, with unimpaired credit, if not cash.

Goodhue & Co., were among that lot; so were Archibald Gracie & Sons. N. & D. Talcott, large cotton merchants — sons brokers in these days. There was Cambreling & Pearson, a great house. C. C. Cambreling was of that firm,—still alive, and many years a democratic member of Congress from this city, in times when it was an honor to be a member from commercial New York. Pearson was Isaac G. — a great real estate operator in later years, and president of the Relief Insurance Company.

Andrew Foster, an old merchant, who was in business in 1800, in Greenwich street — afterward moved to 65 South street, where he was during the war, and long years after. The firm was afterward Foster & Giraud, and still later, Andrew Foster & Sons. Mr. Giraud was once a cooper. His father was a cooper be fore him, and several of his brothers were hard work ing coopers, and a credit to the city.

Another great house that stood through the war, and exists at this day, is De Rham & Moore. Henry C. De Rham was Swiss born. When he came to this country, I do not exactly know, but it was about 1806 to 1808. He started business at 79 Washington street, a few doors from Le Roy, Bayard & McEvers. His residence was at 60 Greenwich street. In youth or in a venerable old age, there probably never was a finer looking man than Henry C. De Rham. He is one of those men that the perfect stranger to him may meet, and will look around after he has passed, and wonder what celebrated man he is. After moving from Greenwich street, Mr De Rham lived many years in that aristocratic quarter known as Park place.

After the war, Mr. De Rham formed a partnership with Mr. I. Iselin, who had been a partner in the house of Le Roy, Bayard & Co. Mr. Iselin was another fine man, and an old school merchant. When De Rham & Iselin kept at 44 Broad street, Mr. Iselin lived at No. 36 Laight street, on the north side of St. John's Park. His fate was a melancholy one. He was drowned in a Swiss lake near Geneva, about the time of the great financial panic in 1837. He had several sons, and fine young men they are. Two sons are of the firm of Iselin & Co. (formerly Mauran & Iselin.) They gave $3,000 to the war fund a few days ago, as their father, Le Roy, Bayard & Co., gave $20,000 in 1812. Another son is a broker in Wall street.

H. C. De Rham married Maria Teresa Moore. Her brother Benjamin was his clerk a long while, and afterward one of the firm of De Rham, Iselin & Moore. He died some years ago. Another brother, William, was taken into the firm, which is now called De Rhan & Moore. These Moores are of a very ancient stock They boast direct descent from Thomas De Moore, a Norman, who went skylarking with William the Conqueror into England, in 1066. John Moore came to this country in 1657. Among his descendants were two very celebrated persons. The great Bishop Samuel Moore, who died in 1816, and the eminent Dr. William Moore, father of Benjamin and William, and of Mrs. De Rham

Mr. De Rham's commercial house has been in existence over half a century. He has done an enormous business, but in a quiet, unobtrusive way, not making half the noise created by a Canal street shopkeeper every spring. He had been the Swiss Consul many years.

The concern has ever imported largely in dry goods, principally from France, Switzerland and Germany. But they have also done a very large commission business, and sold cargoes of all kinds of merchandise.

They have been for many years the heaviest buyers of "bills" in the market. Always buying exchanges to remit to their correspondents in Europe. Recently they have done a large and profitable banking business.

During the most prosperous times of the French packet-ships, the owner, old Francis Depau, built and named one of his crack packet-ships the "De Rham," after his friend, H. C. De Rham. She was commanded by Captain De Peyster, the superintendent of the Sailors' Snug Harbor, at Staten Island.

God seems to bless and prosper patriots, and especially patriotic merchants.

There were hard times in the war with England, in 1812 to 1814. It was with the greatest difficulty money could be had. Mr. Madison was President, and George W. Campbell was Secretary of Treasury. On some occasions, the Government was very glad to borrow small sums from different individuals in this city.

On the 8th of February, 1813, Congress passed an act authorizing the borrowing of $16,000,000.

Proposals were advertised, but it proved a lamentable failure. Only $3,965,400 was offered.

Finally a few merchants, headed by the celebrated Jacob Barker, opened a subscription list, and among them Henry C. De Rham subscribed $32,300.

Many of the names mentioned in these chapters took part in this loan.

Harman Hendricks took $42,000. He died leaving a large property. The loan prospered him. His sons continue business.

Boorman & Johnson took $10,000. That firm still exists.

John F. Delaplaine took $10,000. He is dead, but his son Isaac lives—is very rich, and a member of Congress from this city.

Stephen Whitney took $10,000. He is dead. Henry A. and John G. Coster took $100,000. Both of them are dead.

Bradhurst & Field took $5,000. One was John M. Bradhurst, who died rich. Mr. Field was father of the Fields. B. & F. were wholesale druggists.

Jacob M. & John M. Hicks took $2,000. They died rich. They were Quakers.

W. H. Ireland took $2,000. He is rich and prosperous.

Majahre & Tardy was an old and wealthy French house. John G. Tardy was the partner. He was father to the present John A. Tardy, noticed in a former chapter.

James McBride took $10,000. He was an importer of Irish linens. Lived in College place many years. His daughter married Judge Vanderpoel.

Peter Crary took $10,000. He was one of the great dry goods house of P. & I. S. Crary & Co., in Pearl street.

Peter H. Schenck took $10,000. I wrote much about him in a former chapter. So also of Thomas H. Smith, the old tea merchant, who took $10,000, and died owing the Government $3,000,000.

Thaddeus Phelps took $10,000. He was a great merchant, but awfully profane. He lived in Park place many years. Was a great Democrat in Jackson's time. A daughter married Governor Mason, of Michigan.

Smith & Nicoll, great tea merchants, took $100,000. They failed in after years, but died rich. Their commercial career is all narrated in a previous chapter of the "Old Merchants."

We cannot give anything more agreeable this week, than a list of our patriot citizens forty-eight years ago. Many of them are alive now. Of those dead, their descendants will be proud to read the patriot names.

John Rathbone & Son, $20,000; Jacob Barker, $100,000; Harman Hendricks, $40,000; Gabriel Havens, $10,000; John Bullus, $10,000; Brockholt Livingston, $20,000; John Mason, $5,000; Stephen Whitney, $10,000; Freeman Allen, $25,000; Thaddeus Phelps, $10,000; John L. Brown, $20,000; Smith & Nicoll, $100,000; Walsh & Gallagher, $10,000; Post & Minturn, $50,000; John Howland, $50,000; Benjamin Huntington, $10,000; Wright & Allen, $30,000; Ayer Bremner, $30,000; George W. Murray, $10,000; Robert Chesebrough, $10,000; Jonas S. Roulet, $10,000; John Colvill & Son, $20,000; Norwood & Austin, $10,000; H. C. De Rham, $32,300; Samuel Tooker, $20,000; W. & S. Vandervoort, $10,000; Robert Ainslow, $10,000; Joseph Icard, $20,000; Boorman & Johnson, $10,000; L. Bleecker, $30,000; T. H. Smith, $10,000; J. F. Delaplaine & Co., $10,000; John Taylor, $150,000; Isaac Clason, $500,000; Lawrence &

Van Buren, $10,000; Theodore Fowler, $150,000; Philip Brasher, $50,000; Kelly & Morrison, $20,000; Mollan & Rankin, $20,000; Teterel & Williams, $20,000; Gurdon S. Mumford, $20,000; Benjamin Bailey, $10,000; Peter H. Schenck, $10,000; I. Prall, $10,000; Abraham Riker & Co., $10,000; John Clendening, $20,000; Thomas & Peter Stagg, 25,000; Joseph Dederic, $10,000; Rensaeler Havens, $20,000; James McBride, $10,000; Peter Murphy, $10,000; Walter Morton, $10,000; John Grant, $10,000; James Thompson, $20,000; Thompson & Edgar, $10,000; Peter Crary, Jr., $10,000; Louis Larue, $25,000; Majahre & Tardy, $10,000; Irving & Smith, $50,000; F. & E. Irving & Co., $20,000; James C. Flack, $10,000; James Kelso, $10,000; Kelso & Cromp, $10,000; Bernard Keenan, $4,000; Garrit Storm, $10,000; Jose & W. Dunlap, $10,000; Austin & Andrews, $20,000; Jonathan Lawrence, $23,000; Alanson Douglas, $50,000; Isaac Jones, $4,000; Jeremiah F. Randolph, $10,000; G. B. Vroom, $500,000; Samuel Stilwell, $10,000; David Dunham, $10,000; Van Horn & Morris, $5,000; Isaac Lawrence, $25,000; James Lovett, $5,000; Nicolo Senchich, $40,000; Leonard Bleecker, $20,000; H. A. & J. G. Costar, $100,000; John Grant, $20,000; Peter Feviere, $10,000; Joseph Burr, $6,000; Bradhurst & Field, $5,000; F. Wildman, $4,000; Samuel Flewelling, $257,800; James Van Dyke, $5,000; S. M. Thompson, $10,000; P. & S. Wildman, $6,000; John & Jacob Drake, $10,000; John H. Douglas, $4,000; Philip S. Lebreton, $6,000; Mehitable Hunting, $4,000; Samuel Watkins, $5,000: W. Holly, $5,000; Jacob & J. M. Hicks, $2,000; James Townsend, B. T. U., $2,000; B. T. Underhill, $2,000; John Lefferty, $2,500; B.

Andariese, $2,000; Titus & Avery, $6,000; John Russ, $4,000; Irving & Smith, $5,000; John Shute, $10,000; Henry W. Bool, $6,000; Jeremiah Akerley. Jr., $12,000; James Weeks, $6,000; W. H. Ireland, $2,000; H. Ischer, $5,000; Abraham Bishop $25,000; Luther Loomis, $5,000; Whitehead Fish, $250,000 Fred DePeyster, $25,000; Francis Depau, $20,000 Edmund Elmendorf, $5,000; W. P. Van Ness, $25,000, Walter Bowen, $20,000; William Van Ness, $20,000; Alexander Ferguson, $200; David De la Pierre, $3,000; Federick Brune, $15,000; James R. Wilson, $30,000; Earl De Pearce, $5,000.

The foregoing list should be perserved. The descendants of those old true New York merchants may well be proud of them. Money was not so plenty in 1813 as now, and in those days the merchant who was worth $100,000 was considered well off.

Government could not raise money except at a discount of fifteen per cent.

If the merchants and capitalists of 1861 were to offer a loan to Government as liberally as the list above, it would be one hundred millions, for ten millions loan in 1813 was a far greater affair than a hundred millions would be in 1861.

CHAPTER XXXVIII.

Among the list of names of eminent commercial firms in the city of New York, published in the last chapter, as contributors to the loan to our Government in the war of 1812, will be found many French names, who were members of commercial houses. One was Majah re & Tardy; they kept at 80 Broad street.

They contributed $10,000.

John S. Roulet subscribed $10,000. He was of the firm of Rossier & Roulet, No. 21 Broadway. They were among the largest merchants of the city, and in their day were as eminent as Goodhue & Co. in this. Their house commenced business as early as the year 1800, and their business was immense. They retired about forty years ago. I am not aware that they left any descendants.

Joseph Icard was another. He gave $20,000. He was a heavy French merchant. He first started in business here at 85 Greenwich street, corner of Rector, in 1798. He afterwards moved to 14 Rector street, and lived at 308 Broadway. After the downfall of the Emperor Napoleon, he went back to Paris, and became a celebrated man. He took a contract for cleaning the streets of Paris, and made a million of francs.

Louis La Rue gave $25,000. He was a long time a celebrated merchant. He also came out of France in the time of the French Revolution, came to this city, and started at No. 10 Rosevelt street, near Chatham. He afterwards moved to No. 14 Hudson street, then the aristocratic part of the city. When the restoration in France occurred, he went back, and established in Havre the great commercial house of La Rue, Palmer & Co. This house did an immense business. Palmer was a New Yorker, had been a clerk with Mr. La Rue, and married his daughter.

Francis V. Riviere was another French exile, who contributed $10,000. He kept a large dry goods store at 190 Broadway, and lived at No. 3 John street. He went back to France as soon as Louis XVIII. was restored.

An immense number of Frenchmen came to this city from 1792 to 1802, for different causes. One cause was the Revolution in France of 1792, when heads began to be unsafe. Many Frenchmen went to St. Domingo. From there they were all glad to escape when the negro uprising and massacre occurred in 1799. Some of the French *emigres* landed here without a cent, and, in after years, did a large business. We mentioned some in our last. John Deseze taught music at 12 Reade street. He was of a noble French family He was the father of Mrs. John B. Flandin, whom all New Yorkers will well recollect. J. B. was once a partner in the celebrated dry goods establishment of Vandervoort & Flandin, No. 111 Broadway.

John B. Desdoity was an *emigre*. He lived in Grand street, near Bowery, and was the father of a young man who was afterwards cashier of the Chemical Bank.

B. Desobrey was a French *emigre*. He kept a dry

goods store from the year 1800 to the fall of Napoleon, at 261 William. His wife Madame Desobrey, was the most beautiful woman in New York. The very first sight of her set many men crazy.

Alexis Gardere was a French wine merchant. He kept at 115 Fly Market when he first arrived here, in 1802, (Maiden Lane, between Pearl and Water streets.) From there he removed to 71 Stone street.

Mr. Gardere was a refugee from St. Domingo. He came here twice; once in 1796 on business, and afterward in 1802, when he fled to escape the fury of the negroes. The last time he brought with him all his family, and four slaves. The name of one was Vato, and another named Veronique. She is living yet, though ninety years old, and has great grandchildren, and is much respected by all the descendants of old Mr. Gardere. He freed his slaves after his arrival here, in 1803, Madame Gardere had had three husbands in St. Domingo, Mr. G. being the last. There were children by the other husbands, but the last brought them all with him to New York. By the second husband there was a son, named Lawrence A. Rigail, who entered the United States army. He commanded at one time the Arsenal that in 1806, stood where Madison Square now stands, and where afterward stood the House of Refuge.

In later years he was in command of Fort Moultrie (near Charleston.) There he took the country fever and died. He had married a Miss Walker, of Milledgeville, Georgia. Colonel Rigail was regarded as one of the handsomest men in the Union.

Old Mr. Gardere had an only son, named Peter. He was the beau ideal of a perfect dare-devil; and many who read this will remember Peter Gardere. He was a high strung fellow, had a splendid education, spoke several languages, and, like his half brother Colonel Rigail, was good-looking.

In 1827 or '28, he joined Lord Byron in Greece, and was at Missolonghi when captured. After that dreadful event, he met the ex-Emperor Iturbide in Italy, and joined him. He went with him to Mexico, landed with him, and was with him when Iturbide was caught and shot.

(The Empress and wife of the same Iturbide died in Philadelphia a few weeks ago.) Peter Gardere escaped by declaring himself an American citizen. He finally became District Judge at Key West, where he died in 1845. He died rich. He was one of the favorite beaux of New York in his day.

In those years people in business lived over their stores. Among the rest was Mr. Gardere. In the war period he lived at 120 Pearl street, directly opposite to General Moreau.

This celebrated French General Victor Moreau, who at one time was even more celebrated than Bonaparte, was mixed up in the Pichegrew conspiracy. He fled from France, and came to this country about 1803. He took a house in Hanover Square, that is now, in 1811, where he lived with his amiable lady for three years, or until he went back to France to fight with the allies, and was killed at the battle of Dresden. While in New York he was very popular.

General Moreau lived at 119 Pearl street, corner of Slote lane.

The Bell Tavern, in Slote lane, kept by King, the father-in-law of William Niblo, was directly in the rear of the residence of General Moreau. To understand the precise locality, I must explain that Slote lane was Beaver street, now from William to Hanover, and then took a turn around into Hanover square. In the centre of Hanover square was a block of buildings (torn down 40 years ago,) reaching up as far as where Slote lane came into Hanover square; and Stone street, instead of ending at William, ran up as far as Slote lane, on the north side of what is now Hanover square.

Next door to General Moreau, lived Nicholas Low. He was of the firm of Low & Wallace, merchants, and a great man in his day.

On the opposite side of the square was called Pearl street, the odd number on the west side. There resided at No. 109, L. C. & T. Hammersly, and at No. 111, Luqueer & Vannest, saddler men, celebrated all in history in after years.

But, to the celebrated General Moreau, as I have said before, there was an immense number of high born but unfortunate Frenchmen here at that time. Among them was the celebrated G. Hyde de Neuville. He was a married man, and kept house quietly at 61 Dey street. They had no children.

These two prominent Frenchmen, wishing to do good, started a school for French children. They were assisted by Henry Cruger, a wealthy man, who lived at No. 12 Hudson street, next door to Louis La Rue; also by the celebrated Bishop Chevereuse, of Boston, afterward a Cardinal, and who would have been Pope had he not been poisoned. Also by John B. Lombart, the Chancellor of the French Consulate.

It was called the Economical School — "*L'Ecole Economique.*" Those who were able to pay for children, paid. To others, it was free. The best professors in the Union were employed. Its first location was in Chapel street (West Broadway,) between Duane and

Reed. It was afterward moved to Anthony (now Worth,) opposite the Hospital grounds.

Every morning, Hyde de Neuville and General Moreau would go to the school, and give lectures and explanations to the scholars. This they did as a pastime t gave rise, however, to the absurd story that Gen. Moreau taught school in the United States for a living. It was not so, for he was very wealthy, and entertained at his house in Hanover square in princely style. It was an immense concern. The school had grand examinations every year. It had a regular printing-office attached to it, and they printed all such books as were used in the school — grammars, geographies, dictionaries, Fontaine's Fables, etc.

These books were given to the scholars. One lies before me now. It is handsomely bound, and entitled "Excerpta ou Fables; Choisies de la Fontaine; par M. de la Harpe, New York: d l'imprineried l'Economical School. 1810."

On the back of the cover is the following certificate signed by M. de Neuville, viz:

"Prix de bonne conduite accordè a Miss Hostin le 9 Juillet 1810, par les membres du comitè inspeciteur de l' ecole.

(Signed) G. Hyde Neuville.

(Signed) Lombart. Instituteur."

The young lady above was named Jane, and she was one of the most charming French girls that ever trod shoe leather in this city. Her father was a wine cooper and lived at 59 Fair street (Fulton.)

This great man, Hyde Neuville, after Louis XVIII was restored, went back to France. The King sent him back to this country as Minister Plenipotentiary, etc. When he reached New York on his way to Washington, he put up at the Washington Hotel, a large building that stood in Broadway, where A. T. Stewart's large dry goods store now stands. To his surprise about thirty of these boys, monitors in the Economical school, made their appearance. They had called to welcome their old friend back to America. He knew every one of these American boys, for Americans they were, although of French parentage, and some of the first merchants now bear the names, and are the same boys, though older. Both Monsieur and Madam Hyde de Neuville declared that they had never received so heart-telling an honor. When the Ambassador reached Washington, he sent on an order to divide about 20,000 volumes of the publications of the school, among these monitor boys.

Joseph Denouse was the printer for the school. It declined after the fall of Napoleon and the departure of de Neuville and of Gen. Moreau. Out of it, however arose the celebrated school of Bancel. He was a refugee from St. Domingo. Victor Bancel commenced keeping a boarding-school as early as 1801, in Harrison street. When the great Economical school fell into decay, he secured its "good will." Many of our old merchants will remember Bancel very well.

The house occupied by Gen. Moreau, after he left was made into a hotel by Collet. It was a large doubl house. Collet was a man as celebrated in his day fo superb French cookery, as Mataran, of Beekman street, is now.

In the block of buildings in what is now Hanover square, at No. 120, lived Cebra & Cummings. When the block was torn down, they moved to 106 Pearl, corner of Old Slip. In that region the old concern kept fifty-five years. Fifty years ago, they did an auction and commission business. John Y. Cebra was alderman of the First Ward for years, and a wealthy citizen. He died a few years ago. His partner is yet alive, hale and hearty, and still carries on the business.

L. C. & Thomas Hammersley did business at No 109 Pearl street, sixty years ago.

Their father, old Andrew Hammersley, did business as an ironmonger and dry goods merchant, just after the war in 1784, at No. 46 Hanover square, in about the same place. He had a son named William Hammersley, who was a physician. Later old Andrew moved to 25 Courtlandt street, and left his sons, L. C. & Thomas, to carry on the same business at the old stand —afterward changed to 109 Pearl street, but same shop. The sons went into business in 1801.

Thomas Hammersley left a son Andrew, and a daughter who married the Rev. A. Verren, the rector of the French Episcopal church in Franklin street.

The son of L. C. married a Miss Mason. The descendants of the worthy old iron man do not do any business. They have plenty of money, and are considered at the top of the local aristocracy, have a coat of arms on their carriage, &c. Thomas Hammersley lived a long time at No. 97 Greenwich street.

There are untold lots of French people who came here from St. Domingo to escape the negroes. They were lucky if they saved their lives, let alone money. Hundreds owe their lives to a noble-hearted merchant named McIntosh. He stayed all through the massacres, and spent all he was worth, $250,000, in rescuing and redeeming with money the lives of those condemned to death and crucifixion by the negroes. Sometimes 200 to 300 a day were killed. When McIntosh visited this country in 1810, he was received like a king, by those he had rescued, in Baltimore, Philadelphia and New York. He was an American merchant. He was, however, a Scotchman by birth.

The French Government made Hayti pay for all the property destroyed. By treaty Hayti agreed to pay 60,000,000 in sixty years, in sums of one million annually. This was paid faithfully up to 1850. Then Hayti became utterly impoverished. She owed 12,000,000 on this debt. She was left off for twelve years. In 1862 the balance is to be paid.

There are many French families here who have received their installments regularly, as compensation awarded by the French Commissioners, and who will receive their proportion of the 12,000,000 still due.

CHAPTER XXXIX.

When Gen. Moreau lived at No. 129 Pearl street (Hanover Square,) about every one who was engaged in trade lived over their store or counting house. Most of the neighbors of the General, while he was in this city, were of the first class.

There was much talk about General Moreau when he arrived here. Napoleon was in the ascendant, and the star of Moreau in the decline. He was charged with many crimes. This led him to write and publish a book in this city, in 1806. It was entitled "The Life and Campaigns of Victor Moreau, Comprehending his Trial, Justification, and other Events, till the period of his Embarkation to the United States, by an Officer of the staff." Of course the Officer of the Staff merely wrote what the General dictated. The publishers were Isaac Riley & Co., who kept at No. 1 City Hotel (No. 123 Broadway, between Thames and Cedar streets.) Riley kept a book-store there for many years. David Bliss was a partner, and copyrighted the book. Bliss was a book-binder, and kept No. 6 Slote Lane, right around from Moreau's house, where the book was bound. He afterwards kept a "Library" at No. 235 Greenwich street. A library, "circulating" or other, was a great affair in those days, and nearly all of the booksellers had a "library," and loaned out books at so much per copy, and if the party who wanted a book was unknown, he left a deposit equal to the value of the book. The widow of good old David was alive 35 years ago, and resided at 36 Courtlandt street. A son of David, named Elam Bliss, kept, after the old man's death, at No. 128 Broadway, nearly opposite the City Hotel.

The General was extremely nervous about this book, and when it came out, he presented it to his American friends, and gave away to the first society at least 500 copies. It contained a miniature likeness of himself. John Davis translated the work from the General's French into English. Davis united the functions of translator and accountant, and resided at No. 29 Harrison street. I do not know whether John was a relation of Matthew L. Davis, but I think he was. The latter visited at Moreau's house, and lived at 49 Stone street, where he also did an extensive mercantile business.

The book stated that Victor Moreau was born at Morlaix in Brittany (Lower,) in 1762,—101 years ago. He studied law. When 26 years old, he took up arms for the King against his Parliament in 1788. In 1793 Robespiere's committee made him General of Brigade. In 1794, he served as General of Division on the Rhine under Pichegru. In 1796, when the latter was disgraced by the Directory, Moreau succeeded to the command of the army of the Rhine and Moselle. Moreau was successful in every battle until 1799. It was near the close of that year when at Paris Bonaparte and Moreau met for the first time. The former had just returned from Egypt.

On the 6th of November Paris gave a great fete to

Bonaparte and Moreau in the temple of victory. A song was sung:

"Oh Bonaparte! oh, Moreau,
For conquest preordained;
What pencil proud may hope to show
The glories ye have gained."

A year after General Moreau married a young lady that his father had recommended in his will.

He continued a great favorite of the First Consul, and defeated numerous armies.

General Moreau became mixed up in the Pichegru conspiracies by having the General call upon him in Paris. His name was posted on the walls of Paris in a paper entitled "A List of Brigands in the pay of England to assassinate the First Consul." He was arrested and conducted to the Temple. Crowds of people called on Madame Moreau to express their sympathy. Gen. Pichegru, who could have cleared up all doubts about Moreau, was discovered dead in his cell. For five months General Moreau was not permitted to see his family. On the 30th of May, 1804, he was put on trial with other State prisoners. He was tried on five indictments. One was for not having denounced his old friend Pichegru, when he knew of his criminality."

Moreau himself addressed the court in one of the most eloquent speeches on record. I extract one portion:

"Some events in the life of the most virtuous men living may be obscured by unfortunate circumstances, either effected by chance or by the workings of malice. Finesse and artifice may do away suspicion from a criminal, and may seem to prove his innocence; but the surest way to judge an impeached man is by the general tenor of his conduct through life. In this way, then, I shall speak to my persecutors. My actions have been public enough, I conceive, to be well known. I shall call to your recollection but a few of them; and the witnesses I desire to bring forward on the occasion are the French people themselves, and the nations whom France has conquered."

He closed his speech thus:

"Magistrates, I have now nothing more to say. I solemnly call heaven and earth to witness the innocence and integrity of my intentions. You know your duty. France awaits your decision. Europe contemplates your proceedings, and posterity will record them."

The trial ended June 9, 1804. While others were sentenced to death, General Moreau was sentenced to two years imprisonment.

Napoleon consented that he should banish himself from France. He went with his lady and family, by the way of Barcelona, to Cadiz, where he embarked for the United States. He resided at Bristol, Penn., for a few years. The house and stables are yet standing.

I have told what he did here while living in this city. At 119 Pearl, his house was ever open. He resided in that until he started to return to Europe, to take a part in the downfall of the man who had overshadowed his life — Napoleon.

I do not think Madame Moreau left with him, for the house was not given up until 1814. Previous t that the magnificent furniture was advertised and sol at public auction. Crowds attended the sale.

The battle of Lutzen was fought on the second of May, 1813, between Napoleon and the Allies. Previous to that day, Russia had sent an invitation to New York to General Moreau, requesting him to leave America and join the camp of the Allies. It was a high honor, and he accepted it. Here he and Bernadotte met again in the same camp, and were a great acquisition to the war councils of the allies. Prince Schwartzenberg commanded. On the 23d of August, 1813, the army was at Dresden. The sovereigns of Russia and Prussia, as well as General Moreau, had descended from Bohemia and were on the left bank of the Elbe.

On the 25th, the allies commenced the assault on Dresden. On the 26th, it continued fiercely, and on the 27th, in a tremendous rain storm, Napoleon caused 200,000 of his troops to file out of the city, and diverge upon different points like the stick of a fan when expanded.

A heavy cannonade continued on both sides. Napoleon observed one of the batteries of the Young Guard slacken fire. He inquired the cause. Was told. He said, "Fire on nevertheless."

The firing was resumed, and from an extraordinary movement among the troops on the hill, the French became aware that some officer of high rank had been struck down. Napoleon supposed that the sufferer must be Schwartzenberg.

The next morning, however, a peasant brought to Napoleon more precise accounts. The officer hit, had both legs shattered by the bullet, and was taken from the field on a bier of lances. Both the Emperor of Russia and King of Prussia had expressed the greatest sorrow. The man ended his account by bringing the fallen officer's dog, a grayhound, whose collar bore the name of "Moreau." He died a few days afterwards.

Two doors from the noble residence of Moreau, No. 119 Pearl, lived an old solid family named Goelet, at 113 and 115 Pearl.

The old man, Peter Goelet, was an ironmonger during the War of the Revolution, and in 1786 did business in the same place, then called 48 Hanover square. A few years later, old Peter's eldest son, Peter P. Goelet, took up the same business at No. 6 Great Dock street (Pearl.) Up to 1792, Pearl street that now is, was only Pearl from the Battery to Broad; from Broad to Hanover square, it was Great Dock street. Hanover square had its own name and numbers up to Wall. From there to Chatham it was called Queen street, and from Chatham to Broadway, it was Magazin street. The whole line from the Battery to Broadway, forming a half circle, is now Pearl street. Young Peter P., afterwards opened a store at 63 Water. His brother, Robert R., opened another store at 59 Water, and did business there many years.

Old Peter died about the time of the War at the double number 113 and 115 Pearl. His son Peter P., moved in, and lived there for some time afterward.

Peter P. did business as late as 1826, at 69 Water, and lived at 53 Broadway. When he died, he was a very old man. He had a son, Peter, grandson of and named after old Revolutionary Peter. Young Peter kept up the old business to within 28 years.

Robert Ratsey, the brother of Peter P., went into business upon his own hook in 1792, at 59 Water street, five doors from his brother. He died somewhere about 1820, and left his wife Margaret a large property. He had sons, but I believe they died unmarried. A daughter married some years ago. I think the old lady is yet alive, and if so, she must be nearly eighty years old. Her husband, Robert R., was a stout, fat man, excessively good natured, and a most remarkable swimmer. When Rabinau opened his bath, foot of Harrison street, crowds used to go and see old Mr. Robert Goelet swim. He would lay upon his back, place his hands under his head, and float upon the water, as securely as if on a feather bed.

Both Robert R., and his brother Peter P., married sisters, the Misses Buchanan. Their father was an eminent Scotch merchant, named Thomas Buchanan He lived and did business at No. 41 Wall, and in 1799 he was a director of the U. S. Bank. He came over to this country with Archibald Gracie before the war.

When Peter P. lived at 113 and 115 Pearl, after his father's death, his family were very intimate with General Moreau and his lady.

Peter P. left two sons. One was named Robert. He married a Miss Ogden. She was a daughter of Jonathan Ogden, who lived at No. 4 State street, and occupied many years that old store (still standing a monument of old New York) corner of Whitehall and Bridge streets. That store when built, caused all the citizens of New York a surprise on account of its magnitude. Claffin, Mellen & Co.'s large store in 1861, was not a circumstance to it. Mr. Ogden founded the house of Ogden, Ferguson & Co. Mr. F. also married a daughter of old Jonathan.

Young Peter, the son of Peter R., and grandson of old Peter of Revolutionary times, still lives among us. But, long ago, he left No. 53 Broadway. His wealth is vast — not less than five or six millions.

Are there not tens of thousands of New Yorkers, and millions of strangers, who have passed by a large brick house in Broadway, corner of Nineteenth street, and wondered who dwelt in that spot? The house is in the middle of a third of an acre of grass plot. Several handsome, but unhappy peacocks wander about those grounds — no female old or young — no child of either sex, was ever seen about that spot. I have never seen a man about those premises, and yet there lives the wealthy Peter No. 3, the oldest descendant of old Peter Goelet No. 1 — the ironmonger of 48 Hanover square in 1780.

We like these solid Goelets. Our pen has done more to immortalize three generations of these worthies than was ever done before. Beyond the two lines of record, of death, of marriage, occasionally, their names have not appeared in print.

They are not found among the lists of successful politicians, either in the Common Council, Legislature, or Congress — among militia officers, or in navy registers. Neither are they to be found as directors of banks, insurance companies, houses of refuge, or lying-in asylums, and yet they have lived, and died among us for nearly 100 years, honored and respected, enjoying themselves in their own quiet way, while real estate advanced, and they and our colossal old city got rich together.

May the worthy race keep peacocks in the heart of the city, in 2861.

I have alluded to Riley's book store, No. 1 City Hotel He also kept No 4 City Hotel. There were at one period (60 years ago) stores under the Hotel not known to those who know it only 30 years ago just previous to its being destroyed.

On the Broadway and Cedar street corner under the Hotel, James Hostin kept for many years, (in fact until the Hotel was given up) a large wine cellar. He kept the choicest stock of claret and French wines in the city. In our last we alluded to him as being the father of Miss Jane Hostin, one of the best scholars in the celebrated economical school, and as living at No. 59 Fair or Fulton street.

Many a glass of wine have we tasted at his place. It was a place of resort of old Frenchmen. Mr. Hostin was one of those unfortunate persons driven out of St. Domingo by the Negro race. He lost his all, and like many others, who escaped from that Island, had to commence the world anew in New York. He was the father of twelve children. He died about 18 years ago. His widow lived until within a short time.

His daughter Jane, the scholar, who received the prize, married Quincy Degrove.

She died a year ago, and her husband three months later. They left no children.

That French school was a celebrated one, for many years. It had a regular Board of directors, viz:

"*Economical School.*"

Hon. DeWitt Clinton, President; J. B. A. M. Lombart, Vice President; Charles Wilkes, Treasurer; G. H. De Neuville, Secretary; Clement Moore; Doctor McNeven, Louis La Rue, Doctor Cognacq and Doctor Evrard.

The building was large, has two wings and a steeple, with a bell in it. It stood in the open ground, in Anthony (now Worth), north of the Hospital grounds. When it was pulled down, Doctor Lisle's Christ Church was built upon the same spot.

The printing office of the School was at No. 59 Church street.

Doctor McNevin was an Irish patriot. He practised medicine at 69 Beekman street.

Doctor Cognacq was a French emigre. He had a large practice, and lived at 27 Chatham street.

Clement C. Moore was the only son of Bishop Moore, and grandson of Major Clement Clark. He is still living. His mother was married in 1778, and C. C. Moore must be a very aged man.

Charles Wilkes commenced as a clerk in the Bank of New York when it first started in 1786, and rose to be its President. For many years he was its Cashier. He lived at 31 Wall street a long while; but at the time of the school he lived at Greenwich, where he gave parties. Most of those mentioned in this chapter, especially General Moreau, were frequent visitors at his country seat.

De Witt Clinton lived over at 339 Pearl, in the old Isaac Roosevelt mansion, now occupied by Harper & Brothers.

Mr. Valentine has old Peter Goelet down as one of the most wealthy of merchants in 1795.

By the way, how few are aware of the value of those 'Manuals.'

If I dared suggest some subjects for his Manual of 1863, one would be the old Economical school house in 1810; Peter Goelet's residence in Nineteenth street, Ogden's great store, corner of Whitehall and Bridge streets; and John Murray's (1776) Brewery, between Roosevelt and Catherine streets.

CHAPTER XL.

I have mentioned the names of strong merchants that contributed during the last war with England, in 1813, to support the Federal Government, and sustain it vigorously. Upon the list will be found the names of John Rathbone & Son for $20,000.

That house was in existence and did business in 1804 —long before the war, and long after. Its patriotism prospered it, and has not deserted the name now, for John Rathbone, No. 3, great-grandson of the old founder, still does business under the firm of Rathbone & Havens, at No. 11 Nassau street.

When the house first started, it was at No. 96 Front street, and the old gentleman lived at 45 Dey street— a fashionable part of the town in 1805. He was born in Stonington, Ct., in 1751, and removed to this city soon after the close of the Revolutionary war. He clerked it for some time, as is usual with Connecticut boys, and then entered into business upon his own hook about 1795. He died in 1843, in this city, 92 years old. He had two sons and one daughter.

His eldest son, John Rathbone, jr., who was taken into the concern of John Rathbone & Co. in 1804, was a gentleman of extraordinary good sense and sound information. He was a member of our State Legislature in 1823, and made a reputation for himself in politics.

John Rathbone & Son were largely engaged in the salt trade, as well as in general merchandizing. All their operations were upon an immense scale, and were conducted with such sagacity and prudence as to yield the two partners a handsome fortune. The Rathbones, father and son, were warm supporters of the Government, and would have sacrificed every dollar they were worth if the United States had needed it. Their names stand at the head of the list published a short time ago.

Saml. B. Ruggles, ex-Canal Commissioner, &c., married the youngest daughter of old Mr. Rathbone, and, of course, was a brother-in-law of John, jr., and Thomas. The two were very active in getting a charter and establishing the present Bank of Commerce. Both were among the first directors elected. Thomas Rathbone died early. He left a son named E. Beverley Rathbone. He married a daughter of Capt. Whetton, of the Sailor's Snug Harbor. E. B. R. is dead. He left a son, alluded to as still in business here.

John Rathbone, jr., never married. He died at Albany in 1842. He was on his way home to New York. His age was sixty-eight years.

His father, the old John, who died in 1843 aged ninety-two, was descended from a brother of Col. John Rathbone, who was a colonel in the Parliamentary army of 1658. He was noted for his devotion to Republican principles. So active had been this brave fellow, during the civil war, that he was excepted, by name, from the general amnesty for political offences granted by Charles II, when he mounted the throne.

Col. Rathbone escaped pursuit, and took refuge in "Whitefriars," or Alsatia, where he remained concealed several years. He was finally apprehended, with other ex-officers of the Commonwealth, tried at the Old Bailey, found guilty, and with seven other officers beheaded at Tyburn, on the 26th of April, 1666 — almost 200 years ago. His brother, more fortunate, got over to Connecticut, and was the founder of the old New York merchants we have alluded to.

Aaron, a brother of old John, was engaged in the wholesale grocery business in this city a number of years; about 1815 he removed to Waterford, Saratoga County, and engaged in business with John Knickerbocker, with whom he remained several years. In 1821 he married a sister of Robert Chesebrough; he died in 1845, leaving two sons, Robert C. and Aaron H.; both have been in business in this city a number of years. Aaron H. has been engaged largely in real estate and accumulated a fortune, and is accounted among our millionaires; both are married and have children. Aaron H. married the eldest daughter of Captain Richard F. Loper of Philadelphia, the well-known veteran yachtsman and shipbuilder. His famous yachts Madgie, (now Magic,) Josephine and Palmer, have won more prizes than any others of the New York Yacht Squadron. The Magic having won the Queen's Cup in the late contest, beating the Cambria and the entire squadron. Captain Loper was at one time the largest shipbuilder and owner in the United States, having constructed also a large number of vessels for the government during the Mexican and the late civil war. Robert C. married the youngest daughter of the late James W. Bleecker, one of the original founders of the Board of Stock Brokers of this city; he was its second president, and at the time of his death in 1861 had held the office of treasurer for thirty-three consecutive years.

Another of the same old stock and also born in Stonington, was the well known Captain John Rathbone. For many years he commanded vessels out of this port. What a splendid fellow was Captain Jack. He entered upon a sea-faring life at an early age, and was before the mast in the first English packets in 1804. He was destined in after years to command the finest ships in the line.

When he first came here, the "British Packets," as they were designated, were of about 179 tons burthen. Their sailing to and from the United States was as follows: Their station was at Falmouth, England. The mail for New York, Quebec and Halifax was made up the first Wednesday in the month, and the packet sailed on the following Saturday.

The sailing of the packet from New York frequently depended upon adventitious circumstances, but as often as it could be done, the mail was made up on the first Wednesday, and the packet sailed the Saturday following for Falmouth.

The packets sailed for New York direct from Falmouth in November, December, January and February, the other eight months they went and returned by way of Halifax, Nova Scotia. The return of the American packets was calculated at fifteen weeks to New York and back to Falmouth.

The following is a list of the regular packets employed in 1805 between Falmouth and New York:

"Lord Auckland." Captain Schuyler; "Earl of Leicester," Captain Peell; "Townshend," Captain Dodd; "Princess Elizabeth," Captain Kidd; "Marlborough," Captain Ball, captured in the West Indies by the French. but afterward retaken; "Princess Amelia," Captain Stevens; "Princess Charlotte," Captain Ker; "Chesterfield," Captain Blight; "Lord Charles Spencer," Captain Catesworth; "Duke of Kent,' Captain Dennis, captured by the French in the West Indies; "Lady Arabella," Captain Porteus; "Lady Hobart," Captain Fellows, lost upon an island of ice; "Prince Ernest," Captain Petre; "Prince Adolphus," Captain Boulderson; "Queen Charlotte," Captain Mudge "Windsor Castle," Captain Sutton.

It seems almost incredible that twenty-four years after the Independence was acknowledged, that the city of New York depended upon English packets for communication. Yet so it was. Those little cock boats not so large as a North River sloop made about two voyages a year. Fancy such a list of names to come poking into New York.

The names of all old King George's family — wife, sons, daughters, sons-in-law, ministers and officers of the crown.

What a change since! New York could not sport ships then. Why? Because in 1805 New York contained but a few thousand people. It was a little bit of a place comparatively speaking.

I am preparing a list of the vessels and changes that occurred slowly in the packet arrangements from the year 1804 to the time when great ships of a thousand tons were placed in the English trade as regular liners.

I do not know how long Captain Jack Rathbone was an apprentice to that old line of royal names. This I do know: some eight years later, he commanded a small coasting vessel during the last war with Great Britain, and was one of the foremost in managing "the torpedo affair," with a view of blowing up the British fleet at anchor off his birthplace, old Stonington.

In this enterprise the Captain exhibited the greatest coolness and daring. He afterwards commanded several ships; among them the packets "Crawford," "Talma,"

"Kentucky," and "Nashville;" and he made voyages out of this port to nearly every port in the known world. When ashore he lived up Hester street, at Nos. 81 and 56, from 1815 until 1830.

In one of his voyages in the "Crawford," during a tremendous hurricane, the ship struck on the "Bahama Banks." She had a large number of passengers on board, and the greatest consternation prevailed among them. Every one seemed to give way to the expectation of being lost, except Captain Rathbone himself. With the greatest perseverance, coolness, and presence of mind, he succeeded in landing safely every person on board, and his conduct on the occasion has been spoken of in the highest terms of commendation.

Captain Rathbone was appointed to the command of the "Oxford," one of the old line of Liverpool packets in 1834. I have given the line in which he sailed in 1804. I will now give the list thirty years later of the Liverpool packets alone. In the Old Line, or Black Ball Line, as it was called, ships "Columbus," De Peyster, master; "Hibernia," Wilson; "South America," Barstow; "England," Waite; "Orpheus," Bursley; "Oxford," Rathbone; "North American," Hoxie; "Europe," Marshall.

They sailed from New York and Liverpool on the 1st and 16th of each month. Goodhue & Co. and C. H. Marshall were the agents in this city.

A second line was ships "Roscoe," Delano, master "Independence," Nye; "Washington," Holdridge; "Pennsylvania," Smith.

Grinnell, Minturn & Co., were the agents. The ships left New York on the 8th, and Liverpool on the 16th of each month.

A third line was ships "United States," Holdredge, master; "St. Andrew," Thompson; "Virginia," Har-

Robert Kermit was agent of that line. It left New York on the 24th, and Liverpool on the 8th of each month.

There was yet another, called the "New Line." Some called it the "Dramatic." It consisted of the ships "Shakespere," Collins, master; "Siddons," Palmer; "Sheridan," Russell; "Garrick," Robinson.

E. K. Collins was agent of that line.

There were twenty ships, to take the place of three little English packets of 179 tons.

Some of the above ships were of 1,000 tons. Who does not remember their gallant captains? Where are they all now?

Captain Rathbone continued in the "Oxford" until May, 1846, when he was transferred to the "Columbia," a ship built expressly for him.

He was in the "Oxford" during the great gale at Liverpool in 1837, when the "Pennsylvania," "St. Andrew," "Victoria," and a number of other vessels were lost. On that trying occasion, when his ship was dragging her anchors and rapidly drifting ashore, his coolness, decision, and admirable management saved the ship and every person on board.

Captain Rathbone was washed overboard from the ship "Columbus" on the 13th of January, 1847.

Another large house was that of Jenkins & Havens, shipping merchants. They did business at 198 Front street, as early as 1804. The original partner in founding the house was Philetus Havens. He continued in it a few years, and then, in 1811, Jenkins left Philetus to carry on business at the same spot, which he did to about 1818. Jenkins removed to 189 Front street, and there carried on the same style and firm of Jenkins & Havens, but with Rensselaer Havens for a partner, instead of Philetus.

The latter was a person of somewhat extraordinary character. He was born at Shelter Island, Suffolk county, in this State, where his ancestors emigrated in 1699 from Rhode Island.

Rensselaer Havens had an elder brother, Jonathan Nicoll Havens, who was a member of Congress during Jefferson's administration, and was noted for his fine intellectual attainments.

Rensselaer came to New York in 1794, when just of age, and commenced clerking it with the then great house of Minturn & Champlin, who did business at 214 Front street as early as 1792, and up to 1815 at 286.

I have spoken of the great shipping house in a former chapter. They endorsed Jacob Barker's note for $18,000, and the proceeds went to the Government loan in 1810.

After Rensselaer left the employ of M. & C., he entered into a large dry good business upon his own account, at 169 William street. He continued in that until he became a partner of the old house of Jenkins & Havens, alluded to above, at 189 Front street. His residence was at 100 Chambers street. The house of Jenkins & Havens did a very extensive shipping business. The partnership lasted until after 1815. During the war they fitted out the private armed brig "General Armstrong." Her desperate fight against superior odds in the port of Fayal, has become a matter of history.

This privateer took eighteen prizes during the war, and some of them were of great value. It may not be generally known that during that short war our privateers took from England sixteen hundred and ninety-four prizes.

The claims against the United States for the loss of this dashing privateer in a neutral port, still remains unsettled. Other privateers were fitted out by this firm during the war.

In our list of contributors to the loan of $16,000,000 in 1813, there stands the name of Rensselaer Havens, for $20,000. He came forward promptly when President Madison became embarrassed for want of means to carry on the war.

In 1815, after the war, Mr. Havens withdrew from active commercial life, and devoted himself mainly to works of philanthrophy. He assisted in the foundation, and became a trustee of the Public School Society, the New York Sunday School Union, and Mariner's Church, and for more than a quarter of a century, he served as an elder in the old Brick Church, under the care of Rev. Dr. Spring. The *Times* building now occupies the site of the old church and graveyard.

In 1819 Mr. Havens was appointed on a committee of prominent New York merchants, to enter into a correspondence with citizens in various parts of the Union, with a view to devise some plan for checking the spread of African slavery. Archibald Gracie, General Clarkson, and Henry Rutgers served upon the same committee.

In 1825, Mr. Haven obtained the charter of the Howard Insurance Company. He was chosen president, and held the office twenty-nine years, or until his death in 1854.

He carried that company safely through the terrible fire years, 1835 and 1845, when the city suffered so fearfully, and many fire companies were ruined. He established that institution firmly in public confidence. It has stood over thirty-five years, and now is in as great favor as any company in the city, and has, as it had when Rensselaer Haven was its president, a superior Board of Directors.

When he died he was eighty-one years of age. He left a large family, having been twice married. His first wife was a Miss Jenkins, of Hudson, N. Y. General Worth was a near relative of this family. His second wife was a Miss Webb, of this city. One of his sons is a partner in the firm of Rathbone & Havens, and that concern, not less patriotic than their ancestors of fifty or sixty years ago, are getting up a military company to join the New York legion.

No merchant or citizen ever stood higher in this city than the venerable Mr. Haven. In his old age, his appearance was grand and striking. His death was felt as a public loss.

Some one has sent me a paper of 1805, showing that Peter P. Goelet was one of the directors of the Western and Northern Canal Company. I was under the impression that the Goelets never had their names as directors of public institutions. Of course I am corrected. I certainly cannot make out what canal company that was. Peter Schuyler was president, and John Murray, the merchant described in those chapters, was vice-president. Thomas Eddy was secretary and treasurer. Probably it was the father of the Erie canal.

Townsend, Vanderbilt & Co. were extensive grocers at 165 Fly Market. The head of the firm, Thomas Townsend, kept in the same locality from 1804 to 1815, and lived at 22 Cliff. He afterwards moved to 176 Front, and lived at 92 Beekman, a few doors from his store.

Mr. Joseph Lawrence, a well known merchant, for many years was a partner of the firm of Hicks, Lawrence & Co., and Lawrence & Trimble. He was brother of old C. W. Lawrence. Old Thomas S. Townsend had a son named John Q. Townsend, president of the New York Life Insurance and Trust Company until he died, in 1846. He was forty-six years of age. The elder Townsend was probably the principal capitalist of the house of Hicks, Lawrence & Co., when it first started

CHAPTER XLI.

Passing along slowly to the grave, having traveled eighty or ninety years, we meet every now and then venerable men, who were men of mark in this town sixty or sixty-five years ago. Some, even before Washington died.

As we recognize them in the street, we involuntarily pause, in respectful attitude, and carefully mark their strange, shy look, acting as if strangers, or as if suddenly transferred to Pekin, or the city of the great Mogul, seeming to have forgotten the fact that they were once men of renown here. These very men can hardly realize that their city and its suburbs has grown from 23,000 to over a million of population!

Twenty-three thousand! Why, one can live among 23,000 people, and know almost everybody, even down to the little children, and be known to them, as you take your walk down to the Battery, in 1786 — and that was only seventy-five years ago! The man we have in our mind's eye now was a man with an eagle eye and majestic presence three quarters of a century ago, and the eye has not dimmed yet.

"An old merchant?" ask our regular readers. No — not exactly; and yet so closely allied has he been with them, that I must allude to him. Sometimes I think I will add "and citizens" to "Old Merchants," so as to give me full latitude to write about all the old worthies of the past or present, whose names are familiar and dear to every thorough New Yorker.

A few days ago, a regiment called the "Steuben Volunteers" was presented with a flag made by a fair lady. An address was made by Judge Charles P. Daily — a most excellent and just judge, loved and respected, and in other years dearly esteemed by the great Calhoun.

He made the address. Standing among the crowd of listeners was an old man, absorbed in the words — unknown to every one except "Walter Barrett," who philosophized upon the probable astonishment of both orator and crowd had they known the fact that the tall old man was regarded almost as a son by Baron Steuben, and that for many years he was an aid-de-camp and a member of the family of the Baron. Yet, such was the fact. I allude to John W. Mulligan.

I have no means of judging of the age of Mr. Mulligan, but I imagine he must have been born before the war, and not far from 1769. If I am right, he is now about ninety-two years old.

Baron Steuben lived down at No. 32 Broadway as late as 1792. I had marked out for this chapter, Charles Brugiere, an extensive French merchant, who gave his magnificent hospitalities, well remembered now by many, at No. 32 Broadway, a few doors above the Adelphi Hotel.

After the war, the Baron was a prominent man in the city. He was Vice President of the Cincinnati Society, elected in 1786.

John W. Mulligan was admitted an attorney in the Supreme Court of the State, May 4, 1795, and he opened his office at No. 160 Broadway, where he lived with his father, Hercules Mulligan, an old respected citizen, during the war and many years after. He was one of the most fashionable merchant tailors in his day, and in the war kept at No. 23 Queen (Pearl), not far from Pine. He afterwards moved to No. 3 Vesey street, where the Astor House now stands. He must have died toward the close of the century. He was one of the famed "Sons of Liberty" that my learned friend Henry B. Dawson, of the Historical Society, has written and lectured so much and so satisfactorily about. Besides John W. Mulligan, Hercules had another son named William C. Mulligan. Both sons were lawyers, of extensive practice, for many years.

William C. did business as late as 1833, at No. 38 Cedar, and lived at 118 Chambers street. I remember though, about that time or later, he had an office or dwelling in Nassau, between Maiden Lane and Liberty. He must have died about 1835 or 1836. He left sons. His eldest was Henry Strong Mulligan, William was his second. He had other sons. Old William died rich. He was a very religious man, and a communist of Dr. Mason's Church in Cedar street.

He married Miss Strong, a daughter of Selah Strong, an eminent merchant in 1800. "Selah Strong & Son" had their store at No. 160 Front street. The name of the son was James. Old Mr. Strong lived many years at No. 12 Courtlandt street. James occupied the same house as late as 1832. He married Aletta Remsen, a daughter of Simon Remsen. She is still alive, and resides at some place on Long Island. James Strong, the brother-in-law of Mr. Mulligan, was also a brother-in-law and partner of Peter Remsen, who did business in New York for over forty years, commencing about 1796, and ending August 26, 1836, when he died. He opened a grocery store at No. 15 Coenties Slip, in the fomer year.

About the commencement of this century, the Remsens were numerous as merchants, in this city. An uncle of Peter, named *Rem*, did business at No. 12, Little Dock (now Water street). Rem was a bachelor. His father was Peter Remsen, an old merchant in 1774 and who died in 1771. His grandson, Peter (Rem's nephew, and Strong's brother-in-law), did an immense business in later years. His store was a large double one at No. 109 Pearl, north side of Hanover Square, where Hoffman & Pell, auctioneers, now do business. He had many partners, and they all made fortunes. One was James Strong, another James McCall, and also Frank Olmstead. Mr. Peter lived at No 2 Bowery many years, and after at No. 52 Broadway. His ancestors came here in 1632. Peter Remsen was an extraordinary mercantile man. He was director in many of our important corporations. He, for a long time, was a director in the Merchant's Bank, and associated with David Lydig at that Board.

Old Selah Strong (merchant) was an Alderman of the Third Ward in 1799 and some years following. John W. Mulligan was Assistant Alderman for the Third Ward from 1806 to 1809. He had a large legal practice, and was for many years one of the most popular men in the city, where now few of this generation know him.

Sixty years ago, this young man was master of the Howard Masonic Lodge in this city. No man took a more active part in public affairs than Mr. Mulligan. He married a most amiable lady, and by her had some children. He had but one son — John W. Mulligan, Jr., a most estimable young man, who died a few years ago. Young John was brought up to be a merchant. He clerked it with the celebrated dry goods commission merchants, Horace Waldo & Co., 71 Pine street, and after leaving their employ, entered into business upon his own account, which he continued until his death. He married, but I think left no children. The elder Mulligan had three daughters. Somewhere about 1831 one of them married the Rev. Mr. Hill, and she and her sister Frederica, accompanied that gentleman to Greece, where the great American Mission School, under their charge, became so celebrated. I believe the School is still in existence, and that they are still there. After Mr. Mulligan lost his wife, and a younger daughter, Mary, he, too, went to Greece and resided at Athens many years. I believe he was United States Consul at Athens.

Mr. Hill was a particular friend of the late Dr. Milnor, who was so many years the rector of St. George's Church in Beekman street. Mr. Mulligan was one of the old doctor's favorites, until the death of the former separated them.

I have not spoken to the venerable Mulligan for many years, and I should certainly have not been led into bringing his name up in these chapters, had I not recognized his venerable form — standing alone, on a recent p blic occasion, unknown to the world, and where 70 years ago every one would have known him by name if not personally. Several lawyers of distinction were once students of Mr. Mulligan ; among them was John Leveridge, who for many years had his law office at 145 Cherry street I hope Mr. Mulligan may reach the good old age of 100 years.

I have already alluded to the French people who emigrated from France to St. Domingo in 1792, and from

St. Domingo at a later period to this country. Most of them came to New York, a few went to Philadelphia. Among those who left France in 1792, and went to St. Domingo was Charles Brugiere. He was of a noble French family of that name. After the massacre of St. Domingo, he came to this country with a family of the name of Teisseire, and landed in Philadelphia. Shortly after their arrival in the Quaker City, Mr. Brugiere married Miss Teisseire, and then entered into a business co-partnership with her brother, under the firm of Brugiere & Teisseire, in 1801. Their nominal business dry goods importing and jobbing. They imported French goods to a heavy amount up to the war of 1812. This firm was as celebrated for its enormous business in those years, as A. T. Stewart & Co., of this city are now. They continued to do a large business all through the war, and no firm was more respected than this. They were regarded as the *beau ideal* of safe, prompt merchants, and honored as high minded citizens.

In 1816, when Philadelphia went through that terrible ordeal, when she was nearly ruined by the State of Kentucky, this French house, though it met with immense losses, stood firm.

Philadelphia had given long credits to merchants and traders in the State of Kentucky. In 1816 forty-two Kentucky banks failed, and every body went by the board. Millions were lost by merchants of Philadelphia, and those debts never have been paid. Brugiere & Teisseire went through it all safely, became very prosperous and very rich. Mr. Brugiere was a director in the old United States Bank, when the president of the renowned institution was Mr. Langdon Cheeves, of South Carolina.

In 1823, Brugiere & Teisseire, finding their importations must all come through New York, decided to establish a branch house here, under the style of "Charles Brugiere & Antony Teisseire." That year Charles Brugeire came here first, and opened a place of business at 55 Greenwich street.

Very soon the New York branch became far more important than the original house, and did twice the business, the facilities for doing an importing business being twice as great. In a few years their business became immense. Mr. Teisseire never came on here to live, but continued to reside in Philadelphia.

The year after the house was established in New York, they took a store at 174 Pearl street, and there they kept for years, having a very heavy assortment of French dry goods constantly on hand.

The residence of Mr. Brugiere was at No. 30 Broadway, and his house was famous for its elegant and hearty hospitality. Madame Brugiere was a queenly woman, and she received grandly. She had no superior in this city. Every foreigner who visited the city frequented her home. There are many who will remember with delight her superb receptions. She gave one to bring out the Senorita Garcia, afterward the celebrated Madame Malibran.

She gave, at her residence in Broadway, the first fancy ball ever given in the United States, and set everybody crazy. Up to that time nothing of the kind had been seen in any part of America. Her spacious apartments were crowded with the very elite of city society. Not only that — Philadelphia, Baltimore, Boston and Albany sent its loveliest flowers to grace the occasion. For months before and after every one spoke in raptures of the "Grand Fancy Ball" of Madame Brugiere.

From her house on the Bowling Green went out invitations on the most deliciously perfumed cards to the furthermost extremities of the city. The adjoining house was annexed for the night. The theatres were ransacked for dresses; milliners worked night and day to get up fancy dresses. When the night came off, company poured in for hours, and were welcomed by Madame Brugiere.

Among the guests that night was Mr. Charles King, who was at that time called "the Pink" of good society. I believe Major Noah gave Mr. King that nickname. Noah also added, on the occasion of this fancy-dress ball, that Mr. King went in the dress of a private gentleman, and nobody knew him in that disguise. He afterwards went out and returned three times, changing his dress and disguise each time, and the last time the band played "God Save the King."

A most extraordinary character is that Charles King. He is a son of Rufus King, who was a member of the old Continental Congress from Massachusetts, in 1786. He came to New York afterwards to live, and was sent minister to England from the United States, and was also a senator from New York to Washington. All of his sons were remarkable men. John A. has been governor of this State. James G. was once a merchant in England, a great banker in this city, and a member of Congress. Frederick was a physician, and lived a No. 4 Bowling Green. He died young. Not the least clever of this very clever family was Edward King, who went to Ohio. Had he lived he would have made, not, perhaps, a second Webster, but the name of Edward King would have been known as one of the most famed orators of any age. But not far behind any of his brothers, three of whom have each exercised a greater influence, in their day, and generation, than their father, was Charles King, who has been more abused than any other man in this century. He was a merchant, and formed one of the firm of Archibald Gracie & Sons, in 1808. He had married the old gentleman's daughter. Their store was on the corner of Bridge and Whitehall streets and is still standing That firm continued until 1820. Mr. King was sent out to England after the war, by the President, and had something to do with the prisoners at Dartmoor. Major Noah hated him cordially, and frequently alluded to him in connection with the word "Dartmoor." Few would understand the application now. When Charles King was a director in the Bank of New York, Mr. Wilkes, the cashier, used to say he had the best financial head in the board.

As an editor he had no superior. He edited the *New York American* for many years, and had its financial matters been managed with half the cleverness given to the editorial department, it would have been alive now. For his second wife Mr. King married a daughter of the clever merchant, Nicholas Low, who lived near General Moreau, and has been so often alluded to in these chapters.

Mr. Charles King had several sons, but one especially named Charles, was a noble fellow. It is twenty-five years, or more, since my eyes looked upon him, but I did like him vastly: and I never heard how he was lost, though lost he was in the Pacific Ocean. Charley took to the sea, and rose to be captain. Now I will go back to the grand fancy ball of Madame Brugiere.

Everybody in New York spoke of this most splendid of splendid affairs. The elegance, the liberality, and the magnificence of the entertainment of Monsieur and

Madame Brugiere were the theme of every tongue and the admiration of every heart.

The supper was luxurious, and never since surpassed.

James W. Gerard, famous now as a clever, if not a remarkably handsome lawyer, was then a gay gallant. He was a regular visitor at the mansion of Madame Brugiere. So, too, was Mrs. John McGregor, wife of the McGregor, who was of the famous house of McGregor, Darling & Co. Mr. Gerard was the beau of Senorita Garcia (Madame Malibran,) and he paid her the most devoted attention.

Madame Brugiere was the mother of three of the most lovely daughters that ever lived in this or any other city of the world. They had no superior, either in beauty, education, grace or amiability. Eloise was the oldest, the next was Nathalie, and the youngest was Juliet.

The last was too pure and lovely a plant to live on this earth, and she was transferred to a different sphere in the very flower of her young life. She was an angel while she was here. Everybody loved her — every one who knew her admired her. When she died, and the brief notice announcing her death was sent to the office of *The New York American*, it caught the eye of Mr. Charles King. He added to it the following — "who never caused her parents grief but when she died." Mr. King knew the sweet girl well.

After her death the parents went to Europe, where hey resided some time. Previous to this, however, they moved from 30 Broadway to 48 Bond street, then a very fashionable part of the town. They used to give private concerts. Everybody of note attended.

They went to Europe after Juliet's death, and resided in Paris, the commercial house doing a large business all the while in this city. In 1838, Charles Brugiere retured to this city. Shortly after he was taken sick suddenly, and died. Madame lived but a few years after. Mr. Teisseire, his partner, had died a few years previous.

I believe the two daughters are still living.

So well thought of was Mr. Brugiere in Philadelphia, when he was a director of the U. S. Bank, that the president, when Mr. B. removed to New York, wrote to Morris Robinson, who then controlled the United States Branch Bank in this city, to make Charles Brugiere a director. It was done.

Brugiere & Teissiere were regular importers of silks and all the French dry goods. If they did a business of half a million of dollars annually, thirty years ago, it was equal to four millions to-day.

In their day was the old packet-ship times, and they were constant buyers of French and English bills of exchange to remit to the parties of whom they made their purchases in France. Their credit was unquestioned, and they could have bought a million of dollars of bills of exchange *on time*, had they wished to do so.

It would be safe to say that there was one constant scene of domestic confidence and happiness between these two persons, Monsieur and Madame Brugiere, from the time of their marriage until the day of his death — a period of over thirty-five years.

They were remarkable for their attachment to each other, and their sympathy — both having apparently the same purposes in life, the same pleasure in society, and frequently the same idea. Eickholt, the painter, used to tell a story about them, illustrating this idea in a beautiful manner. On one occasion, Mr. Brugiere called upon the painter, a short time previous to New

Year's Day. He ordered a painting, and sat several times for his likeness. He made it a condition, however, of strict secrecy. He wished no one to know of his intention. It was to have been painted, framed and placed in the parlor of his house on New Year's eve, so as to give Madame Brugiere an agreeable surprise the next morning. All was done as he wished. When the New Year's morning arrived, he asked his wife to go in the parlor. She did so. Both stared, for there were two portraits — his and her own. She had given the same order. Both charged the painter with betraying purposes that both had confided to him. He at last satisfied both that he had faithfully kept their secret.

CHAPTER XLII.

Many of our residents, in passing down Pearl street, beyond Chatham, towards Franklin square, may have observed over the door of store No. 426, corner of Madison, an old board sign, with the letters partly faded, I. & N. Robins & Co. Over that house that sign has been for fifty-one years. It was once a wooden building, No. 428 and (before Banker street was opened and name changed to Madison), was what is now 426 and 428. It was rebuilt by Mr. Robins in 1838, and the present double building was erected.

John Robins erected his first sign at No. 446 Pearl, as early as 1799. He has now been in business in New York sixty-two years, and he is still a merchant, capitalist, and as active, useful a citizen as we have among us.

After being a short time alone in business, he took in his elder brother Johnson, and the firm for a few years was J. & J. Robins. John was born in 1779, and Johnson in 1778. Later, in 1803, the firm moved to 450, and John also lived in the rear of 440, while Johnson lived at 434. Johnson afterwards went to the East Indies, where he died.

Besides Johnson, John had a younger brother, Nathan, who was born in 1783, and was in business with him from 1812 until 1840.

The way that John Robins came to start a dry goods store in Pearl street, on the east side of the block between Chatham and Madison streets, and within a few doors of where this spry young merchant of eighty-two now keeps, is curious.

But I must preface a little. He was born as I said, in 1779, in Monmouth county, New Jersey. When a lad he wandered to Philadelphia. Congress met there at that time. They were discussing the propriety of rejecting or confirming "Jay's" treaty. Meetings were held in different parts of the city, and young John Robins attended them to hear what was going on. On one occasion, Mr. Dallas, the father of the late minister to England, was speaking. He had a copy of the treaty in his hand, and after venting his indignation in the most fiery language, he flung it from him and exclaimed "kick the d——d thing to hell." The boys picked it up and made a bonfire of it, in front of the British Minister's house.

Where John was born there was game. He caught a muskrat, skinned it, and took the skin with him to Philadelphia on his first visit. He bartered the skin off for two books — one was Robinson Crusoe and the other a bible. He keeps the bible yet.

John was idling about Philadelphia, waiting for something to turn up, when the Whisky Rebellion broke out in Pennsylvania. A proclamation was issued to raise troops. There had to be notices served upon the military privates raised. He did this business, and received seventy-five cents, the first money he ever earned.

Not long after this, John Robins came on to New York, then quite a town, but not so large as Philadelphia. He had an elder brother named Enoch, who kept in Old Slip.

Enoch Robins owned several vessels, and was quite a shipping merchant of those days. He loaded his vessel with all sorts of assorted provision cargoes, pork, beef, onions, etc., and sent them to the West India Islands. He owned no vessels larger than 150 tons In fact, the largest ship owned in New York in 1796 did not exceed 250 tons burden. One of 200 tons was an uncommonly large ship.

Enoch owned one brig called the Mary, of 150 tons burden. He loaded her with staves for wine casks, dried codfish, and other truck, to make up the assorted cargo, and despatched the "Mary" from New York to Bilboa, in the Bay of Biscay. He sent his brother John out as supercargo. At that time the United States was at war with France, and the brig "Mary" had a narrow escape from a French privateer. She lay at Bilboa three months, selling cargo. Then the "Mary" went to Lisbon, disposed of her staves, and took on board a quantity of gold and silver for New York. The exportation of silver was prohibited by Portugal, but Mr. Robbins had a belt made, and every trip he made on board his vessel, he would take a thousand Spanish dollars. In this way he got on board $16,000.

At that time the British fleet was anchored at Lisbon, and among the vessels was the 64 gun ship "Asia,' that had given the city of New York so much trouble in the dark days of the Revolution.

Finally the brig "Mary" went to St. Ubes, loaded with salt, and got back safe to New York, making a splendid voyage. The salt sold for a dollar a bushel. The supercargo had saved several hundred dollars, which he put away in a safe place. On his return the supercargo, in 1797, had the yellow fever in Oak street. It was then called Rutgers street. But as that Rutgers street was rather a hard street, to please Colonel Rutgers, who wanted a nice street named after him, old "Rutgers" street was changed to "Oak," and the Rutger's name was given to the street that bears it even now.

After he recovered, the merchant Robins made up a voyage for the West Indies, and John Robins again started as supercargo. The vessel carried out an assorted cargo of provisions and vegetables. She cleared at New York for Surinam. Thence she went to Barbadoes, and afterward to Port Royal, Martinique. That island had been captured by the British.

Alongside of Robins' vessel lay a Connecticut craft, commanded by Baldwin Boardman, of New Haven.

"Do you want to see Benedict Arnold, Robins?" said Boardman to the supercargo.

"Benedict Arnold, the traitor? Why, what is he doing here?" asked Mr. Robins.

"He is one of his English Majesty's Commissary Generals at Port Royal. He comes alongside of my vessel every time I arrive here, and also to every other vessel that brings live cattle on here from any port in Connecticut. He never goes on board. He is fearful he might be knocked down, or be kept a prisoner and taken to the United States. He always asks for news and about different people in Norwich, New London, and other places, where he has relations, or where he used to be acquainted," remarked Captain Boardman.

The vessel of Mr. Robins went to St. Kitts, and afterwards to Turks Island, where she traded with salt, and returned to New York, making a capital voyage for her owner, and adding a few more dollars to the stock of our supercargo.

When John Robins got back, he made up his mind not to go to sea any more.

He was afloat in the city after his return about 1797. He had no resources except his few dollars. No trade, and his only available knowledge was picked up while voyaging for his brother.

He made up his mind to go into the dry goods business. He fancied he should like it, but of course, it would be necessary to learn the business before attempting it on his own account.

Now I come to the reason why John Robins came to start a dry goods store in that particular part of Pearl street, near to Chatham, No. 446. John was passing along Pearl from Chatham looking at the various stores, and the tasty manner in which the dry goods were temptingly displayed in front and in the windows. At that time, that part of Pearl was the fashionable shopping quarter. Old George Clinton who was a great hand at shopping, used to visit and buy at all those stores. So did the fashionable women of sixty years ago. Fancy such a state of things, as high born dames shopping in Pearl near Chatham! But at that time and for thirty years later, all the most famed millinery establishments were in William street, as low down as Maiden Lane. Young John Robins stepped in at one of these dry good stores and asked if they wished to get a young clerk. He had no success.

Finally, he halted at the door of 430 Pearl, where was kept a large stock of dry goods. It was a wholesale as well as retail store. Robins asked the owner the usual question:

" Do you want a clerk ? "

"What to do?"

"I want to learn the dry goods business."

"What wages do you expect?"

"None. I want to learn the dry goods business."

The proprietor of the store looked at him. He was earnest and honest. He liked his appearance.

"Very well, you may come; I'll try you."

That merchant was the celebrated Henry Laverty, who in after years became a renowned merchant and very rich. He was of the firm of Laverty & Gantley, No. 173 Pearl, thirty years later, and for many years he resided at No. 247 Broadway, between Park place and Murray street.

Who does not remember Harry Laverty? John Robins went to work for Mr. Laverty. He slept in his store on the counter. He got up at daylight, opened the store, swept it out, dressed out the windows with dry goods, shut it up at night, was busy every hour of the day, and constantly employed in learning the value and qualities of dry goods. Very soon such clerkly devotion began to be appreciated by Mr. Laverty. After the year or eighteen months for which he was engaged was up, he told Mr. Laverty he should leave him. Mr. Laverty was not ready to part with him.

"Oh, yes, John, you'll stay. I'll give you a good round salary."

"No, I know how to handle goods. I have acquired a good deal of knowledge, and I will try and do something for myself," said John.

Mr. Laverty offered a still more tempting salary. John still said "No." Then he was offered a partnership. John still said "No." His mind was made up. He was astonished at the partnership offer, but he firmly declined it. Mr. Laverty parted with him regretfully.

He had found out his sterling integrity, and his industry and care made him invaluable to anybody who was doing so large a business as Mr. Laverty.

After leaving the employ of Henry Laverty, John Robins determined to start a dry goods business on his own account. He had saved up carefully the money earned by him while supercargo for his brother. It was quite a little sum. He took a store at No. 406 — a few doors from Mr. Laverty — in August, 1799. It was an exceedingly small store, and at a low rent. As soon as he had hired it he went to "vendue" and bought dry goods for cash. These goods he carried from the auction to his new store himself, and that was the commencement of our merchant's fortunes, one year before the commencement of this century.

He adopted a rule then, that he has never since deviated from, viz.: not to run in debt. Unlimited credit was offered to him but he would not accept it. He preferred doing a small, secure business, until by economy he had accumulated a large capital, and could be better able to expand.

His mother was an uncommonly smart woman. She lived to be a very old lady, and kept house for her son John, who never married. She was a good, old-fashioned, Dutch-looking dame. In these days, the front door was cut in two in the middle, and swung on separate hinges. The upper part swung in, the old lady used to lean over the lower part closed, and watch what was going on in the street.

She was famous for making capital coffee, and in every other respect was an excellent cook, and could make good pies and cakes. She was an energetic, hard-working dame, and an early riser. She lived to be ninety five, and died the year after the cholera of 1832.

Mr. Robins continued on his quiet, snug business, until the War of 1812 broke out. Until then he had been successful, but in a small way. Now a new field was opened; and, after the blockade commenced, he was able to compete with some of the largest houses in the city. He purchased entire cargoes of such vessels as had successfully run the blockade and come into the harbor, or were smuggled through Canada.

His competitors at that time were men of large capital. There was old Laurence Salles, of whom I have written in other chapters. He kept his store at 136 Water street; Jotham Smith, who kept at 214 Broadway, where the museum now is; Harry Laverty, who had removed to 454 Pearl, although he had established himself with D. W. Gantly, at No. 149 Pearl, below Wall, and King & Mead, 175 Broadway, heavy dry good dealers.

All of the dry goods dealers bought cargoes of the great shipping houses such as Le Roy, Bayard & Co., Jacob Le Roy, Jonathan Goodhue, Astor and others.

Frequently old Salles and Mr. Robins would join together and purchase a cargo of valuable French goods — silks, velvets, laces, &c. &c. — paying therefor as much as fifty cents a franc (18 cents) on the advance cost, or more than 300 per cent. profit!

Those were gay, lively times, and money was made.

There never resided in the city a more lucky fellow than John Robins. Few have done business sixty-two years, and fewer still have had a constant run of uninterrupted prosperity from the beginning. He is the richest merchant in the city who has acquired his immense property in a legitimate business. Other merchants have become millionaires by the rise of real estate, which they happened to own in large quantities.

This is not the case with Mr. Robins. I am not aware that he ever owned real estate, except to a very limited amount.

His fortune has been made by his regular business and his knowledge and judgment in regard to the value of mercantile paper. He was content with profits, no matter how small. He was very economical, very saving, and very industrious. These great qualities, exercised for many years, have made him, as they will make every other man who practices them, very wealthy.

During the last year, (1861) Mr. Robins, who is hardly known to New Yorkers of the present generation, paid a larger *personal* tax than W. B. Astor, Mr. Stewart, or any other rich man in New York city ; and those who doubt it can ask Mr. James Kelly, the Receiver of Taxes, who will confirm what I say, and yet it is so contrary to the generally received opinion of who is most wealthy in our midst, that my assertion will hardly be credited.

But a man with the habits of John Robins, in a period of years embracing more than the full life of most men, must accumulate immensely.

He has never thrown away money. He is a bachelor, dresses plainly, and wears his clothes carefully. He has washed his hands and face daily in the same shilling tin basin for sixty and odd years, and in the open yard. He has done his own marketing all that time. Not niggardly, but has lived on plain, healthy fare. The furniture of his abode is very moderate, and the loss of interest on its original cost has never been much. Mr. Robins is no believer in the rich velvet carpets and costly furniture of a Fifth avenue palace.

He has never fooled away his money on beggars, or squandered it on institutions of a doubtful value. What he has given away in the last half century he has kept to himself, and has not placarded his name in the public papers in any such connection.

As I have said before, no merchant in this city ever possessed so correct a judgment. He rarely erred. He never made a hazard in his life, and but one bet. That was a hat between him and the celebrated Matthew L. Davis.

During the war, when property, and especially merchandise, was so precarious, he sold out his entire stock of merchandise on three several occasions at a great profit. One of these occasions was to Tredwell & Hone. Isaac S. Hone, 172 Pearl, was a partner. These transactions were very common. "What will you sell out for?" was asked. "Thirty thousand dollars," was the reply.

Isaac Hone and his partner bought out Mr. Robins. He was a great speculator. Tredwell & Hone failed, and old John Hone, his father, had to pay $130,000 for them. He was obliged to sell his United States stock to save the name of Hone from dishonor. He felt so deeply, and had so much pride in keeping the commercial name of his sons untainted, that he cheerfully made any sacrifice. Old John Hone was a trump in his day.

CHAPTER XLII.

During the last month of 1814, previous to the close of the war with England, every one was aware that when peace should be declared, all persons who had a large stock of goods on hand would suffer terribly, as prices would fall at once; but no one dreamed then of an early peace.

Sometime in January, 1815, a large lot of dry goods was advertised to be sold at auction, at the Tontine Coffee House, on a specified day, by Hones & Town, 61 Wall street, who were the auctioneers. The members of that great firm were John and Philip Hone and Charles Town.

I do not recollect the precise day when the sale was to come off, but it was a Saturday. There was a thousand cases of dry goods to be sold. Whether they had run the blockade safely, or been smuggled through Canada, I cannot say.

The goods were at a warehouse in Pine street. They had been exhibited a week. There were buyers here from Baltimore, Philadelphia, Boston, Albany, and every city around.

John Robins had examined the goods, and expected to buy largely, and had so marked his catalogue. He, Philip Hone, and Pelatiah Perit, now president of the

Chamber of Commerce, all belonged to an Artillery Regiment stationed at the West Battery (now Castle Garden.) Philip was a corporal, but John Robins and Perit were only privates. Mr. Robins served in the artillery company nine years and all through the war, obtaining his warrant for one hundred and sixty acres of land, which he now holds, and would not part with at any price.

Between whiles Mr. Robins soldiered and examined the dry goods to be sold. The day came — it was Saturday. The great sale commenced at ten o'clock, in the great bar-room of the Tontine Coffee House. There was a large crowd of buyers congregated — the bidding was very spirited, and the highest prices of the war were reached: the commonest samples of unwashable calicoes brought fifty to seventy-five cents a yard, such as to-day would sell at three cents.

Everybody outbid Mr. Robins. At one o'clock the sale adjourned, as was customary, that the buyers might go home and get their dinners, and be back by two, when the sale recommenced.

John Robins went home rather down in the mouth, and quite disheartened that goods had gone so high.

"Have you bought nothing, brother John?" said Nathan.

"No," was the surly reply, and he went back to the Tontine. His bad luck continued. Prices were higher than ever. Not a lot was struck down to Mr. Robins. Henry Laverty bought over $30,000 worth. About dark the sale closed. Every package had been sold. John Robins nad bought none. He felt annoyed. His stock of goods on his shelves did not amount to but a few dollars, a few remnants of calicoes, which he could have carried on his shoulder. He went to bed about eight o'clock, sick of his hard luck. He had just begun to drowse, when he heard some one down William street shout "peace." He opened his window — a man was running at the top of his speed. When he reached the corner of Pearl and Chatham streets, he screamed out again "peace," and as he sped on up Chatham street, once more the voice was borne through the air, with the simple word "peace," and the disappointed merchant lay down in his bed again, and wondered what it meant. The next day was Sunday, and it was a lovely morning. Mr. Robins rose early, and hurried over to the barber shop on the opposite side of Pearl.

While waiting for his turn, a friend came in and said: "Glorious news, eh, Robins?"

"What is the news? I have heard nothing," replied John Robins.

"Why a vessel reached Sandy Hook last night, and she brings news that on the 24th of December last, at Ghent, the commission signed a treaty of peace between Great Britain and the United States. There is no doubt it is true."

"Perhaps I was lucky in not buying yesterday at auction," thought John Robins, and he begged the barber to hurry with the shaving. That done, he hurried across the street, and told his mother the news. "Get breakfast as quick as possible," he added, "and I will hurry down to the printing office and see if it is true."

First he visited the office of *The Mercantile Advertiser*, at No. 150 Pearl street, near Wall. Already there were solid masses of delighted people, hearing and talking of the thrilling news. There was no longer a doubt about it. The vessel that bore the news had reached the dock, and the bearer of the dispatches for Government had passed on his way to Washington

All the stores in the neighborhood were opened. Among them was that of Henry Laverty, at No. 149, just below Wall.

His store was heaped up with goods bought at the auction sale on the previous Saturday. Mr. Laverty was walking rapidly up and down the store, and swearing like a trooper.

"John, did you buy any goods yesterday?"

"Not a dollar's worth."

"Well, that is always the way with you; you know when to buy and when to let alone. It is all dickey with me. I am ruined. I am going to have all these goods (the first floor was crowded) hoisted up into the lofts. I can't bear the sight of them."

By-and-by other merchants and large purchasers at the sale came in. "I bought $8,000 worth. I'll sell out for 4,000." There were no buyers. Another had bought $10,000 worth. He would sell for half price.

Mr. Laverty was nearly crazy. That night, Sunday night, cartmen were busy hauling goods to the auction store; and the next morning, Monday, every auctioneer was busy selling goods of all kinds for a mere song.

Lewis Hartman, one of the wealthiest and most prosperous grocers in the city, was nearly ruined by the peace. He had speculated without limit in coffee, sugar, teas, etc. He kept at 423 Pearl, corner of Rose, from about 1800. That same man lived in the house as late as 1837, but he had previously removed his store to 227 Front, where he did a grocery business, under the firm of Lewis Hartman & Son, as late as 1835.

By the year 1815, the credit of John Robins, in this city was unlimited. It stood on a basis too solid to be shaken. Yet rules of trade required an indorser. Laverty was the indorser, and Mr. Robins indorsed for Laverty. So great was the confidence in each other's stability, they never even took a memorandum of the extent of their indorsements for the other, but indorsed *ad libitum.*

John Hone & Son were then in business, and Myndert Van Shaick was Collector. He once said to Mr. Robins:

" Hereafter please to draw your notes to my order."

" Why so ? " asked Mr. Robins.

" Because it is too much trouble for me to go and get Mr. Laverty's indorsement."

This is convincing proof of a high mercantile standing. In later years he gave no notes, and it afforded persons a great deal of amusement to hear him threaten that if parties did not make a discount of six per cent., he would give his note. Any bank would cash his note for six per cent. per annum.

Mr. Robins never had any ambition to be known as a down town merchant, even after the character of that part of Pearl street where he lived had changed. He was known as a monied man. He was elected a director of the Phœnix Bank, and at one time when Mr. Boggs, the President, was in Europe, on account of his health, was elected vice-president. It is not generally known that "Phœnix" is a very appropriate name of the bank. In 1812 it was chartered as the " New York Manufacturing Company," with a capital of $1,500,000, with twenty years to run. In 1817, it had run so low that ts capital was cut down to $700,000, and its name was changed to " Phœnix" Bank. Again, in 1820, the capital was cut down to $500,000.

Mr. Robins was in it from that time to 1833, and regarded as one of the best directors the bank had. His knowledge of the value of mercantile paper was extraordinary, and to this day is so. John Delafield was cashier of the Phœnix. He was a great schemer, and ambitious to be president. Mr. Robins discovered that such was his aim, and determined to thwart him. He was for some time successful, but after a while the Board of Directors coalesced with Delafield, and he carried his point. Of course, the influence of Mr. Robins in the Board was somewhat weakened. During the time that Mr. Robins had been an active director, and his wishes predominated, the bank had met with great success. Its stock had gone up to 130 at the Broker's Board.

As soon as he discovered that Delafield would succeed, and had a majority of friends, he determined to resign. He told the other directors so, and added, "I have been a long time a director — I live a good deal out of the way — I am getting older than I was — I have neglected my business, and I now want to give way and make room for some younger man. I will resign and not be a candidate for re-election."

However, when the election came he was re-elected.

That very afternoon three of the directors, Henry Parish, Moses H. Grinnell and one other, called upon Mr. Robins and informed him that he was re-elected.

"I am sorry, for I was not a candidate," said Mr. Robins.

"You must serve," said Moses H. Grinnell. "We can't get on without you. Your knowledge of the value of dry goods commercial paper, makes you invaluable It is indispensable that you should serve."

"I'm sorry. But I told you I would not serve."

"We will not take 'no' for an answer," said Grinnell.

"I will not accede to your request," said Mr. Robins.

"Very well, will you say that you will not decide not to accept until to-morrow?" asked the directors.

"Very well. I will not," said Mr. Robins.

After they had stepped out, Mr. Robins went to work and made a list of every dollar of bank stocks that he held, including, of course, a heavy amount of Phœnix shares.

The next morning Mr. Robins went with this list to the office of his old friend, John G. Warren, the broker who kept then at No. 46 Wall street. He handed him the list: "John, sell every dollar of the stock on that list at the Board to-day."

It was done. All his Phœnix brought 130, and other stocks in proportion.

That afternoon the committee from the bank called to get his acceptance of the position as a director.

"Gentlemen," said Mr. Robins, "I believe the charter of the Phœnix Bank requires that all its directors shall be stockholders?"

"Certainly."

"Then I cannot serve, for I am no longer a stockholder."

The committee said no more. Phœnix Bank stock fell to 70.

Old Mr. Robins said that John Delafield would ruin the bank. He did. Again the capital stock had to be reduced one-quarter to get it to par.

After that Mr. Robins never would own a dollar's worth of any kind of bank or insurance stocks.

John Robins was once associated with John Jacob Astor, Nathaniel Prime and John Hone, as a committee to examine into the condition of a proposed loan asked for by the State of Ohio, to carry on her internal improvements. That great State had witnessed the success of the Erie Canal in this, and became anxious to follow in the track. Commissioners came on to Wall street to raise money. The subject was referred to the above persons. The true reason why Ohio state credit is to this day better than any other Western state, is doubtless due to the report of these financial gentlemen, and to the advice they gave the legislature of Ohio.

The Commissioners first applied to old Nat Prime, of the great house of Prime, Ward & King. He selected the other names, Robins, Hone and Astor. The Ohio agents left all their papers with these men, and they spent one night and day in a room together, carefully examining every document, and with fidelity searching into the true condition of Ohio. Fancy that scene! Watch the wrinkles on the faces of these venerable financiers as they carefully read the laws of Ohio!

Only one of these four shrewd, long-headed old men, yet lives, and that is Mr. Robins, the subject of this chapter.

They reported unanimously in favor of loaning to Ohio every dollar she asked for, provided the legislature of that state would insert in the law creating said loan a clause prepared by them relative to taxation, such as had been agreed upon by the four rich men, who stated that if this suggestion was perfected, the money should be had — the loan should be made.

The Ohio agents called at the time appointed to hear the report. Old Mr. Prime told them what was wanted to be made a law. That night the agents started for the capital of Ohio. The legislature was in session. That body promptly amended the law, as suggested by the money kings of Wall street. The agents again returned to New York, and got all the money Ohio wanted; and her credit has been A 1 from that day until now.

Mr. Astor and Mr. Robins were great friends, and the latter used frequently to purchase almost entire cargoes of the former, and particularly about the time of the war. On one occasion Mr. Robins had bought an immense quantity of long nankeens of John Hone & Sons. There was but one lot more in the market. This was held by John Jacob Astor. Mr. Robins went around to his store. It was then at 69 Pine street, corner of Pearl. Robins told Mr. Astor what he wanted. John Jacob went to a long counter in the middle of the floor, then took a duster, and brushed off all the dust or dirt; then laid down a sample of the nankeens. He was a very methodical man was Mr. Astor, and did his own business. He told chop-grade, and all that sort of thing.

"How many have you got?"

He named the quantity. "What is your price?"

He replied.

"I'll take 'em, said Robins.

"Have them to day?"

"Yes, send them up to 450 Pearl street."

Mr. Astor asked but one price, and he never departed from it. He represented everything as it was, and never deceived anybody. He never told a lie even by implication, to sell a lot of goods. They were always found to be as he had represented them. Mr. Astor and Mr. Robins were both directors in the celebrated Globe Insurance Company.

Mr. Robins always prided himself upon his thorough knowledge of dry goods — especially cloths. He knew the value of the finest broadcloths to a fraction. Up to 1855, he attended every auction sale where they were to be sold. He was never at all avaricious. He would work as hard to make a profit of a few cents a yard on a costly broadcloth as on a cargo of silks and nankeens. He was a capital judge. To those he liked, Mr. Robins was a thorough and a good friend. Those he disliked, never received favors at his hands, but they were pretty sure to get little notice from him.

He never carried an umbrella.

Once he sold some property in the Bowery, at No. 15½, for about $5,000. It was afterwards re-sold for $27,000. A friend made some comments upon it. Mr. Robins replied: "I got a high price. I could have bought lots in Chambers street at the same time for less than I sold mine in the Bowery."

I have said, in the last chapter, that Mr. Robins had but little to do with real estate; his first purchase and sale of a lot, however, is worth recording. A lumber merchant, by the name of Baker, doing business near Corlaers Hook, on the east side of the town, owned a lot of ground in the Bowery, No. 15, near Chatham Square; it was 30 feet wide and 100 in depth; there was upon it a small, comfortable dwelling house, and a stable in the rear, to which access was had by an alley way. The owner was anxious to sell, and had tried to do so at auction, but there were no bidders. Mr. Robins was applied to to purchase the premises. This was at a period not long after the commencement of the present century, before the present City Hall was built. Negotiations were not long pending; Mr. Robins was desirous of furnishing his mother with a comfortable home, convenient to his own business, and having already a deposit in bank of a few thousand dollars which he did not require in his business, bought the property for $4,500. The deed had hardly been delivered before a Scotchman, whose name is now forgotten, called upon Mr. Robins to know if he would sell the property in the Bowery which he had just purchased. Before the interview closed, the Scotchman became possessed of that which he had long coveted, but not without an advance of some hundreds of dollars, which went into the pockets of the then youthful Robins. The late Gen. Robert Bogardus who was the grand marshal on the occasion of the obsequies of President Harrison, in this city in 1841, drew up the conveyance to the new owner, and now the formalities of deliverance were to be gone through with. The Scotchman with his check, and young Robins with the deed, met by appointment. Certified checks were unknown in those days, so they agreed to go together to the bank. It was the old United States Bank, located at No. 164 Pearl street.

When the Scotchman presented his check to the teller (who, by the by, was connected by marriage with the family of Col. Rutgers), he said to him, "I acknowledge that check to be mine, and I want you to pay it;" the money was counted out and paid, and then the title was to be searched. They left the bank and went to the City Hall, which was then located in Wall street, on the site now occupied by the Custom House. They entered the County Clerk's office, and finding that dignitary, the Scotchman inquired in an audible voice, "Are there any judgments against John Robins?" After a short alphabetical search, the clerk answered in the negative. The Scotchman was not aware that there would be any charge for such a service and was about to retire, when he was politely reminded that he must pay 5s. 6d. He reluctantly paid the amount, and the twain went in pursuit of the Clerk of the Supreme Court, whom having found, the same formal demand was made, and being answered in the negative, Scotchman turned to leave, but was again reminded that it was necessary to pay the accustomed fee. He replied that he had already paid a considerable amount, and could not see any good reason for paying again.

It was, however, of no use to argue the matter — the clerk pocketed the usual fee. Mr. Robins said there was still another court for them to visit. The Scotchman inquired if there would be anything more to pay; the reply was he supposed there would be. "Well," said the Scotchman, "in that case I'll be d——d if I will go any further," and he did not. That ended the search of the validity of the title of the property known as No. 15 Bowery, which, it is believed, is still vested in the descendants of the penurious Scotchman.

As I have said before, Mr. Robins had no ambition to be called a down town merchant." He has kept upon the same block for over sixty-two years, and for half a century in the same building — for Nos. 426 and 428 are really under the same roof now, and the old building was upon the same plot of ground, thirty-three feet wide.

His trade, that was once immense, insensibly diminished — partly from indisposition to keep up with the times, but more probably from the fact that his old customers, in the long lapse of time, dropped one by one into the grave, and left him alone in the old store, with the same old shelves, but now empty. Of his old, intimate business acquaintances, but one lives, and that is John Haggerty.

Still the spry and active man, with fourscore and two years on his white head, goes regularly to market every morning; stopping first at the baker's for his loaf of bread for breakfast — and this, too, in all kinds of weather, in winter and summer. He never wore a pair of gloves in his life; but in very cold weather he wears his woolen mittens. Every morning, early as the light, he is in his store. He opens it, sweeps it out, and makes the fire. There is no aristocracy, no false pride, and yet he is a proud man; he is proud of his independence from want—proud that he has been a true old New York merchant—proud that he never failed—proud that he never lied or wronged a human being out of a dollar—proud that he has kept the "talents" entrusted to him, and has more than doubled them—proud that he has never squandered or wasted the property accumulated by his energy in legitimate trade, and that he has never given way to a false weakness, like some men who have become poor to enrich others.

Mr. Robins has never been a slave to luxuries, or felt their necessity. He never had a fire in his sleeping apartment, and he never had a wash-stand there.

He did without Croton water for many years, and was content with the old-fashioned pump water, which was good enough for any old New Yorker. He never would have allowed Croton to be brought into his yard, had not the spirit of innovation removed the good old pump from his neighborhood.

He was the very opposite of his old friend, Henry Laverty. Laverty did love luxuries, from early strawberries and green peas to the finest woodcock and tenderest game.

I remember him, an old man, long years ago, and yet with a remarkably keen eye for a young and pretty girl. His house in Broadway was once the seat of hospitality and festivity. I remember the son who accidentally killed Sykes, at Windust's saloon, near the old Park Theatre. By the way, Ned Windust himself is still a handsome, lively young man, and keeps in the same place, or very near it, in Park row.

I remember D. W. Gantley and Cutter, both of the firm of Laverty, Gantley & Co. But they have all gone.

dead, or out of town. Henry Laverty was crippled in means for years. He was never out of trouble. He died poor and left nothing, comparatively speaking. Rufus H. King, Vice President of the State Bank of Albany, married one of his amiable daughters.

Gantley blew up. What ever became of dapper little Cutter, I never knew.

Mr. Robins never paraded his name before the public. People have no idea how low United States sixes were during the war with England in 1812 to 1815.

At that time all the banks South, West and North, had suspended specie payment, except New England. The banks in that section paid specie.

There was a difference of twenty per cent. between New England and New York money. United States sixes in 1814 were worth fifty cents payable in specie, or seventy cents if paid in New York bank currency.

Mr. Robins was one of the builders-up of our city. One of the oldest of the Old Merchants shall not pass away from the scene of his labors without seeing more said of himself than was ever said, before these chapters were written, of any of his cotemporaries — Astor, Hone, Prime, Laverty, Nat Griswold and George, Stephen Whitney and others, whose names will be found here.

His brother, and for many years partner, died in 1859. He left a large family of sons and daughters. Thomas was cashier of the Vicksburg Bank. Amos is collector at Perth Amboy, N. J. George is a manufacturer of army utensils. John, the eldest son, died about eight years ago. Nathan is living at the old homestead. Wright, another son, is married, and living in a beautiful cottage on the farm left by his father. He is the youngest nephew of the subject of this interesting narrative, and is his constant companion. He can be seen almost daily in Wall street, watching with keen discernment the movements of that important locality; he keeps closely in his own counsels, and, like his uncle, rarely errs in judgment. He is the confidential adviser of his mother and sisters, and his advice is their rule of action. There are few of his age in this emporium who have more responsible duties to discharge, and fewer still more capable than he to discharge them. He is now reaping the rich reward of those uncompromising principles of honesty and integrity in which he has been educated.

Indeed the name Robins has become to a degree synonymous with upright dealing and straightforward business principles, combined with a clearness of conception which has made the members of this family good and trustworthy citizens, to whom friends and neighbors apply for advice and counsel, confident in the belief that the judgment which sustains an honorable career will not fail a friend in time of need.

Such characteristics are the ties which bind the members of a community together and make possible the general advancement rather than the embittering effects of isolated successes.

I have mentioned above, young Thomas Robins, cashier of the Vicksburg Bank.

Thomas was a teller in the Phœnix Bank of this city. At the time the Vicksburg Bank was chartered, the directors sent on to New York to procure the services of the most able financier that could be had, for cashier.

Young Thomas Robins was the man selected. He went out. Of course, he had not long been there, before the same attempt was made to crowd him, that is usually made upon all Northerners who go South.

But Tom Robins would fight, most boys brought up in the Fourth and Sixth Wards of New York, will. In three duels, Tom wounded his opponents severely.

He and the celebrated S. S. Prentiss were bosom friends, but finally the Southerners worked upon Prentiss to challenge Tom. It was accepted. The night before the meeting was to come off, Prentiss went to Tom's residence, and frankly said: "Tom, I am in the wrong, and I will not fight you any way." To the hour of his death they were friends.

When the Mexican war broke out in 1846, Tom Robins raised the celebrated Mississippi regiment, and was elected its colonel. By some very dishonorable means, he was induced to resign in favor of Jefferson Davis.

Thomas Robins challenged him, but he knew his man, and refused to fight. Upon what slender strings important events hang! Had Davis not got the command of that regiment, he never would have been heard of again.

From the many incidents connected with the history of John Robins with which I am familiar, the following is selected, demonstrative of his honest impulses in his business transactions. At the close of the last war with England in 1815, the English manufacturers, the moment the embargo was raised, and all restrictions had been removed, which had obstructed our commerce, sent to this port large cargoes of dry goods invoiced at *war prices*, with instructions to sell on arrival. The auction rooms were literally crowded with them, prices gave way, and this market offered no inducements for other shipments. At that period Mr. Henry Barclay, an older brother of Anthony and George Barclay, the latter now retired from active life, and who resides at No. 8 Washington place, was largely engaged in the importation of dry goods. Seeing that great sacrifices were being submitted to by many of his neighbors in their hurry to dispose of their consignments, and the general panic created by their great haste to sell, he conceived the idea of investing a hundred thousand dollars in purchasing dry goods at auction, thinking it would prove a profitable speculation. It would not answer for him to make the purchases in person, and while thinking to find some trusty person, one on whom he could rely for honesty, and one, too, who was a good judge of the quality and styles of English fabrics, he selected John Robins as his man. With a fixed purpose to carry out his project he called upon Mr. Robins and made known to him the object of his visit.

"I want your services Mr. Robins," said Mr. Barclay, "to carry out a project which I have conceived and which I think will result to the advantage of both of us."

"Pray, Mr. Barclay," said Robins, "in what way can I render you a service?"

"Don't misunderstand me, Mr. Robins," said Barclay, "it is purely a business arrangement I wish to perfect with you. I find the market is largely overstocked with dry goods, they are now selling at ruinous prices, and instead of being a seller I have concluded to become a purchaser."

"Indeed,"said uncle John Robins.

"I have come to propose to you, to attend the auction sales and exercise your best judgment in selecting and purchasing goods in your name for my benefit to the amount of one hundred thousand dollars, which sum I have appropriated for that purpose, and for which services I will pay you 2½ per cent. commission."

"It is a very heavy operation, Mr. Barclay, and I hope you have well considered it," observed Mr. Robins. "I have indeed, the profits which will result from this speculation must be large, don't you think so?" replied Mr. Barclay.

"I am not so clear upon that point, I have generally found that where there is a chance to make, there is also a chance to lose," said Mr. Robins.

"What," said Barclay, "can you for a moment doubt that the speculation will not prove profitable?"

"Well," replied Robins, "since you have put the question to me, I will answer it in all candor. My advice to you is to abandon the scheme, it will result unprofitably to you, you will lose money by the operation, for be assured the price of the very goods which you desire me to purchase for you will fall much lower, and I advise you instead of becoming a purchaser in this market, that you turn your attention to the disposal of what stock you have on hand, and banish the idea from your mind which you have proposed to me."

Mr. Barclay was so disappointed and yet while he was astonished with the boldness and frankness of this advice, he was induced to reconsider his plans, at any rate to delay the execution of them for a few days. In the meantime the market became more and more overstocked, prices went down still further, and Mr. Barclay instead of realizing a golden harvest from his favorite project, acted upon the advice of Mr. Robins, and disposed of his own stock as speedily as possible. These gentlemen met accidentally many years afterwards, when Mr. Barclay remarked, "I can never be too grateful to you, Mr. Robins, for the advice which you once gave me, and the large amount of money which I saved by following it."

"I think," modestly replied Mr. Robins," the price of dry goods has not advanced since the day we had a talk upon the subject, which if I mistake not is now more than twenty years ago."

It is quite refreshing to dwell upon such sterling worth in these degenerating times of shoddy contracts.

CHAPTER XLIV.

Thomas Robins who went to Vicksburg and became the cashier of the Vicksburg Bank, fought eleven duels. One was with the editor of the Vicksburg *Sentinel*. I forget his name. A trench was dug, and both parties descended into it by means of a ladder. Each man was stripped naked, and both were armed with a six-shooter and a bowie-knife. An account of that duel filled four columns of the New York *Herald* at that time. Tom Robins married a niece of Jefferson Davis. Tom Quick has a capital notice of the old gentleman Robins. He speaks of *Breeze* Robins, " a Sport he loved in his younger days." Tom says, writing of old John Robins:

We would bet high he walks out of nights, and hunts up poor families, and, after being sure of it, pays the grocer's bills unknown to them. If he don't, he ain't like his nephew, Breeze Robins, a Sport whom we knew in our younger days, when Fulton Engine Company Twenty-one lay in Cedar street, with the bulliest set of quick men that ever held a pipe, or had men enough to stand by the butt, were it One, Fourteen, Fifteen, Twenty-seven, Thirty, Thirty-nine, Forty, Forty-two, Forty-five, or any other crack machine with a fighting crowd. Breeze was handsome, broad-hearted, and always had lots of money and sweethearts. I have seen him crack his dozen to treat his friends, who would meet nightly at the Clarendon, near Jimmy Gemmel's house — Bob Walker, Dan Berrian, Mathew T. Brennan, Jimmy Green, and a heap more.

We lost him of a sudden; he went out West, and took to business, and is now a model merchant. Good uck attend him, for his heart was in the right place.

Tom Quick's *Breeze* Robins is Amos Robins. Thomas Robins married a daughter of Joseph Davis, brother of Jefferson Davis. He died leaving no children. He was game to the last. He was a great favorite with General Taylor, who made Tom's home at Vicksburg a stopping place in the summer season.

He challenged Jeff. Davis, not about the Mississippi regiment, of which Tom was Colonel, but about some family matter. Jeff. had clandestinely married a daughter of General Taylor.

Jeff. Davis was not the man to meet the New York boy, who had fought eleven duels, and who did not know what fear was. It is a pity that Jeff. and Tom did not fight. Very likely it would have saved President Lincoln a vast amount of trouble.

After Tom Robins had fought his way through all opposition, no one had so many friends and admirers as he. Had he lived he would have been Govenor of Mississippi, or held any other position he wished in that State.

He did good service in trying to get that State to pay her bonds. He went to Europe for that purpose, and visited most all of the European bondholders to try and make an arrangement.

I cannot but respect old age, and a letter from one who has passed 88 is really a luxury to me, especially if the venerable writer has passed a great portion of his time in New York city.

I shall publish in this chapter a long letter from Grant Thorburn.

I do not precisely remember when Grant arrived in this country, but I know it was before the year 1800, for then he was established in a well-to-do grocery, at No. 20 Nassau street. He was there some ten or twelve years, and then he moved to No. 22, and about the time of his removal, in 1810, he changed his business, and kept garden seeds, and was a florist, and lived at 41 Liberty street.

There was another Thorburn, who lived in New York a great many years, at No. 50 William street. His name was James, and those who remember him will call to mind his dignified appearance. I believe he was a Quaker. He was porter to the Bank of New York for twenty years at least. He succeeded to Daniel Thorne somewhere about 1812.

A very prince of a man was James Thorburn. I met him every day the year after the cholera season (1832.) He then lived in 28 Courtlandt street, with his family, at George Monell's. His daughter was one of the loveliest girls in the city. I have never met the stately James Thorburn since then.

Previous to James Thorburn being a porter in the Bank of New York, he was a wood-ware seller and grocer, at No. 32 Maiden Lane, and opened business there as lately as 1800. In those days there were very few merchants who did not keep an assorted stock of goods. While James kept "woodware and groceries," Grant kept "seeds and groceries." I am quite sure that James was a Quaker. He kept in Maiden Lane many years, and I am sure that Grant must remember all about him.

Grant Thorburn has sent me a letter containing what follows:

Anecdote of Robert Hoe, Inventor of the Printing Press. I have read with pleasure your notice of Old Merchants. My business as seedsman brought me in contact with most of them. In the same period lived Robert Hoe, who, though only a mechanic, his name will live while woods grow and waters run. In 1805 the yellow fever swept the streets of New York like a Turkish plague. I never left the city during seventeen summers that the fever prevailed. I kept a grocery store at that time on the north corner of Nassau and Liberty streets. One afternoon I sat on a chair outside of the door, with one of my children by my side. I saw a strange man coming from Cedar street, and reading the signs. He stood by my side.

"Mr. Thorburn," said he.

"Where did you get my name from?" said I.

"I read it on the sign-board," said he; and he continued, "I am just come on shore from the ship 'Dragon,' from Liverpool. I am a carpenter by trade, but can't get work on account of the fever. If you can tell me where to board, I will pay them when I get work."

"How old are you?" I asked.

"Eighteen years," said he.

"Did you serve out your apprenticeship?"

"I never was bound. My father was a carpenter."

"If my wife is willing, I will board you myself," said I.

I stepped to the foot of the stairs. My wife stood at the head.

"Good wife," said I, "a stranger standeth at the door. He has no money; he wants board; will you take him in?"

"If thee pleaseth," she replied.

"If he takes the fever, will you help me to nurse him?"

"I will," she replied.

"Thank you, my dear," said I, "For this God will bless you."

Before a week, he was seized with the fever. I got

the best medical advice. My wife and I nursed him. On the fourth day of the fever, he was under the operation of powerful medicine. The fever ran through his veins, and drank his English blood. I stood by his bedside. He fixed his eyes on mine.

"Oh, Mr. Thorburn, I shall die! I shall die! I can never stand this!"

"Die!" said I. "Robert, we must all die, but you won't die this week." [In this I spoke unadvisedly, but I thought the end would sanctify the means.] "I hope to see you marry one of our bonnie Yankee lasses, and to carry your grandchild in my arms."

I saw this prediction fulfilled to the letter. From that hour the fever left him. His worthy sons continue to improve on their father's invention. Hoe's improved press is another proof that the Bible is true. When printing was first discovered, three hundred years ago, good men hailed the event as a messenger from God, preparing the way for the King of the East, when knowledge would be increased over the world. Hoe's improvement is another message, carrying peace and good will to men on earth. By it, books have become so cheap that he who runs may read. Before the improvement, bibles used in schools were sold for one dollar. Now they are sold for twenty cents. Thus the Bible is found in ships, shops, and granaries, in India, in Japan, and in the islands of the sea. Soon knowledge will be over the earth.

Yours, GRANT THORBURN, SEN.,
Aged eighty-eight years and three months.

NEW HAVEN, 6th *June*, 1861.

That letter is a very just tribute to the oldest Mr. Hoe, and I will add a few lines to it of my own, to keep Mr. Thorburn company.

Robert Hoe started a carpenter shop at 89 Fair (Fulton) street (at that time it only ran from Broadway to Cliff street, not being cut through to the East river, and from Broadway to the North river, what is now Fulton was called Partition street). The next year, Mr. Hoe moved to 44 Barclay street, from this to 79 Nassau street, near Fulton, in 1808, still carrying on the carpenter business. He kept that business in different places as late as 1824, when his carpenter shop was in the rear of 84 Maiden Lane, and he lived at 90 William. Previously, for some years, his shop had been in the rear of his dwelling.

In the year 1825, Mr. Hoe openly announced his business as printing-press maker, at 64 Pine. His brother Richard, who was a mason, kept at the same place, and lived in Eldridge street. Many a day have we sauntered among these old buildings, in the middle of the block where Hoe's establishment was, and looked with admiration at the model works. There was an alley-way from Pine to Maiden Lane, through a lot of old wooden buildings, about the middle of the block, between William and Pearl. The Hoes were there some years, when they moved into Gold street.

In one of the chapters I spoke of the old concern of John Rathbone & Son. I have before me one of the autographs of the old gentleman, written fifty-six years ago. Sometimes the name is Rathbun as well as Rathbone, by children of the same father. The family is very ancient, having been distinguished in Great Britain for more than 500 years.

A wealthy branch of the family has resided in Liverpool for more than 300 years, and a large commercial house there for many years is that of Rathbone, Brothers & Co., and a large American business they have always done.

It was John Rathbone, of the Liverpool family,

who emigrated from that city to America with the Pilgrims in 1625. The name is one of the sixteen that settled Block Island (Rhode Island.) One of the descendants, Elijah, was born in 1740, and settled in Groton, Connecticut. He died in 1825, aged eighty-five years. His eldest son was Captain Benjamin Rathbone He died of yellow fever, in this city, in 1795, leaving two children, a son and daughter.

Nathan, the son, was born in 1794, in August. When the war of 1812 broke out, he attached himself to an organized water or coast guard, and was instrumental in the capture of a number of vessels, caught in the act of giving assistance to the enemy. This guard annoyed the English fleet very much. He was present at the bombardment of Stonington, Conn., with a regiment of the state militia. He came to New York city in 1822, went into business, and continued in it until 1860. He was at the earliest and latest periods of his life engaged in the fish business. He was at one time in the dry goods business, in Greenwich street. He wrote his name at different periods of his life Rath bone and Rathbun. He was extensively known over forty years in this town, and very much respected by all.

He married in this city, and had a number of children; three of them were sons, Nathan James, William and Charles. The first died young. William now commands the steamship "Bienville," the trader between here and Havana. He commenced his sea life and made his first voyage, in the old packet ship "George Washington," belonging to Grinnell, Minturn & Co's line of Liverpool packets. She was commanded by Captain Ambrose H. Burrows.

Captain Walter Rathbone is well known in New York, having been connected for a number of years with the California and other lines of steamships. He is a skillful seaman, and a gentleman. Charles, another son, resides in this city.

In the notice of John W. Mulligan, who is still alive, I omitted to state a few items of considerable interest. He was Surrogate of the County in 1810.

Mr. Mulligan is also the oldest living graduate of Columbia College. He is the oldest lawyer in this city.

When Alexander Hamilton was a student at Columbia College, he boarded with the father of John W. Mulligan, old Hercules Mulligan alluded to in a former chapter, who lived in Broadway, but kept his store at No. 3 Vesey street.

In confirmation of what I have stated in a previous chapter in reference to the intimacy between Baron Steuben and Mr. Mulligan, I have since met with a capital work, entitled "The Life of Frederich William Von Steuben, Major-General of the Revolutionary Army, by Frederick Kapp, with an introduction by George Bancroft, and published by Mason & Brothers. 1859."

This clever work of 735 pages, ought to be in the hands of every member of the Steuben regiment, and a more acceptable present to a member than this copy of the Baron's life, could not be made.

It says: "In 1791 Steuben made the acquaintance of John W. Mulligan, a young and promising man, whose father had been an active whig in New York city during the Revolution. Mr. Mulligan, after having finished his studies in Columbia college, became Steuben's secretary, and served him with a fidelity and love which won him the friendship and confidence of his protector. Steuben concentrated all the tenderness of his heart on his friends, as he had no family relations, and there are few examples to be found in which the feeling of kindness and good fellowship were so fully reciprocated as between Steuben and his friend."

In 1807, when Mr. Mulligan was Assistant Alderman for the Second Ward, he wrote the following letter in reference to a plan for fortifying New York, that he knew Baron Steuben had prepared in 1793, after examining all the ground between Hell Gate and the Narrows, looking out for the best place to erect forts. His plan was produced and used previous to the war of 1812:

"In the present state of our political affairs, the subject of fortifications to defend our city naturally excites considerable anxiety and attention. Various plans are devised and proposed, but that which includes the defence of the Narrows seems to have most advocates. One has been published which I believe to be an entire plagiarism from one framed by our excellent friend, my benefactor, Baron Steuben. In the year 1793, as I believe you are informed, he devoted one or two days to an actual survey at the Narrows, and formed a plan which, with a memoir, he presented to the Corporation. After particular search, it is not to be found. I hope that he may have left a copy among his plans and papers in your possession. The object of my present application is that you will have the goodness to search, and if you find either the plan or memoir, to send them on, as far as your search may be successful, as soon as you possibly can, to me, by some safe hand. Being a member of the Board, I wish to procure it, as we are at present on the look out for a plan for the purpose of meeting the wishes of the citizens, to erect fortifications without delay, at the Narrows, relying on Government for future reimbursements, as their Commissioners have not thought it proper, or, rather, within the scope of their instructions, to expend at present any money to fortify that point. Many inducements make me anxious to have this plan, and, notwithstanding the importance of the object it was intended to effect, I confess one of my leading motives is to prevent any person from bearing the credit of what is due my friend."

The Baron died in November, 1794; and Mr. Mulligan gives an account of it in a letter to Mr. Walker. He says:

"On Tuesday morning our friend, my father, was struck with a palsy which deprived his left side of motion. The evening before at 11 he was perfectly well. At 4 A. M., he was struck—at 6 P. M., he was speechless. On Thursday he died."

When the will was opened, it was found that he had bequeathed most of his property to his adopted children and aid-de-camps, Benjamin Walker and William North. "To John W. Mulligan I bequeath the whole of my library, maps, and charts, and the sum of two thousand five hundred dollars to complete it."

CHAPTER XLV.

Those who pass down Broadway in 1862, and admire the solid-looking building called the "Astor," extending the whole front of a "block," can have very little idea of the events that have transpired, and the names that have figured in the city history, who resided where the hotel now stands.

Among the most eminent, of course, was John Jacob Astor. He lived at No. 223 Broadway, in a large double house. He lived in the house a great portion of his life — certainly commenced to live there as early as 1802. I think Rufus King, the founder of the King family of this city, built the house and sold it to Mr. Astor.

When Mr. Astor started in this city he resided at No. 40 Little Dock Street (now Water). He then moved to 149 Broadway. He kept his store at 71 Liberty street.

In 1802 he moved his residence to 223 Broadway, and there he lived as late as 1826, when he gave up that house to his son William B.

His neighbors who occupied houses facing upon Broadway, where the Astor House now stands, were all prominent men. I think the numbers were 213 to 227. Mr Astor, as I have said, lived at 223 — north of him, on the corner of Barclay, was 227 That house was owned and occupied by John G. Coster. It was the last property purchased by Mr. Astor to give him all the land required upon which to build his contemplated hotel He had purchased all the other portions at very low prices. Not over $15,000 a lot and house of 25 x 100 feet. Mr. Coster would not sell at any price. There was no chance of his ever wanting money, or of being forced to sell. Mr. Astor, while he was making the purchase of other property, had let no one into his secret intentions. Finally he went to Mr. Coster and told him frankly: "Coster, I am going to build a hotel. I want the ground upon which your house stands. It is of no particular use to you; you can go up Broadway, above Canal street, and build a palace with the money I will pay you. Now I wish you to name two friends, and I will name one. The three shall fix the value of No. 227. When they have done so add $20,000 to it, and I will give you a check for the total amount, and you can give me the deed of that property."

The proposition, so fair, and so much more than Mr. Coster expected, was accepted at once. Mr. Coster immediately made his arrangements to build the house — palace it was — No. 517 Broadway. There he lived until he died. Then it was rented to the famous Chinese Museum, brought from Canton here. The house was finally called the "Chinese Building," and still stands, a portion of it let to model artists, or some similar amusement, that would horrify the worthy old gentleman could he return from the spirit world.

Between the house of Mr. Astor at 223 and of Coster, 227, lived at No. 225 the celebrated David Lydig. I do not know what price Mr. Astor paid him. He moved out of the house preparatory to its being torn down in 1830, to No. 34 Laight street, and there he lived until he died in 1840. I think his son lives there yet. His name was Philip.

David Lydig was one of the bold old race of merchants that built up New York, and I will not pass the name now without further mention. It is almost extinct, and yet no "firm" has been more honored.

David Lydig must have been an older man than John Jacob Astor, for he started in the flour business, on his own account, in 1790, at 21 Peck Slip, and lived over his store. He afterwards took a residence at 55 Beekman; and there he lived for many years — in fact, until 1819 — when he moved to 225 Broadway.

In 1824, old David took into business his son Philip, at 160 South street, and the firm was for many years after, David Lydig & Son.

David Lydig was in every prominent bank and insurance company for nearly half a century. He was a prominent merchant in 1790, and died in 1840. I believe he had only retired a few years previous to his death from active business. Judge Charles P. Daly married a daughter.

In 219, old Michael Paff had his celebrated picture gallery. Who among old New Yorkers does not remember the famous "Old Paff?" Were he alive now, he would be a world's wonder. I wish I had time to say more of him.

Aaron Fountain occupied a store on that block, so did Jonathan Smith. Wagstaff kept his store in one of the numbers; and I cannot recollect, at the moment, the other prominent men who lived in that celebrated block.

About the time Mr. Astor lived last at 223, the firm was John Jacob Astor & Son, and also the American Fur Company. That office was at 8 Vesey, and extended back, so that the rear wall was on a line with the north side of Mr. Astor's dwelling at 223 Broad way. William lived at 17 State street.

In the war, and many years after, Mr. Astor had his store at 69 Pine, corner of Pearl street.

At 223 Broadway he could go from his yard into the store. There was an open piazza, supported by pillars and arches, where he frequently sat of an afternoon, after he had had his dinner, at three o'clock. He would play three games of checkers, and no more, and drink a glass of beer. He did not drink anything else, in his working days.

Those who suppose Mr. Astor had an easy time in money matters, are greatly mistaken. He has often paid old Prime, in Wall street, very large interest and a large commission to get long paper discounted.

He (Astor) loved to tell anecdotes connected with his early difficulties. One was about a bargain he made with his brother Henry, when the latter was much better off than his brother John; for Henry was owner of butcher stall No. 57 in the Fly market — valuable property in the commencement of this century. Henry then lived at 37 Bowery Lane.

John, in his financial difficulties, frequently went to Henry for a loan, or for an endorsement. This was a source of annoyance to Henry, who did not like to borrow or lend to anybody. On one occasion, John wanted to borrow $200 very badly. He went to Henry, and asked him to lend him that sum.

" John, I will give you $100, if you will agree never to ask me to loan you any money, endorse a note, or sign a bond for you, or be obligated for you in any manner whatever."

John says he hesitated for a moment, rapidly passed

the proposition through his mind, saw its advantages, for $100 was $100 in those days. He accepted the proposition, and he never did ask a favor of that character of his brother in after years.

A business acquaintance of Mr. Astor one day asked him what particular transaction or peculiar kind of business first gave him his great start. Mr. Astor never claimed any great sagacity or intelligence over his fellows.

He said, in reply, that at one period of his life, he had accumulated quite a quantity of unsalable furs in this market, such as beavers. The common furs that he or his agents picked up, viz., musk-rat, mink, rabbit, squirrel, &c., he could sell in this city and at good prices. The other and costly he had to buy, but could not sell here, and they were packed away in whisky casks down in the cellar. He had no correspondent in London to send them to, and no disposition to send them if he had had. After talking over the matter with his wife, they concluded it would be best for himself to go out to London with the choicest kind of furs. He did so. The prospect of the trip was uncertain, and to economize as much as possible, he went out as a steerage passenger.

When he reached London, he found a ready market for his choice furs, and sold them at a very high rate. He made a list out of such goods as he thought would make money by being taken to the New York market, purchased and shipped them by a vessel bound hither. After he was all through with his business, he was detained a couple of weeks by the ship not being ready to sail. The idle time he spent in looking about London, and picking up all the information possible, especially such as was likely to advantage his business in New

York. Among other extraordinary places he visited, was the great East India House. He visited the warehouse, and offices. On one occasion he asked one of the porters what the name of the Governor was. The man replied, giving a German name very familiar to Mr. Astor. He asked his informer if the Governor was an Englishman. He replied, that he had come from Germany originally when a boy. Mr. Astor determined to see him — watched an opportunity, and sent in his name. He was admitted. When he entered, he said to the Governor:

"Is not your name Wilhelm ——? Did not you go to school in such a town?"

"I did, and now I remember you very well. Your name is Astor!"

After this, they had a long chat, and talked over old school matters. The Governor insisted that Mr. Astor should dine with him. He declined for that day, but the next they met again. He asked Mr. Astor several times if there was nothing he could do for him. Mr. Astor said no; he had bought all he wanted; he needed no cash, or credit. Almost every day they met. The Governor kept urging Mr. Astor to name something that he could do for him. He asked what present would be acceptable. Astor declined any. Finally, they met two days before the vessel was to sail, and again the Governor asked Astor if he would accept any present he mad him. Mr. Astor, seeing the Governor so anxious, said "Yes."

When he called to bid the Governor good bye, the 'atter was really quite affected at parting with his old German schoolmate.

"Take these," said he, "you may find their value."

One of the documents was simply a Canton prices current.

The other was a carefully engrossed permit on parchment, authorizing the ship that bore it to trade freely and without any molestation, at any of the ports monopolized by the East India Company.

Mr. Astor bade his friend good bye, and returned to this city, never giving the *present* a second thought. He had no ships, and never had any trade with the East Indies, and never expected to have. He little dreamed that in the parchment would be the foundation of vast shipping operations, and a trade amounting to millions, and embracing the Pacific Ocean. The permit was No. 68.

When Mr. Astor got home, he showed these documents to his wife, and advised with her, as he always did, what to do in the matter.

"I have no ships — it's no use to us," he said. At that time, there was a very celebrated merchant named James Livermore. He was largely engaged in the West India trade, particularly to Jamaica. He owned vessels — some of good size.

Mrs. Astor recommended her husband to go and have a talk with the merchant. Mr. Astor went — showed the East India Company ship pass and the Canton prices current.

"Now," said he, "if you will make up a voyage for one of your largest ships, you can have the pass and have the prices current, on one condition. You are to furnish ship and cargo, but I am to have one half the profits for my pass and for suggesting the voyage."

"Pah, pah!" said the great West India merchant. He laughed at it — would not listen to such a one-sided operation. Astor went home and reported progress

For a time, the matter was dropped. Not many weeks after the great West India merchant thought over the matter. He had made money in the West India trade, and he saw an opening for the East Indies.

At that time no vessels traded to Canton. It was just after the Revolutionary war, and the East India ports were as hermetically sealed to American commerce as if it had not existed.

He called at Mr. Astor's store. "Were you in earnest the other day, when you showed me the pass of the East India Company?"

"I was. Never more so." Again they talked over the matter. The merchant finally thought he saw his way clear, and an agreement was signed, agreeing to to give Mr. Astor one half the result or profits. He to have no outlay.

The ship was selected and loaded. Partly with specie—Spanish milled dollars, about $30,000, and the other half was ginseng, lead and scrap iron.

She went to Canton. The pass enabled her to anchor at Whampoa, a few miles below Canton, where she loaded and unloaded her cargo the same as if she had been a vessel belonging to the East India Company.

Her ginseng, costing 20 cents per pound in New York, she sold at $3,50 per pound in Canton, lead 10 cents, scrap iron at an enormous price. Tea was purchased that sold here at $1 per pound profit on the Canton cost.

When the return cargo was sold, the accounts were made out, and Mr. Astor's half share, which was $55,000, all in silver, was packed in barrels, and sent up to his store. When Mrs. Astor saw the barrels, she asked what was in them.

"The fruits of our East India pass," replied her husband. He went to the shipowner, and got back his pass. He then bought a ship, and loaded her with an assorted cargo. On her way out, she touched at the Sandwich Islands to take in water and fresh provisions. They also laid in a large stock of firewood.

When this ship reached Canton a mandarin came on board, and noticing their firewood, asked the price of it at once. The Captain laughed at such a question, but signified that he was open to an offer. The mandarin offered $500 a ton, and every part of it was sold at that price. That was *sandal* wood.

For seventeen years Mr. Astor enjoyed that lucrative sandal wood trade without a rival. No other concern in the United States or England knew the secret. Nor was it discovered until a shrewd Boston shipowner detailed a ship to follow one of Mr. Astor's, and observe the events of the voyage. Then, for some time, that house was a participant in this valuable trade.

It was a curious fact that Mrs. Astor knew more of the value of furs than he did. She would select a cargo for the Canton market, and make no mistake.

When they became very affluent, she used to make him pay her $500 an hour for using her judgment and knowledge of fur to promote his commercial plans. He paid her whatever she asked.

John Jacob was a great free mason. In 1801, he was Grand Treasurer of the knight Templar Encampment, and was "*Sir John Jacob Astor.*"

Besides the bachelor, Henry Astor, John Jacob had another brother, who came out here, I think, in 1816, just after the war. His name was George. He kept a store in 144 Water street, and at 22 Cliff street he lived. He died in 1832.

Henry Astor must have died about 1831. He left a widow, but no children.

He was in the habit of selecting young girls, adopting, educating, and starting them in life when they married. He gave them his name. I recollect one of them, Eliza Astor, married Mr. Constant, the oil merchant.

Henry left a large fortune. I believe it went mostly to Wm. B. Astor.

These facts concerning the renowned John Jacob Astor are true, and are far more interesting to the general reader than the dry stuff published in his "Life," and, what is more, no man would enjoy their publication more than Mr. Astor himself, were he now alive.

CHAPTER XLVI.

The subject of this chapter will be a merchant of singular incorruptible integrity and extraordinary sagacity. I do not believe he ever did a dishonest action in his life, and probably no earthly calamity — not even death itself, in any way or shape — would be regarded by him with such horror as a failure to pay his mercantile obligations.

I am writing about William Whitlock, a merchant of the first class — a ship owner and a man of business, and in business, on his own account, for full forty-five years in this city.

His firm for many years was William Whitlock, Jr. His father's name was William Whitlock. Old Captain Whitlock was a sea captain out of this port as early as 1790, when he lived at 136 Queen (Pearl) street, near Frankfort. He afterwards removed to 31 Frankfort street, and lived there until 1800, when he removed to 189 William street, and there the old captain lived until 1832, a period of thirty-one years. His son, for many years, lived at 187, next door, or until 1827, when he bought a house near St. John's Park. I remember those two houses, Nos. 187 and 189 William street very well. They were plain houses, and stood near the corner of Spruce. They were torn down long ago.

I think old Captain William Whitlock lived to be a very aged man. I know he was connected with insurance companies for some years of his life.

I believe Wm. Whitlock, Jr. was started in business by his father when young. I think he went into the grocery business when he first started, at No. 71 South street. That firm, under the name of Whitlock & Jenkins, was soon dissolved, and then William Whitlock, Jr. went to Augusta, Georgia, where he remained one or two years, buying cotton on commission.

What prejudiced him against partnerships I do not know, but after his first unsuccessful partnership with Jenkins, he would never have a partner. Even in ship owning he preferred to hold an undivided interest if he could. If there was a loss, he could stand it, and if a profit, he did not wish to divide it with anybody.

In 1824 Mr. Whitlock started the line of Savannah packets in connection with James C. Seguine. I presume this line originated in connections made while in business at Augusta, a city that stands on the banks of the Savannah river. Scott & Morrell, afterwards Scott, Shapter & Morrell, continued this line for many years after Mr. Whitlock gave it up.

Mr. Whitlock married a Miss Scott, the sister of the Scott of the above firm. Benjamin Richards married another sister; he was of the celebrated firm in South street of Richards & Richardson, and now of the firm of Richards, Benkard & Co., in same building with Mr. Whitlock. Previously Ben Richards had been the agent of William Whitlock at the Rio Grande in the Brazils. Mr. Whitlock for many years sent out cargoes and vessels to his consignment.

Captain Richardson was originally in the command of the ship Salem. She was owned by the celebrated merchant in South street, William Osborne, who, when he failed in this city in 1830 or thereabouts, created quite a panic. After his failure the Salem was sold, and Mr. Whitlock bought Osborne's share. Richardson was her captain, and owned a portion of the ship. That was the way he and Mr. Whitlock became acquainted. She was a fast sailer, made quick passages, and coined money. Captain Richardson owned one third and Mr. Whitlock two thirds of her. Captain Richardson was a flashy sort of man. He afterwards commanded the new ship Poland in the Havre line. This ship belonged to Mr. Whitlock. Captain Anthony afterwards commanded her. I think he is now President of the Sailor's Home.

About the first real estate purchase Mr. Whitlock made was the store and lot 46 South street. He bought it of old John Aymar, in 1830, and has continued to occupy it from then until now. It is a singular fact that a merchant rarely buys real estate. In the long run no property pays so good an interest as the store he occupies himself, if he owns it. Almost every large merchant keeps his capital in active business, and will not lock it up in a store and lot. Probably if merchants for the last thirty years who have failed, had commenced to lay by every year a little to pay for a store, costing $12,000 or $15,000, they would have been saved and in business now. Very few merchants of the past fifty years have stood up, and retired with means, unless they have invested largely in real estate. Many others, who, like Stephen Whitney, have done a very small mercantile business, yet a portion of their business profits they invested in real estate, became very wealthy. Others that did an immense business, but made no investments in real estate, became bankrupts. I suppose Mr. Whitlock, if obliged to pay rent, would have paid $33,000 in as many years. The store was burned in the great fire of 1835, but was insured sufficiently to rebuild it.

I do not think the property at No. 46 South street has advanced a dollar. I believe there is a dock with it, or that Mr. Whitlock leased it. At any rate his ships of the Havre line always lay at that dock in front of his store.

Hundreds of the old-fashioned stores can still be seen in this city. A high steep roof, with an immense garret and a bad fall, are the marked characteristics of these old time stores.

Mr. Whitlock did a very heavy business in 1825, and after, with the Brazils.

Then he got into the Havre line about that time. Old Francis Depau, Crassous & Boyd, and Wm. Whitlock, Jr., owned one or more vessels. I do not think there was more than six Havre packets in 1825, in the line.

One famous ship was the "Cadmus." She belonged to Mr. Whitlock. She brought out to this country General Lafayette. She was to sail from Havre to this country with a full freight, and a long list of passengers All were patriotically sacrificed to make room for General Lafayette, "the Nation's Guest," his suite, and their baggage. The "Cadmus" brought them all over safe and landed them at Staten Island; but for this trouble and real loss, Mr. Whitlock received no compensation whatever. I do not think he ever carried another great man free after this trip, in the "Cadmus," or any other ship that he has since owned. The "Cadmus" was a ship of about 350 tons. She was commanded by Francis Allyn. The same captain afterward lost the Liverpool packet-ship "George Canning." That last ship was built for a Capt. Stoddart, but he was not allowed to take command of her on account of his having been caught smuggling broadcloths in bales of hay. He was coming down the wharf towards his ship, when he saw a bale of hay going on a cart.

"What are you going to do with that hay?" he asked of the custom-house officer.

"Send it to the public store," was the reply.

Capt. Stoddart was surprised, and addressed the mate, who was ignorant of what was doing (had he been trusted by the captain, all would have been right), asking what had happened. The mate told him. It seems the cow had been kept aboard and not "struck ashore," as she ought to have been. The mate had ordered the cabin-boy to go and cut some hay for the old cow from one of the bales. The boy returned and told the mate, in presence of the custom-house officer, that he had cut through hay into fine broadcloth. Custom-house officer immediately smelt a very large mice, and ordered all the bales of hay sent to the public store, where a large quantity of first-chop broadcloth was confiscated. Owing to the fact that Captain Stoddart stood at the head of his profession, the affair was hushed up. The ship belonged to Fish & Grinnell. Capt. Stoddart never went to sea again. His disgrace preyed upon his mind. He retired to Yonkers, became very dissipated, and died poor. Capt. Allyn, of Mr. Whitlock's ship "Cadmus" retired, after he lost the "George Canning," to New

London, Ct., and then went extensively into the whaling business.

The ship "Montano" was another of the early ships of that Havre line of packets. They earned money for all parties. Old Mr. Depau retired from the line very rich, and so did every one connected with it. Mr. Whitlock made a mint of money, in his share of the line.

He did not confine his ship owning to this line. Whenever he could buy a ship he did so, and placed her in the general freighting business. This was also very profitable to him, and he coined money in it, when others would have lost.

In 1827 or 1828, he bought the house at No. 26 Beech street for $13,000. His friends thought he was ruined to pay such a price. He afterwards bought No. 31 Beech street, opposite to the Park, and lived there many years. His wife and his only son died in that house. Afterwards he bought a country seat near Washington Heights, but I believe he left that years ago, and now lives at 25 East Thirty-sixth street.

About thirty years ago, when Mr. Whitlock first moved to St. John's square, it was one of the most famed spots in the city. Some of our largest merchants resided around it in Varick, Beech, Laight and Hudson streets. Many of the old race who own their houses, still continue there. But the greater part have moved to more fashionable parts of the town, and these noble residences are given up to the dominions of boarding-housedom. Each of those houses that surround the Park, own an equal quantity of real estate in the enclosed park, and if it should ever be sold, (which it can be by consent of the owners of the adjoining property) the proceeds will be shared among the opposite lot owners. The houses now are entitled to a key to the Park, and to the pleasure of walking there.

Mr. Whitlock was one of the independent ship owners, who when freights were dull, had capital to invest in cargoes, so as to load his ships quickly. He was always fortunate in such purchases, and not only made good freights for his ships, but a good per centage on the investments. His name is rarely used for any purpose except in banks and insurance companies, when he could facilitate his own business by being a director, and getting aid if he needed it.

He never had a note lay over in his life, and regarded his commercial credit as beyond anything except life. His business is his only pleasure, and it is not probable that he will ever give it up while life lasts. He was for many years a member of Dr. Milner's church, in Beekman street, (St. George) and regularly attended there while the good old doctor lived. He has several daughters married to some of our most useful citizens. Mr. Whitlock built the ship "Formosa." Her commander was Captain Orne, now a port warden. His first acquaintance with Captain Orne was commenced in a singular manner.

William Whitlock, Jr., and his brother Sidney B., bought a corvette. I do not know but it was one of those built for the Columbian government. The brothers fitted her up and sold her to Commodore Fornier of the Buenos Ayerean navy. She was to be paid for part in cash, and the other part by a draft of Commodore Fornier upon the Buenos Ayres Government. The Commodore had a letter of credit, authorizing him to draw for such a purpose. The cash and the drafts had just got into the possession of the Whitlocks, when Jonathan Thompson, who was then collector of the port, seized this corvette, on the ground that she was going to sea to act in hostility towards a power friendly to the United States.

Here was a stumper for any man but Wm. Whitlock, Jr. He at once, but very quietly purchased the schooner "Rehoboth," and loaded her with flour. Orne was a smart young fellow who had been recommended to him, and he at once placed him in command of his new schooner, and gave him orders to proceed to Buenos Ayres — anticipate the news of the seizure of the corvette by the United States, get the money for the drafts, and come home as speedily as possible. The schooner made a splendid run out, run the blockade of the *Banda Orientale*, and got into Ensanada. From that port Captain Orne went up by land to Buenos Ayres. It was with the greatest difficulty he could do anything. But finally he paid a liberal discount to the nephew of the Governor of Buenos Ayres, got his drafts cashed, and hurried away to Ensenada, dreading every moment that the news of the seizure in New York, of the corvette would arrive. He sold the outward cargo at a tremendous profit, loaded the schooner with hides and specie, and returned to New York, making a famous trip, for which he deserved and received great credit.

The corvette was eventually released, and proceeded to sea through Long Island Sound. The news came down to the collector, that boats were constantly passing from her to the shore. He supposed she was shipping a war crew, and he gave orders to a revenue cutter to go up to the Sound and bring the corvette back to the city. The cutter reached the Sound, but found no corvette. The bird had flown. She had proceeded to sea the night previous, and from that day to this has never been heard of.

By that operation the two Whitlocks made a large sum of money, but it led to a quarrel between the two brothers, and from that year they never spoke to each other.

Sidney Whitlock went up to Southbury, Connecticut, and purchased a beautiful place, belonging to Simeon Mitchell, for a very large sum. Simeon Mitchell had a father who was one of the most extraordinary men of this or any other country. Old Sim was a venerable old joker, and a great believer in Lorenzo Dow. Old Sim determined to die, be buried, have a monument, and to have Lorenzo preach the funeral sermon.

Southbury is an extraordinary place of itself. It is about twenty miles north of New Haven, on the Litchfield road. Nearly all the *Grahams* in New York came from Southbury, since two hundred and thirty years ago, when the original Scotch Grahams located there.

Old Sim died, or rather made believe so. He was laid out in regular Connecticut fashion. A copper cent was placed over each eye. He was put in the coffin, after being encased in a shroud. The meeting-house bell tolled. The solemn procession went up the hill to the burying-ground. The coffin was taken off the bier and placed by the side of the tombstone, and then old Lorenzo Dow preached such a funeral sermon as I never heard before or since. It was witty, elegant, complimentary, severe, and made everybody cry. Old Sim listened attentively, and when it was through declared he was satisfied, and the crowd, dead man, and Parson Dow, all went home. A few years later, old Sim did die for good, and left a handsome fortune to young Sim, who invested nearly every dollar of it in the expensive house which he was so lucky as to sell to Captain Whitlock.

With that money young Sim came to Brooklyn, bought a small farm somewhere near where the present Brooklyn City Hall stands, and ought to be worth a million. It is nearly half a century since I first, and nearly a quarter of one since I last saw him, and he was one of the handsomest men I ever saw on both occasions.

Old Lorenzo Dow stopped, for weeks at a time, at his father's house.

The Sidney B. who bought Sim Mitchell's place was a ship chandler. Another brother, Samuel, was a ship captain; he died at sea. Another brother, Augustus, was a grocer, in partnership with Daniel Bonnett, his brother-in-law, under the firm of Whitlock & Bonnett. For many years both lived at 80 Franklin street. Mr. Bonnett has a son, who was an accomplished surveyor, in New Jersey, some years ago. The firm of W. & B. was for many years at 165 Fly Market.

I think Augustus is now in the ship chandlery business, at 57 South and 117 Wall street, and lives in the country.

None of these Whitlocks are any connection to B. & M. Whitlock, the Southern grocers and sympathizers.

William Whitlock, Jr. has jogged along, a practical, thorough business man, for many years — nearly half a century — and is far more worthy of a chapter among the "Old Merchants," and to be honored with a public notice, than any politician, or man who makes a great noise in the papers.

CHAPTER XLVII.

It has often occurred to the author of these chapters, that it would add much to their interest if some of the old merchants who have departed this life could be sent for, to talk over old times and old matters, even through the "medium" of a clever spiritualist. If one of those old commercial worthies would condescend to communicate in that manner, it would add greatly to the attraction of my chapters, and I certainly would believe in spiritualism, if we could be assured by some spiritual chieftainess that she could produce from the spirit world any old merchant I called for.

This morning it would be John W. Kearny. If the spirit had indication that the old worthy was present, I could test the medium and spiritualism very quickly, by the following questions:

1. "Mr. Kearny, where were you born?"

2. "In what year?"

3. "With what celebrated commercial house was you a clerk between the years 1790 and 1800?"

4. "What year did you go into business on your own account?"

5. "What was your firm?"

6. "What was the name of the eminent citizen and '’76 Liberty Boy' whose daughter you married?"

7. "What Emperor interfered seriously with the extensive commercial arrangements of your firm?"

8. "In what manner?"

9. "What sum of money did you eventually receive from the successor to that dynasty?"

10. "Is that your handwriting to this paper for $412, which I have in my pocketbook, signed by your firm fifty-eight years ago?"

If the spirit medium rapped out — or wrote out — rapidly in reply, to

1. "Near Newark, New Jersey."

2. "In 1776."

3. "Le Roy, Bayard & Co."

4. "1803."

5. "John W. & Philip Kearny.'

6. "Robert Watts."

7. "The Emperor Napoleon No. 1."

8. "By his celebrated Berlin and Milan decrees.'

9. "$18,000, when we ought to have received 150,000."

10. "No, it is in the handwriting of my brother Philip."

Then and now and forever more I would believe in spiritualism. I know Judge Edmonds, Horace H. Day, George B. Turrell, Barney Corse, and others who have faith in spiritualism, as millions have, — I have seen mediums, but I have never yet had the slightest evidence that I could converse with the dead — not evidence such as it would be to me, were I to ask to converse with sc venerable an old merchant as Mr. Kearny, and get such truthful answers as a proud New York merchant of the olden time would give, whether dead or alive.

I would like to have such evidence as the above that

the dead are *not* eternally dead. We see our friends laid out cold — the spirit power that moved their machinery — enabled their hands to grasp ours, their voices to speak lovingly, their eyes to look tenderly — gone somewhere, we do not know where, and it is painful. But if I knew, from such evidences as I have named, that could *not* be doubted, it would make millions of human beings happy on earth — death would cease to be dreaded, and I certainly should be very much assisted in my "Old Merchants," by being able to call upon the old merchants themselves for information upon subjects that I am not positive about.

I remember these old Kearny merchants very well. Splendid looking men they were forty years ago. John and Philip resembled each other very much. Philip was a very little slighter built than his elder brother.

The answer to the imaginary questions are fairly answered. They are facts in relation to the firm.

The great house of Le Roy & Bayard gave a commercial education to young Kearny from 1792 until he went into business upon his own account ten years after. The counting house of L. & B. was at 3 Hanover Square, and old Herman Le Roy lived over the store as was customary. His partner, William Bayard lived at 43 Wall street.

The Kearny brothers went into business in 1803, at the corner of William and Garden (Exchange) street. Their house and yard occupied a large plot of ground.

Their father was a very wealthy Irishman, and heir to the Garrison estate. He settled near Newark, on the west bank of the Passaic, and the old mansion is still possessed by his descendants. He had a brother, Edmund, who came out with him. They were both rich. These two brothers were the progenitors of the Kearny family in America. A family that has always maintained the highest respectability, and many of its members have risen to the highest rank in the American army and navy. Both General Kearny, U. S. A., and Commodore Kearny are of the above stock.

John W. & Philip Kearny did a very large business for some years after they had commenced. They sold merchandise on commission, and did a large West India trade. They also owned ships. Their largest trade was to Antwerp. To that city they were large shippers of produce. When Bonaparte issued his celebrated Berlin and Milan decrees and confiscated all the property he could find, the firm of J. & P. Kearny were large sufferers. Ships were taken and coufiscated, as well as a large amount of American produce they had shipped to Antwerp, and which was lying in the warehouses when seized. Their loss was over $150,000. In the time of General Jackson's presidency, they received about $18,000 of their claim.

Philip Kearny, the senior partner, went out to Paris, to get at the facts. It is a very curious circumstance that the French Emperor had perfect method in his confiscations. To this day can be seen, in Paris, the mark of every box, bale, or package of merchandise confiscated. Its shipping mark, the name of the vessel by which it arrived, name of the owner, name of the consignee, prices the articles brought, and the day of sale Everything was put down with the utmost exactness, so that the most humble person, in a distant land, who suffered by the severe policy of the first Napoleon, who tried to ruin England, can ascertain how much his goods brought, and get redress.

John W. Kearny married a daughter of Robert Watts, very celebrated in his day, and who, until 1814, lived at

33 Pearl street, then a fashionable part of the city. Robert was a brother of John Watts, who lived for many years at No. 3 Broadway.

Robert Watts married a daughter of the celebrated Earl of Stirling, of revolutionary times.

After his marriage John W. Kearny, in 1810, built the house 2 Greenwich street. At that time the North River came about up to the rear of the house. Kearny's house was built on piles, as were all the houses on the west side of Greenwich street, below Albany basin.

Philip Kearny married a daughter of John Watts, of No. 3 Broadway. He was married in that house. He continued in business with John W. for some years, but after the war, he started in business at 40 Wall street, where his brother, Archibald K. Kearny, was a ship broker. After that he retired to the old homestead, which became his after the death of his father, and there he died.

Philip left two children; one comes to my view now as a pleasant little girl of ten years old, with a very sweet face. I have never seen her since. Her name was Susan. She married a son of General Macomb, of the United States Army. She is dead, but her children own the old Kearny mansion on the west banks of the Passaic.

Her brother Philip entered the American army. He was out in the Mexican war, and behaved very gallantly there — lost an arm in one of the battles. He was aid to General Scott. Possessed of an income of $25,000 a year, he some time ago resigned from the army, and went to Europe. He served as a volunteer in the French army, and was, if I am not mistaken, at the great battles of Magenta and Solferino. When our rebels commenced operations, Major Kearny was in

France. He at once came home, and offered his services to the President. His services were accepted, and he is now a Brigadier General. Major Kearny built a beautiful "chateau" on the New York side of the Passaic, a short distance above the Newark road. He must have spent a small fortune upon it. It is directly opposite to the old Kearny mansion, now owned by the children of his sister. It is now rented by Ex-Governor Price of New Jersey. I have not seen Philip since thirty years. He was a fine young fellow then.

John W. Kearny, the old merchant, after he got through the confusion occasioned to his business by Napoleon's confiscation arrangements, started again in 1818, at No. 27 William street. His dwelling house was at the Bowery Hill. At that time business was very dull in the city. The effects of war lasted some years. The Post-office was close to his place. One evening the old gentleman sent a lad, with money to pay the postage on a letter. The office was closed, and he put the letter and postage-money in the letter box. The next morning, when he went for his letters, the clerk told him the circumstance, adding, "We knew the money flung in the box must have been to pay the letter you sent, for there was no other letter put in the box during the night."

Fancy such a thing in the New York Post office of 1861!

Mr. John W. Kearny kept on in business in New York until 1830, when he moved up to Saugerties, on the North River, and there he resided until he died, in December, 1849.

His friend, Henry Barclay, had previously moved there, and made that village increase from 700 to 7,000 inhabitants. He built dams and mills, and made great improvements. He took up Moses Y. Beach (afterwards of the *Sun*), and made him the superintendent of the Saugerties paper mill company.

Mr. Kearny married a second wife. She was the daughter of George Hammeker, who had been a consul at Denmark in Washington's time, and retired to Saugerties.

John W. Kearny had several children. His eldest son was named Philip. He married a daughter of John G. Warren, celebrated as a broker in Wall street, so many years under the firm of John G. Warren & Son.

The old man was one of our most eminent merchants for many years. He commenced business as early as 1795, at 44 Greenwich street. He afterwards removed to 30 South, and lived at 19 Broad street, when all that street was occupied by dwelling-houses. He then lived at 31 William, near Cedar, where his family own property yet. He changed his business and went to 53 Wall, in 1813. He lived at Bowery Hill. Afterwards he removed to 339 Broadway, near Anthony street, and lived there until he died, in 1833. His son John was the partner of John G. Warren & Son, and now the firm is John Warren & Son, 65 Wall. The last son, being grandson to the old John G., and the house has now existed and continued sixty-six years. What a fine lot of old fellows lived along that block, on the west side of Broadway, next to John G. Warren! There was James Heard, five doors above, at 349; Myndert Var Schaick, at 335; John Mason, next door to Mr. Warren, at 337. They are all gone to the spirit world.

John Warren married a Miss Kearny. She was a daughter of Robert Kearny, a cousin of John W. Robert was a merchant in this city for about six years. In 1806, he kept at No. 1 Garden street, and lived in the house with his brother at 10 Liberty. Then I believe he went to Amboy. Commodore Kearny was, I think the son of that Robert Kearny.

John G. Warren had but one son, and, if I recollect correctly, seven daughters. One married Cornelius L. Hardenbergh, a lawyer of New Brunswick, N. J.; and one was next married to Philip Kearny, John W.'s son. Another married a fine fellow, long ago dead, named Francis J. Spooner. He did business at 82 South street. Shipped heavily of cotton and such stuff to European ports. He lived in Mr. Warren's house, 339, with the old gentleman. One daughter married a Mr. Rice of Albany. Another Mr. Nelson, of Virginia, and one married Richard S. Coxe, a celebrated lawyer in Washington city.

Philip Kearny was secretary of the Union Insurance Company for many years. He died in 1841, leaving a son named Watts, who is a clerk with his uncle Alfred, for many years a merchant in New Orleans on his own hook, and recently head of the house of Kearny, Blois & Co.; and a daughter named Evelina. I met Alfred in New Orleans in 1833, when he first commenced there.

The second son of John W. was Edward Kearny, who continues to do mercantile business at No. 139 Front street, the same as his father did sixty years ago, at the corner of William and Garden streets.

Old John W. and Philip Kearny had other brothers. One was Archibald K. Kearny, who is now alive, a bachelor, and very much respected by those who know him. He was placed in the U. S. Navy early in life, served gallantly in the war of 1812, and afterwards resigned. He was out in the Algerine war, and on one occasion, when there was great danger to the magazine on board his ship from a fire close to it, he was the first officer that reached the dangerous neighborhood and put out the fire. He was the one I alluded to as a broker in naval stores at 40 Wall street for some years. He is a regular visitor to the old city library in University Place.

Another brother, Robert, was a farmer at Aquacka neck, New Jersey. I am not aware that he was ever in business in New York. If he was, he is the Robert, written about above, who was in business at 1 Garden street.

This Robert has three sons in this city. Philip R. and Joseph are in the New York Life and Trust Company, and John R., another son, is assistant cashier in the Bank of the State of New York. All of these sons are married, and have children. John R. married a daughter of Robert Cheesebrough, an eminent merchant of this city for many years.

Stephen W. Kearny was another brother of the house of J. W. & P. Kearny. He entered the United States army in 1812 — served gallantly in Canada and during the late war. He was only eighteen years old when he entered the service. He was a gallant fellow, served in the war with Mexico and in California. He died a general, in St. Louis, in 1850, leaving a very large family.

In the days of John W. & P. Kearny, or before 1812, notes were not protested as now. I do not know when the institution of "notaries public" came into vogue, but it was certainly after 1810. Previous to that, if a merchant did not pay his note the day it became due, he paid it as soon as he could, and it was all right.

It continues a custom in all parts of Spain and South American countries. A merchant pays when he agrees to do so, if he can. If the custom was so here, millions of dollars would be saved to a merchant's legitimate business that are now spent in them to give three per cent. a month shave, in order that his note may *not be protested.*

I have to notice two deaths among our commercial names. Both of them have been alluded to in previous chapters. I gave a history of the house of Davis, Brooks & Co., of which Mr. Dehon was a member.

He died in London on the 24th of June, 1861, aged forty-seven years. He was a clerk with Davis, Brooks & Co. from 1830 to 1837, when he was admitted a partner, the senior partner, Charles A. Davis, having retired, and Mr. Dehon and Charles Davis were admitted into the concern.

Mr. Dehon was a son of the late Bishop Dehon, of South Carolina.

He was also a brother-in-law of Sidney Brooks of the firm.

Since the dissolution of the old house, Mr. Dehon carried on mercantile business under his own name. He was a prominent man in the Chamber of Commerce. He was also a devoted "Union" man, and was treasurer of the Union Defence Committee. He was so active in the Committee that his labors injured his health, and he sought relaxation in a trip to Europe. There he died. Present with him, in the last dread hour, was his brother, William Dehon, his brother-in-law, Sidney Brooks, and his two sisters. His body came home in the steamship "Edinburgh."

Abraham B. Sands, of the drug house of A. B Sands & Co., corner of Fulton and William, died on the 6th of July, aged forty-six years. He was a vestryman of Trinity Church.

CHAPTER XLVIII.

One of the most prominent and most useful of mercantile occupations was the book business. In former years, or as late as 1823, the regular book merchant and stationer were the same. There was no separation in the business. He published books and pamphlets, sold them wholesale and retail, and also kept a complete stationery store, and manufactured immense ledgers, journals, day-books, and other account books, for the great merchants, as well as selling goose quills of every variety, inks, inkstands and wafers.

The two largest men in the business were Peter A. Mesier and Thomas A. Ronalds. The latter kept his store many years at No. 188 Pearl street, and afterward at No. 203. The former building was owned by Peter Lorillard, and the latter by Mr. Ronalds. The relation of landlord and tenant led to the nearer one of father and son-in-law, and Mr. Ronalds married Miss Maria Lorillard.

The respective firms published many books during many years previous to 1823.

Thomas A. Ronalds was a son of James Ronalds, who was a carpenter during the Revolution. He lived at 107 Queen street (Pearl), and for many years afterward was a joiner and house carpenter at 89 Fair (Fulton) street.

He lived as late as 1811. He had the contract with Samuel Thomson to build the church in Murray street (now standing in Eighth street, in sight of Broadway,) to which spot it was removed some years ago. Thomson kept his shop at 75 Church street, and it was about the first "big job" he had ever been engaged in. He rose to be one of the largest builders in the city. As late as 1835, I remember Nathaniel Prime employed the firm of Samuel Thomson & Son to put up stores Nos. 22 and 26 Broad street. I think Thomson bought the lot and put up No. 24 for himself. Their carpenter shop was then at No. 68 Lumber street, back of Trinity Church.

The original name of Ronalds was Ronald, Scotch. He added an *s* after they came to this country.

The store No. 188 Pearl street was started in 1803 by John Ronalds. He kept it three years, when he gave it up to "James & Thomas Ronalds," who kept at No. 188 for many years.

Finally, James his brother, and the latter carried on the business upon his own account, until within a few months of his death, twenty years later. James was the oldest. The younger, Thomas, commenced business before he was of age.

Thomas A. Ronalds was a great friend of John Phyfe, Jr., who kept at No. 19 Murray street many years, under the sign of an immense golden elephant, a wonder in its day. Phyfe had served his time with James Ruthven & Son, who were the great ivory and hard wood turners of their day (1801). John was in some business in Barclay street, No. 30. Old John Phyfe kept a grocery store in same place. Young John moved afterwards to 19 Murray street. I believe John, junior, who must be John senior, now, and a very aged man, is still alive, and resides somewhere in the city.

Being son-in-law to so wealthy a man as Peter Loril lard was no drawback to Thomas Ronalds. He was many years a director in the Mechanics Bank, of which his wife's uncle, Jacob Lorillard, was President.

Mr. Lorillard had several daughters. Besides the one married to Mr. Ronalds, another, Dorian, married Mr. John Dash Wolfe; she is yet living. Elenora married William Spencer. I think he was a lieutenant in the navy. When she died, he married Catharine, another sister, and the youngest daughter of Petér Lorillard. She was fifty years old when she became the second wife of Spencer.

I have mentioned in another chapter that Mrs. Peter Lorillard was one of the most excellent mothers, and one of the finest women that ever lived. When a visitor called upon her, when she lived at No. 40 Chatham street, although she had plenty of servants, yet she preferred waiting upon the guests herself. She would hand around the apples, cracked hickory nuts, and nice things she always kept on hand.

Thomas A. Ronalds had another brother, named Mason Ronalds, who established himself at Tuscumbia, Alabama. The brothers had heavy operations in business together; the result was that when the Alabama brother became embarrassed, he involved the New York one; and when the former died, Thomas A. was obliged to go to Alabama and spend several months settling up those affairs.

As I have said before, in the early part of his career, Ronalds published largely, but finally gave it up and confiued himself strictly to the "stationery" part of it.

He retained "Cicero Delphini," and other Latin books he had published himself, but gave up the old fashioned book business that united stationery, and confined himself exclusively to stationery. Other book concerns stuck to the book part and gave up the "stationery." Among the latter concerns who did merely a book selling business, was G. & C. Carville, T. & J. Swords, W. B. Gilley, Samuel Wood & Son. The last published medical books, and kept all kinds for sale.

Thomas A. Ronalds was a very active citizen and engaged in every laudable work. He was a prominent military man, especially during the war of 1812, as was also his friend, Thomas L. Rich, who was a merchant tailor at No. 166 Pearl street in the war time and a neighbor of Ronalds. Mr. Rich afterwards moved to No. 9 Wall.

For many years the latter had a clerk who was and is one of the most extraordinary men of the age. I allude to John Allan now living, and who must be full 90 years old. He was what was called an *accountant* in the early part of this century, and for many years after. In those days it was a distinct business. Many large commercial houses had no regular book-keeper. They hired one who was designated an "Accountant." He sometimes called once a week, and wrote up a particular set of books. To others he went twice a week, staid an hour or more. Mr. Allan accumulated a snug property, and for many years has been engaged in settling up complicated accounts. Probably he has settled more estates than any other man or ten men in this city.

Everybody among the old residents was aware of his stern, uncompromising honesty. It was never questioned in a period of over sixty years of active business life. He is the most accomplished book-keeper that ever lived in the city. He looks young yet. No one could imagine that he was over forty-five years old. He is more lithe and active than half of our youths of twenty. He is famed for an antiquarian collection of everything relating to our city.

I now return to Mr. Ronalds. He continued his stationery business with great success for many years, but in the old routine way, and to a limited extent. In those years a stationer rarely imported goods, and no importer ordered out any particular kind of stationery. One imported quills — another ink-stands — another sealing-wax — another paper — another wafers. It was necessary for the stationer to visit twenty different importers before he could purchase his principal articles. Mr. Ronalds was the first stationer who changed all this. He determined to import himself. For this purpose in 1834, he went to Europe and visited all the principal manufactures of stationery articles in England and France. He had in former years ordered goods in his line through an importer, paying the latter a commission ; but when he reached the manufacturers in England, he found he had been greatly deceived. For instance, he had paid the importer six dollars a dozen for glass ink-stands. He found he could get them of the manufacturers for three dollars a dozen. It was so with nearly every thing in his line. From the moment he made that discovery, he ordered all goods direct from the manufacturers in Europe. He was absent nine months, and had sent home, as he supposed, stationery enough to last six years. When he reached New York, it was all sold. The prices were so low, that everybody flocked to his store. Even rival dealers could do better with him than by the old mode. He extended his orders everywhere. Even to

China, ordering out from Canton lacquered ink-stands Mr. Ronalds had prepared matters for doing a large business, when his health broke down, one year after. In 1835, while on his death bed, he sold out to David Felt, who jumped in and reaped the fruits of another's planting. Had Mr. Ronalds lived, he would have become immensely rich. As it was, he died worth half a million, besides the sum his family received from the Lorillard property.

Felt, who bought out Mr. Ronalds, was a small dealer at No. 245 Pearl. He commenced in New York in 1825. His purchase of the Ronalds business made his fortune. In two years after he did the largest wholesale stationery business ever done in New York. But he became careless with his customers, and they left him Some of them in New Orleans had been in the habit of purchasing $50,000 a year of him. In order to punish them, he established a branch in New Orleans. This flung business into the hands of some of the clerks of Ronalds here, who had established themselves in business on their own account.

One was Geo. C. Morgan. He had been in business before he had been with Ronalds. He staid a short time only with Felt, and is now, I believe, with Ames & Barnes, book-sellers, 41 John street. He must be sixty-five years old. He is one of the most esteemed and useful citizens.

Another of these clerks of Mr. Ronalds, was James V. Rich. When Ronalds died, he started the same business with Edward S. Mesier, a son of Peter A Mesier (already mentioned,) under the firm of Mesier & Rich. They continued in business some time, when the firm was changed to Rich & Loutrel, and that concern continued twenty years. That clerk of Ronalds still continues the old business at 82 Nassau street.

David Felt became so rich, that he established the village of Feltville, in New Jersey, but finally, I believe, he swapped off that town with Dr. Sarsaparilla Townsend for some Fifth avenue property.

When the grand celebration of the Erie Canal occurred here, Mr. Ronalds was grand marshal of the book-sellers and stationers. The procession passed down Pearl street on its line of march. Old Peter A. Mesier was one of the assistant standard bearers.

Thomas A. Ronalds left children. One, named Thomas, married a magnificent Boston lady. They have resided in Paris some years, where his style of equipage equals, if it does not surpass, that of the Emperor Napoleon.

Mrs. Ronalds is a splendid skater. It was her that attracted the attention of the Empress Eugenie last winter. The latter stopped some time, and entered into conversation with the beautiful skater.

Mr. Ronalds left three sons and three daughters. Thomas I have alluded to. Peter Lorillard was the second son. He is unmarried.

One daughter married Captain Thomas, who had been a West Point cadet. He is not the *Secesh* Thomas of 1862.

One daughter died before the death of her father, and the other shortly after.

I intended to have made a sketch of Mr. Mesier, but leave it for a future chapter.

It is not likely that Grant Thorburn will write many more articles, and I cannot refuse to make room for the following interesting communication, and place it in this chapter:

He writes about the 4th of July: — "The first one I saw in New York, after I arrived from Scotland, the 4th of July, 1794. I landed in New York on the 16th of June, 1794, then in my twenty-third year, but being very small I looked ten years younger. A wrought-nail maker by trade, and having my shop in Liberty street, between Nassau and Broadway; the schoolboys belonging to the "Society of Friends," kept on the opposite side of the street. When the boys arrived before the school doors were open, they assembled in my nail shop, which was a large frame building, and I was the only occupant. Here commenced a friendship with the sons of the Leggets, the Foxes, the Franklins, the Wrights, the Willets, etc., which thirty-five years after put eighty thousand dollars in my pocket — but we'll describe the 4th of July 1794.

On the morning of the Fourth the bells rang one hour at sunrise, and thirteen guns were fired on the Battery, at the foot of Broadway, at 11 A. M. A company of old veterans marched from the Park to the Battery, and fired another salute at 12; they wore the old, tattered uniforms and pinched-up cocked hats which they wore when fighting by the side of Washington at the Battle of Monmouth; some had lost a leg, some an arm, and others leaned on crutches. In 1801, when Jefferson became President, I saw some of these men dismissed from the Custom House in New York; their places were filled by imported patriots — but such is the gratitude of a model republic. At 3 o'clock P. M. the Cincinnati Society dined at the Tontine Coffee House, which stood on the north corner of Wall and Water streets. The Society was composed entirely of Revolutionary officers and their sons; they dined on the first story; the windows were opened; a cannon called a six-pounder fired a shot when each gun toast was drank. At 4 P. M. I stood at the lower end of the Fly Market, foot of Maiden Lane; people were stepping on board a small boat, which the oarsmen said was the Brooklyn ferry boat; it held twelve passengers, and was rowed by two men. After waiting fifteen minutes for passengers, we started; a strong tide setting in, carried us up as high as Grand street; we made Long Island shore near the Wallabout, then rode down close on the Long Island shore, and landed in Brooklyn after a passage of *one hour and ten minutes.*

I stood for the first time on Long Island. I looked through the four winds of heaven, standing on the wharf. I was not able to count over twenty dwellings in all directions. About one thousand feet from the wharf, right in the middle of the road, stood an old Dutch church. The wagons going to Newtown, drove on the right; the wagons going to the river, drove on the left side of the church. The church stood in the days of Governor Stuyvesant. I went forward on the road towards Newtown. A thunder shower commenced. I took shelter in a cottage by the wayside. After conversing half an hour with the inmates, the rain ceased. On returning, I noticed a field of Indian corn on the wayside, the leaves and tassels hanging full of large drops of rain; the sun was going down, which made the rain drops like pearls. It was the first time I had seen corn in the blade. I thought it looked a field whom the Lord had blessed. We had sky rockets in the Park at 8 P. M., which closed the 4th of July, 1794.

GRANT THORBURN, Sen, aged 88 years.

NEW HAVEN, *July* 8, 1861.

Mr. Thorburn had a very good memory.

I have now merely to say, that of all the merchants written about in this Book, much more could be said but it would have made the work too lengthy. Still as a new edition will most likely be published, those who can add to its interest or to its correctness, by additional information, will oblige by communicating the same to the publishers.

THE END

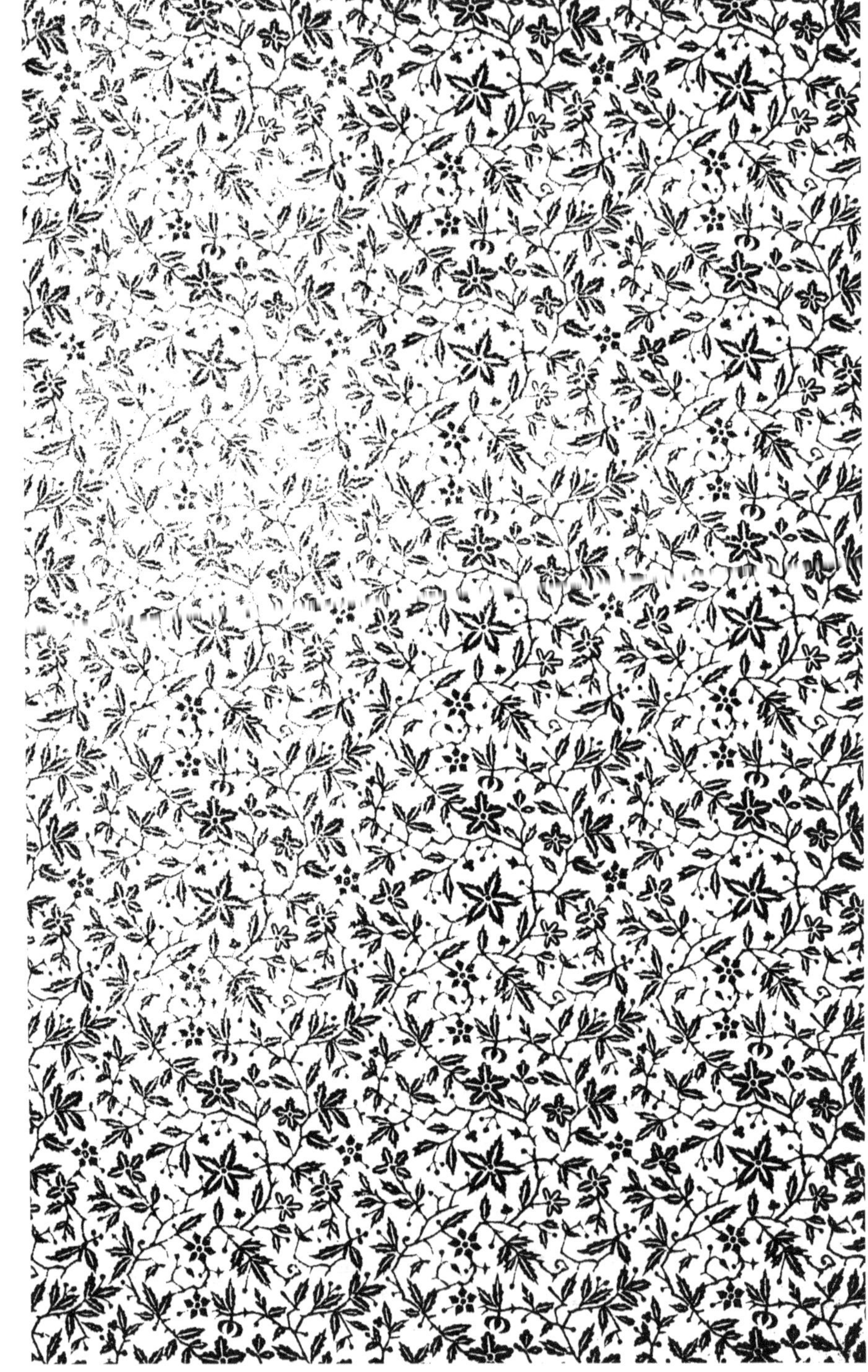

www.ingramcontent.com/pod-product-compliance
Lightning Source LLC
LaVergne TN
LVHW010527100826
845148LV00001B/117

* 9 7 8 1 4 2 5 5 8 5 9 7 6 *